THE RATIONAL MALE

VOLUME III

POSITIVE MASCULINITY

ISBN-13: 978-1548921811
ISBN-10: 1548921815

Published by Counterflow Media LLC, Reno, Nevada
Design and layout by Rollo Tomassi.

CONTENTS

AFTERWORD

ACKNOWLEDGMENTS

Dedicated to the memory of Andrew Hansen,
The Private Man

FORWARD

It was the first week of August, 2013, when I first listened to the actual voice of Andrew Hansen. I'd known Andrew as an online personality for some time before this, but I'd never really listened to the guy's voice. Andrew was a fellow blogger in what's popularly known as the Manosphere today – an online community of men that spans the globe and seeks to develop a better understanding of conventional masculinity, the nature of women and how best to develop oneself with this collective knowledge. Andrew was The Private Man and was the proprietor of a blog of the same name. Private Man was his handle on Twitter as well as many other online forums. That name was going to stick with him, and likely will be the one he's remembered by the most.

Before this particular podcast I'd had some inspired debates with Private Man. He was always a good guy to hash out ideas with because he'd had such a wealth of experience with regards to intersexual relations, divorce and dating as a 'mature man' after his divorce. I'll say right now, there were some issues I'd had strong disagreements with him about. More than once I had to take issue with his take on things from a watered down, Purple Pill perspective. That was always the concern, the want to temper one's Red Pill message to be more palatable to a larger audience (usually for the want of not offending women) at the expense of broader truths. But with Private Man, there was always a willingness to listen to the uglier side of things, the more objective, less palatable truths and to embrace them in spite of what his experience was. He'd have a penchant for writing an article critical of some fluff piece he'd come across, try to measure his response and I'd be there to push him to see the real latent message in it and why it was really bothering him enough to write about it.

Andrew's Manosphere niche was his appeal to older gentlemen. That may seem like an easy fit for a guy who really came into the sphere already in his late 50s, but you have to consider that the men who he was connecting with were largely guys like himself coming into a very rude awakening of their Blue Pill conditioning well past middle age. This is a hard demographic to reach. When a guy's been plugged in since the early 1970s and has based his intersexual existence on a set of rules that he discovers no one has really been playing by for as long as he's been around, it's very easy to fall into the 'bitter' and 'burned' category of men. Private Man could've easily been one of the same guys he was trying to reach, but his own unplugging, late as it was in his life, was something different, something positive, for him. In a way I think his positive Red Pill awareness was something unavoidable for him. This hopeful, though educated, attitude is something he brought to his writing. When I wrote the last book, *Preventive Medicine*, I did so in an attempt to address a common question men had been asking me for as long as I've been writing:

"Where was all of this knowledge when I was younger? Why didn't someone make me aware of all this before I got married, got divorced, had a messed up relationship with my kids, etc.?"

This question is usually a casual joke amongst older men in the Manosphere, one that usually stems from a need to reconcile regret for not having realized the truths of the Red Pill sooner. But with Private Man, I never really got the same sense of regret from him. It was as if his unplugging were something he accepted without much regret for the experiences and decisions he'd made for his life up to then. He acknowledged and accepted his role in his own plugging-in without much pause for the nihilism that comes with it.

We often talk about the several phases a man usually progresses through when he's processing the new awareness the Red Pill presents to him. One of these is a phase of nihilism, where a man must reconcile that his past decisions were uninformed (or deliberately misled) and from there on it's up to him to remake himself. This nihilism comes from a sense of lost investment, lost value, and the prospect of having to rebuild himself after being cut away from Blue Pill idealism. Private Man never really seemed to go through this phase – or if he did he did a good job of hiding it. In fact, if there was one thing that defined Andrew's character it was his positive attitude about damn near everything. That may seem like the 'right' thing to say about a guy in retrospect, but for Andrew it was true. I'd encourage my readers to peruse his blog and decide for themselves.

So, there I was on an August day, hobbling my way back to my car, iPhone and earplugs listening to Private Man on a podcast called, I think, Manosphere Radio or something. I say hobbling because I'd suffered a dancer's fracture on my foot a week earlier and I usually had a slow, mostly painful, walk to my car in a parking lot at a casino I was doing contract work for at the time. I downloaded the audio and listened to it while I walked and drove home that day. This may seem kind of insignificant, but it's the memory I'll always associate with Andrew because here was one of a few men from my online life who was putting himself out there. Sure, there was Roosh and a few others, but Private Man was a guy I already had a connection with. You have to remember this was about 3 months before I'd published The Rational Male. It was at a time when I didn't know how it would be received, and while I had confidence in what I was doing, it was still something new for me. There were a lot of 'what ifs' I had to consider then. Hearing Andrew go into what he always did, I knew then that he'd be a guy I could share a beer with. A guy that was accessible.

I think that's important, accessibility. It's very easy to get wound up in the idea that the text we read on our monitors are just cold expressions of ideas. It's easy to forget there's a human behind those ideas. Sometimes that human might be someone you'll click with immediately, sometimes it's a person you're glad to get away from. Their ideas may be genius, but who they are is very much subjective. Hearing Andrew's delivery, much of it dead pan, you just knew he was a good dude. I wish I could say I know more than I do about him. He was a very open guy and I honestly wondered what woman would ever have a reason to divorce the guy. It certainly wasn't his lack of approachability.

It makes you wonder why he chose the moniker Private Man. He was anything but private.

Between 2013 and Andrew's passing this year, 2017, I'd talked with him personally on several occasion. It was actually Andrew who'd hit me up for my cell number. He lived alone with a dog and I'm fairly sure he just wanted to talk with someone outside his immediate circle the first time we connected. He'd hit some tough times financially, asked me to help him with a cell phone bill, but moreover it was about the time he knew he'd be losing an eye to cancer. It's interesting to see pictures of him now without the eye patch since it quickly became the look that made him most recognizable. Cancer is a shit disease. It's alters you in many ways even if you beat it. Talking to Andrew on this occasion, I knew there was likely something more he was holding back, but even in a time he was obviously hurting and sorting things out for himself he still pressed on with the same upbeat determination I'd always known.

Then came the announcement that his cancer had become aggressive enough that he knew and accepted that he'd be taking the last train home. Mortality is something very personal. If I'm honest, it's not something I like to contemplate too often or too deeply. I'm not too good with death. It's easy for men to come up with heroic speeches about the importance of living life well and facing death strength and honor, but after all of that, dead is dead and gone is gone. I'll be addressing this in more detail in the chapters of this book, but suffice to say that precious few men leave a sizable dent in the universe during their time in this life. Private Man may not have been up there with Steve Jobs, but he did leave a dent in the Manosphere.

As with everything else he did, Andrew accepted his fate and still pressed on, with little words of regret. Just as he'd accepted his Red Pill awareness with grace and positivity, so too did he accept his imminent end. In fact, he had a 'going away' party for himself not but a few weeks before his passing. You can see the video of this party on his blog (saved for posterity).

Once he'd announced his life was coming to an end I immediately asked him if he'd do me the honor of writing the forward of the book you now hold in your hands. I had wanted nothing more than for Andrew to be memorialized with this book. The Rational Male has become a cornerstone of Red Pill awareness and dare I say the most influential work on intersexual dynamics in the Manosphere. It was my hope that this installment might serve as a tribute to Private Man, written by his own hand here. Alas, it was not to be, so thus I write his eulogy here in his place.

I renamed this volume *Positive Masculinity* in tribute to what Private Man brought to our collective consciousness. As you read through this book keep this theme in mind. Far too much is made by critics of the Red Pill – the true Red Pill founded in brutal, but enlightening truths of intersexual dynamics – that its readers, its proponents, its awakened men are simply a collection of angry, bitter, nihilistic guys railing at their social ineptitudes. It's all too easy to believe there is nothing positive to masculinity in an age where boys and men are taught to hate anything looking like the conventional definition of it. But there is more to the Red Pill aware man than this, and it's my hope that this book will serve as a counterbalance to that, often deliberate, misconception.

The Private Man was a good example of this positivity, so it's in his name I dedicate the following text. God willing, this will serve as his memorial.

– *Rollo Tomassi*

April 13, 2017

INTRODUCTION

"Good decisions come from experience, and experience often comes from bad decisions."

One of the major hurdles I had to really come to terms with when I decided to start getting involved with the new male paradigm – the Red Pill – was why I was so passionate about it in the first place. Ever since I began contributing on the SoSuave forum and the manosphere in general, I've always tried to make a point of not emphasizing my past sexual and personal experiences to base more global ideas upon. Women's default position is often just this; personalize the instance then come to a universalized conclusion. Not only is it the height of solipsism to think your experience should define the frame for everyone else, but it myopically ignores that exceptions usually prove a rule.

That was my basis for not wanting to relate too much of my own experiences. People can draw too easy a conclusion from the conditions that molded your point of view. This is actually one of the easiest ways to *read* a woman because their experiences and sense of self-importance tends to define their reality. I wanted a more pragmatic approach, and all this came at a time for me when I decided to explore behavioral psychology. *Game*, or what would become a form of practical intersexual awareness, influenced this decision for me. Back in my earliest writing, as far as Red Pill awareness went, I wanted to know how the television worked instead of that it just worked when I turned on the power. I wanted to be able to take it apart and put it back together again.

All that said, I was still left with the question, 'why the hell do you even care whether guys unplug?'

I 'unplugged' largely without the support of a global Internet community of men comparing their experiences, so why even bother? At the time of this writing I have had what most men would consider a very good marriage for over 20 years now. I have a whip-smart and pretty, grown daughter, I make good money, I'm successful at what I do, I'm well traveled, why is it so damn important to make my voice heard?

My detractors will say it's all about ego appeasement. There's always some truth to that I suppose; every writer has some ego-investment in their work or they'd never do it. However, it's when I'm forced to answer questions like this that I have no choice but to apply my own personal experiences to the equation. I'm loath to do so because it's far too easy for critics to mold them into some intent and purpose that serves their perspective – he's bitter, he got burned, this is his catharsis, he's vindictive, etc. However, it's necessary to present these experiences as observations for a better understanding. I wont pretend to be unbiased, no one is, but I do take the pains to be as self-analytical as I can in what I offer.

So you want to know what my problem is?

My problem is living in a world teeming with young men who've become so conditioned to believing that anything remotely masculine is to be ridiculed, vilified or subdued until they have no concept of what conventional masculinity truly entails much less pass off even the possibility that it could be something positive and attractive.

My problem is when a personal, Beta friend swallows a bullet because he, literally, "can't live without" the girlfriend who left him.

My problem is watching a pastor's pretty wife leave him and 4 children so she can pursue her Hypergamous instincts after 18 years of marriage because he pedestalized her and deprecated himself (and men) every day of their marriage.

My problem is when a 65 year old man, steeped in his Blue Pill conditioning for his long life, cries in my lap about how he's been consistently blackmailed with his wife's intimacy for the past 20 years of their marriage and won't risk offending her for fear of losing her.

My problem is talking a close friend out of killing both the wife he married too young and the man she just cheated on him with in the parking lot of the motel he's spent all night tracking her down to with their three children crying in the backseat of their minivan at 4am.

My problem is civilly sitting down to Thanksgiving dinner with a hyper-religious woman and the new millionaire husband she married just 8 months after her former Beta husband of 20 years hung himself from a tree when she decided "he wasn't the ONE" for her. My problem is staring at the brand new tits and Porsche she bought herself with the money from the home he built for her, that he busted his ass for, just 3 months after he was in the ground. My problem is emphatically teaching a nephew how not to be the Beta his father was, while

18

tactfully pointing out the Hypergamy of his obliviously opportunistic mother.

My problem is watching my father, though decaying from Alzheimer's, still playing out a *Savior Schema* in an effort to get laid that he's thought should work for his entire life at 68 years old. My problem is watching him feebly default to a behavior that had obsessively motivated him to succeed until he was forced into early retirement at 53 and his second wife promptly left him after that.

My problem is consoling a good friend who fathered three daughters with two wives and is being emotionally manipulated by his third (another single mother), who's become so despondent that he dreads going home from work to deal with his personal situation and waits with anticipation for the weekends to be over.

My problem is counseling a guy who thought the best way to separate himself from "other guys" was to be 'chivalrous' and date a single mommy, also with three children from two different fathers, only to knock her up for a fourth kid and marry her because "*it was the right thing to do.*"

My problem is dealing with a 17 year old girl who witnessed her new boyfriend being stabbed 30 times by her ex-boyfriend because he believed "she was his soul-mate" and "would rather live in jail without her than see her with that guy."

My problem is trying to explain to 'Modern Women' that – after 20 years of marriage, my wife could still model swim-wear and confidently respects my judgment and decisions as a man – and that I didn't achieve this by being a domineering, 1950's caveman-chauvinist who's crushed her spirit, but that it is an understanding and adherence to living a positively masculine, Red Pill aware role in the marriage.

And my biggest problem is seeing 14 year old Beta boys all ready to sacrifice themselves wholesale to this pitiful, mass-media fueled, pop-culture endorsed, idealized and feminized notion of romantic/soul-mate mythology – all because some other Betas trapped in the same quicksand are affirming and co-enabling each other to further their own sinking and spread this disease to other young men. It's infectious, and complacency, like misery, loves company. If I have a fear it is that I'm only one man, and I can't possibly be enough to kick these guys in the ass like their fathers were unable or unwilling to do.

This is why I bother. It really is a matter of life or death sometimes.

Understanding Game, for lack of a better term, and how and why it functions, is literally a survival skill. Think about the importance of the decisions we make based on uninquisitive, flimsy and misdirected presumptions we have been conditioned to believe about love, gender, sex, relationships, etc. Think about the life impact that these decisions have not only on ourselves, but our families, the children that result from them, and every other domino that falls as a repercussion. We rarely stop to think about how our immediate decisions impact people we may not even know at the time we make them. What we do in life, literally, echoes or ripples into eternity. That's not to go all fortune cookie on you, but it is my reasoning behind my desire to educate, to study, to tear down and build back up what most would ask, "why bother?"

Do we really need another book?

In September of 2015 I dared to make my first public appearance in Las Vegas at the *Man in Demand Conference* hosted by my good friend Christian McQueen. He, myself and bloggers Goldmund and Tanner Guzy came together for a Saturday we wanted to bill as a TED talk for the manosphere. Sort of a meeting of the minds for the Red Pill aware. As it worked out it was a very well balanced collection of men's experience.

At this conference I was privileged to meet many different men from all walks of life who'd made great efforts to attend. I was introduced to men in their early 20s all the way up to their late 60s. I met some 9 to 5 office workers, some college students, a private investigator, a cop, and some men who'd flown in from an Air Force base in South Korea. I was honored to have one of them personally hand me an Air Force coin for my work. I met men in the military and a guy who'd ridden a bus from across the country in order to meet with me. I met fathers with kids who they told me would be handing them my first book as soon as they were old enough to understand it. I also met men who'd brought their own fathers with them to hear my first in-person talk. Needless to say it was an unqualified honor and easily one of the most humbling experiences of my life to meet men wanting to thank me and my writing for improving or saving their lives – literally and figuratively.

At the conference I had a fellow ask me, "What are you going to write about once you've covered everything from a Red Pill perspective?" I kind of paused at this; it'd never occurred to me that I might ever run out of dots to connect with respect to intersexual dynamics. If anything, the very fact that so many men from such diverse backgrounds and experiences had come together in Vegas to hear us speak and to get some one-on-one live time with myself and my fellow bloggers was a testament to how Red Pill awareness applied in so many contexts. There's a running joke going on with myself and my Twitter followers that says there is a *Rational Male* post for every circumstance, issue or difference between men and women today. I'm not sure I entirely agree with that, but I do understand the sentiment – I have quite a bit of material collected over the fourteen years I've been writing. It's become a habit of mine to simply link past articles as answer to some seemingly new intersexual contention or story readers will ask for my take on. Needless to say I don't do 140 characters very well.

So have I tapped everything out? Have I written all there is to be written? At the time of this writing I'm beginning to get people unfamiliar with 'Rollo Tomassi' sending me links to my own quotes as a response to something I may talk about on a Red Pill forum. My work, it seems, precedes me as an author. This is a very strange place to be I assure you; to have your message overshadow you as a writer as it becomes endemic to the large Red Pill narrative.

All that said, I don't for a moment believe I've tapped out everything there is to say about intersexual dynamics and Red Pill awareness. Intersexual dynamics, the differences between men and women's sexual – and really life – strategies is very broad. In the three and a half years since my first book published there have been countless other writers starting blogs to focus specifically on various aspects of how Red Pill awareness affects particular social sets, ethnicities, married men, men going their own way (MGTOW), religious and political considerations.

The Red Pill – in it's original definition of being about the psychological, sociological and interpersonal dynamism between and women – isn't something I've ever thought I would need to categorize. I'm happy that my work is the foundation for so many offshoots of Red Pill specialization, but my first, most important role in this sphere is to stay as attuned as I can to the broad questions and the foundational truths.

My purpose in writing what I do for as long as I have has always been to benefit other men, to hopefully unplug the guys who are on their last nerve, but have a desire to really understand the *whats* and the *whys* that have led them to the point in their lives where they are ready to dissolve the barriers that have prevented them from becoming Red Pill aware.

Praxeology

The Red Pill, from the respect that I interpret it, is a praxeology. Simply put, it's the deductive study of human action, based on the notion that humans engage in purposeful behavior, as opposed to reflexive behavior like sneezing and inanimate behavior. With the action axiom as the starting point, it is possible to draw conclusions about human behavior that are both objective and universal. For example, the notion that humans engage in acts of choice implies that they have preferences, and this must be true for anyone who exhibits intentional behavior.

This is primarily why I continue to use the phrase '*Red Pill awareness*' throughout what I write. Once a man truly unplugs and reorders his life according to what it presents to him, this developed awareness extends to many other aspects of his life than just his intersexual relations. This awareness makes men sensitive to others around him who, like he was, are caught in the same Blue Pill conditioned way of interpreting his personal and social existence. With a *Red Pill Lens* he begins to see the sales pitches, the ego-investment defenses, and the predictable responses of men and women whose lives have been colored by a feminine-primary social conditioning that has defined their lives for so long they are unaware of it, but would cease to exist without it.

In this volume I would ask that you keep the idea of the Red Pill as a praxeology in mind. It is a loose science at best, but as a science it is always open to new data, new input from the larger whole of men's experiences. And as such it is always open to reinterpretations, more experimentation and new assessments. The Red Pill is still evolving. It is very much a 'living study', so to speak.

Positive Masculinity

When I began writing, compiling and rewriting this book I had an initial working title – *The Rational Male, The Red Pill* – however, as I progressed I shifted this to *Positive Masculinity*. There came a point in my compiling and editing where I'd taken a different path in the purpose of the book. Where I had wanted to explain and/or defend the initial, intersexual, definition of what the term 'Red Pill' has increasingly been distorted away from, I found myself leaning more into expressing ways in which this Red Pill awareness could benefit men's lives in many ways, both in and apart from intersexual dynamics.

I'd hit on this in my Red Pill Parenting series from a couple years ago and I knew I wanted to revisit and make that series a prominent part of this book. As it sits now, it accounts for a full quarter of the book's content, but as I moved into my writing more I decided that the best way to really define 'The Red Pill' as I know it was to go into the various ways men might benefit from redefining masculinity for themselves in a conventional, Red Pill aware sense.

When I finished the parenting section I realized that I was really laying out general, if not prescriptive, ideas for ways men might better raise their sons and daughters in a feminine-primary social order that's determined to raise and condition them. My purpose with both the series and section was to equip fathers with Red Pill aware considerations in making their sons and daughters Red Pill aware themselves in order to challenge a world that increasingly wants to convince us that fathers' influence is superfluous or dangerous.

It was from this point that I'd made a connection; what I was doing was laying out a much-needed reckoning of sorts with regard to what conventional, positive masculinity might mean to future generations of Red Pill aware men. Since my time on the SoSuave forums and the inception of my blog I've used the term *Positive Masculinity*. I've even had a category for it on my side bar since I began too. From the time I began writing I've always felt a need to vindicate positive, conventional masculinity (as well as evolved conventional gender roles for men and women) and separate it from the deliberately distorted "toxic" masculinity that the *Village* of the Feminine Imperative would have us believe is endemic today.

I've always seen a need to correct this intentionally distorted perception of masculinity with true, evolved, biologically and psychologically inherited aspects of conventional masculinity.

As you may guess this isn't an easy an task when a Red Pill man must fight against many different varieties of this masculine distortion. We live in an age where any expression of conventional masculinity is conflated with 'bullying' or 'hyper-masculinity'. Blue Pill conditioning teaches us that inherent strength ought not to be considered "masculine". If a boy acts in a conventionally masculine way he's to be sedated and boys as young as four, it's accepted, can decide their gender to the extent that doctors are chemically altering their physiologies to block hormones and transition them into (binary) girls.

To the Blue Pill *Village*, a definition of masculinity is either something very obscure, subjective and arbitrary or it's something extraordinarily dangerous, ridiculous and toxic. As I said, even the most marginal displays of anything conventionally masculine are exaggerated as some barbaric hazing ritual or smacks of hyper, over the top displays of machismo. With so much spite arrayed against masculinity, and with such an arbitrary lack of guidance in whatever might pass for a form of masculinity that feminine-primary society might ever find acceptable, is there anything positive about the masculine at all?

There is only one conclusion we can come to after so much writing on the wall – there is a war on conventional masculinity that's been going on in 'progressive' western societies for generations now.

I found it very hard to describe what exactly a *Positive Masculinity* might mean to Red Pill aware men. One of the more insidious ways that Blue Pill conditioning effectively neuters masculinity is in the recruiting of men to effect their own emasculation. Usually these men themselves have had no real guidance in, or embrace of, conventional masculinity precisely because this Blue Pill conditioning has robbed them of maturing into an understanding of it. Blue Pill fathers raise Blue Pill sons and the process repeats, but in that process is the insurance that Blue Pill sons are denied an education in what it means to be a man.

This book is a loose attempt at giving men actionable ideas in how to apply Red Pill awareness in their lives. This book is not intended to magically convert you into an 'Alpha Male', nor is it a step-by-step program about how to "change your mindset" in order to make your life better. If you make that transition, great, but I don't have a cure for you or any other man and I would caution against taking to heart the formula or program of any other Life or Dating Coach who wants to sell it to you. The Red Pill is not one-size-fits-all. Individual men will have individual solutions for their own particular circumstance, advantages and disadvantages.

What I do have for you is a series of ideas, concepts and observations that will help you fashion your own solutions to the most common problems that vex most men in this era. I offer you tools to build a life based on a new awareness which hopefully frees you of the consequences of making uninformed choices that will affect your own life, and the lives of those you choose to include in it.

Different men have differing needs from Red Pill awareness, this book's intent is to give you some ideas as to how best to implement it whether you're married, single, dating non-exclusively, divorced, a parent or planning to be one someday. As I mentioned in the beginning of this introduction, there are many faces and demographics of the Red Pill and while I cannot cater a plan for every man, my hope is to give you a firm grasp of how this awareness can affect you and be utilized by you at various stages of your life.

In the second book in the *Rational Male* series, *Preventive Medicine*, I outlined what men could likely expect of women at various phases of their maturity and station in life. In this book I will venture to outline what a man might expect from themselves in a feminine-primary social order, from women, kids, academia, and to interpret this within the context of Red Pill awareness.

Furthermore, it's my hope to give you a few 'ah-ha' moments that not only shake you from a Blue Pill illusionment, but to also spark an idea about how you might put that information to best use in your own life. One of the more satisfying aspects of the reader feedback I've received from the past two books has been listening to the 'moment of revelation' stories men have told me they had in reading a particular passage that directly spoke to them. I expect there will be similar epiphanies in this book, but when you come to one it's my hope that you begin to think of ways in which you might apply it to your life in the most immediate sense.

Guidelines, not rules

As most of my reader know, I don't deal in prescriptions. I've never believed in cookie-cutter, bullet point lists meant to teach men the 12 habits of highly effective Alpha men. In fact, my mission statement isn't really even about improving or correcting mens' lives per se. My purpose is exploring ideas and dispelling misconceptions (often deliberate) about intersexual dynamics. In all of my books I make a point of reiterating that I'm not in the business of making better men, I'm in the business of men making themselves better men.

My hope is that this book will help you make better choices based on a broader understanding of the intersexual dynamics, but also a better understand of how those dynamics affect the other aspects of your life. That may be reflected in your workplace, your family, or perhaps it motivates you to become active in a social respect; maybe it redirects your education, career or how you (will) approach parenting your sons and daughters. Maybe this information helps you reconstruct yourself, or your marriage, however, it may also destroy the more unhealthy relationships you've been as yet unable to assess your part in. The Red Pill has a very discomforting way of exposing the long-term results of a life that's been founded on Blue Pill illusions and a lack of wanting to confront them.

For all of that, remember that, as a praxeology the Red Pill is about suggestions, not hard and fast laws. Since the advent of what's become the Manosphere there has been a laboring effort to force fit this otherwise amoral, loose science, into various doctrines, codes of ethics and ideologies that distort the objectivity of the Red Pill. There is a definite want to justify whatever a man's pet ideology is by aligning it with the term "Red Pill". It's a hot moniker to call whatever you happen to believe in "Red Pill" in 2017. After all, it's just an abstraction for 'truth', right? I would very much warn against anyone using the term Red Pill to foster an agenda. This is why I believe in guidelines, suggestions and objective truths that are open to future interpretations rather than rules that straitjacket the Red Pill to accommodate ideology, or justify Blue Pill idealism that's too uncomfortable to disabuse oneself of. The Red Pill should always be 'open source' and any grab at ownership or any need for specificity should always be suspect of another motive.

How to read this book

When I wrote the first *Rational Male* book I had no plans to write even a second or third book, however, as the popularity of the first book still continues to spread I've come to see the *Rational Male* as a core source book of sorts. *The Rational Male* represents a foundation upon which supplemental volumes might follow. After I'd published *The Rational Male, Preventive Medicine* it dawned on me that any 'sequels' ought not to be sequels, but rather supplements to the first book. When I was writing and compiling *The Rational Male* my instinct was to put as much into the book as possible since I figured it would be my only work. Unfortunately, this also meant I was cramming as much into the book as possible without a thought to interpretation or what might follow after it.

It became apparent to me that *The Rational Male* would be a kind of source book for Red Pill intersexual dynamics after publication. Thus, *Preventive Medicine* followed it using the same resources set forth in the first book. As such, I would advise readers to read *The Rational Male* before delving into this volume. Much of what I'll outline in this book presumes a familiarity with the material in *The Rational Male*. You can still get a lot out of this book 'as is', but there are established Red Pill principles, acronyms and idioms that only make sense with an understanding of the ideas in the first book. So, for as much as this will sound like a marketing pitch, please, read *The Rational Male* first. After that, read, *The Rational Male, Preventive Medicine* if you like. Certain ideas, like Mental Point of Origin, are discussed in that volume. However, *Preventive Medicine* is one more supplement; not an absolute necessity, but it will further your understanding in Red Pill awareness. I should also add that reading this volume before *Preventive Medicine* won't necessarily throw off some prescribed reading order or linear understanding.

Lastly, I'm going to make an appeal to you to read this (and really all my writing) as free from distractions as possible. That's tough to do these days, I know. I'm asking you this because it's my belief that introspection is a necessary part of understanding Red Pill awareness. You have to give yourself the opportunity to digest this material and see how it's applicable to your own life.

Today we live in what I call the TL;DR generation. That stands for Too Long ; Didn't Read in case you weren't aware. TL;DR is a summation meant to give a reader only the most basic information about a particular forum post or blog entry. I can understand why this info bite is popular in an online world where our attention spans are constantly distracted from one stimulus to the next. It seems like pragmatism to just run off a few salient bullet points about what you just spent the better part of an hour to compose, but with regard to understanding Red Pill intersexual dynamics it actually puts a reader at a disadvantage. I'll explain.

In so many forums, in so much media TL;DR pervades our thought process. We want to get to the important parts to see if we agree or disagree and rarely invest our online time in sussing out all of the particulars that led to those TL;DR points. This corrupts our method of really learning something, and in the case of changing one's life with a full understanding of Red Pill awareness it's simply impractical to hope to get the ideas without putting in the effort. And that's the point, education takes effort.

I've had many requests from my readers on the Red Pill Reddit forum to just distill down ideas I've put a lot of time and insight into developing. Speak more simplistically, give us a TL;DR summation and we'll take it from there. The problem with this line of thinking is that in the Red Pill praxeology, the process in coming to foundational ideas and principles is equally important as describing the dynamics themselves. I find it ironic that the same critics who endlessly request several peer reviewed long-form experimental studies in order to give my ideas any credence are often the least likely to actually read them due exactly to this TL;DR phenomenon.

On the few occasions I've made an honest attempt to strip down a post for easy digestibility the process goes like this: I make a TL;DR summation of the points I think best exemplify what my ideas are about and an under-informed reader turns into a critic of those points. They say, "Yes Rollo, that's all fine and well, but Aha! I got you because you didn't think of reasons X, Y and Z and I don't believe you." These reason I did, in fact, factor in to my ideation process of coming to those points, but because I've just catered my process to the 8th grade attention span and reading comprehension of readers who want the TL;DR convenience I've bypassed the process of how I came to my conclusions. What happens next is I then go into a more detailed explanation of reasons X, Y and Z and reexplain what would've been made clear had a reader simply invested some time in enriching themselves with both the process and the conclusions.

So, you see, TL;DR is actually the less pragmatic approach in that it takes more time to grasp a concept with the back and forth need for explanations. In other arenas, in other subject matter, this may be a convenience, but with the sensitive nature of Red Pill awareness, and the veritable certainty that the ideas will challenge a person's deeply ego-invested Blue Pill beliefs, making a commitment to devoting the time needed to understand the material is key. So, that said, I would humbly request that you ensure that you're distraction-free when reading any of my books.

The Rational Male is weighty stuff. Not a week goes by that I don't get an email or a Tweet from a man praising my work, but moreover, they tell me how they keep returning to reread key parts of the book as their lives' circumstances change. This is a good thing. It's actually how I intended the books to be read – with a highlighter pen to pick out the parts that jump out at a man and with a pencil to scribble in liner notes in the margins.

As I mention in all of my books' introductions, *The Rational Male* is meant to be a kind of living text that a man can keep coming back to. I want men to discuss it with other men (and women if warranted). The knowledge and insight is something that needs to be constantly debated and developed. I always imagine just the title, *The Rational Male*, on the cover being enough to get sideways glances or scoffs from women and feminized men, but this was intentional. It's triggering to be sure, but it's also meant to prompt discussion. I'd never want *The Rational Male* to be some banner or icon of some 'new masculinity' movement to be waved in the faces of feminists and social justice warriors. With some men I get the impression that *The Rational Male* could turn into some kind of Bible to thump in the presence of 'plugged-in' men and women. That's not the sentiment that I wrote this and my other volumes in.

Personal Development

Always remember, the material herein is meant for conversation. I understand the eagerness of men who've had their lives changed for the better to want to 'share the gospel' so to speak, and I'm glad for that, but I also know that changing the minds of others only comes from open discourse and conversation. I'm fond of saying that I only hold up a mirror, you've got to want to look into it. This is the approach I take when it comes to 'unplugging' men; they have to come to it and I can only be ready to discuss ideas when they are. Hopefully this, and my other works, will help facilitate that discussion when the time comes for you as well.

I'm prefacing this here because in this book the emphasis is more focused on men's personal development. I'm kind of reluctant to classify this book as "personal development" because, to me, that smacks of the Power of Positive Thinking schtick of positive mindset gurus selling old, formulaic optimism in whatever book or seminar program they're selling. I've never been interested in telling men how they can go about becoming better men or Real Men®.

I am interested in giving men the tools with which they can create better lives, individually, by applying Red Pill awareness to their individual states. I have always been wary of 'coaches' who claim to have a step-by-step plan to make men better at life, career and love, so I'll state here that this book's motive isn't to improve your life. I sincerely hope that your own betterment is a byproduct of this, but the intent is to inform and educate you.

I've separated this book into four main sections: Red Pill Parenting, The Feminine Nature, Social Imperatives and Positive Masculinity.

Red Pill Parenting is primarily aimed at the men who've asked me to go into some depth about how to go about raising their sons and daughters in a Red Pill aware context. Of the sections in this book I feel this will be the most potentially controversial. I say this not because Red Pill men will have any problem with what I outline in it, nor is it due to the ideas and suggestions I offer, but because it is a direct affront to how mainstream society hopes to socialize the coming generations of both genders. I'll let the material do the talking, but I expect a lot of flack for it from a feminine-primary social order to which this parenting advice is a threat. Much of it undermines most pop-psychology pablum about parenting today.

The Feminine Nature is a collection of essays I've rewritten and curated from my blog that specifically address the most predictable aspects of female psychology. In the sense that it outlines and explores the evolutionary and socialized reasons for women's most common behavior this section reads the most similar to my first book. In that book I touched a lot of what I believe constitutes the female mind (and expanding it to become the Feminine Imperative), but in this section I explore some more specific aspects of the female psyche.

In Social Imperatives I detail how the female psyche extrapolates into western(izing) cultural narratives, social dictates and legal and political legislation. This is the Feminine Imperative writ large and in it I'll explore how feminism, women's sexual strategy and primary life goals have molded our society into what we take for granted today. The 'women's empowerment' narrative, and the rise of a blank-slate egalitarian equalism, masks a form of female supremacy that has fundamentally altered western culture. These essays directly address and illustrate this phenomenon in an organized reading flow.

Finally, Positive Masculinity is comprised of essays I've reformed and expanded on that will give you a better idea of how to define masculinity in a conventional and rational perspective for yourself. I saved this section to be the last in the book because everything that leads up to it is descriptive and written to increase your 'Red Pill' awareness about the true personal and social environment in which you live. Positive Masculinity (and really this book in whole) are ideas from which I expect you'll want to apply in your own life at some point. In my second book, *Preventive Medicine*, the idea was to help men to know what they might expect from women, and what prompts them to it at various phases of their maturity. I wrote it in response to the common refrain "I wish I'd known all of this stuff before I got married, got divorced, I was dating (or not) in my 20s, etc." In Positive Masculinity I make an effort to give men some food for thought about what they might expect from themselves at certain stages of their own maturity.

While I'm not suggesting a codified return to 'traditional masculinity' or to lay out some rule book for "real men", I am going to suggest an outline of what I believe might constitute a retaking of a conventional masculinity for men. In what we call the Manosphere there have been various efforts to define real masculinity. Most of these are really just rewriting of what old school, old social contract, traditional masculinity was about before the sexual revolution and before mass social feminization. What I'll suggest in this section is a reclaiming of conventional, evolved, biologically prompted masculine nature by men. Furthermore, I believe this masculinity, founded in Red Pill awareness, can be a net positive for men, the women they involve in their lives, their families and society on whole.

It's my hope that we can push away tropes like "toxic" or "hyper" masculinity that our feminine-primary social order would have us characterize masculinity as. To be a man today is to be poisoned by testosterone. Masculinity is a bad word for men, while women make it something they dallyingly believe makes them greater. For men, this social order would have us believe that masculinity is something to be avoided or something that can be defined in feminized ambiguity. Even just suggesting you know what it is to "be a man" or you've embraced your masculine nature makes you a suspected criminal – or a ridiculous child with fantasies of manhood.

My hope is this book can change that perception; if not for larger society then for the sake of the individual and his family. Masculinity can be a positive, even (especially) including the aspects that feminized society finds so scary. The aggressive, sometimes hostile, aspects of masculinity have a place in the whole of it, but I believe we have to accept the entirety of conventional masculinity. When we only take the parts of it that we're comfortable with we're left with an inauthentic, unoffensive watered down masculinity that only serves the feminine reinterpretation.

Western culture has never had a greater need for risk takers and emboldened men who instinctively understand their masculine nature. After having read this volume I would ask that you take stock of both yourself and the social environment going on around you. In this book you'll read about what I call the *Red Pill Lens*. My hope is that you'll apply this new way of seeing things to a constructive effort of your own in understanding that raw, conventional masculinity can be a positive for your life.

As always, please pass on this book to a man you think needs it. I make the least amount of royalties from the printed version of my books, but these are what I encourage the purchase of the most because they inspire men to share this knowledge. You can't really do that with a digital or audio copy, but share this with other men. Discuss the contents, even the parts you strongly disagree with. There will again be parts you'll have an 'Aha!' moment reading, and there'll be parts that might make you angry. Thats good, that's what sparks insight, and that insight is what helps change us.

– Rollo Tomassi
June, 2017

Why do my eyes hurt?

You've never used them before.

THE RED PILL PARENT

AN INTRODUCTION TO
RED PILL PARENTING

The importance of fathers is something of a love-hate relationship in our feminine-primary social order. In our inner-cities the narrative is one of lamenting the lack of fathers' involvement in their kids' lives – especially boys' lives.

This is the go-to narrative whenever some kid commits a criminal act. If only men would be more involved fathers this kind of thing wouldn't happen. The call is always for more responsibility on the part of men who, according to narrative, are little more than irresponsible boys themselves. We're told their only imperative is to have indiscriminate sex and leave the consequences of an "unplanned" pregnancy to the poor girl he must've deceived in order to get laid.

This is one impression of modern "fatherhood", the deadbeat Dad, the 'Baby Daddy', the guy who needs to 'Man Up' and do the right thing after his girl '*accidentally*' got pregnant. And these fathers are, of course, the products of deadbeat Dads themselves, with no thought of seeing the larger forest for all the trees with regards to the social climate that's inspires this fatherly archetype.

When we watch the most consistent portrayals of fathers in popular media, sitcoms, movies, etc. we see another archetype of fatherhood; the buffoon, the bumbling Dad so thoroughly out of touch with the mainstream he requires his wife's uniquely female problem solving to set him straight – usually saving him from himself. This is the father who is essentially a dependent child himself and an archetype women believe they contend with in real life because it confirms their superiority in the *Strong Independent Woman*® identity – the same media has sold them for generations now.

This fatherhood archetype is reserved for Beta male fathers who are only too happy to play along with it because it neatly fits into their preconceptions of an egalitarian equalism between the sexes. However, this is only to the point where his humorous self-deprecation of his maleness coincides with his own impressions of fatherhood. Then all notions of equalism fall away in favor of his ridiculous maleness as a father.

The third archetype is the asshole, abusive father preconception. This Dad is easy to feel good about hating. Around Father's Day this is the father who gets the hate cards that explain to him (as well as salve the egos of his kids and wife) how unnecessary he really was after all. His wife, the mother of his kids, was always more than enough of a 'man' herself to make his influence superfluous if not detrimental to his kids' lives. In *Promise Keepers* I'll outline how this father-hood archetype is responsible for predisposing young men to a Beta mindset in the hopes of avoiding becoming the father he hated.

I'm not sure if most guy's really understand the irony of celebrating motherhood and fatherhood in some organized fashion, but it serves as a poignant highlight to the feminine-centric society in which we live.

The contrast between Mother's Day and Father's Day is now perhaps one of the most easily recognizable evidences of the code in the feminine Matrix.

As per the dictates of feminine social primacy, Mom is celebrated, loved and respected by default if only by virtue of her femaleness. Dad, if not outright vilified or publicly excoriated, is constantly reminded that he should always be living up to the servitude that defines his disposable gender. Father's Day is his reminder that he's still not living up to his feminine-primary expectations.

For children who blame their social indiscretions and psychological hangups on their mother, there is a certain degree of forgiveness. It's difficult to blame a mother since the impression is that mothering is a supreme effort and sacrifice – particularly when the popular idea is that she must go it alone due to uncoopera-tive fathers and *not* by her own designs or personal choices. If she fails to some degree it's excusable. For a man to blame his life's ills on Mom smacks of latent misogyny, and even then it's suspected she's a bad mother *because* of a bad father. However, when you lay the blame at Dad's feet, the whole world wails along in tune with you. A mother failing in her charge is negligent, but often forgivable; a man failing as a father is always perceived as selfish and evil.

When the next Father's Day rolls around make a mental note to visit the *Post Secret* blog. There you'll find that week's batch of anonymously sent, and hand-crafted, postcards revealing the inner workings of the feminine-primary mind of both men and women. The usual fare for Father's Day is a hearty "Fuck You Dad!" or "You're the reason I'm so fucked up!" interspersed with a couple 'good dad' or 'at least you tried' sentiments so as not to entirely degrade the feminized ideal of fatherhood – wouldn't want to discourage men's perpetual 'living up' to the qualifications set by the Feminine Imperative. There has to be a little cheese in the maze or else the rat won't perform as desired. I always see a marked difference in attitude between Mother's Day and Father's Day, especially now that I've been one for more than 18 years. Father's Day is a slap in the face for me now – not because my wife and daughter don't appreciate me as a father, but because it's become a big "fuck you" or "try harder". It's now a reminder that masculinity, even in as positive a light as the Blue Pill world might muster, is devalued and debased, and we ought to just take it like a man and get over it.

The more I hear how feckless fathers' perceptions are today only makes me want to be that much better a father to my daughter (even as she's an adult now), and I can't wait until I've got a grandson to help raise as well. That is until the reality sets in. The reality is that the only reason I feel the need to outperform other men in the fatherhood department is because a feminized social convention briefly convinced me that it's my responsibility to compete with other men in a game where the rules are fixed to make better slaves of disposable men. Of course the bar is set so low, and men are so debased now, that even the most mediocre of dads can play along and still get the feeling that they're marginally qualifying. The social convention plays into the same "not-like-other-guys" identification game most chumps subscribe to in their single years. The same desire-for-uniqueness groundwork is already installed.

After realizing this, I stopped worrying about "being a good dad". I'm already well beyond the fathering quality non-efforts of my own father, but that's not the point. A good father goes about the business of being a father without concern for accolades. For Men, like anything else, it's not about awards on the wall, but the overall body of work that makes for real accomplishment. A Father is a good father because he can weather an entire world that constantly tells him he's a worthless shit by virtue of being a Man with a child. He just 'does', in spite of a world that will never appreciate his sacrifice and only regard his disposability as being expected. And even in death he'll still be expected to be a good dad.

I outlined these father archetypes (there are a few more) to illustrate the various ways in which, as with all men, fathers are again caught in the same *Masculine Catch 22* I outlined in my first book.

One of the primary ways Honor is used against men is in the feminized perpetuation of traditionally masculine expectations when it's convenient, while simultaneously expecting egalitarian gender parity when it's convenient.

For the past 60 years feminization has built in the perfect Catch 22 social convention for anything masculine; The expectation to assume the responsibilities of being a man (Man Up) while at the same time denigrating anything asserting masculinity as a positive (Shut Up).

What ever aspect of maleness that serves the feminine purpose is a man's masculine responsibility, yet any aspect that disagrees with feminine primacy is labeled Patriarchy and Misogyny.

Essentially, this convention keeps Beta males in a perpetual state of chasing their own tails. Over the course of a lifetime they're conditioned to believe that they're cursed with masculinity (Patriarchy) yet are still responsible to 'Man Up' when it suits a feminine imperative. So it's therefore unsurprising to see that half the men in western society believe women dominate the world (male powerlessness) while at the same time women complain of a lingering Patriarchy (female powerlessness) or at least sentiments of it. This is the Catch 22 writ large. The guy who does in fact Man Up is a chauvinist, misogynist, patriarch, but he still needs to man up when it's convenient to meet the needs of a female imperative.

Fathers (and male mentors) in this social order walk a very fine line. As you'll read in the next section, fathers are viewed with contempt and suspiciousness when they assume an active role in parental investment and their influence in a child's life. Yet, fathers, and particularly the masculinity they represent, are also blamed for every social ill when they are absent from a child's life.

Fathers are simultaneously a vital ingredient in a kid's life, yet still superfluous to a kid being raised by a *Strong Independent®* mother. The Feminine Imperative is all too happy to assume authorship of a child's successes, and if not through its mother herself, then through the feminine-primary 'Village' that we're told is necessary to raise a child. A father or men's influence is only valued insofar as it coincides and agrees with the feminine-primary plan for that child's upbringing. Anything else is just teaching what the narrative deems to be an institutionalized misogyny or '*toxic*' masculinity.

The National Center for Fatherlessness estimates about a third of American children live absent their biological father. The statistics are even worse for African-American families. Estimates vary, but everyone agrees that somewhere between half and three quarters of black children grow up without their dads.

The epidemic of fatherlessness is so pervasive we tend to forget about it. It stays in the background when we consider other social ills. Even so, fatherlessness lies near the bottom of our increasingly dire cultural problems. The conscious awareness of fatherlessness only arises when some tragedy occurs that requires Dad as a convenient foil for it.

Watch any video clip of rioting and social unrest. What you'll see is young men behaving in a heinous and disgusting manner. Look deeper, and you'll see boys who grew up without fathers or, alternatively, fathers who did little but tutor them in criminality.

But this is only one example of the consequences of absent fathers. When you look at the boys and girls of what I call the "Participation Trophy" generation you see disempowered, disenfranchised, gender-loathing boys who all too eagerly wish they could become girls. And due to the priorities our culture places on *Fempowerment* and feminine-correctness in our education methods we have a generation of girls growing up to be male-entitled in their self estimations.

In my own estimate, Beta fathers basing their parenting on this same Blue Pill feminization posing as egalitarianism ideologies are every bit as damaging to the next generation's upbringing as uninvolved or absent fathers. Perhaps even more so. Fatherlessness can exist with a father present in the home.

The denial of the effects of fatherlessness also supports the larger cultural narrative about the irrelevancy of men. The idea that fathers are not really necessary for children is everywhere. When we laud women who choose to have a child on their own, while we infer that fathers don't matter – nice to have around if he's useful, but entirely unnecessary. These days, a pet is typically considered a more crucial part of a complete family than a man.

That's the way some people have wanted it for a long time. The entire feminist project has been devoted to unseating the father from his role in the family. Now that they have achieved their objective we see the results. We see this even within the modern church; men's family authority is only a liability for them and, along with that a father's "headship", has lost all meaning.

Despite what all the propaganda claims, fathers are necessary for a stable family. Authority and order in social relationships start with him. Without him, things fall apart as we are now seeing. The patriarchy has been smashed, and along with it the patriarch. And, contrary to feminist promises, once the patriarchy has been smashed, what emerges is not a peaceful world of equality and rainbow-draped unicorns. Rather it's the burned out hell-scape we'll see on display on the streets of the next riot, and on the faces of boys and girls wherever the father is missing. And we'll nod together and ask, "Where are these kids' fathers?"

THE RED PILL PARENT

In September of 2015 I spoke at the *Man In Demand* conference in Las Vegas. One thing I found encouraging to see was fathers and sons attending together. I honestly wasn't expecting this. It was a humbling experience to see fathers and sons coming to a Red Pill awareness together. I hadn't anticipated that more mature men would've been 'unplugged' by their sons, but I met with quite a few men who told me their sons had either turned them on to my books or that *The Rational Male* would be required reading for their sons before they got out of their teens.

One of the greatest benefits of the conference was the inspiration and material I got from the men attending. A particular aspect of this was addressing how men might educate and help others to unplug, and in that lay a wealth of observations about how these men's upbringings had brought them to both their Blue Pill idealisms and ultimately their Red Pill awareness.

I feel I have to start this chapter with some of these observations, but as I mentioned in the introduction, I'll be breaking protocol and be a bit more prescriptive here with regard to what I think may be beneficial ways to be a Red Pill parent.

In *The Rational Male – Preventive Medicine* I included a chapter which outlined how men are primarily conditioned for lives and ego-investments in a Blue Pill idealism that ultimately prepares them for better serving the Feminine Imperative when their usefulness is necessary to fulfill women's sexual (and really lifetime) strategies. If you own the book it might be helpful to review it after you read this section.

For the Kids' Sake

One of my regular blog readers (and conference attendee) *Jeremy* had an excellent observation for me about men's prioritization in the hierarchies of contemporary families:

There's a certain book that my friend's wife read, which told her to place her husband above her children. Children come first for a mother, and they should for the father too. I'm not advocating to neglect her husband, but he needs to accept some biological facts and not be hurt because of it.

What's happening here is actually the first steps of a hostage crisis. That is a textbook first-wave-feminism boilerplate response. This is the first redirection in a misdirection perpetuated by women in order to sink any notion that men should have some authority on matters in their marriages or relationships.

Think of the children. It's been repeated for so long, it's a cliché.

This is typical crab-in-a-basket behavior. Women seek power over their lives and somehow instinctively believe that the only way to achieve power is to take someone else's power away. So they attack male authority by placing children above men. This then becomes a stick with which to beat male authority into submission, as only the woman is allowed to speak for the needs of the children. This default feminine-correct authority is also intimately associated with women's *mystique* giving them insight to mothering no man would ever be considered to have a capacity for.

This is literally textbook subversion. When the children's needs become the *"throne"* of the household, and only the wife is allowed to speak for the children's needs, then the authority of the household becomes a rather grotesque combination of immediate child(rens) needs and female manipulation. A father's only contribution to these mother-determined needs is his support and acquiescence to what she's decided they are.

Worse still, the children are now effectively captives of the wife because, at any time, she can accuse that father of anything the law is forced to throw him in handcuffs for and take away the kids. While that may never be the first recourse it is always the unspoken 'nuclear option'.

This is the first step in that hostage situation. Equalists will try to convince you of the logic that children come first, that children are the future, it takes a *Village*, and that all of that which makes them better is more important than anything else. This is bullshit.

Our paleolithic ancestors didn't sit around in caves all day playing and socially interacting with their babies. They didn't have some kind of fresh-gazelle-delivery service that allowed him to interact with the children directly. Mothers were not under exactly the same survival conditions, needing to forage for carrots, potatoes, berries, etc, while the men hunted and built structures. If you think the children came first in any other epoch of humanity you are very sadly mistaken.

44

Children were more than capable of getting everything they need to know about how to live simply by watching their parents live a happy life together. This is how humans did things for eons, changing that order and putting the children first should be seen as the equalist social convention it is and the beginning of the destruction of the family.

Children are more than information sponges, they are relatively blank minds that often want desperately to be adult. Children want to understand everything that everyone around them understands, which is why a parent telling a child that you're 'disappointed' in them is sometimes more effective than a paddling.

If you focus on children, you are frankly spoiling them with attention that they will never receive in the real world. If instead you focus on yourself and your spouse, you will raise children that see you putting yourself as your *Mental Point of Origin*, and your marriage/partnership as an important part of what you do each day.

Don't put the children first. That sounds selfish because we've been acculturated in a feminine-primary social order that seeks to disempower men by making children the leverage with which to do it. This is not to say men ought to be uninvolved or disinterested in the raising of their kids, quite the opposite, but rather I'm stressing the need to be aware of the dynamic of disempowering men, fathers and husbands by women and mothers' essentially pedestalizing their children above yourself and your relationship with the mother.

I'll expound upon this later, but as most of my readers know, I am a proponent of what's called *Enlightened Self-Interest* – I cannot help anyone until I help myself. I doubt that most of the men of the previous, *Old Books*, generations would associating their parenting style with such a term, but this is exactly how they used to approach raising children. They came first, and wife and child followed in his *headship* and decisions.

Your Mental Point of Origin should never waver from yourself, whether you're single, monogamous, married, childless or a father.

American Parenting is Killing American Marriage

During the time of my writing this I came across a fantastic article on Quartz. com titled, *American Parenting is Killing American Marriage*. The money quote follows here, but I thought it was a good explanation of how well we parent in western culture is measured by how well it serves the Feminine Imperative:

Of course, (Ayelet Waldman's) blasphemy was not admitting that her kids were less than completely wonderful, only that she loved her husband more than them. This falls into the category of thou-shalt-have-no-other-gods-before-me. As with many religious crimes, judgment is not applied evenly across the sexes. Mothers must devote themselves to their children above anyone or anything else, but many wives would be offended if their husbands said, "You're pretty great, but my love for you will never hold a candle to the love I have for John Junior."

Mothers are also holy in a way that fathers are not expected to be. Mothers live in a clean, cheerful world filled with primary colors and children's songs, and they don't think about sex. A father could admit to desiring his wife without seeming like a distracted parent, but society is not as willing to cut Ms. Waldman that same slack. It is unseemly for a mother to enjoy pleasures that don't involve her children.

There are doubtless benefits that come from elevating parenthood to the status of a religion, but there are obvious pitfalls as well. Parents who do not feel free to express their feelings honestly are less likely to resolve problems at home. Children who are raised to believe that they are the center of the universe have a tough time when their special status erodes as they approach adulthood. Most troubling of all, couples who live entirely child-centric lives can lose touch with one another to the point where they have nothing left to say to one another when the kids leave home.

I think these quotes outline the dynamic rather well; a method of control women can use to distract and defer away from Beta husbands is a simple appeal to their children's interests as being tantamount to their own or conflating them with their husband's interests. If the child sits at the top of that love hierarchy (*see Preventive Medicine*) and that child's wellbeing and best interests can be defined by the mother, the father/husband is then relegated to subservience or superfluousness to both the child and the mother.

This gets us back to the myth of women's supernatural gift for *Empathy*; Women, by virtue of just being a woman, are imbued with some instinctual, empathetic insight about how best to place that child above all else. That child becomes a failsafe and a *Buffer* against having to entertain a real, intersexual relationship and connection with the father/husband and really consider his position in her Hypergamous estimate of him.

If that man isn't what her Hypergamous instincts estimates him being as optimal (he's the unfortunate Beta), then she's defaults to tolerating his presence for the kids' sake and you have marriages that have only one common interest.

The first case here was about an incident where a woman was being encouraged to put her husband before her kids in a conventional love hierarchy priority. The fact that this would appear so unnatural for a woman – to the point that it would need to be something necessary to train a woman to consciously consider – speaks volumes about the ease with which women presume that their priority ought to be for her kids. It's never a consideration that a husband's concern, importance or appreciation would supersede that of a child's. In fact, just the suggestion of it reduces a man to being equally as needy as any child, thus infantilizing him.

Most men buy into this prioritization as well.

It seems deductively logical that a woman would necessarily need to put her child's attention priorities well above her husband's. What's counterintuitive to both parents is that it's the health of their relationship (or lack of it) that defines and exemplifies a complementary gender understanding for the child. Women default to using their children as cat's paws to assume primary authority of the family, and men are already Blue Pill preconditioned by a feminine-centric upbringing to accept this as the normative frame for the family.

As with all your relations with women, establishing a strong relational *Frame* is essential. The problem for men, even with the strongest initial *Frame* with their wives, is that they cede their relational *Frame* to their kids. Most men want the very best for their children; or there may be a *Promise Keepers* dynamic that a guy is dealing with where he makes every effort to outdo, and make up for, the sins of his father by sacrificing everything. But in so doing he loses sight of creating and maintaining a dominant *Frame* for not just his wife, but the state of his family.

Most men, being conditioned Betas, feel uncomfortable assuming any kind of authority, thus, weak *Frame* is a handicap for them even before their first child is born. This creates a (sometimes impossible) challenge for them once they have a kid, become Red Pill aware, and then seek to assert or reassert a needed *Frame*.

It's important to bear in mind that when you set the *Frame* of your relationship, whether it's a first night lay or a marriage prospect, women must enter *your* reality and *your* frame. The same needs to apply to any children within that relationship – they also must exist in your *Frame*.

Far too many fathers are afraid to embody this strong authority for fear of being seen as a "typical man" and expect their wives (and children) to recognize what should be his primary place in the family on their own accord.

The preconditioned fear is that by assuming this authority they might become the typical asshole father they hoped to avoid for most of their formative years. Even for men with strong masculine role models in their lives, the hesitation comes from a culture that ridicules fathers, or presumes they're potentially violent towards children. Men internalize this acknowledgment of ridiculousness or asshole-ishness and thus, the abdication of fatherly authority, even in as positive a sense as possible, is surrendered before that child is even born.

Comfort in Frame

One of the most basic Red Pill principles I've stressed since I began writing is the importance of *Frame*. This was the first *Iron Rule of Tomassi* for a reason:

Iron Rule of Tomassi #1

Frame is everything. Always be aware of the subconscious balance of whose frame in which you are operating. Always control the Frame, but resist giving the impression that you are.

The dynamic of *Frame* stretches into many aspects of a man's life, but in a strictly intergender sense this applies to men establishing a positive dominance in their relationships with women. In a dating context of non-exclusivity (*plate spinning*) this means, as a man, you have a solid reality into which that woman wants to be included in.

Holding *Frame* is not about force, or coercion, it's about attraction and desire and a genuine want on the part of a woman to be considered for inclusion into that man's reality. Being allowed into a man's dominant, confident *Frame* should be a compliment to that woman's self-perception. Being part of a high-value man's life should be a prize she seeks.

This is a pretty basic principle when you think about it. The main reason women overwhelmingly prefer men older than themselves (statistically 5-7 years difference) is because of the psychological impression that men older than a woman's age *should* be more established in his understanding of the world, his career, his direction in life and his mastery over himself and his conditions.

From the Alpha Fucks perspective of Hypergamy, the air of a man's mastery of his world makes an older man preferable, while a Beta older man represents the prospect of dependable, if somewhat unexciting, provisioning.

In our contemporary sexual marketplace I think this perception – which used to hold true in a social climate based on the old set of books – is an increasing source of disappointment for women as they move from their post-college *Party Years* into the more stressful *Epiphany Phase* where they find themselves increasingly less able to compete intrasexually.

And, once again, we also see evidence of yet another conflict between egalitarianism vs. complementarity. Because, in an egalitarian utopia, all things should be equalized; equalism espouses that this age preference should make no difference in attraction, yet the influence of this natural complementary attraction becomes a source of internal conflict for women who buy into equalism.

Women's self-perception of personal worth becomes wrapped up in a tight egotistical package.

It's an interesting paradox. On one hand she's expects a Hypergamously better-than-equitable pairing with a self-made man who will magically appreciate her for her self-perceptions of her own personal worth, but also to be, as *Sheryl Sandberg* puts it, "someone who wants an equal partner. Someone who thinks women should be smart, opinionated and ambitious. Someone who values fairness and expects or, even better, wants to do his share in the home."

In other words, an exceptional, high value man, with a self-earned world and *Frame* she wants to partake of; but also one who will be so smitten by her intrinsic qualities (the qualities she hopes will compensate for her physical and personal deficits) that he will compromise the very *Frame* that made him worthy of her intimacy, and then reduce himself to an equality that lessens him to her.

The Red Pill Father and Frame

The reason I'm going into this is because of a basic tenet of *Frame*:

The *Frame* you set in the beginning of your relationship will establish the tone for the future of that relationship.

That isn't to say men don't devolve from a strong Alpha frame to a passive Beta one, but the *Frame* you enter into a relationship with will be the mental impression that woman retains as it develops. This impression also becomes the basis from which you will develop your persona as a father.

Your establishment and maintenance of a strong control of psychological and ambient *Frame* is not just imperative to a healthy relationship and interaction with a woman, but it's also vital to the health of any family environment and the upbringing of any children that result from it.

I've been asked on occasion about my thoughts on the influence family plays in conditioning boys/men to accept a Beta role in life. In specific, the question was about how a mother's dominant *Frame* influences her children's upbringing and how an unconventional shift in intersexual hierarchies can predisposes her to imprinting her Hypergamous insecurities onto her children. It gave me a lot to think about.

A common thread I've occasionally found with newly Red Pill aware men is the debilitating influence their domineering mothers and Beta supplicating fathers played in forming their distorted perceptions of masculinity. I made an attempt to address this influence in the *Intersexual Hierarchies* section of the last book, however, I intended those essays to provide an outline of particular hierarchical models, not really to cover the individual health or malaise of any of them.

From *Frame, The Rational Male*:

> *The default pedestalization of women that men are prone to is a direct result of accepting that a woman's frame is the **only** frame. It's kind of hard for most 'plugged in' men to grasp that they can and should exert frame control in order to establish a healthy future relationship. This is hardly a surprise considering that every facet of their social understanding about gender frame has always defaulted to the feminine for the better part of their lifetimes. Whether that was conditioned into them by popular media or seeing it played out by their beta fathers, for most men in western culture the feminine reality IS the normalized frame work. In order to establish a healthy male-frame, the first step is to rid themselves of the preconception that women control frame by default. They don't, and honestly, they don't want to.*

Post LTR Frame

> *In most contemporary marriages and long-term relationship arrangements, women tend to be the de facto authority. Men seek their wives's "permission" to attempt even the most mundane activities they would do without an afterthought while single. I have married friends tell me how 'fortunate' they are to be married to such an understanding wife that she'd "allow"*

him to watch hockey on their guest bedroom TV, ... occasionally.

These are just a couple of gratuitous examples of men who entered into marriage with the Frame firmly in control of their wives. They live in her reality, because anything can become normal. What these men failed to realize is that frame, like power, abhors a vacuum. In the absence of the Frame security a woman naturally seeks from a masculine male, this security need forces her to provide that security for herself. Thus we have the commonness of cuckold and submissive men in westernized culture, while women do the bills, earn the money, make the decisions, authorize their husband's actions and deliver punishments. The woman is seeking the security that the man she pair-bonded with cannot or will not provide.

*It is vital to the health of any LTR that a man establish his frame as the basis of their living together **before** any formal commitment is recognized.*

The primary problem men encounter with regard to their marriages is that the dominant, positively masculine *Frame* they should have established while single (and benefiting from competition anxiety) decays (or reverts) to a Beta mindset and the man abdicates authority and deference to his wife's feminine primary *Frame.* This is presuming that dominant *Frame* ever existed while he was dating his wife. Most men experience this decay in three ways:

- A gradual decline to accepting his wife's *Frame* via his relinquishing an authority he's not comfortable embracing.

- An initial belief in a misguided egalitarian ideal redefines masculinity and conditions him to surrender *Frame.*

- He was so pre-whipped by a lifetime of Blue Pill Beta conditioning he already expects to live within a woman's *Frame* before marriage.

Of these, the last is the most direct result of an upbringing within a feminine-primary *Frame.* I think one of the most vital realizations a Red Pill man has to consider is how Red Pill truths and his awareness of them influences the larger dynamic of raising and instructing subsequent generations.

Hypergamy is both pragmatic and rooted in a survival-level doubt about women's optimizing it. When a woman's insecurity about her life-determining Hypergamous decisions are answered by a positive conventionally masculine Man, who is both her pair-bonded husband and the father of her children, that doubt is quieted and a gender-complementary environment for raising children progresses from that security.

In a positively masculine dominant *Frame*, where that woman's desire is primarily focused on her man, (and where that man's sexual market value exceeds his wife's by at least a factor of 1) this establishes at least a tenable condition of quieting a woman's Hypergamous doubt about the man she's consolidated monogamy and parental investment with.

In a condition where that husband is unable or unwilling (thanks to egalitarian beliefs) to establish his dominant Frame this leaves a woman's Hypergamous doubt as the predominant influence on the health of the overall family. That doubt and the insecurities that extend from Hypergamous selection set the tone for educating and influencing any children that result from it.

In the past I've made the case that deliberately single, primarily female, parents arrogantly assume they can teach a child both masculine and feminine aspects equally well. In the case where a wife/mother assumes the headship of family authority, both she and the *Frame* abdicating father/husband reverse this conventional gender modeling for their children.

That woman's dominant *Frame* becomes the reality that not just her husband must enter into, but also their children and, by extension, their family's relatives. That feminine-dominant *Frame* is one that is predicated on the insecurities inherent in women's Hypergamous doubts.

Hypergamy Knows Best

I think this "putting the kids first" phenomenon is very simple to explain. She doesn't want to fuck you! She is using the kids as a shield, a barrier, to deflect your unwanted Beta sexual advances.

It is generally accepted that women are only interested in the top 20% of men, and if you are talking about as marriage partners I would agree with this.

However if you are talking about as sex partners that they are genuinely hot for, I would estimate this percentage to be north of 5% add in the frame required to maintain her sexual interest in a marriage / long-term relationship and your probably closer to 1-2%.

It's really that simple.

*The women that are with these top tier men, the top 1-2% don't need to be told to put them before the kids, they do it because he **is** more important to her than her kids, because if he leaves she will never be able to replace him with another top tier man now she has his kids in tow.*

Top tier men don't raise other mens children and she knows this instinctively. If you think you can mitigate this by being top 20% and reading a few articles on frame and dread game then I think you will be disappointed.

Sure you can improve your relationship but you're probably not going to be able to command the visceral, raw, desire that women have for the top tier men that makes them do this shit naturally under their own volition.

This was a comment from one of my regular readers that sums up the basic point; for women there is a natural, desired, recognition of a man's *Frame* that is attached to his fundamental sexual market value in contrast with her own.

"Is he really the best I can do?"

In a feminine-primary *Frame*, that question defines every aspect of that woman's family life and development together.

It's important for Red Pill aware men to really meditate on that huge truth. If you do not set, and maintain, a dominant masculine *Frame*, if you do not accept your role in a conventional complementary relationship, that woman will feel the need to assume the responsibility for her own, and her children's, welfare. Women's psychological firmware predisposes them to this on a visceral, limbic, species-survival level.

I've met with countless men making a Red Pill transition in life who've related stories about the burdening influence of their domineering mothers and Beta supplicating fathers leading to them being brought up to repeat that Blue Pill cycle. I've also counseled guys who were raised by their single mothers who had nothing but spite and resentment for the Alpha Asshole father who left her. They too, took it upon themselves to be men who sacrifice their masculinity for equalism in order to never be like *Dad the Asshole*. I've met with the guys whose mothers had divorced their dutiful fathers to bang their bad boy tingle-generating boyfriends (whom they equally despised) and they too were molded by their mother's Hypergamous decisions.

And this is what I'm emphasizing here; in all of these upbringing conditions it is the mother's Hypergamous doubt that is the key motivating influence on her children. That lack of a father with a positive, strong, dominant *Frame* puts his children at risk of an upbringing based on that mother's Hypergamous self-questioning doubt. Add to this the modern feminine-primary social order that encourages women's utter blamelessness in acting upon this Hypergamous doubt and you can see how the cycle of creating weak, gender-confused men and vapid entitled women perpetuates itself.

Finally, to the guys who are psychologically stuck on the shitty conditions they had to endure because of this cycle, to the men who are still dealing with how mommy fucked them up or daddy was a Beta; the best thing you can do is recognize the cycle I've illustrated for you here. That's the first step to pushing past it. Acknowledging Red Pill truth is great at getting you laid, but it's much more powerful than that. It gives you the insight to see the influences that led to where you find yourself today.

Once you've recognized the Red Pill truths behind your Blue Pill conditioning, then it's time to realign yourself, and recreate yourself in defiance to them. The longer you wallow in the self-pity condition that your mother's Hypergamy and your father's passive Beta-ness embedded in you, the longer you allow that Blue Pill schema to define who you are.

Ectogenesis

At the *Man in Demand* conference I had a young guy ask me what my thoughts were about a man's being interested in becoming a single parent of his own accord. In other words, how feasible was it for a guy to father his own child with a surrogate or some other technology (artificial womb tech), much in the same way women can via sperm banks and artificial insemination?

I had this same question posed to me during an interview with blogger and podcast personality Christian McQueen. At present this essentially breaks down to a man supplying his own sperm, buying a suitable woman's viable ovum to fertilize himself, and, I presume, hire a surrogate mother to carry that child to term. Thereupon he takes custody of that child and raises it himself as a single father.

I'll admit that when I got the question about single fatherhood I was a bit incredulous of the mechanics of it. Naturally it would be an expense most men couldn't entertain. However, I did my homework on it, and found out that ectogenesis was yet another science-fiction-come-reality that feminists have already considered and have planned for.

In theory, this arrangement should work out to something similar to a woman heading off the sperm bank to (once again, Hypergamously) select a suitable sperm donor and become a single parent of her own accord. It's interesting that we have institutions and facilities like sperm banks to ensure women's Hypergamy, but men, much less heterosexual men, must have exceptional strength of purpose and determination to do anything similar.

Despite dealing with the very likely inability of the surrogate mother to disentangle her emotional investment in giving birth to a child she will never raise (hormones predispose women to this) a man must be very determined financially and legally to become a single father by choice. In principle, I understand the sentiment of Red Pill men wanting to raise a child on their own. The idea is to do so free from the (at least direct) influence of the Feminine Imperative. I get the reasoning, however, I think this is in error.

My feelings on this are two part. First, being a true Complementarian, it is my belief that a child requires two healthy adult parents, male and female, with a firm, mature grasp of the importance, strengths and weaknesses of their respective gender roles (based on biological and evolutionary standards). Ideally they should exemplify and demonstrate those roles in a healthy fashion so a boy or a girl can learn about masculinity and femininity from their respective parents' examples.

Several generations after the sexual revolution, and after several generations of venerating feminine social primacy, we've arrived at a default, collective belief that single mothers can perform the function of modeling and shaping masculinity in boys as well as femininity in girls equally well.

Granted, the definition of masculinity is a distorted one, defined by egalitarianism and the Feminine Imperative, but the underlying social message in that is that women/mothers can be a one-woman show with respect to parenting. Thus, men, fathers or the buffoons mainstream culture portrays them to be, are superfluous to parenting – nice to have around, but not mission-critical. This belief also finds fertile ground in the notion that men today are largely obsolete.

Secondly, for all the equalist emphasis of Jungian gender theories about anima/animus and balancing feminine and masculine personality interests, this presumptions is evidence of an agenda that suggests a woman is equally efficient in teaching and modeling masculine aspects to children as well as any positively masculine man could. With that in mind, I think the reverse would be true for a deliberately single father – even with the best of initial intents.

As such, I think a father would serve as a poor substitute for a woman when it comes to exemplifying a feminine ideal. The argument then of course is that, courtesy of a feminine-centric social order, women have so divorced themselves from conventional femininity that perhaps a father might teach a daughter (if not demonstrate for her) a better feminine ideal than a woman. Conventional, complementary femininity is so lost on a majority of women it certainly seems like logic for a man to teach his daughter how to recapture it.

Raising Betas

This was the trap that third wave feminism fell into; the belief that they knew how best to raise a boy into the disempowered and emasculated ideal of their redefined masculinity. Teach that boy a default deference and sublimation of his own gender interests to feminine authority, redefine it as 'respect', teach him to pee sitting down and share in his part of the *choreplay*, and well, the world is bound to be a better more cooperative place, right?

So, it is for these reason I think that the evolved, conventional, two-parent heterosexual model serves best for raising a child. I cannot endorse single parenthood for either sex. Parenting should be as collaborative and as complementary a partnership as is reflected in the symbiotic relationship between a mother and father.

It's the height of gender-supremacism to be so arrogantly self-convinced as to deliberately choose to birth a child and attempt to raise it into the contrived ideal of what that "parent" believes the other gender's role ought to be.

Yet, this is what single mothers often elect to do, and as a society we laud them for it. We encourage and facilitate mothers in their raising children with the idea that they can be effective in teaching both genders' aspects. This should put the institutionalized, social engineering agenda of the Feminine Imperative into stark contrast for anyone considering intentional single parenthood. Consider that sperm banks and feminine-exclusive fertility institutions have been part of normalized society for over sixty years and you can see that Hypergamy and its inherent need for certainty has dictated the course of parenting for some time now.

This amounts to a unilateral control of what new generations will define as masculine and feminine; this is the very definition of social engineering.

THE RED PILL FATHER

"If I'm not going to have children, she told herself, then I'm going to have lovers." – Robin Rinaldi, The Wild Oats Project.

In the last section I put an emphasis on men's understanding women's rudimentary doubt of their Hypergamous choices with regards to rearing children and the overall health of a family. There are a great many social factors in our westernized feminine-centric social structure that encourages women to delay both marriage and becoming a mother well past their prime fertility windows.

In my essay, *Myth of the Biological Clock* I detailed the misconceptions women hold with regard to their own capacity of having children later in life:

Popular culture likes to teach women and, by association, unenlightened men that there is an innate biological clock inside each woman that slowly ticks down to a magical period where her maternal instincts at long last predispose her to wanting a child. Perhaps, not so surprisingly, this coincides perfectly with the Myth of Women's Sexual Peak as well as conveniently being the age demographic just post or just prior to when most women hit the Wall.

[...]I wont argue that women actually possess maternal instincts, I will argue that their understanding of when they manifest has been deliberately distorted by a feminine-centric cultural influence. If women are angry about the revelations of their inability or difficulty to conceive that their post-Wall biological conditions presents, their anger is misdirected. Rather than come down from the heady pedestal of ego-invested female empowerment psychology, they'll blame men for not being suitable fathers at exactly the time that conveniences their sexual strategy, or men lacking a will to "play-by-the rules" and satisfy the dictates of the feminine imperative by whiling away their time in porn and video game induced comas.

The have-it-all mentality popularized by feminism has led to some very bad social effects for women on whole. While a great deal of having it all is couched in messaging that appeals to enabling '*Empowered®*' women to get a similar deal from career life that men are supposedly enjoying, the subtext in this message is one of never settling for a less than Hypergamously optimal (better-than, not equal-to) monogamous pairing with a man.

The "have it all" advertising is about life fulfillment from a distractingly equalist perspective. The sales pitch is that women can expect equitable or better fulfillment than what the Feminine Imperative would have women expect that men are getting from life.

Women want to *be* men. Thus, we see the push for female college enrollment that imbalances men's enrollment, dangerously reducing the standard physical requirements for combat in the military or being a 'fire-person', or any number of other arenas in life where men seem to have it all. However, in so doing, the life course women are directed to by the imperative also limits their Hypergamous optimization efforts by putting unrealistic expectations upon it.

Women are taught that it's possible to serve two masters, male-comparable achievement *and* Hypergamy.

As a result women either delay childbearing until ages that put them and any offspring at a health risk, or they simply forgo marriage altogether and birth a child with the foreknowledge that the father (though maybe an adequate provisioner) will never be a contender to quell her doubts of his Hypergamous suitability.

If Momma Aint Happy Aint Nobody Happy

I'm fleshing out this aspect of Hypergamy here because I believe, as with all things female, a broad understanding of Hypergamy is essential to a man's life and has far reaching effects that go beyond just learning Game well enough to get the lay on a Saturday night when a woman is in her ovulatory peak phase.

A byproduct of the societal embrace of openly acknowledged Hypergamy is the degree to which women are largely disposed to delaying commitment until what I call their *Epiphany Phase* and then transitioning into a need for security once their capacity to attract and arouse men decays and/or is compromised by intrasexual competition (i.e. hitting *The Wall*). I detailed this child-birth postponement process in *The Rational Male, Preventive Medicine* where I outline women's Party Years through their *Epiphany Phase*, however it's important for men to understand that this phase is largely the result of women believing they *should* have a similar window as a man in which they can have both a career and find the "right guy" to partner in parenting with.

Equalism's fundamental flaw is rooted in the belief that men and women are both rational and functional equals, separated only by social influence and selfish imperatives (uniquely attributed to men). The grave consequences women accept in this belief is that their sexual market value declines with age, both in terms of intrasexual competition and fertility.

As such, we entertain the complaints of generations of women frustrated that they were unable to consolidate on a Hypergamous ideal because they believed they had ample time to do so while pursuing the Alpha Fucks aspect of their Hypergamy in the years of their prime fertility window.

Today's women also believe that the men who are available and ready to fulfill the Beta Bucks aspect of Hypergamy simply don't measure up to their socialized, overinflated, sense of Hypergamous entitlement (and particularly in comparison to the men who made them *Alpha Widows* in their Party Years).

So distressing is this prospect, and so keenly aware of it are women, that they are beginning to mandate insurances in anticipation of not being able to optimize Hypergamy – such as preemptive egg freezing and legislating that men pay for their infertility while married in alimony settlements.

It's getting to the point where the ages of 29-31 are no longer being considered a crisis point for women with regard to child bearing. With the popularization of the false hope in frozen ovum extending a woman's birthing time-frame, now, even 35-38 years old seems to magically grant women some bonus years in which to secure a man for parental investment. The question is no longer one of a woman making herself suitable for a man's parental investment (by his late 30's no less), but rather, she believes, a magical-thinking proposition of waiting out the Hypergamously 'right' father for her children.

Parental Precautions

I'm stressing these points here before I move on to Red Pill parenting ideology so men who are, or want to become fathers, husbands or invested boyfriends, understand the importance that Hypergamy plays in any family arrangement they hope to create.

Just to head off all the concerns about marriage being a raw deal for men reading this; Don't get married. Under contemporary western circumstances there is no advantage for men in a state of marriage and 100% advantage for women. Unfortunately, as things are structured, marriage will always be a cost-to-benefit losing proposition while women insist on making marriage a legalistic contract of male-only liabilities.

That said, also remember that an entire world steeped in feminine-primary social imperatives is arrayed against your efforts in being a positively masculine father to your kids. Those anti-father efforts start with women's own feminine-centric conditioning that leads them to push for Hypergamous optimization personally and societally. Yet, they will delay that optimization until all opportunities for her have been exhausted. If you are considering marriage and starting a family with a woman between the ages of 27 and 31, statistically, this will likely be the situation and mentality that your would-be wife is experiencing.

I'm presenting these things to you as a father or potential father, because it's important for you to discern what women have been conditioned to believe and expect from men and for themselves. In the coming chapters I will elaborate on the complementarity both sexes have evolved for to make our species what it is today; and that conventional complementarity is something idealistic equalism would distort for men. However, for now, it's important to realize that women have been thrust into this zero-hour, jump-at-the-last-second, cashout of the sexual marketplace schedule of mating that their very biology rebels against.

Single Moms and "Good" Fathers

It is also important for men to understand that, while there is a constant 'Man Up' berating of fathers for their lack of involvement in a child's life in popular culture, men are simultaneously presented with the female 'empowerment' meme. As I mentioned in the last section, there is a meme that proposes these fathers' parental involvement is effectively superfluous to that child's maturation because *Strong Independent Women®* can reportedly fulfill that fathers' role equally as well as any man (this is the 'equalist' narrative).

For all the public awareness campaigns extolling fathers to be more involved Dads, the message is always one of being "better" fathers and placing them into a default position of being 'bad' by virtue of their maleness. If men are as ridiculous or potentially violent as popular media has taught us they are, men are already starting their fatherhood from a negative position. In fact a 'good' father is a rarely appreciated commodity because that 'good' quality is always tied to a man's never ending and ever shifting qualification for female 'correctness'.

On the other side, the single mother empowerment meme is endemic. It's very important to use our Red Pill Lens with this meme because the message is one that forgives women of their inability to make themselves appropriate prospects for men's parental investment. At the same time this meme also foist the blame for men's *'typical'* unwillingness to parentally invest squarely on men's responsibility to women in optimizing Hypergamy to their satisfaction.

The following quote is from an article titled *I'll Probably Always Be a Single Mom* by Leah Campbell.

I'm Stupid Picky.

In my 15 or so years of dating, I've been around. I don't mean that to sound skanky, but ... it's not like I haven't given love a chance. The problem? Out of all the men I've ever dated, there has only been one or two that I felt a genuine connection with. It is a rare thing indeed for me to meet someone I feel like I could picture spending forever with. Sadly, I can't even remember the last time I met a man who gave me butterflies. It's definitely been years.

I Want the Fairytale.

There are very few relationships I've witnessed in my life that I would actually want for myself. Which begs the question, what do I want? Well, I want a man who is great with kids and totally open to adopting a houseful with me. I want a man who is smart and driven, sexy and hilarious. One who gets me, and who challenges me, and who makes me weak in the knees. Basically ... I want everything. And I'm not sure the image I have in my head of what love should be is something that actually exists in real life.

My Daughter Will Always Be Priority Number One.

If you think my expectations of what I want for me are implausible, we probably shouldn't even discuss my expectations of what I want for the man who steps into that paternal role for my daughter. Truthfully, as much as I want that father figure for her, I am also absolutely terrified of choosing wrong, of messing up our dynamic by choosing a man who isn't worthy of being her father.

I add this here because it illustrates many of the common misgivings women have with understanding their Hypergamous choices and their consequences. This article's entire checklist read like a manifesto for the *Strong Independent®* single mother with no consideration given to how single men, potential fathers or husbands might interpret it. As expected, it perpetuates the 'put your kid first' religion of motherhood here, but after reading through her single-mom rationalizations, and then combined with men's presumptive servitude to the beneficiaries of the Feminine Imperative, it's easy to see why most, if not all men, might be hesitant to sign up for the duty she expects of them.

Preparations

My point here isn't to dissuade men from wanting to be fathers, but rather that they enter into being a parent with their eyes open to how Hypergamy, and a cultural imperative that's built around it, influences women's life choices today.

I mentioned earlier about women between the ages of 27 and 31 experiencing the first harsh realities of the consequences their choices have predisposed them to. Understand, as a man, your desire, your potential, for parental investment puts you into a position of being the most sexually selective with women during this phase. So much in fact that the Feminine Imperative has created long-held social conventions all pre-established with the purpose of convincing men they are not only obligated to fulfilling women's Hypergamous strategy, but should feel lucky to do so.

The truth is that it's women who are at their most necessitous of men during this phase of their lives – thus placing men with the means and desire to become a parent into a prime selector's position. Feminine social conditioning has done all it can to predispose Beta men to wait out and forgive women their short-term Alpha Fucks indiscretions during their Party Years, but as Red Pill awareness becomes increasingly unignorable in society the pressures of maintaining an image of being the prime selector will wear on women.

That said, I've had many men ask me how best to go about becoming a Red Pill parent. I've had many men express that the only advantage to men in marriage is in creating a healthy, hopefully complementary, environment in which to raise children. However, I'm not sure even women would concur with this assessment in the face of a social narrative that tells them they can raise a child as well as any father can. Yet, by the definition of the Feminine Imperative, a 'good' father is one who will sublimate his masculinity and assume a feminine, subservient gender role, thus making him superfluous whether he's available or not.

I generally emphasize establishing a strong, dominant, yet positive masculine *Frame* for men. This is the vital starting point for any long term relationship a man might hope to raise children in.

The next imperative a man must confront is the Herculean obstacles he faces in a western culture that devalues him as a father, but obligates him to be an involved 'good' father who can only ever qualify himself to the mother of his children (who are taught they should place them above his interests) and qualify himself to a society that's been conditioned to hold him to her standards.

Finally, a potential father needs to understand the circumstance in which women's never ending quest to satisfy their Hypergamous doubt places them in at various phases of their maturity. For Red Pill men, a lot gets made of 'vetting' women for personal attributes and character to make them contenders for being the mother of their children. While this is important, I can't stress enough how important it is to account for the Hypergamous choices women make prior to his consideration – as well as the consequences she should be held accountable for, yet attempts to avoid by his obligated graces.

If knowing is half the battle, taking action is the other half.

The Vetting Process

I could care less who I'm talking to. In my opinion, if you're looking to disqualify a woman based on her sexual history you're doing yourself a disservice because you better believe that the high quality chicks have been fucked in every way imaginable. If not you it's somebody else... Might as well be you!

This was a comment from one of my blog readers, but it's a fairly common refrain amongst men dealing with our modern sexual marketplace. Men ought to just sack up and accept that, statistically, women are going to have had more than a few lovers prior to getting together with you.

One of my most widely linked blog posts on *The Rational Male* blog was called *Saving the Best*. In it I detailed the increasingly more common situation of Beta husbands discovering that their seemingly sexually-disinterested wives were far more sexually adventurous with the Alpha men of their Party Years when they discover evidence (online or digitally recorded) or personal admissions of it. The money quote was this:

"I married a slut who fucks like a prude."

I understand this sentiment. Too much overt concern (i.e. asking or torturing oneself) about a woman's sexual past is indeed demonstrating lower value for a man. Men who women consider Alpha, the men that women already have a mental impression of, don't overly concern themselves with women's sexual pasts because those men generally have multiple romantic options going.

On some level of consciousness women know that if what a man can glean from interacting with her about her sexual past is off-putting to an Alpha he'll simply eject and move on to a better prospect.

An Alpha mindset is often very minimalist, blunt and direct, but there are aspects of interacting with women that come as a default for a man who is his own *Mental Point of Origin*. One of those unspoken aspects of an Alpha mindset is a self-understanding that he's got options (or can generate more) and this is manifested in his indifference to a woman's long term sexual suitability. If she doesn't enter his *Frame*, to his satisfaction, he moves on to the next prospect with very little, if any, communication.

However, we're not discussing non-exclusive dating/fucking; we're discussing making an investment in a woman we're vetting for our own parental invest-ment. When you consider the all-downside risks a man must wager on that investment it behooves a man to be at his most discerning about that woman's sexual past and the consequences that *you* will be burdened with if you don't vet her wisely.

Most men (myself included at the time) have very sparse prerequisites when it comes to their considering a woman for marriage or even a long term relation-ship. Most men simply transition into it. The hot one night stand or the fuck bud-dy becomes his de facto girlfriend and then his long term partner without any real consideration or introspection about her suitability as a wife or mother. And by then, certain emotional and familial investments make any real, hard vetting a biased prospect.

This lack of insight is the result of a constant battery of shame and precondition-ing by the Feminine Imperative that tells men any requisites they would have of a woman for marriage are 'passing judgment' on her character. He should consider himself "lucky" that any woman would have him for a husband (or "put up with him") and his concerns about her are shameful, typically male character flaws on his part.

Consequentially Blue Pill men self-censor and rarely permit themselves the luxury of putting their own considerations above that of a potential mate.

Vetting

If you asked a woman whether she would be wary of marrying a man who was a recovering alcoholic or a cleaned up heroin addict she'd probably disqualify him as a marriage prospect from the outset.

And were she to go ahead and marry him anyway with full disclosure of his past addictions, would we be sympathetic with her if he were to relapse and she to bear the consequences of his past indiscretions?

Now suppose that woman married this former addict, but due to his being offended about her prying into his past, she was actually ignorant of his old addictions. She has her suspicions, but society tells her it should never be her purview to hold him accountable for anything that happened in his past.

He's moved on and so should she, right? Any lingering consequences from his addictions (such as a DUI, criminal record or his unemployability) shouldn't be held against him, nor should she *judge* him, nor should she consider those consequences whatsoever when she's assessing his suitability for marriage now.

In fact, she should feel ashamed to even consider his past with regard to her feelings about who he is. Her judgmentalism only points to her own character flaws.

Now, would we praise that woman for "following her heart" and marrying him? Would we hold her accountable for the decision to marry him if he relapses?

Reverse the genders and this scenario is precisely why women become so hostile when men even hint at 'judging' women's past sexual decisions. There is a very well established operative social convention that the 'Sisterhood' will all unanimously get behind; and that is the ruthless shaming of men who would ask any questions about any woman's sexual past. This is the degree of desperation that women feel during the *Epiphany Phase* when they acknowledge that men are becoming aware of their long term sexual strategy.

They understand that, in their *Epiphany Phase*, the clock is ticking down to zero. That's the cause of a lot of anxiety. They are just beginning to understand that their marriageability (Beta Bucks priority) now conflicts with their previous short-term mating strategy (Alpha Fucks priority). Women of this age cannot afford to have their short term sexual strategy count against them at a time when they are at their most necessitous of what that Beta can provide towards her long term security.

Again, on some level of consciousness, women understand that, were the ignorant Beta she's decided to marry (start a family with or help her raise her prior lovers' children with) to become aware of what she'd done in her sexual past, he too might expect that same degree of sexual performance. And that performance she reserved for the men she perceived as Alpha then and freely gave to them the sex which he had to earn, and still must constantly qualify himself for now. As such, women are required to keep the details of that past secret and obscured.

So grave is this anxiety that men must be punished for having the temerity to be curious about it. It is vitally important because a woman's capacity to bond with a man is reduced with every new sexual partner. This is a statistical dynamic; the more lovers a woman has prior to her marriage is proportional to her odds of infidelity and divorce.

According to a study by the National Survey for Family Growth, collected in 2002, 2006-2010, and 2011-2013. For women marrying since the start of the new millennium:

* Women with 10 or more partners were the most likely to divorce.

* Women with 3-9 partners were less likely to divorce than women with 2 partners; and,

* Women with 0-1 partners were the least likely to divorce.

This is a well-studied phenomenon. Every new sexual partner for a woman is a potential Alpha for her to be 'widowed' by, but the man who marries her must be kept ignorant of those men, and the impact they had on her, if she is to secure his resources and his parental investment. These are important facts to consider for a man looking for a mother of his children. Those childrens' lifetime wellbeing depends on the stability of the family.

This non-judgementalist social convention operates on absolving women's past indiscretions by redefining them as a period of learning. It was her "journey of self-discovery" and she's "not that person" any more. Cleverly enough, this is exactly the same convention and the same rationale of women who divorce their husbands later in life to then "take the journey of self-discovery" a la *Eat, Pray, Love* that she passed up when she was younger.

> *"When looking for a life partner, my advice to women is date all of them: the bad boys, the cool boys, the commitment-phobic boys, the crazy boys. But do not marry them. The things that make the bad boys sexy do not make them good husbands. When it comes time to settle down, find someone who wants an equal partner. Someone who thinks women should be smart, opinionated and ambitious. Someone who values fairness and expects or, even better, wants to do his share in the home. These men exist and, trust me, over time, nothing is sexier."*
>
> — *Sheryl Sandberg, Lean In: Women, Work, and the Will to Lead*

It is also vitally important for men to keep women's dualistic sexual strategy in mind at every age of their maturity.

Open Hypergamy is triumphantly crowed about when women are at their peak sexual market value, but when a woman is in her *Epiphany Phase*, (between 28 to 31 years old) when she's anxious and frustrated in securing her own long term provisioning, that is when she will fall back on the social conventions that shames men for their own awareness of the same *Open Hypergamy* they would otherwise flaunt for men.

Within this convention, men are expected not only to accept that a woman's sexual past is not any of his concern, but that any interest in it as something he might vet a wife over, is perceived as a sign of his own insecurities (i.e. a Beta tell). Many Red Pill men will see this convention as some fiendish plan to exploit his niceties and resources, but it's important to keep the latent purpose of it in mind. This is women's sexual strategy conflicting with men's sexual strategy.

Once we understand the latent purpose of this social convention, let me explain to every man reading – vetting a woman's sexual past is not just your prerogative, but an absolute imperative to the health of any future relationship you hope to have with her. When you consider the significant risks you are essentially setting yourself up for, risks no woman can ever acknowledge, empathize with or appreciate, the single most important thing you can do is vet her according to that woman's sexual past.

This doesn't mean you make weak, overt inquiries about her past. It means you subtly, covertly and discretely pick up on the many cues and *tells* she will reveal about that past. Most men would rather use a direct approach to this, and while there's merit to that, it's far better to do your vetting by drawing out freely offered information from a woman. It's also much more honest and reliable. Once you go the direct route, the jig is up and she will play the role she thinks you expect from her, not the honest one you need to make your determinations.

Sex is the glue that holds relationships together. It's the height of irony that a woman would place so high a priority on her own sexual experiences while in her sexual market value's peak yet completely disqualify that importance when she gets to the phase where it becomes a liability to her. As a man it is vitally important for you to know whether you'll be her apex Alpha lover, somone in between, or if your burden of performance will be measured against the ghosts of Alpha men from her sexual past – and all while you endure the stresses and joys of raising children with her.

Alpha Widows

As an aside here, I should add that I'm completely aware of the studies indicating a woman's capacity to bond monogamously is inversely proportionate to the number of sexual partners she's experienced prior to monogamy. I wont argue the merit of that concept, but I also don't think this fully encompasses the dynamic. I say this because even one prior lover (or even unrequited obsession of hers) can be Alpha enough to upset that bonded monogamous balance.

These then are the *Alpha Widows* – women so significantly impacted by a former Alpha (or perceptually so) lover that she's left with an emotional imprint that even the most dutiful, loving Beta-provider can never compete with. A woman doesn't have to have been an archetypal 'slut' in order to have difficulty in pair bonded monogamy.

So how many prior lovers is too many? For an Alpha Widow, one's enough. It's my contention that the *Slut Paradox* isn't a numbers game so much as it's an Alpha impact game. What if your new partner has only banged a mere two men before you, but had an intense relationship with them and engaged in such intense sexual experiences she feels self-conscious about doing with you? Is she a slut?

When it comes to vetting women for a long-term decision of monogamy, most men fall into two camps; the guys who take that process to a largely imagined, egoistic extreme, and the men who will scarcely give themselves permission to consider judging any woman's character for suitability to be his spouse or live-in girlfriend.

A few caveats need to be addressed here; the first is for men to understand the risks involved in marriage from the outset. In this era there are no appreciable advantages for men to marry even the most ideal of women. On the contrary, marriage is a losing proposition for men from all perspectives. Legally, financially, socially and evolutionarily, marriage represents an all-downside prospect.

The first conversation you should have with yourself is whether or not having and raising children is worth this virtually all risk proposition. It's also important for men to understand that even in the best of circumstance he's always at risk of having his kids and his influence as a parent removed at any time.

I began this section, and really the point of this book, with the intent of educating men on the modern realities that will make his role as a Red Pill parent difficult. No decision will impact your life more than the one you make in determining who will be the mother of your children. Very few guys see a hot girl in a club and think 'wow, I bet she'd be a great mom'. Their concern is the most immediate; that of getting the lay and experiencing sex with her.

However, this is exactly why most men, more commonly, have this decision made for them with no real insight into how a woman might be a great or horrible prospect with which to sire children. The pregnancy was "accidental" or maybe the result of the make-up sex you had after you were determined to leave her because she was such a terrible prospect. As of this writing the rate of all births to unmarried women is 40.2%.

Put this statistic into perspective. The vast majority of these unwed births is due more to how men and women prioritize their mating habits according to the dictates of Hypergamy, not pre-envisioned long term relationships. As a result we have 4 in 10 children without a father or a greatly reduced influence of that father on the child's life. The consequences of a feminine-primary social order and its prioritizing the optimization of Hypergamy can get very complex.

But, as I mentioned, most men follow a couple of more or less extreme attitudes with their regards towards vetting women. The first is the guy who takes himself and this decision so seriously that it conflicts with his true self-worth and sexual market value. The guy with this self-impression is easy to spot because his qualifications for women are more like demands which he really doesn't merit and can't enforce. This is usually the guy who, like most women, maintains a mental checklist of appropriate traits he *needs* his woman to have - a list that he's always happy to rattle off for anyone who'll listen in the hopes that the right woman will be listening too and step up for his consideration. I should add that this guy is usually given to spiritual notions and justifications.

The other guy is far more common. This is the properly trained and conditioned Blue Pill Beta who would never dream of presuming his self-worth would ever merit his being selective with a woman. His fear is being thought of as 'judgmental' and this runs very much parallel to his Beta Game of trying to identify himself as much with the feminine as possible.

This man never gives himself permission to vet a woman and follows along with most of the preestablished feminine social conventions that would shame a man for ever being so bold as to believe a woman ought to make herself suitable for any man. For our purposes, I think the Beta perspective of vetting women is likely the most common men will have to deal with.

If children are your priority, and you want to be the best Red Pill aware, positively masculine influence you can hope to be for them, it is vitally important you coldly and dissociatively vet any woman you believe might be a candidate for being the mother of your kids. As I said, most men never do this and fall into the trap of allowing things to happen instead of designing them to happen. A big part of that design is to understand that your risks as a father and husband (if you choose to be one) are life-threateningly great. So great in fact that you *must* vet women for suitability.

The first step in this vetting is to unlearn the idea that it's wrong or judgmental for you to do so. This is a Blue Pill conditioned mindset that is in place with the sole purpose of benefiting women in consolidating on their sexual strategies in the long-term, and at the cost of men's long-term parental investment.

If it is wrong for a man to vet or to judge a woman's character and worth, it places women as the only arbiters of what an acceptable, "good", mother ought to be for a man. As a positively masculine, Red Pill aware man it is your prerogative to vet women for long term suitability.

PRACTICAL RED PILL PARENTING

One of my more prolific readers left me this comment about parenting:

Being a dad isn't all that great in many ways these days. At best it's mostly thankless, but for most men, they are fathering into a culture that denigrates them, laughs at them and makes saints of mothers and motherhood. If you think this won't effect how your children see you as a father, you're not applying your Red Pill awareness.

I used to ride the train back and forth to the city – leaving my home at 6:30 in the morning and returning at 7:30 or later, wondering if my daughter would ever realize all I sacrificed to provide for her and her mom? I'd wonder if she'd ever get that I sacrificed being as close to her as her mother is to her for her wellbeing? That her closeness with her mom as a result of having a stay at home mom until she was 5 was a consequence of my efforts, not her Mom's?

Guess what – nobody wants to hear it. Nobody gives a shit what sacrifices you make to be a good father and provider – it's all about Mom. It's all about the kids. Dad's are at best seen as second-best Moms most of the time. And even when we are "in charge", we can be dismissed as superfluous in myriad ways.

Many men adapt by becoming second mothers and wives in the household – and the entire culture encourages this. Try being a traditional male at parent teacher night or at the preschool or even the Boy Scout troop... Fatherhood and a family is not what it once was either. Trust me, learn from my experience. Your kids will very likely not appreciate all you've done for them.

Just like men subscribe to two sets of books – old and new social rule sets that contradict the other – I think our ideas of marriage fall into this same contradiction. When marriage was a social contract and not so much a legal one involving the state, the old set of books applied well to that institution. This old set of rules about marriage and what men could expect from that largely socially-enforced institution worked well and in a complementary paradigm. From the Little House on the Prairie days up to the post-war era, the first set of books worked well with regard to marriage and fatherhood.

After the sexual revolution, the second set of books took social preeminence. Optimizing Hypergamy and all of the social and legal paradigms that make it the foundation of our present social order took priority. Yet, both men and, ostensibly, women still cling to the old order, the first set of rules when it comes to a man's role as a husband and a father, and simultaneously expect him to adopt and promote the feminine-primary interests of the *new* feminine-primary order.

Fathers are expected to follow the edicts of conventional masculinity with regards to their provisioning for a family and obeying the liabilities for not acting in accordance with it, but they are also expected to adopt, embrace and internalize their popularized role of being superfluous, ridiculous or even angry and abusively resistant to the second set of rules – those that prioritize the importance of the Feminine Imperative.

In other words, the expectation is that a man should find happiness in his sacrificial role of provider, be happy in his lack of appreciation for it, and happy to have the 'village' of society raise his children into the next crop of confused, frustrated adult men while he's doing it. He should be happy in his presence being devalued, but be held responsible for the lack of presence his sacrifices demand.

Oh, and he should also feel a sense of smug pride when he sees another man being pilloried for the same lack of his superfluous presence in his family's life.

'Village' of the Damned

I'm sure all of this sounds like a bridge too far for most men. Yes, the prospect of becoming a father is depressing, and I can see how these truths would make the average man despondent about becoming a new parent. However, I feel it's incumbent upon me that I'm honest with men about what they're up against before I advocate for being a Red Pill aware father.

You will *never* be appreciated for your sacrifices, and certainly not while you're making them. However, your presence is only as superfluous as you allow it to be. While you will never be appreciated for it in any measurable sense, you will be liable for it, so my advice is to make the most of it in a Red Pill respect.

Your reward, your motivation, for being a Red Pill parent and a positively masculine example in your kids' lives needs to come from inside yourself because it will never be rewarded by a feminine-primary social order outside yourself.

If you don't think you will ever find being a parent intrinsically rewarding, get a vasectomy now because it will never be extrinsically rewarding. Understand now, the Feminine Imperative wants you to be despondent about your role.

Understand this too, your presence, your influence, will only be as valuable or as appreciated as you are willing to make it to yourself. Just as with making yourself your mental point of origin, your Red Pill aware influence in your kids' lives needs to matter to you first because it will never be appreciated in your time, and in fact will be resisted by a world saturated in feminine-primacy.

Being a mother and birthing a child is a constantly lauded position today. By virtue of being a mother, women are rewarded and respected in society. Men, on the other hand, must add fatherhood to their burden of performance just to avoid the societal default of being demonized.

The Feminine Imperative wants you to give up and allow the 'village' to raise your sons and daughters to perpetuate the cycle of the second set of rules. It *wants* you to feel superfluous; the Feminine Imperative's maintenance relies on you feeling worthless. The reason men commit suicide at five times the rate of women is due in part to this prepared sense of male-worthlessness cultivated by the Feminine Imperative.

In *Preventive Medicine* I detail part of our present feminine-primary conditioning and how the imperative raises boys to be Betas and girls to be caricatures of the *Strong Independent Women®* narrative. All of that begins at a very early age. The first, most primary truth you need to accept as a father is that if you don't teach your children Red Pill truths there is an entire western(izing) world that is already established to raise them in your absence.

'The Village' will raise your kids if you don't. You will be resisted, you will be ridiculed, you will be accused of every thought-crime imaginable to the point of being dragged away to jail for imparting Red Pill awareness to them (in the future I expect it will be equated with child abuse). The Village will teach your boys from the most impressionable ages (5 years old) to loath their maleness, to feel shame for being less 'perfect' than girls and to want to remake their gender-identity more like girls – to the point that *transitioning* their gender to girls' will be the norm.

The Village will raise your daughters to perpetuate the same cycle that devalues conventional masculinity, the same cycle that considers men's presence as superfluous and their sacrifices as granted expectations. It will raise your daughters to over-inflate their sense of worth with unmerited confidence at the expense of boys as their foils. It will teach them to openly embrace Hypergamy as their highest personal authority (publicly and privately) and to disrespect anything resembling masculinity as more than some silly anachronism, or reverse it into being all about men's insecurities.

The good news is that for all of these efforts in social engineering, the Feminine Imperative is still confounded by rudimentary biology and our evolved psychological firmware. That basic root reality is your greatest advantage as a father. If there's one underlying truth upon which to base your parenting it's this; children are still motivated by influences that are relatively predictable. Begin from the root truth that we evolved our psychology and our behaviors from intergender complementarity that made us the preeminent species on this planet. It takes a global Village to distort this by teaching failed notions of egalitarian equalism.

Raising Boys

I'm often asked when I believe the best time would be to introduce a boy to the Red Pill. A lot of guys with teenage sons want to hand them a copy of *The Rational Male* before they hit 18, or maybe when they're 15, some even say 12 is really a good time. While it's flattering for me to hear men tell me how they gave their teenage sons a copy of my book, I have to think that this is too late.

I've been a father to a teenage daughter for a while now and in my 20's I was a mentor (big brother figure) to a young man I watched grow from a ten year old boy to a mid-30s man today. One thing I've learned from dealing with kids as I have is that the Feminine Imperative conditions children from the moment they can understand what's playing on a TV or in a movie. By the time that kid is ten they already have the ideological conditioning that came from a decade of meme's and messaging taught to them by schools, Disney, Nickelodeon, popular music, feminine-primary parenting from their friends' parents, even your own extended family members.

By the time that kid is ten they've already internalized the stereotypes and social conditioning of the Blue Pill and they will start parroting these memes and behaving and 'believing' in accordance with that conditioning. By the time they are in their 'tweens' and beginning to socially interact with the opposite sex, the Blue Pill feminine-primary conditioning will be evident to any man with a Red Pill perspective to hear and see it. You'll see the 'tells' of their Blue Pill conditioning more starkly because they so readily exaggerate them as a deductive, though adolescent, form of Game. Red Pill aware men must also consider that in just the five years or so a ten year old boy has to develop a capacity for abstract thought. He's already learned Blue Pill terms and has molded his identity around the ideas he's picked up from the Village. That Blue Pill internalized ideology will seem natural and logical to them even though they couldn't tell you how they came to their formative beliefs. And the Village will reinforce this acceptance by congratulating him for being more 'mature' than his peers.

The time to start exemplifying Red Pill awareness in a parental capacity is before you even have kids. As I detailed in the beginning here, an internalized Game that results from strong Red Pill awareness and a positive, dominant *Frame* control are imperative before you even consider monogamy. That *Frame* becomes the foundation for your parenting when your children come along.

I realize this isn't exactly helpful for men who came to Red Pill awareness after their kids were in their teens, but it needs to be addressed for men considering becoming a father. Ideally you want to impart that same Red Pill awareness during a boy's formative years. Children completely lack the capacity for abstract thought until their brains fully form and they learn from experience to develop it. The age of 5 is the time when kids are most impressionable and learn the most, but they do so by watching behavior. So, it's imperative for a Red Pill father to demonstrate positive, conventional masculinity during these years.

Include your son in exclusively *Male-Space*, where only men (and boys) are allowed to participate. Even if all he does is sit and play, it's important for him to understand male-only tribalism (detailed later). Eventually, as he gets older, he'll feel more a part of that collective. In a feminine-primary world that is bent on his devaluation as a male human it's important for him to feel valued in male-space and to institute his own male-spaces as he gets older.

Within this male-space your son needs to learn about his eventual burden of performance. I'd also advise you institute some kind of rite of passage for him from being a boy to being a man. This rite of passage needs to be something uniquely male for which only boys are qualified for. It should also be something which is earned and meritorious of unique, male-exclusive, rewards and respect, as well as responsibilities and accountabilities.

There needs to be a delineation point at which his manhood is marked. This is important because it not only teaches him to value his masculinity, but also to accept the responsibilities of his burden of performance.

Most Beta men are conditioned for gender-loathing in the guise of normative egalitarian equalism. Thus, they become uncomfortable even calling themselves '*men*', so the earlier a kid understands this the better he is in accepting his manhood. The Feminine Imperative is all too ready to teach him his masculinity is a mask he wears; something he puts on and not the 'real' him to hide his presumed insecurities just for being male. Your son needs to unapologetically reject this notion that his masculinity is an act.

He needs to learn that men and women are different and only deserving of earned respect, not a default respect simply granted to the female sex. Eventually he needs to learn to accept his own dominance and mastery in a world that will tell him his sex, and conventional, constructive masculinity is a 'toxic' scourge on society.

Your presence in his life is an absolute necessity if you are to thwart the efforts of gynocentrism. As such, it is important that you do things with your son. Even if that's something you have no interest in, being the Man, his model for masculinity is vitally important and to impart this to him you need to have a mutual purpose. As I've written before, women talk, men do. Men get together socially with a purpose, an action, a hobby, a sport, a creative endeavor, a problem to solve, etc. and *then* they communicate while working towards that purpose.

Your son must learn this from a very early age, particularly when he's likely to be forced into feminine-primary social structures and conditioned to communicate like girls do in school as well as in popular media. One of the tragedies of our age is a generation of Blue Pill men and women teachers raising their sons to adopt feminine-primary communication preferences because they themselves had no experience with conventional masculinity. They can't teach what they don't understand.

Our modern systems of teaching and learning has become highly gender-specific to the point that the only 'correct' way of learning is in the ways that encourage feminine-primary learning. Unless you home school or pay for private education, your boy will be taught this feminine 'correctness' in school. Know that you will have to bend your will as a parent to countering this influence by teaching him in male-specific ways.

Demonstrate, do not explicate, is true of dealing with women, but it is also an imperative of Red Pill parenting. Your son (and daughter) needs to see his mother's deference to your dominant *Frame* and beneficent authority. He needs to understand on a rudimentary level that his mother responds to your positive masculine *Frame*. Again, this is imperative since your kids will see a different narrative being displayed in popular culture and their schooling.

Exemplify for him how a man presents himself, how a man reacts to a threat, how a man commands a dog, how a man interacts with, and helps, other men he values, and how he avoids men and situations he does not.

Don't make the mistake of thinking that you'll start teaching him Red Pill awareness when he's old enough to understand it. By then it's too late, his conditioning makes him resistant to it and thinks his Beta Game is more appropriate.

Your son will follow your lead, but that must start from day one, not age 12. I have a good friend now whose 16 year old son is literally following the same path as his Beta father. His boy moved in with his estranged ex wife because he'd be closer to his ONEitis girlfriend. Now his girlfriend has left him and he's stuck living with his neurotic mother.

The consequences of a Blue Pill conditioned mindset also start early. I've seen ten year old boys despondent over not having a girlfriend. I've counseled a girl whose former teenage boyfriend stabbed and killed her new boyfriend 32 times because she was his *soul mate*. They fall prey to the soul-mate myth because they are taught to be predisposed to it.

As your son moves into his teenage years, that connection you began in his formative years should strengthen. You can begin to introduce him to Red Pill awareness, but in all likelihood you'll notice him using his own Red Pill lens when it comes to dealing not just with girls he likes, but his sister, his mother and the girl 'friends' who would like to be his girlfriend. Be sure you praise him for it. His grasping the fundamentals of women's dualistic sexual strategy, Hypergamy and how this will be used against him in the future is something imperative that he learns later.

His young-adult years are the time to reinforce that Red Pill sensitivity and capitalize on his own awareness, the awareness you planted in his formative years, by introducing him to Red Pill ideas he wasn't cognizant of. Bluntly, overtly, declaring Red Pill truths in his teenage years might make sense to you, but plucking out bits of his own Red Pill observations, praising him for them and expanding on them in his teen years will probably be received better and more naturally. Red Pill awareness should come to him as a product of his own curiosity and connecting the dots you put in front of him during his formative years.

One thing I know about teenage boys and girls is that if you try to tell them something profound they roll their eyes and blow you off, but if you wait for the right moment to let them come to that thing you want them to learn on their own then they're receptive to it. Your demonstrating Red Pill awareness doesn't stop when they're teens. For as much as you'd be excited to share the truths of the Red Pill and how best to apply them with your boy, understand that he will be prone to make the same mistakes you made when you weren't aware of the nature of women and how men might avoid the worst of it.

Raising Girls

Much of what I've outlined for raising boys would cross over into raising a daughter, however there are some differences in approach. Exemplifying a Red Pill ideal, and demonstrations of positive, dominantly masculine *Frame* control are still the highest priority, but more so is the modeled behavior of the girl's mother toward you and her acknowledgment of your *Frame*. If your wife resists, ridicules or mocks your *Frame*, if she feigns acceptance of it, devaluation is the lesson your daughter will be taught about masculinity. You must model for and mold her perceptions of masculinity while your wife models the aspects of femininity – for better or worse.

A lot of how you approach raising a daughter can be based on your Red Pill understanding of how to deal with women, and based on much of the same basic gender-complementary foundations. The same Game principles you would use with women are actually founded on behavior sets that little girls learn and enjoy while they're growing up. *Amused Mastery* is a prime example of this. The idea is to model the type of man you would be happy to accept into your own family as her husband. This then is reflected by how you interact with a son.

You will notice that root level Hypergamy manifests itself in girls at a very young age. In *Dr. Warren Farrell's* book, *Why Men Are The Way They Are* he notes that girls as young as 7 already have a definition of the (celebrity) "boys they'd like to kiss and the boys they'd like to marry." No doubt girls' accultura-tion influences their preferences, but the Alpha Fucks and Beta Bucks archetypes are part of their mental firmware. Popular culture is ready to exploit this nature, and in so doing it eroticizes girls from a very early age, but it still exploits a base nature in women that is inherent.

As a father, your primary role will be one of modeling the provider security seeking aspect of the Hypergamous equation. While that comfort and control is necessary it tends to be a trap for most Betas. The challenge most Beta fathers fail at is embracing and owning the very necessary Alpha / Dominant role that makes up the other side of that equation. That isn't to say you directly assume the Alpha Fucks role that Hypergamy demands, but it is to say that you adopt and own the Alpha dominance that makes that aspect sexy in other men.

The challenge is exemplifying *Amused Mastery* with your daughter, but in such a way that it balances Alpha dominance and control with rapport, security and comfort. In *Myth of the Good Guy* I make the case that adult women don't really look for this Hypergamous balance in the same man. Alphas are for fucking, Betas are for long term security, and men who think they can embody both are neither directly sought after nor really believable. The root of this mental separation of Hypergamous, purpose-specific, men can be traced back to the impression of masculinity that a woman's father set for her in her formative years.

Lean too far toward Alpha dominance and you become the asshole abuser who domineered poor mom while she was growing up. Lean too far to the Beta, permissive, passive and feminine side of the spectrum and the future men in her life will be colored by your deferring to the feminine as authority – thus placing her in the role of having to create the security she never expects men to have a real command of.

The challenge of raising a boy is modeling and exemplifying the positive, dominant masculine role you want him to boldly embrace in spite of the same fem-centric world arrayed against yourself. The challenge of raising a girl is embodying the dominant masculine man you will eventually be proud to call your son-in-law. Your daughter needs to be able to identify that guy by reflexively comparing him to the masculine role you set for her.

Most contemporary men (that is to say 80%+ Beta men) are very uncomfortable in asserting dominance with their daughters for fear of being perceived as misogynists according to their feminine-centric acculturation. The zeitgeist of this era's approach to fathers parenting girls is one of walking on eggshells around their little princesses, or treating their daughter as if she were a son. The fear is one of avoiding instilling a crushing of their independence or limiting their future opportunities by being more permissive with girls. The gender-correct hope is that in doing so they'll all go on to be the future doctors and scientists society needs, but that permissiveness and coddling does them no favors in the long run. To the equalist father of today there is no greater sin than to think of their daughters, or have any man think of their own daughters, as anything less than co-equal entities as boys.

If you were uncomfortable experimenting with Red Pill concepts while you were single, you'll be even more so in raising a daughter. The most important impression you need to leave her with is that men and women are different, but complementary to the other. She needs to know that your masculine dominance is beneficial, protective and valid to both her and her mother, and your personal mastery of you conditions and environment are an aid to her and the family.

She needs to understand that girls and women are, sometimes, excluded from male-spaces, particularly if you also have a son. In fact, it's boon if you have a son to teach while you bring up a daughter as she'll see his upbringing as a model for positive masculinity.

Lessons for My Son

As many of my readers know Mrs. Tomassi have raised a daughter for the past 19 years. We had one child by design, and in all honesty I'm rather relieved it was a girl. Take this however you'd like, but I think raising a girl has allowed me more insight into how women grow and mature into young women, and it's been through this experience that I've based more than a few of my theories.

I have one younger brother, so the maturation process of growing up female was something I've never been familiar with until the past 19 years. I suppose the possibility exists that I may at some point be able to pass on my Red Pill wisdom to a future grandson, certainly my brother's son, and many older male relatives, however I don't really have any regrets since I've had more private messages and consult requests from the sons I never had.

One of the best compliments I get from Red Pill fathers is when they email me about how they've bought an extra copy of *The Rational Male* that they plan to give to their sons or some other male relative. Nothing encourages me to keep writing than the stories I receive like this.

So, it was with some admitted pride that I came across a post on the Red Pill *Reddit* forum detailing lessons a Red Pill father hoped to impart to his soon to be born son. This guy had come to Red Pill awareness late in life.

There is a definite want in the manosphere to help other men, and particularly the coming generations of young men, to awaken them to what to avoid and how best to proceed in a Red Pill awareness. Most of these men's father's advice consisted of, "I don't care who you do, just don't do it under my roof." Either that or they were raised on the Blue Pill idealism and misguided presumptions of equalism from their thoroughly feminized Dad's.

So it comes as no surprise that today's Red Pill men would find one of the most important things they can do is prepare their own sons for manhood.

The following is a list collected from the suggestions of Red Pill men as to when (sometimes how) it's best to introduce a son to Red Pill concepts.

1. **(13 & up) Non-Exclusivity**
   Whatever you do, don't settle for one girl (oneitis) until much later in life. Play the field, spin plates, date lots of girls. This is the only way you'll be able to separate the wheat from the chaff and realize what you really want in an LTR relationship down the road if/when you want a family.

2. **(13+) Physicality & Alpha Character**
   Your physical characteristics matter (looks, body type, etc.)... An alpha attitude matters more.

3. **(13+) Don't Chase**
   Set yourself apart. Let girls come to you. If you do pursue, do so in a carefully calculated way: Pursue and retreat. Push and pull.

4. **(13+) The Value of Ambiguity**
   Keep her constantly guessing. Always imply that you have options.

5. **(13+) Say less than is necessary - Avoid Social Buffers**
   Texting, phone calls, etc... Be disciplined in your response. Use the 1-3 ratio in responding to her texts, phone calls. Give her one short text response/phone conversation for every three she gives you.

6. **(13+) Girls are a complement to your life, not the focus of it**
   Define your mission and pursue it (not girls) passionately. Admittedly, this will be undefined and in flux for an adolescent, but whether it's sports, studies, extracurricular activities, make those your first priority.

7. **(13+) Bigger & Better Deals**
   Develop a keen understanding of the psychological/biological nature of women... Understand how girls think. They are always looking to upgrade. If you're not always the "best in show", they will cheat on you to find someone who is.

8. **(13+) Nice guys finish last.**
   There's a reason all the girls like the boy who teases them. You don't have to be a 'jerk', but you do need to harness the jerk's energy.

9. **(17+) Niceness will never get you laid**
   If it is a friend she sees, that will be her lasting impression of you. Even if later in life you think she's finally come around to finding you attractive, her impression of your personality will be that of the Beta she rejected initially.

10. **(17+) Establishing Frame – Be a leader in every relationship**
    If you're on a date, make sure you're doing something that *you* want to do. She can come along for the ride.

11. **(17+) Rejection is better than regret**
    It is better to have attempted something great, to have defied the odds, to have approached that girl, than to live with the regret of never having attempted it.

12. **(17+) Shit Tests**
    Understand shit tests and learn to master them. Girls will always be qualifying you to make sure you're of the Alpha mindset she wants. If you start getting a lot of shit tests, re-evaluate your frame — you're probably coming across as too needy.

13. **(17+) Know the plumbing**
    Understand female physiology and how to bring a woman to orgasm.

14. **(17+) Understand the Long Game**
    Girls' sexual market value will peak around 22-24. Men's doesn't peak until their early to mid 30s. Do not be disheartened by her rejections now, in 8-10 years it will be you doing the rejecting. Remember what she was like during this phase of her life, it will give you greater discernment of women when you are doing the choosing later in life.

15. **(17+) Men and women have different concepts of love**
    Don't believe the lie that men and women mutually share an idealistic concept of love-for-love's-sake. Girls will love you, but only opportunistically. If you demonstrate lower value, their love for you will evaporate.

16. **(17+) Vulnerability is NOT strength**
    Your character should be Alpha to the point that this is women's overall estimate of it. Show your Beta traits sparingly and use extreme caution when dong so. Girls will want to see that you are stoic, self-reliant, and confident. If you want a shoulder to cry on, get a dog. Use Beta comfort only as a reward for good behavior.

17. **(17+) The Medium is the Message**
    Women don't send men "mixed messages", their behavior *is* their message. The only practical way of judging motivation and intent is observing

women's behaviors. Believe what they do, not what they say.

18. **(17+) Smile less, smirk more**
   Agreeableness, virtue, generosity and kindness make for a man of noble character, but they are never traits or behaviors that women find arousing.

19. **(17+) Charm is treating women like little girls**
   Tease relentlessly. Women find comfort in men who are so in control of their frame that they are fearless in treating women like their older brothers did when they were children.

20. **(17+) Experiment with Game**
   Learn what style of game works best for you: Are you the extroverted "cocky-funny" type? Are you the introverted "aloof-amused mastery type?" Are you the asshole type?

21. **(13 & up) Stay away from online porn**
   Learn the dangers of instant gratification. Realize that the build up of testosterone is what gives you your masculine energy. Don't masturbate as a crutch to avoid meaningful interactions with real women. That guy who sits in his basement fapping to online porn all day? Women are repulsed by him because his masculine energy is depleted and he has not learned to focus that energy on real women.

   As an adolescent, you will be consumed with thoughts of sex. Control your masculine energy so that it can be harnessed outwardly instead of inwardly in the realm of fantasy.

22. **(15+) The greatest risk you can take is no risk at all**
   Men's great fear ought not to be aiming too high and failing, but rather aiming too low and succeeding. This applies to all aspects of life.

23. **(17+) Never apologize for your sexual nature**
   Embrace the fact that men have huge sexual appetites. Never be ashamed of this and fully appreciate your masculine sexuality.

24. **(17+) Ovulatory Shift – Menstruation is your friend**
   Understand the behaviors and evolved functions of the female menstrual cycle and what it means for them, and more importantly for you (e.g. up the Alpha during ovulation, throw in some rapport during her down cycle.)

25. (17+) Learn the cognitive process of women's arousal
Understand that for females, sexual arousal typically takes place in the brain and that they are less visually aroused than you are. Men's sub-communication and emotional impact (good or bad) are vital aspects of female arousal.

26. (17+) Be aware of SMV ratio
Make sure that your sexual market rank is at least 1-2 points above hers at all times. This can be done either with attitude, physical fitness, your life passion or some combination of the above. Never be beholden to the idea of 'leagues', but do understand how SMV affects women's attachment to you.

27. (17+) Practice makes confidence
Approach and open often. The more girls you talk to, the more you'll refine your specific style and what works for you. Your Game success is directly proportional to your practice.

28. (13+) You cannot negotiate genuine desire
Don't think doing nice things for girls (giving them flowers, valentines, carrying their books, etc.) will make them like you more. It won't. Women will not rationally fall in love with you because you provide some material value. Obligation is not desire.

29. (13+) Adolescence sucks
You will likely be filled with insecurities, you'll be self-conscious, you'll think you look like a goof, you'll say dumb things to girls and then obsess about it. It's only temporary… You're learning and practicing the skills to be a man and there will be failures and mistakes. Always remember that everyone of your peers is going through the exact same thing, but you have the benefit of a Red Pill father.

30. (17+) Life is risk
Push boundaries, take risks and be exciting… Even when you're scared shitless. There's nothing sexier to a woman than a man who is unafraid to embrace challenges.

31. (15+) Respect is earned, but respect is all with women
The minute a girl disrespects you call her on it. And if she continues to disrespect you "next" her immediately no matter how emotionally difficult it is. This is absolutely critical to build your long term self-respect/self-confidence.

Admittedly, this isn't an exhaustive list, but it is an actionable start.

If you cannot teach your son positive masculinity from a Red Pill perspective, rest assured, the Feminine Imperative and a fem-centric world will teach him its version of masculinity. This is a version that will convince him any aspect of masculinity that isn't directly benefiting the Feminine Imperative is "toxic" masculinity. It will teach him that any definition of masculinity that is a benefit to himself or places his interests above that of women is a detriment to society.

Blue Pill conditioning will teach him to despise being male and to mock conventional masculinity as an act, a facade, that hides men's *real* insecurities. That the egalitarian equalist ideology has promoted this notion for the youngest boys isn't really an issue – the very fact that western(izing) educational systems have opted for learning methods that favor a feminine-correct basis is something even liberal academics have a hard time arguing against. What *is* at issue is why and how this pacified, feminized and feminine-correct idea of masculinity should need to be validated as the *real*, genuine, definition of masculinity in young boys.

At no time in history has it been more advantageous to be a woman in western cultures. Author *Hannah Rosin* acknowledged the advancement of women at the expense of men in her book *The End of Men* as far back as 2010. I add this here because it outlines the degree to which society has opted for the betterment of girls and women, while simultaneously affirming the idea that men and boys ought to become more feminine since the time of the sexual revolution.

Since this time there has been an effort in social engineering not just to feminize boys and men, but to fundamentally, and fluidly, redefine 'genuine' masculinity as a feminine-correct ideology. Ostensibly, egalitarianism has been about gender neutrality; a leveling of the playing field that ignores the inconveniences of human nature and evolved biology and psychology. The truth is that the Feminine Imperative uses the cover story of egalitarianism while it attempts to geld conventional masculinity by defining anything inconvenient about male nature as "toxic".

Is it mere coincidence that men have been encouraged to "get in touch with their feminine side", to identify more like, and as, women? To alter their ways of communication to be more female-accommodating, and to redefine conventional masculinity as "toxic" while reinforcing a new feminine-correct definition of masculinity for men?

Is it coincidence that 90% of all transgender children are boys being encouraged and affirmed by their parents and teachers to switch to being girls? And is all of this coincidence in an era when the social condition is one that provides benefits and entitlements to girls; one in which teachers presume a feminine-correct bias in their teaching methods? This of course is all speculative, but these are unignorable observations about our feminine-primary social order. I believe that the Red Pill men of today will be in the perfect position to exploit this, or to inform the next generations of men how to exploit this shift for themselves.

At present, boys drop out of school, are diagnosed as emotionally disturbed, and commit suicide at four times the rate of girls. They get into fights twice as often, murder ten times more frequently and are fifteen times more likely to be the victims of a violent crime. Boys are diagnosed with Attention Deficit Disorder at six times the rate of girls, Boys get lower grades on standardized tests of reading and writing, and have lower class rank and fewer honors than girls.

At universities women now constitute the majority of students, having surpassed men in 1982. In the next eight years women are predicted to earn almost 60% of bachelor's degrees in U.S. colleges. Women now outnumber men in the social and behavioral sciences by about 3 to 1, and they've moved into such traditionally male fields as engineering (making up 20 percent of all students) and biology and business.

Elementary schools have been 'anti-boy' for several decades now, emphasizing reading, communicative feminine learning styles and restricting the movements of young boys. They feminize boys, forcing active, healthy, and naturally rambunctious boys to conform to a regime of feminine-correct obedience and pathologizing what is simply normal for boys. As psychologist *Michael Gurian* argues in *The Wonder of Boys,* despite the testosterone surging through their limbs, we demand that boys sit still, raise their hands, and take naps. We're giving them the message, he says, that "boyhood is defective."

In *The Rational Male, Preventive Medicine* I outlined the institution of socialization classes wherein 9 year old boys were asked to list all of the reasons they dislike being boys:

- Not being able to be a mother
- Not supposed to cry
- Not allowed to be a cheerleader
- Supposed to do all the work
- Supposed to like violence
- Supposed to play football
- Boys smell bad

- Having an automatic bad reputation
- Grow hair everywhere

It used to surprise me how young boys knew exactly the right feminine-centric terminology when asked how they ought to deal with girls. Not anymore. I've had boys as young as ten rattle off buzz words and catch-phrases I would expect from a women's studies major whenever I've asked them what they think of girls or some intergender situation. Each of these boys was eager at the opportunity to 'prove his worth' to any girl in earshot by parroting the mantras of the Feminine Imperative he'd learned in school.

However, this eagerness was always tempered with a hint of fear; fear that, as young as ten, he might slip up in relating 'his beliefs' about women and be perceived as a misogynist. And that *is* the word they'll use. Blue Pill conditioning of boys begins from a very early age. I get asked constantly what exactly constitutes a "Blue Pill" conditioned mindset by my critics, this training for gender loathing is why it's such a arduous task to explain it.

Part of the feminine-primary social re-engineering western cultures have endured for over sixty years now is raising generations of boys to hate conventional masculinity. At the same time those cultures' educational charter has been one of empowering girls at the expense of boys. Thus, we have largely female (or feminized male) teachers molding the minds of generations of boys to despise being male (who will become potentially despotic men) and simultaneously defer to the feminine.

This is the cultural narrative that you, as a father, must continually be vigilant of in raising your sons. This understanding needs to color every interaction and every teachable moment you have with him. I cannot emphasize this enough. While it's important for you to embody, demonstrate and live out a Red Pill aware model for him, you must always recognize that your example will be exactly the opposite of what he's being taught is the feminine-correct model in school, not only by his teachers, but by his feminine-identifying peers.

Emotional Control

The basis of all the feminine-correct messaging your boy will be fed is founded on the idea that emotion and emotiveness are the only legitimate way of communicating. As I mentioned earlier, he will be conditioned to believe that the more he concerns himself with expressing his emotions the better a boy he will be viewed as in the hopes that this carries into his adulthood. It's gotten to a point where boys' natural competitiveness creates a competition among them to 'out-emote' one another.

The counter to this is a necessary step on the part of fathers to teach their sons emotional control. Ironically though, a father teaching his son to contain and reserve his emotionalism constitutes the other half of the conflicting messages boys are conditioned to think is fundamentally wrong with them. Boys are sedated by any number of methods (drugs, behavioral modifications, etc.) to get them to contain their natural masculine energies, yet are encouraged by their feminization to be *more* emotive, to cry more, to roll over and be more vulnerable and to believe that is strength. This is masculinity defined by the feminine.

As a Red Pill father it's your duty to teach him that vulnerability and expressions of insecurity or weakness are not a well of strength. Instead you must encourage your sons to develop real inner strength of both mind and body and to acknowledge it as such despite a world arrayed against them doing so. They need to understand that withholding feelings and controlling their emotive states are security measures that have preserved men for millennia. They need to know that true, conventional masculinity is derived from inner strength and resolve.

Red Pill fathers must stay media literate and make constant efforts to understand just how boys and men are portrayed as ridiculous or moronic, while simultaneously aggrandizing women and the feminine. Your boys need to develop their own Red Pill Lenses through which they will instinctually filter the feminine narrative. When a boy sees an ad or a TV show in which negative male stereotypes are present, make sure you point it out. When they see media that inflates the feminine narrative as being the only correct one, point it out to them too.

Teach them that there is more to men than what the feminine narrative wants him to believe. Teach him that everything he sees around him was conceived, designed and manufactured by men with creative, intellectual and physical strengths. Discuss famous men who have done, and are doing, important things – that should include athletic accomplishments as well as men who are examples of intellectual, strategic and creative achievements.

Engage him with questions about the differences between boys and girls, and men and women. Illustrate for him examples of how men and women differ in their thinking, their manner of solving problems and how girls manipulate boys to do things for them. Make sure your son knows the consequences of making girls his highest priority. Teach him that respect is earned and never granted without merit for either men or women – there is no default respect for women.

Teach your boy to fight and to know when it is appropriate to use force to defend himself. This is tough for many Beta fathers striving to raise their boys in a Red Pill paradigm. Most Beta men are conditioned to believe that masculinity is equated with a potential for unsolicited violence. Most Beta men are confrontation averse. If you don't know how to fight, learn a martial art with your boy. It's an excellent example of doing something male-specific and you both learn together. This also illustrates a man's willingness to submit to the experience of a master in order to become a master himself.

Mental Point of Origin

Let your son know he is to make himself his mental point of origin. This is perhaps the most important lesson you can impart to a boy in an era when he will be debased for just being male. Endowing him with the bearing of putting himself first is one of the most vital gifts you can leave to your son.

For some Fathers it may seem like a good idea to insulate your son from a world that is determined to condition him to what the Feminine Imperative would make of him, but it's far healthier to arm him with his own sense of enlightened self-interest. His feminine-centric world will make every effort to convince him to put the needs of "others" (really women and female interests) before himself, but he needs to know that he cannot help anyone until he first helps himself.

This deference to others is a key component in the conditioning that the Village would have him internalize. It is the central part of feminization's push to have his mental point of origin be extrinsic, if *any* thought is ever given to his own wellbeing. But more importantly, it is determined to have him internalize the idea that emoting like a female and considering girls' needs before his own is the correct, rewarded, first thought he should have in any gender-specific exchange.

This isn't to say a Red Pill father should encourage sociopathy in his son, but that his own wellbeing and his own interests need to be the first thought that originates in his mind. The Blue Pill mindset always jumps to binary extremes, thus, the criticized fear is that encouraging enlightened self-interest in a boy will lead to Dark Triad personality traits in him later in life. However, he should know that teamwork and cooperation, while valuable in his male world, need to pass through the filter of his self-centric mental point of origin.

Men face challenges in order to feel that men we respect hold us in the same esteem. It happens wordlessly. The sense of what is expected of us in these situations, and of what our choices mean arises naturally for us. So many men who struggle with shame do so because they know they have failed these tests more often than they have passed them.

This dynamic is lost on most people. Feminists and the culture they have influenced generally portray this aspect of masculine nature as pure foolishness; the stupid attempt of overgrown boys to "out-macho" one another. The male need to face challenges and to feel acceptance in a band of brothers, a tribe, who have also faced them 'valiantly' is derided in popular culture, in schools and in pop psychology.

Many young boys are confused by these messages. They suffer needlessly because their inner desires for respect and a sense of purpose conflicts with their social conditioning. The nature of a boy inclines toward bravery, risk and a desire to control his surroundings, but his teachers praise weakness and call cowardice good. His feminine-correct teachers seek what women primarily seek in the long term, security, safety and regulable stability. This is what they hope to condition your son for – to suppress that natural risk-taking and replace it with placating to the cause of providing women a sustainable sense of security.

The result is young men who either shrink from every challenge and seek to retreat from life behind a wall of video games, junk food and porn, or those who act out their natural inclinations through all manner of dissipation and base self indulgence. We end up a society where men are divided into cowering, compliant sheep or callous, untutored boy-men driven by testosterone and an unending quest for making their burden of performance *entirely* about qualifying for the approval of women..

Without a culture of mature, conventional masculinity to train boys' inner instincts, things fall apart. This is just another way that feminine-instituted fatherlessness drags civilization toward its destruction. It's a self-perpetuating process – Blue Pill conditioned boys become the Blue Pill compliant fathers who became disenfranchised with the exploitative roles they were raised to believe were correct. Fatherlessness then becomes a social mandate by a societal order that believes fathers are superfluous.

A society with a chance of survival supports, rather than targets for destruction, organizations like the Boy Scouts. Such groups train boys' desires for respect and recognition by placing them under the watchful eye of mature men who keep them from undue danger, give them a model toward which to aspire, and a troop of brothers.

But this is too 'toxic' now. Men banning together in male-exclusionary tribes is far too risky for a feminine social order. Those old groups are practically gone now. Either that or the integrity of those male-spaces has been redefined. In their place, we have transgender day camps for boys, a million Snapchat stories and gender -neutral bathrooms. The Boy Scouts have become an object illustration in how the Feminine Imperative recreates male-space to better effect weakening conventional masculinity. We have decided the trade off was worth it.

We are left with the illusion of freedom and a pervasive sense of some unavoidable decline. We all tremble to behold the boys we have made, boys deliberately confused about their natures, anxious about belonging, and unable to join or even understand that company of conventional men upon whom the future so desperately depends.

Despite all of this social conditioning, despite all of the interests that would condemn you for even considering raising a boy in a Red Pill manner, remember this, for all of it there is a root level hunger for a positively masculine father.

One of the first preconception we have about strippers or 'damaged' women is that they have "daddy issues." We presume the root cause of a woman's personal problems lies in some deep hunger for a father that never fit the mental model her evolved unconscious mind wanted for her life. *"Fatherless"* young men bear a similar 'damage'.

Once the deep longing for a father takes root, the ache never goes away. Instead of disappearing, it goes underground, often so deeply we don't recognize it for what it is. The desire for a father, for a steady masculine presence to guide and anchor boys and girls masquerades these days as numerous other maladies: social anxiety, anger, purposelessness, and emptiness.

But, our culture makes it easier to talk about anxiety than about father hunger. Fathers are considered disposable or ancillary to the child rearing process. To admit we suffer from their absence would be to challenge the cultural narrative of equalism and to have oneself branded a traitor to the consensus. So, we keep quiet and compound our sullen anxieties with the shame of knowing deep in our hearts we long for the archetype of a conventional Dad. Take the effects of father hunger on a personal level: the directionlessness and weakness in men and, in women, the desperation, the fear, the pitiful, never-ending search for affirmation and multiply them by millions. This is where we are now.

General cultural attitudes toward fathers that veer between indifference and open hostility. It magnifies these personal problems and makes them pervasive cultural threats. Fatherlessness is an easy foil for social ills, but masculinity and men's unique influence is always suspect. It's always one degree away from 'toxic'.

When an individual kid losses his father, he suffers, his spouse may suffer, his own future children might. But, if he lives in a culture that recognizes the inherent goodness of fatherhood and fathers' necessary contribution to his development, he may be able to find a surrogate – a mentor.

Not so now. Father hunger and its consequences are now so widespread we take it to be normal. At the bottom of our many of our social ills lies the hunger for a father who has been displaced by the state or by other the proxy of the Village. That father has been supplanted by the attacks against him launched by a thousand feminists in the name of the Feminine Imperative and amplified by every media production of the last fifty years and by the decision to make divorce easy, expected and grossly beneficial to a mother.

All this makes the importance of what fathers do even more important. For those of us who still have young children, we must not be persuaded by Village culture to doubt our own importance. Instead, we must double down on our commitment to do our duties. We must be there in the knowledge that we are not superfluous and our mere presence satisfies.

If you aren't a father, even your Red Pill aware mentorship of young men is supremely valuable and needed. Look for opportunities to educate young men. An intentional dedication to mentoring young men in Red Pill awareness is admirable, but even just a casual involvement goes a long way. It is only by your involvement that young men's Blue Pill conditioning can be interrupted.

We cannot father a whole world. The damage is done. Generations without fathers are now ascendant and their hunger for conventional, positive masculinity will drive civilization down if we neglect to act. The best we can do is set the example, refuse to compromise, keep on doing what fathers have always done: provide, educate and protect in a collapsing world.

There is much from which we must protect those in our charge. A fatherless world is a dangerous one. But, in the middle of this dangerous, dying world, we can cultivate pockets of healing and resistance. This is part of the bottom-up approach needed for Red Pill awareness on a societal level.

When we can, we can reach out. We can be a Red Pill mentor, a friend. At the very least, we can tell people that fathers are good and our hunger for them is real. We can be the shoes thrown into the machinery of the feminine-primary social order. We cannot save them all, but we can save some.

PROMISE KEEPERS

I once had a 25 year old guy relate to me about how disappointed he was with himself. He'd gotten together with a new girlfriend, made a commitment of exclusive monogamy, and had all the noble intents most Betas assume when they enter that form of quasi-marriage.

His problem was he'd had a 'fuck buddy' for some months prior to his *'legitimately'* dating his now girlfriend and regrettably had to cut her out of his life. The 'friend with benefits' was upset as most usually become when presented with losing the investment of all those sexual encounters unencumbered with little or no emotional rewards. The guy was determined to honor his arrangement with the new girlfriend, but the fuck buddy persisted and became more emotionally invested until they settled upon a 'just be friends' solution to their prior intimacy.

After a week the guy had doubts about the girlfriend and since he and the fuck buddy are 'still friends' they got together to discuss said doubts. Needless to say this discussion then led to comfortable, reliable, "sure thing" sex with the former fuck buddy and now we come to the regret and disappointment he feels about himself. One might think that this is a simple case of a 25 year old sorting out what works for him sexually and his struggling with monogamy in the light of having other actionable options, but his disappointment didn't originate in this.

"I feel like a piece of shit because I promised myself over ten years ago I would never do this. I broke my only promise to myself that I always stuck with."

I found it interesting that a, then fifteen year old, boy would have the prescience to make some vow of fidelity to a future girlfriend (or wife) to himself. For obvious reasons he didn't strike me as particularly religious – he didn't have a 'promise ring' on either for that matter. So what was it?

"I can pick up girls and bed them with no problem, but when it comes to relationships, I'm lost completely. And yes I do feel like something is missing with my current girlfriend."

This explains part of it. Alpha while single, Beta when monogamous is a very common theme for the feminized, preconditioned youth of today. And of course in light of having (and having had) other sexual options that Alpha-when-single / Beta-when-monogamous conflict about a girlfriend is to be expected, but that still didn't explain the self-promise or the disappointment adequately.

"I felt like a piece of shit. Over ten years ago when my Dad cheated on my mom, I promised myself I would never be like my father and cheat.

I never cheated ever, until tonight. I feel numb, confused, and don't know what to do."

Slay the Father

One common theme I've encountered amongst the more zealous Beta White Knights I've counseled over the years has been exactly this obsessive determination with outdoing the life / relationship performance of their asshole fathers.

Before I go on, many of these guys did in fact have legitimately rotten, alcoholic dads, who were abusive to them and their mothers. Others had the perception of their fathers colored for them either by the bad mouthing of their '*Strong Independent®*' single mothers, or by watching their fathers resolve their own Beta mindsets and tendencies in a post-divorce life.

Whatever the case, each of these guys had a mission – to be a better man than their father was, protect their mothers, and by extension victimized women and the future mother their girlfriends and wives would become for them. His *father's* personal failings would be *his* personal triumphs.

The problem in this modern day Oedipus scenario is that the Feminine Imperative is more than happy to use this promise to its universal social advantage.

Feminization and its Blue Pill conditioning of boys to create better "men" is defined by how well that "man" is acceptable to a feminine-primary culture. Thus, we get gender blurring and boys are taught to pee sitting down by single mothers because "your asshole dad always made a mess and left the lid up." Better 'men', uniquely feminine-acceptable men, pee like women.

Now, that's just an allegory of the mindset behind women raising future men solo, but the father-hating boy becomes the masculine-hating adult Beta male. Feminine social conditioning of boys is cruel to be sure, but nothing cements that conditioning in better than having a living example of the role of what a man is *not* to be and then committing your life to not becoming it. And as I stated earlier, those considerations may be legitimate, but the end result is the same; a Beta who thinks women will categorically appreciate his devotion to identifying with the feminine by his promise not to become like *"typical men"* – like his asshole dad.

This is an extension of the Blue Pill presumption that women will view him as unique amongst other men for being so well adapted to identify with the feminine. And, it follows, the majority of women, who care more about dominant Alpha characteristics, have no appreciation for his 'promise to be a better man' then become "low quality" common women to him. Shoot the arrow, paint the target around it.

This is the root of the conflict the guy in my example was experiencing. He's likely coming into a more mature understanding of what his father experienced with his mother and women in general, but it's clashing with that adolescent declaration of devoting himself to what he believed, and what his conditioning taught him, ought to be his imperative.

"If I'm a better man than dad I'll be deserving of love the way I envision it.

I'll be appreciated and hypergamy will be inconsequential due to the equity I'll invest in our relationship."

Only at 25, he progressively finds that he is just as human, and just as male, as his father was.

Beyond Oedipus

Unsurprisingly this is one very tough psychological schema to dig out of a Beta who's invested his ego in it for so long. Even when he experiences first-hand the trauma of realizing that women aren't the way he's always believed they would be, and despite Red Pill awareness, this 'promise to be better' persists. Layer onto this the social reinforcement of the ridiculous / reprehensible male archetype, then compound it with either his mother's vulnerability, popularized ideas of female victimhood, or her consistently negative characterization of his asshole father, and you have a recipe for a permanent Blue Pill existence.

That said, it's not impossible to unplug 'promise keepers' with enough harsh, experiential reality to awaken them out of their adolescent paradigms. Making them aware is the toughest task, but introspect on their own part is the next step.

It's very important to recount the ways 'bad dad', and a child's reaction to him, has directed and influenced their interactions with women (or men in the case of girls). It is a supremely uncomfortable epiphany for 'promise keepers' to realize that Mom is just as common as the women rejecting him, who are helping him realize his adolescent presumptions were naive. Most 'promise keepers' get shaken awake by two sources: the consistently incongruous behavior-to-stated-motivations by women, or by his own internal struggle with keeping his promise in the face of what he can't quite place is what's in his best sexual interests.

Father Knows Best

I received a request from a father petitioning me for advice on how a Red Pill divorced father might best go about re-initiating a relationship with his estranged son. I thought this might be valuable here for the Red Pill parent.

How a might a newly Red Pill divorced father approach his son, especially if there has been a period of estrangement?

I have a "date" for a phone call with my son after quite a long period. You might imagine my relationship with my "old family" is sort of "interesting", to put it euphemistically. My daughter has dropped my last name from social media accounts. My son calls himself "Younger Surname" and his assumed "middle name" is "Fucking". Sort of a throwback to mine back in the day, but he seems quite pissed though.

I have been told these things can be quite emotional, and then a flurry of contact, but then a "backsliding" away from contact. Inevitably and probably rightfully so, he has innate loyalty to his mother. And he grew up in one of places that is so liberal it is often referred to as "The People's Republic of ..." So the question is "How to bring him along?"

If by "bring him along" it means convince him you're not the asshole he's convinced you are, that's really subjective to your personal history and how amenable he is to listening to your side of the story. That said, there's a world aligned against you that's likely conditioned your son not just to hate you, but to loath his own sex by association with your past decisions and circumstances.

This then begs the question, how does a father go about reestablishing a lost or misguided connection with a son or daughter, from a post-Red Pill awareness perspective?

Being the father in this scenario and attempting to reestablish an after-the-fact, positive connection with a son is a very tall order. It's almost easier to address the particulars of a daughter with 'daddy issues' whose absent father contributed to her 'victim status' condition than it is to right the corrupted upbringing and feminine conditioning a boy receives in his father's relative absence.

The difficulty being that a son will have every negative perception of his father reinforced for him by a feminine-primary social order. Even in the rare instances when an insightful mother doesn't resentfully color her son's negative perceptions of his father during his formative years, there is an entire world of feminine social conventions and popular culture pressing and affirming that impression into him.

Furthermore, it's also likely your feminine-conditioned son will see the utility in playing along with that 'victim-of-dad's-misogyny' narrative as a way to highlight his Beta Game. The idea being he will believe women should find him overcoming *your* failure as some source of attraction for girls/women. It's sort of a '*better hope for the future of women*' narrative he mistakenly thinks will make him unique in the view of women.

It's a difficult task to unplug a man who is a friend and open his eyes to Red Pill awareness. That guy has to be seeking answers to really be open to having his ego-investments in his conditioning challenged and realigned – you can't really *make* a man Red Pill aware, he's got to come to it in some fashion. This is a very important distinction to make when the man you're attempting to unplug is your own son.

A father in this predicament has the double jeopardy of clearing his name as a father and as a representative of masculinity – the representation of all the negative aspects the Feminine Imperative has ever embedded into his son about the taint of his own masculinity. Some of the most ardent anti-conventional-masculinity crusaders I've ever encountered all had the common denominator of a 'bad dad'. 'Deadbeat mothers' don't spoil conventional femininity for men.

One of the more painful aspects of waking up and accepting Red Pill truths is coming to terms with the consequences of basing your past decisions on a Blue Pill paradigm. I can empathize with younger unplugged Betas getting angry with themselves for having wasted part of their lives with the effort of chasing after the carrot of Blue Pill goals, but it's an entirely different anger older men feel after coming to realize that their lives and the lives of their children (the *only* reason to get married, remember?) are the results of their Blue Pill decision making.

This is doubly so for the Red Pill awakened father since part of his Blue Pill disillusionments meant coming to accept that his children's personalities and their own Blue Pill choices are a direct or indirect result of his own Blue Pill idealism.

Fortunately I had my Red Pill awakening prior to my daughter being born and had the foresight to live by example. However, I know enough men in similar straights to see what an impossible task it is to untangle and reconcile the past Blue Pill version of themselves with the Red Pill aware men they've become.

I do not envy them.

So what is the solution then? The first step is coming to terms with the task that's been set before you as I've done here. These are some things to consider before you set out to make your son's unplugging a mission for your life.

I hate to come off as callous from the start here, but it's entirely possible that your son, nephew, younger brother, etc. may simply be too far gone. One of the *Rational Male's* maxims is that unplugging men from the Matrix is like triage; save the ones you can, read last rites to the dying. What's important in this assessment is that you use your Red Pill lens as objectively as possible. That will require an almost clinical evaluation of your family member, and one that's particularly difficult because it forces you to set aside all of your emotional investment in him.

This is a very tall order for most men and more than a few have found themselves compromising in areas of Red Pill awareness in an effort to placate a very Blue Pill invested son they desperately want a new connections with. Be hyper-conscious of the pitfalls I mentioned above in this section, and make your clinical assessment accordingly.

Is your son (male relative) too far gone already? Is his estimate of your character an accurate one in light of what his mother, his school, his sister(s), popular culture and more importantly, the girls he wants to get with have conditioned him to believe about you? Remember, you're not just fighting his preconceptions, you're fighting a social order that *needs* you to neatly fit into its archetype of your *kind* of man.

There are a few angles you need to consider when you plan an approach with your estranged son. This starts with doing an accurate assessment of yourself with regard to how popular conception of your type of guy is perceived.

Are you the asshole father who left mom to get with some 'arm candy' trophy wife? That's a popular cultural meme. It's one that's an exaggerated distortion, but a popular one because it feeds women's innate need for indignation. For the moment, it makes little difference if it's accurate or not, what's important is that you understand that's how you are perceived by your son according to what fem-centric culture has fed him.

Are you the 'nice' accommodating, let-everything-slide Blue Pill kind of father who never had *Frame* (or even knew what it was when you got their mother pregnant)? Are you the guy who bought into the egalitarian-equalist belief that it was no man's 'right' to presume he ought to be dominant or be concerned with his own interests? Are you the type of father who deferred to the mother of his kid's will and as a result she assumed the dominant masculine role because 'bumbling Dad' could never be trusted with the family's security?

Are you the father who never put himself as his mental point of origin and only later became Red Pill aware? This is almost a more difficult position to be in than the Asshole Dad because you're attempting to recreate your Beta impression of your character while simultaneously attempting to unplug your son with a Red Pill awareness that may be new and uncharacteristic to you.

While I cannot give you a specific recipe or map to follow for your individual situation, I can give you some important things to consider before you make your attempt. I should add here that these are equally important to acknowledge when you're re-establishing a connection with your daughter there are some differences in approach for daughters – I'll mention these in a bit.

• Assess your previous Blue Pill impression you held with your son/daughter, their mother, your extended family (her and your sisters, mothers, fathers, close friends, etc.) and consider that impression based on what you understand from a Red Pill aware perspective.

• Assess your son's acculturation in the same Blue Pill conditioning you had to unplug yourself from. Consider how his mother's influence (bad and good), his schools, his friend, the music and media he's into and the girls he hopes to impress have created his persona.

• Assess how resistant he will be to your implementing some sort of reconnection effort based on what your Red Pill awareness would have you reasonably predict. If you're the Asshole Dad and he's the Beta nice kid, or he's bought into a Promise Keepers' mentality this will require a different approach than if you're perceived as the weak Beta Dad who's establishing himself as a Red Pill assertive father.

- Did you have *Frame* when you were involved with your son's mother? If so, did that *Frame* slip while you were together or is it still a part of the personality your son expects from you now? Consider how your son has been trained to perceive his own masculinity both as a result of your (strong or poor) example as well as how feminine primary society has distorted and confused him about it. These will be the things you'll be up against when you try to reconnect.

- Is your son amenable to reconsidering your recreated persona? It's likely your son's concept of masculinity was molded by his mother's false interpretation of a masculine ideal, which is to say a feminine-correct ideal. Thus, his conditioning centered on identifying with, and appeasing of, women. As such, your conventional, complementary, masculinity is likely to be offensive to his trained sensibilities.

- Would a covert, understated approach over time be better than an overt, blunt declaration of your intent? It comes down to your persona, but which would be more believable in conveying your Red Pill awareness?

These are a few things to consider before devising a time and a way to reconnect with your boy. I should also say that these are considerations a father ought to take into account before he attempts something similar with a daughter. In the case of daughters I would also advise considering much of the same Game foundations with the associated principles you would when dealing with women in general.

Most fathers with sons, assholes or not, will be disappointing to them in some (or many) ways at some point. Not to downplay the difficulty, or the headwind of the Feminine Imperative, or the divorce toll, but I'd do my best to see this as an opportunity for both of you. Which isn't to say it is all pleasant or nice even. You still have each other and it is a significant event for an estranged father to have his time to present his side of things while, hopefully, educating his son in Red Pill awareness.

As with most 'unplugging' it is likely that your son's most receptive moment will be when he's hurting from some woman's rejection of him. It's a bitter pill to swallow for a father to see his son suffer for the same Blue Pill misgivings (or outright exploitations) he endured himself – particularly if the consequences were also what led to his son's birth.

The Prodigal Son

A Red Pill father should always be sensitive to moments of opportunity like this. Often it's a personal trauma that leads men to seek out the Red Pill community, even if they don't know they're actually looking for it. This seems horribly opportunistic for Red Pill men, but it's the experience of that personal trauma that breaks up a Blue Pill man's comfortable, normal, ego-investment in what he expects will be rewarded or punished in a feminine-primary social order.

Learn to see these signs in men (your son) you think may be ready to hear Red Pill truths, but more so, be ready to be there for your boy when this trauma shakes his comfortable preconceptions. This will make your story and Red Pill awareness that much more poignant for him. This could be your teenage son reeling from having his soul-mate girlfriend dump him for a new college lover during what I call the *Break Phase* in *Preventive Medicine*. It could also be that your young adult son is stinging from a similar disillusionment from a woman who'd used him as a useful Beta to get what she needed at a particular phase in her maturity.

A very common situation is a young adult having his ideal of Relational Equity destroyed for him by a woman in which he believed he'd done everything the right way and played by the set of rules he believed women would universally appreciate and universally reward.

His invested equity is based on how well he believes he's doing what women have always told him would be valued (i.e. equity) only then to have Hypergamy destroy that notion for him. It's at this time a young man might seek out his father's perspective, particularly if something similar happened to him.

As a Red Pill father it is important to be prepared for these occasions. They make the reconnection you hope for, as well as your hope for opening his eyes to the Red Pill, that much easier. They're sure to be stressful times, but see them for the opportunity they are.

One of my regular readers of *The Rational Male* blog related a very inspiring reconnection story that I simply cannot omit from this section.

My dad passed before we could ever have these conversations. He was a self-made man; solid granite. But through the years of Feminine Imperative driven hailstorms and my bipolar mom, with hammer and chisel, I watched him become a crumbling statue of his former self, a draft horse whose only pleasure was sneaking into the basement to watch TV.

He was no asshole. But I held some anger in me over him – for him; his lack of spine, his constant laboring to serve the female needs, his complete lack of self-regard. He was a true giver. But it was painful to watch his gifts just send him further into oblivion. Together, he and mom, passed it on to me. I was to be respectful, full of character, "nice", but never aggressive, never flexing my strengths unfairly. Blue. So Blue. And so, of course, I became that pain.

Before he died (I was 30) when I would visit, we would sequester ourselves in the work shed to build. He wanted to tell me things, I wanted to ask him things, neither of us finding the words. I was moments before being divorced and he was moments before the beyond. It was too late for both of us.

But we spoke some through our bodies, hands turning the wood this way or that; our conversations would follow, circuitous arcs and tangents cut from linear minds. The words eventually began to hold some shape. The lathe was setting loose years of unspoken things, along with long curls of pine gathering at our feet.

He insisted that I cut, not waning to admit that his hands were already too weak. I let him tell me how; instructing me in the same way he did 20 years back when I'd first checked out on the machine. Those words that annoyed the living shit out of me back then were welcomed. "Jeeze, I know dad!!" became "Oh, I forgot about that trick, thanks."

He always wanted me to be a better man than him. I always wanted him to be better man for him. No, for me too. I wanted him to be the rock not the puppet. It's not just women who feel unease at seeing a man not hold his ground; it is also future men. But beneath the crushing weight of that much Blue Pill conditioning, those conversations are just bubbles rising up.

There was no Red Pill wisdom that day or any that followed. There was an understanding though. A beginning. For me, it would take more time. More pain. But I was on my way to becoming some version of him, a lot closer to the one that I always wanted him to be. He saw it in me. And in so many words, that was his gift to me that day.

Now, RP aware, I both understand his choices as well as my own. For me, a lot of it is about the principle of giving of self; it can be both beautiful and destructive. We need fathers to tell sons these things, these words that give steerage to navigate past the treachery and on to the joy that awaits them.

*A boy becoming a man will likely hold ill feelings for his father for some
reason, for some time. Better it be for truth, the hard lessons leading to
workable skills, the tough conversations that unbind manhood from the
Feminine Imperative, and those small moments together that will feed his
soul when you are long gone and he is looking at his future – or holding it
in his arms. Be that kind of asshole.*

*Learning the "right" way to cut wood will result in some splinters, but re-
moving splinters is not nearly as painful as a lifetime of never truly knowing
how the machine works.*

This story is part of why it's so important to maintain yourself as a Red Pill
aware man and father, unafraid and unapologetic to the feminine-correct social
paradigm that's prevalent today. The narrative of the Feminine Imperative, the
Village that is so ready to emasculate your sons, will see this as some open
communication touchy-feely moment that reinforces their religion of emotions,
but what this should serve as is a stark reminder of what happens because of
the machinations of the Feminine Imperative. This is a warning, not a heart-felt
moment of reflection between father and son, a warning of what awaits fathers
who never unplug and sons who follow in his feminine-correct path.

Just to start, try to engage your son in comfortable, non-emotional events.
Remember, women talk, men do, so have a common purpose prearranged to
complete. It's likely he may be uncomfortable '*doing*' because he has no concept
of conventional masculinity, he may even ridicule it. Be prepared for that.

Don't mention his mother. That should serve to provide some contrast between
her influence and your own. He needs to see, to experience, how a man behaves,
and men should be able to move on and make the best of things without harbor-
ing enfeebling resentment.

I'd be remiss if I didn't mention referring your son to the manosphere or reading
my prior books, but do so only if you believe he's at a point of being receptive
to what I or other Red Pill authors might open his eyes to. Introducing him to the
manosphere prematurely will only reinforce his previous mis-perceptions of you
and genuine masculinity. It's better if his unplugging comes from you.

Be patient, wait it out and keep the door open. Don't *play* Daddy with him if
you've never been a significant influence in his life up to this point. You're not
his father. The Feminine Imperative is his father and has plans for him to fulfill.
This is the an important part to understand.

If at all possible do not talk things out over the phone. In my opinion the phone, texts, emails are all a buffer against real personal rejection and a terrible medium for serious conversations. Any hope of rebuilding your relationship with your son will have to be face to face, over a period of years. Demonstrate, do not explicate. Actions speak louder than words, like with a woman, you'll never convince her why she should be with you through debate or explaining yourself adequately. You show you're a man worth being with, as well as respecting by your character, achievements and accompanying behaviors.

Parental Alienation

There is a related issue to consider in all of this too. It's known as Parental Alienation that is also well informed by the Feminine Imperative. It's how father's who don't abandon their children and meet their financial responsibilities have their parenting role whittled away over the years down to nothing. The short story is that if your ex-wife remarries when your kids are young, the new guy will functionally be their Dad.

Essentially, the new guy is treated like Dad when you aren't around, but when you are this fact is often hidden. This is another important consideration since in many instances you're dealing with the mindset and temperament of the step-father and the influences this embeds in your son or daughter's persona as they mature into adulthood.

If you're dealing with a Beta stepfather you may be tempted to think that your task of reconnection might be that much easier from a Red Pill perspective, but unless your kids are more enamored by your Red Pill cavalier spirit it's likely both he and your kids' mother will have doubly reinforced a Blue Pill, feminine primary belief-set in them. Needless to say, this can make your reconnection a tougher go if you're trying to unplug your son from their Matrix.

Oddly though, if your task is to reconnect with your daughter this Beta stepfather dynamic can work to your benefit. Most estranged daughters will be looking for that positive masculine dominance that their Hypergamy demands. On some level of consciousness her hind-brain understands that Beta Step-Dad is a less than Hypergamously optimal model of masculinity.

Even the most ardent feminists and thoroughly indoctrinated girls still pine for the dominant masculine authority that they'd hoped their fathers would be. Providing this contrast for her against the role of the emasculated Beta stepfather and your reconnection will likely be easier.

Live the Red Pill for Your Son

A divorced father can also help his young son by becoming a more Alpha and masculine leader in his own life as an example, live a social life that his son would like to emulate, and invite his son into that life. Put plainly, that dad gets a younger/hotter/nicer girlfriend or step-mom, by acting like a Man. Let your son bond with her, see how nice she is, and transfer some of his attachment and interest as a "love object" onto her. As I always say, demonstrate, do not explicate. You need to demonstrate the possible for him.

The Oedipal Complex might reset over this new woman. Without a verbal argument on the father's part, the son will start comparing his own mother, or the Village women who've influenced him, to this new woman. Eventually, the son will desire whoever is more appealing and learn to pattern his life accordingly to attain that type of relationship. If the father is being conventionally masculine and creating a more desirable relationship, then the son will desire his new woman, emulate him to get something similar, successfully resolve the complex, and learn to be masculine himself.

Adopting a Red Pill awareness and internalizing it as a way of life is something that a man must come to of his own accord. If your relationships with women can serve as a contrast to the uglier side of the feminine-primacy he's learned, coming to this 'on his own' is made much easier.

Be a Mentor

Finally, I've got to advocate for Red Pill mentorship for boys who aren't your sons. Casual, indirect mentoring is something I've been doing with young men for some time now. It may be you only have daughters or it may be you have sons, but their friends or other young men in your life would benefit greatly just from interacting with a Red Pill aware man as a role model. Embody this positive conventional masculinity and serve as a counterbalance to the Village indoctrination these young men are being taught.

For the guy who has internalized this awareness to the point that it's become a way of life it may simply comes as a matter of course for you to exemplify it in your lifestyle, mannerisms and interactions with men and women. However, always remember that your attitudes and behaviors are what young men are interpreting against the backdrop of what they're learning from the Feminine Imperative in school and in media. Your example, even with sons who are not your own, will serve as a contrast to his conditioning. You need to be aware of this impression. In your absence, you will be talked about. You will occupy head-space of young men, young women and that of the Village women who would try to disparage your persona.

Whether you're aware of it or not, you will serve as a mentor to young men. Far better to be conscious of this and understand your Red Pill effect. Do be careful, however, to understand the contrast you may provide with respect to that boy's father's impression on him. Statistically, that kid's father is likely a Blue Pill conditioned Beta and / or an uninvolved (perhaps absent) father himself. Your impression maybe his only example of a positively, conventionally masculine man.

That's going to be a stark contrast for a boy raised on Blue Pill ideals embodied by his father or those instilled in him by a single mother as well as that of the Village. Keep this in mind too. A Red Pill parent needs to counter the Village by being a Village to himself. This is an important task to remember; you may be able to invest yourself in your own sons' development as men, but if you serve as other boys' mentor, including them in the same Red Pill upbringing as your sons', you serve as a Red Pill teacher for men beyond those you personally created.

Look for opportunities to mentor. That doesn't mean you have to sign up to be a Boyscout troop leader, just look for the opportunities that present themselves.

RAISING DAUGHTERS

When my daughter was about fifteen years old I got into a debate with an allegedly Red Pill wife/mother who was determined not just to home school her own daughters, but to only fund their college aspiration if they chose the local state university and lived at home while attending it. The "dorm life" experiences and online stories of alcohol-fueled orgies on campus played prominently in her fears, but more so, her hesitancy to cut the apron strings were about worries that her little darlings would have socialist/feminists/cultural Marxist ideologies implanted in their impressionable brains.

I found this interesting because her fears were founded on the presumption that her daughters would still default to being indoctrinated in all of the *Village's* teachings despite all her carefully planned homeschooling intended to make them resistant to such influences. This is the same woman who meticulously screened and censored her girls' exposure to the 'corrupting' influence of the cultural narrative in various forms of media – TV, online, music, movies, etc. Yet, despite all of this concern, she still felt an almost obsessive need for control even when her daughters were well past the age of young adulthood. The fear was so great that she insisted she would not pay for, nor help pay for, any university tuition that was outside of the two or three in-state colleges she felt she could monitor her girls at.

Part of this was, ostensibly, motivated by the overly publicized 'rape culture' (and the entirely debunked 1 in 4 women are raped on campus myth) she believed was so prevalent it required her parental supervision well into her girls' adult years. The other part was a tacit acknowledgment of the behavior she'd engaged in herself while in college and her acknowledgment of the nature and predispositions of young women when allowed unfettered freedom to pursue them. There was an unspoken understanding that she knew what she herself had the capacity for, but in the post-millennial era she contrasted this with the lack of direction and lack of accountability for women.

Back when he had a terrestrial radio show, I remember talk-show personality Tom Leykis did a topic about this: He had everyday women call in and tell their stories of how they used to *be* sexually (i.e. slutty) and how they are now. He came up with this after driving past a grade school on his way to the studio and seeing all of the women there waiting for their kids to come out and wondered about what their lives used to be like in their childless 20s. This was a wildly popular topic and the confessions just poured in like all of these women had been waiting for years to come clean anonymously about the sexual past that their husbands would never dream they were capable of. Each of these women sounded proud of themselves, almost nostalgic, as if they were some kind of past accomplishments.

Mothers today know what their daughters are positioning themselves for in their young adult years because, often enough, they too want to relive their *Party Years* vicariously through them. Even if it's not to 'relive' them, it's to experiences, in part, some of what their romantic notions have convinced them might be possible in this era. That's not to say mothers want their little girls to be slutty hedonists – far from it in the case of the woman I described – but it is to say that in their daughters women recognize an opportunity to direct the lives they wished they'd had the foresight to guide for themselves.

According to the Census Bureau, U.S. women now lead men in educational attainment for the first time since the Census began tracking the measure in 1940. A lot gets made about this 'gender gap' in college enrollment, but what usually gets lost is the social dispensations made available to women and the increasingly steep prerequisites for men to attend college. In 2017 where more than 40% of children are raised by single mothers it's interesting to note how the rise in female higher education contrasts with falling birth rates and the longer and longer delay of marriage to older ages for women.

As a Red Pill father of girls it's vitally important to get your head around two very important elements; the evolved gender-specific biological imperatives your daughters will be subject to and how a feminine-primary social order, the *Village*, will seek to accommodate them at every strata, every opportunity in society. While similar in intent to how the *Village* seeks to condition your sons, so too will it raise your daughters into its own image. That image is usually one founded on convincing them of their limitless potential, ignoring any evolved reality particular to their sex and masking it all in ideological premises of egalitarian equalism.

Equalism is the call sign of the *Fempowerment* narrative of today. You'll read about this more later in this book, but as a contrast to how your boys will be taught in a feminine-correct context about their inherent male flaws, girls are conditioned to embrace their roles as strong, independent and ultimately blameless of any consequence for the decisions based on these impressions of themselves. Girls are taught that they are 'correct' as a default.

First and foremost this is a social dynamic fathers must bear in mind at every stage of their daughter's development. Asking a Red Pill father to be a child psychologist is a tall order, I know, but most men are often taken unawares as to how early their girl's *Fempowerment* indoctrination begins. Whether that's how Disney Princesses openly carry the water of the Feminine Imperative, or how the Girl Scouts mold impressionable minds to prepared them for a feminine-primary social order, the purpose is the same; immerse young girls in a sense of their default social, personal and moral superiority above boys (and later men), irrespective of realistic limitations and devoid of any consequence of their actions or decisions.

It's vitally important for a Red Pill father to keep in mind that the *Village* will at every opportunity seek to convince you and her of its ideology. This is where many a Blue Pill father loses his Frame with both his daughter and her mother. Any man, particularly a girl's father, is ruthlessly shamed for not being supportive of his daughter's independence and "strength" should he even marginally disagree with what schools, media, care-providers and an 'empowered' mother would inculcate in his daughter. One of the vicious cycles Blue Pill men become trapped in is transferring their sense of self-sacrificing "supportiveness" duty from their wife/mother seamlessly to their daughter. It's an easy shift for a *Frameless* Beta provider to convince himself that he's also duty-bound to make sure his girl becomes the focus of his support. In doing so he becomes an active participant in his own daughter's conditioning by the Feminine Imperative.

This is likely to stir something up in most fathers, Red Pill or otherwise. What am I getting at here? Should fathers not be a positive, supportive encouraging element of his girl's life? Of course, but this sentiment is exactly how the *Village* convinces fathers (often unwittingly) to foster its ideology in their girl's lives. Who wouldn't want the best for their daughter? I certainly do and I've made the mistake of sparing no expense for it many times. Yet, this is exactly the natural loving attitude that the imperative uses to promote feminine supremacism in girls as well as a supplicating father. There is so much guilt invested in fathers in general today that avoiding it, avoiding the epitaph of being an uninvolved, unsupportive father is so imperative, that (largely Blue Pill) fathers will make efforts to *give* their girls "the world".

Earlier in this chapter you read *Promise Keepers*, and the same dynamic of wanting to avoid the legacy of a 'bad dad' applies to raising daughters. Blue Pill fathers worry that if they don't foment the ideals of feminine social primacy they too will be just like 'bad dad' and their girl will suffer for it as he and (he believes) his own mother suffered.

Raise a Daughter, not a Son

For all of the effort the *Village* goes to in order to convince us of some infinite number of non-binary genders, it is often very specific in its identifying girls and women in as binary-masculine a way as would remove men from embodying it. Part of this ceaseless drumming of girl's superior potential to boys is an endless encouraging of putting girls into conventionally masculine positions. Thus, we see father's enthusiastically encouraging their girls to involve themselves in what we might think of as boys sports, hobbies and interests. If you want to have your girl become a boyscout today there is an active engagement to in the organization to get girls in. Needless to say there is absolutely no similar effort in the girlscouts to recruit boys, rather boys are forbidden from joining (probably for the best). As part of the imperative to get girls into male-space you'll have no trouble finding special programs that'll allow your girl to join everything from a football to a wrestling team where she can show the boys how "girls can do anything boys can."

Even for a Red Pill father there's an element of wanting to encourage a girl to participate in traditionally boy's endeavors. In and of itself this isn't necessarily a bad thing until that desire interferes with your daughter's natural development as a girl. Being Red Pill aware means you also must be vigilant in determining how the *Village* will attempt to shame both you and her for encouraging her to traditionally female, conventionally feminine interests. And even within what you believe are conventionally feminine organizations or interests the influence of the *Fempowerment* narrative will be there. Look at any pageant (no longer "beauty pageant") organization, any girls-club, especially the girlscouts, and you will hear this feminine-primacy message loud and clear.

When you read the section Male Space you'll get a better understanding of why this push is so strong today. For now, it's important that you be aware that not only is this push directed at foisting masculine adequacies on your daughter, but it's also intended to make a father feel ashamed for not joining in that effort.

For the Blue Pill Dad it becomes a point of pride to get his feminist merit badge by proving how 'with it' he is in redirecting his daughters natural feminine interests to what's generally male spaces. There may be nothing wrong with that if a girl has a genuine desire to participate in something she feels passionate about, but from the Blue Pill perspective it becomes less about the endeavor and more about the desire to one-up anything and everything male-associated. This becomes a real concern when that endeavor involves pitting girls against boys on a physical level. While I'm all for women learning martial arts or contact sports there is a reason the sexes are segregated in competition – there is a real danger in the difference of boy's physical nature and aggressiveness compared to that of girls. The *Village*, being founded on the misguided ideals of egalitarian equalism, would have fathers believe that fundamental biological differences between boys and girls is insignificant. They want gender parity and this means ignoring the nature of the male and female biology.

For Red Pill fathers the temptation is one of wanting to relate to your girl as if she were a son. This is an interesting predicament for fathers who may have all sons and a single girl, or only girls and no sons. It's easy to fall into the trap of investing your positively masculine self into a daughter. This may be particular challenge if your wife happens to lean towards the *Fempowerment* narrative herself.

Even a well-meaning "red pill" woman will still be given to the *Strong Independent Woman*® narrative that's become part of her ego investment, and usually, this is just something she takes for granted. She may want a strong Red Pill son to handle his own business, but she also wants a daughter that a feminine-primary social order has convinced her needs to be "just as tough as a boy." Again, this is the result of the equalist narrative that believes gender is a social construct and that any biological influences of gender are simply obstacles to be overcome. I should also point out here that if the mother of your children likes to think of herself as "Red Pill" she will still expect your sons to have a default, unearned, respect for women and this will extend to your daughters, their mother or women in general. There is a growing trend to conflate *Red Pill* with traditional conservative (trad-con) values, and as such the idea of *Red Pill* (however it's defined by trad-cons) becomes more appealing to women who believe men should be conventionally masculine, but also to defer *Frame* to women as is convenient.

She's a Girl who will become a Woman

We live in an age where the most common complaint amongst women is the lack of any marriageable men. We've come to a point where women feel the need to freeze their eggs due to their lack of long term prospects with regards to men with whom they believe will be their 'relationship equal'. We know this status really refers to women's doubt of optimizing Hypergamy in a single man, but what we're seeing now is a generation of adult women, women well past their sexually competitive years, who were raised by the *Village* and fed a steady diet of the *Empowerment* message. These are women who were raised to believe that it was men's duty to be ready and available for them once they'd pushed the boundaries of their "limitless potential". In fact that used to be the old answer as to why women might want to freeze their eggs or look for a sperm bank to have children without a real father – they were "so career focused they never had time to think about motherhood until now." The real truth is now in fashion though; it's really due to their inability to attract and settle into a secure long term relationship with a man who could meet her impossibly high Hypergamous optimization prerequisites.

So the Feminine Imperative arranges convenient social conventions to help them salve the pain brought on by the prospect of never becoming wives or mothers with an equitable man. The *Village* taught them never to settle from the time they were little girls. Boys were ridiculous, men even more so, and all of them needed the correcting influence of the feminine. Now, in their post-Wall years, it's men's fault once again for not having properly prepared themselves to accommodate their long term sexual strategy. Disney taught them they were Princesses, yet they were raised to also believe that they would be self-sufficient, autonomous, self-fulfilling individuals – who would grow into *Strong Independent Women®*, never to be in need of a man for anything. Yet, here they are freezing their eggs because of exactly this "independence".

This is what the *Village* will teach your girl and this is what you must prepare her to expect. She must learn that eventually there will be a price to be paid for her decisions. This is what the *Village* never wants her to believe; that with decision comes consequence. The *Village* will tell her to reject the idea of likabilty and embrace her innate solipsism. Never do anything for a man, never prepared yourself for his pleasure or his acceptance; it's his privilege to even be taken into your consideration. What the *Village* will not teach her is that there are long term consequences for this enduring mindset, one devoid of real appreciation, one devoid of even the idea that men are to be respected for their experiences.

As I mention early, the best education you can give your girl is to give her an example to mold her ideal of a positive masculine man upon. It's so easy to say, lead by example, but the same fundamental core dynamics of Red Pill awareness and Game in practice can (must) be used to teach your daughter that a man is deserving of respect and deserving of her desire to be a better daughter, wife and mother *for* him. Exactly the same Red Pill-aware psychological core, exactly the same understanding of Hypergamy that will help you be the dominant masculine figure with your girlfriend and wife will help you model the type of man you'll hope your eventual son in law will be. Demonstrate positive masculine dominance, never explicate it to your daughter. She will be taught that "girls rule" and boys are sad saps. She'll be taught that men are ridiculous, but not Daddy, never Daddy.

There are a hundred different studies that indicate women without a father or with a weak (Beta) father becomes adults with "daddy issues". They often become 'broken women', rudderless and prone to all the stereotypical tendencies you've probably come to expect – early promiscuity, depression, life-long insecurities, etc. And of course the *Village* is already prepared to vilify fathers (or insist on his superfluousness) and play to women's default victimhood. The truth of this father-daughter dynamic is that girls and women are fed a self-perpetuating, self-defeating cycle of empowerment and victimhood with the weak-man father mixed somewhere into the blame cycle. This, first and foremost, is what you will have to be prepared to fight while being the living example of the positive masculinity she'll never know unless you live it for her. You are vitally important in her development as a woman. You are an example of masculinity that no single-mother will ever be able to emulate. And you must be so fearlessly in the face of a world that'll accuse you of being abusive, typically male, chauvinistic and misogynistic for your conventional masculinity.

Be the Example in your own Marriage

Finally, you need to be the example of positive masculinity in your own marriages. Assuming you're married to the mother of your children and you've initiated a relationship model based on your own Red Pill informed Frame, you also have to know how important it is that your wife reflexively responds to you as the masculine example. It's important that both your sons and daughters recognize your authority as such, but doubly so in the case of daughters. How your wife interacts with you, how she gender-communicates with you, defers to your decisions, how she responds to your *Amused Mastery* is vital to your daughters perception of a masculine role model.

I would argue that having a weak *Frame* with your wife or living in a power dynamic such that it's her to whom all defer to for decisions and authority is almost more damaging to children's gender perceptions than if a father were absent from the home. A weak, Beta, Blue Pill masculine role sets a weak perception of masculinity for girls who will as adult women be seeking out men who either embody a man who will dominate them or one whom they can dominate themselves as their mother did. Considering the direction that Open Hypergamy has set us on, I'd say both.

RELATIONSHIP GAME - A PRIMER

To cap this section off I felt it incumbent upon me to finish with a few basics I think are necessary to promoting a Red Pill defined relationship. How you choose (or not) to effect it, whether in marriage or a sustained long term relationship (LTR), is up to you, but these are some basics I think are likely to help men enter or develop a relationship based on Red Pill fundamentals.

Going Alpha

Before I dig in here I think it's important to bear in mind that the principles of Game do not change in an LTR, only the context does. Every behavior set, every frame control tenet, every aspect of *Amused Mastery* and even Pick Up Artist (PUA) skills like *Cocky & Funny* are all necessary, if not more necessary in an LTR. One of the greatest failings married men begin their nuptials with is starting from a position of Beta-ness. I've encountered, and counseled, far too many men with the same story; they entered into their LTR or marriage from a default position of being the "supportive" submissive partner only to discover Game later in their relationship and then fight the very uphill battle of convincing their spouse that they've 'genuinely' experienced a radical shift in their outlook and personalities.

If all she's ever known is the Beta you, convincing her you've gone Alpha is a tough row to hoe. An Alpha shift in a long term relationship is threatening to a woman who's built a lifestyle around the predictability of the Beta guy she committed to. It stirs up the competition anxiety she's been numbed to for a long time, and while that's beneficial in prompting her genuine desire for you, it also upsets her sense of security. It's for this reason that Beta men are reluctant to experiment with being more dominant; they carry over from their single-hood the same mistaken belief that women require comfort, familiarity and security in order to become intimate or "feel sexy". They still fail to grasp, even in marriage, that sex by definition requires anxiety to be grounded in genuine desire. Sexual tension requires urgency, learn how to stoke it in your woman.

So from the outset it's important to acknowledge that going Alpha from a Beta default is going to require a measured, practiced effort. The ideal position is to begin an LTR from an incorrigible, irrationally self-confident, Alpha frame and encourage the belief in your partner that it was she who 'mellowed' you. It's ingratiating and ego-flattering for a woman to believe that she has the capacity to charm the savage beast with her feminine wiles.

The Outline

It never ceases to amaze me how readily divorced women (and sometimes thrice divorced) are to dispense tips on the makings for a great marriage. Or more fascinating, to hear pussy-whipped husbands parrot these same lines. A divorced guy's marriage advice is usually "just don't get married." So allow me to toss in my two cents here.

In all the years I've been counseling men I have yet to have a guy tell me he's getting more sex now than when he was single or dating his wife, but sex isn't the issue here – *desire* is the root of the problem.

As I've stated in many previous essays, properly motivated, women will move across the country, crawl under barbed wire and out a 2 story window to fuck a guy she has the genuine desire to fuck. This applies equally to your wife of 10 years. Before marriage women look for ways to get laid with a guy they want to fuck, after marriage they look for ways to avoid it, but it's *desire* that motivates it.

Chris Rock says it best when he goes into sex after marriage –

> *"If you like fucking, marriage aint for you. I haven't fucked in 8 years. I've had 'intercourse', but I haven't fucked since I got married. I haven't had a blow job in 8 years. I've had 'fellatio' but I haven't had my dick sucked in 8 years."*

This is the essence of desire after marriage; it generally becomes another chore to add to a woman's to-do list. Get the kids to soccer practice, go get groceries, fuck her husband and fold the laundry. Add a full-time job to that list and sleep becomes the new sex. But it's not about being tired or overwhelmed, it's about desire. My wife used to work a night shift and if she came in at 2am and woke me up telling me she felt like having sex, I could be in the deepest of REM sleep and wake up to knock it out with her and be ready to go for two, because I want to have sex with her. Women love to play the "but I really want to, I'm just not into it now" card to counter this, but as always, never forget it's her behavior that defines intent, not her words. Remember, a woman will fuck; she might not fuck you, she might not fuck me, but she will fuck somebody. She just needs to be properly motivated.

Desire Levels

All of those preconditions she had for you to accept *your* offer of marriage –
a good job, be a good provider, a good listener, be funny, have status, being
reliable, a good physique; all of that does nothing to increase her desire to have
sex with you. The single, bachelor is concerned with Interest Levels, the married
man should be concerned with Desire Levels.

So how do you prompt this *Desire*? How do you get a woman who knows every
intimate detail about you for the past 10 years properly motivated to fuck you
like she did when you were 20-something? Women will offer the Oprah-correct,
"more romance!" and men will roll their eyes and murmur "more alcohol." Put
out of your head right now all of these feminine-correct notions that you need
to "rekindle the fire" or find some gimmicky ritual that will lead you back to
that desire she picked up from some article in Cosmo – I've gone down that
road before. 'Date Night' is a band-aid for a symptom of a larger ill and this is a
prolonged lack of Desire. There is nothing worse than going through the motions
of a preplanned, prescripted, 'date-like-you-used-to-have' only to have your wife
lay on the bed like a dead fish. Starfish sex. No amount of opportunity (which is
what a date night is, scheduled opportunity) will lead to her wanting to have sex
with you.

It's not about frequency, it's about quality. Frequency declines after marriage,
it's just logistics (especially after kids), but spontaneity doesn't have to. Would
your wife fuck you in the car like she did when you were dating? Would she be
up for fucking in the great outdoors if you were hiking together somewhere?
Would she be down for anything kinky that she hasn't done before or in ages, or
is it all just 'vanilla' sex now? Here's a list of things you should do from a man's
point of view:

Make her want it

If you've been married for years, she probably feels pretty secure with you
and whatever degree of control she has in regards to regulating the flow of sex.
Make her uncomfortable. As counterintuitive as it sounds, this is the single most
important advantage you can take. Begin to incrementally take the power that
her intimacy has had sway over you for the past 10 years back from her. When
you were unmarried even the slightest bit of anxiety that she may be put off for
another, better, prospect than herself prompted that desire to fuck you better than
the others.

Most important though is to do this covertly. If you go popping off about how you're taking your balls back and she'd better shape up or you'll be looking for a woman who is into fucking you – you'll just come off as inauthentic. You have to imply with your attitude and behavior that something has changed in you. The best principle to remember in marriage is that you will only get what you've gotten if you keep doing what you've done before.

The power of the 'takeaway'

In one form or another PUAs use the takeaway to shape desired behavior. This is behavioral psychology 101, reinforce the behaviors you want and punish the ones you don't, all the time remembering that too much reward leads to satiation and cessation of the desired behavior. Don't buy your wife flowers in order to get her to fuck you, buy them *after* she's performed accordingly and to your satisfaction. So many married men I know (even in their 60s) still attempt to *purchase* sex from their wives by 'allowing' them to buy expensive things thinking it will lead to 'appreciation sex'. In reality it will invariably lead to negotiated, obligatory and desire-less 'debt sex'. Remember, the personal trainer that your wife cheats on you with didn't buy her a goddamn thing to make her want to fuck him.

Your attention is your best tool in this regard. One thing I tell recovering Betas is not to give away the farm on the first date and that women are by nature attention craving. When you give away your attention without her having to seek it, it devalues your attention. This is a paradox in marriage because she was taught to expect that she 'should' have 100% of your attention and over the years there is zero mystery about you. When you begin to take away attention she's grown accustomed to she will seek it. And again you must do this covertly as she will respond to it covertly. You have to be sensitive to the adjustments she makes in her attention seeking, in conversation, in posture, in habit and behavior, because she wont overtly tell you "oh please pay attention to me." This will add to her desire to have sex with you in order to reaffirm this attention. Sex then becomes a reinforcer for her in this attention seeking which you can then use to modify her behavior – in this case being genuine desire.

Other forms of the takeaway may include certain regularities she's grown used to over the years that she takes for granted. One of these is a regular kiss. I used this to a great effect with my own wife. I would regularly come home from work and go kiss my wife as soon as I saw her, she became accustomed to this and after a few years I came to realize that I was like a puppy dog in this regard, immediately seeking affection as soon as I got home so I began to take this away.

Eventually she covertly recognized this and began to greet me at the door with a kiss. She was prompted to desire that connection by a takeaway.

Stay in shape

Nothing kills married sex faster than one or both partners letting themselves go physically. Most married Mothers who do so love to use their pregnancies as justification for their lack of motivation and obesity. Arousal is the important component to desire. If your wife kept herself in bikini model shape after she'd been overweight your desire to fuck her would undoubtedly increase. The same applies to you. Every day I'm in the gym I see countless 30 and 40 somethings straining and training as if their lives depended on it. Actually their sex-lives depend on it. For far too long we've been taught that "it's what's on the inside that counts" and how wonderful inner beauty is. Funny how hard men and women will train once they're divorced eh? The question is, what is it about their situation that would make them take care of themselves physically that they wouldn't while married? Before the divorce, they never had the time or motivation, but now it seems they have plenty of both.

By staying in shape – and by that I mean better shape than your spouse – you send a message, not only of confidence, but a covert understanding that she'll have some imagined competition for your attention via social proof. Thus, you not only create genuine desire by physical arousal, but you simultaneously create a psychology of desire by prompting her natural competitive impulses (i.e. Dread).

Dont drive drunk

"It provoketh the desire, but taketh away the performance."

Alcohol is *not* an aphrodisiac. I know that sounds odd coming from a guy who's worked in the liquor industry for 12 years, but it's true. Alcohol does lower inhibitions and perhaps predisposes your wife to lovemaking. After years of experimentation I've perfected the 'pantydropper' – that magic formula of just enough alcohol to get her going, but not so much as to have her passed out over the toilet bowl. Still, sex is better sober and the obvious setback of whiskey-dick isn't going to improve her already dubious desire to have sex in the first place. Understand the dynamics of her sexuality too. Strike while the iron's hot and be sure to be up and ready to go at the peak of her menstrual cycle. Catch her right after a good workout and after you come back from lifting and that's the benchmark for 'real' genuine sexual desire. You simply cannot inspire her to a standard of desire if one or both of you have a depressant in your bloodstream. If anything you want to accelerate blood flow not impede it.

Spontaneous combustion

Predictable is *boring*. There's nothing more predictable than sex with the same person you've been getting after it with for over 10 years. Oddly enough the spontaneity principle is exactly why garbage advice like 'date night' and "keeping it fresh" articles in *Marie Claire* sell magazines and don't save marriages. All of these "freshen it up" ideas are predictable. For all of the wacky ideas you can come up with for 'new' sex, you're still fucking the same old lady you married 10 years ago. You've got to be willing to push the envelope with her expectations of predictable sex. Suggest it when she least expects it. Tell her to flash you her boobs or some other cheap thrill when the opportunity presents itself at the beach or somewhere semi-public. Creating a condition of desire doesn't have to directly and immediately lead to intercourse. Ask her for a blow job in the parking lot before you go to dinner one night. Even the asking is arousing. Even if she turns you down you can still use her rejection to your advantage since it implies that, perhaps at some point in time, she (or some other girlfriend you had) used to do this because she wanted to (i.e. assume the sale). When you do proposition your wife make it seem as if it just popped into your head at that very moment. Again, think covert, not overt. Overt requires planning and planning = predictable and boring. Covert implies spontaneity.

The Cardinal Rule of Relationships

In any relationship, whether romantic, personal, business or familial, the person with the most power is the one who needs the other the least.

This may sound Machiavellian, but it holds true, especially in marriage. If you wonder who has the greater degree of control in your relationship the answer is always her. She must come to you. If you are the *prize* and she recognizes this, you will inspire genuine desire. So many married guys I know have walked their entire married lives on eggshells because they put their wives in a position of being the gatekeeper of his own sexuality. "She's got the vagina man, I don't wanna piss her off" is the mantra they repeat to them and themselves. This then flows over into other aspects of their lives and places a woman into becoming the authority in the marriage. Just as in single life, if her intimacy is used as her agency to get a desired behavior from her husband that's the value it has. When you can prove to her that her pussy is no longer a rewarding reinforcer for her desired behavior of you, you remove this agency and reset yourself on at least a partial footing of your prior bachelorhood.

THE FEMININE NATURE

FEMININE SOLIPSISM

Solipsism (from Latin solus, meaning "alone", and ipse, meaning "self") is the philosophical idea that only one's own mind is sure to exist. As an epistemological position, solipsism holds that knowledge of anything outside one's own mind is unsure; the external world and other minds cannot be known and might not exist outside the mind. As a metaphysical position, solipsism goes further to the conclusion that the world and other minds do not exist.

"Women have always been the primary victims of war. Women lose their husbands, their fathers, their sons in combat. Women often have to flee from the only homes they have ever known. Women are often the refugees from conflict and sometimes, more frequently in today's warfare, victims. Women are often left with the responsibility, alone, of raising the children."

– Hillary Clinton

There was a time I had planned on using Hillary's now infamous quote for an essay outlining the distinction between women's innate solipsism and a learned, acculturated narcissism. However, fate delivered me a much more profound use for this quote here.

Before I dig in, I feel it's kind of incumbent upon me to point out that I in no way align with, nor endorse Hillary's political or ideological perspectives, and I think it should go without saying that I disagree with her feminine-primary social agendas.

That said, if you ever need a better quote to explain the realities of feminine solipsism I think I'd be at a loss to give you one. A lot of men, even Red Pill aware men, have a hard time understanding how women's innate solipsism fits into the feminine psyche. The social conditioning and upbringing that predisposes us to an egalitarian-equalist mindset conflicts with the thinking that women and men would have different psychological firmware. Equalism teaches us to expect that men and women's needs share mutual origins and our impulses are so similar that any difference is insignificant. Biologically and sociologically this is provably untrue.

That same egalitarian frame predisposes us to consider that '*not all women are like that*' or to disassociate the idea that men and women could be anything but functionally equal agents. As a result we get convenient distractions to confuse our looking for comparative states should anyone (or thing) challenge an easy equalist answer.

Simply put, we get rationales like "*Oh well, men do it too*", or worse. We're taught to doubt any opposite comparison that leads us away from considering the truth that men and women are psychologically, biologically and sociologically different; with different motives and different strategies which we employ to meet different imperatives. And often these imperatives are at odds with the best interests of the other sex.

Separating Differences

I've elaborated on this rule in *The Rational Male, Preventive Medicine*, but for now lets reconsider:

The Cardinal Rule of Sexual Strategies
For one gender's sexual strategy to succeed the other gender must compromise or abandon their own.

It is the fundamental differences in either sex's imperatives, acculturation and biology that creates this conflict. Of course, men and women have come together for each other's mutual benefit (and love, and enjoyment) to create families and sustain our race for millennia, however, this mutually beneficial union does not originate from mutual imperatives or mutually beneficial sexual strategies between the sexes.

In my first book when I explained how women hold an opportunistic concept of love, while men hold an idealistic one, the resistance to accept that this observable, behavioral, reality is rooted in a blank-slate belief that men and women are fundamentally the same. So, when we read a statement from a woman of Hillary Clinton's status, we either scoff at the oblivious audacity of it (because it is so counter to our (male) imperative's interests) or we nod in ascension in the feminized belief that what best serves the female imperative *necessarily* is the best interest of the male imperative. This is the logic which Hillary hopes men will concur with.

Hillary's is an illustration of the fundamental difference in the interpretation of experience between the sexes. From a solipsistically oblivious female perspective what Hillary is expounding on here is entirely true. From a perspective that singularly prioritizes feminine Hypergamy above all else, these three sentences make perfect, pragmatic sense. The idea that men losing their lives in warfare would make them victims at all (much less the primary victims) isn't even an afterthought; all that matters is the long term security and continued provisioning of women and their imperatives.

Solipsism, not Narcissism

A lot of newly Red Pill aware men get confused at my using the term 'solipsism' when I refer to this female-specific obliviousness to any concern – or lesser prioritized concern – of anything outside their immediate existential needs. The confusion comes from men who want for a similar justice where women are responsible for their own moral agency. Self-importance, arrogant self-interest or narcissism would seem to be a more appropriate term for this dynamic, but I disagree. All of these terms carry a negative connotation and with them the obligation of women (hopefully) bearing the burden of personal responsibility for their behaviors based on them.

As Red Pill aware men, we need to guard against attributing to social constructivism that which is better explained by women's innate, evolved predisposition.

Female solipsism in and of itself is not necessarily a net negative in the larger scope of human survival and evolution. On the surface that may seem a bit outrageous, but it's only outrageous insofar as women's solipsistic natures come into conflict with the biological and social imperatives of men. Much of what constitutes women's solipsistic nature today is founded in evolved self-preservation (and by extension the preservation of any of their offspring). This solipsism is the necessary result of a feminine survival instinct that's helped preserve women and their offspring in the violent, chaotic and uncertain environments of pre-modern eras.

A lot of my critics take me to task on this, however, it's important to keep in mind that recognizing the importance of feminine solipsism is not an endorsement of the anti-social, and often cruel, byproducts of it. Acknowledging women's solipsistic nature is not an endorsement or license for behavior or decisions it influences.

No doubt, men who've been on the sharp end of this nature will grind their teeth at the inevitable narcissism that becomes an extension of women's solipsism. I'll agree. Socially we're living in an era of unprecedented (western) narcissism manifested in a vast majority of women.

At no other time in history have women become more accustomed to perceived entitlements of personal security, ubiquitous social control and relative assurances of optimizing Hypergamous imperatives. At no other time have women's sexual strategies been of such primary importance to collective society. However, this narcissism is the result of an acculturation and learned social priorities that predispose women to expectations that border on arrogance. Over recent generations that narcissism has become learned and fostered in women to the point that narcissism is openly embraced as a feminine strength – women believe it's their due after a long suffering.

Women's solipsistic nature however is an integral part of their evolved psychological firmware. Solipsism is the evolved, selected-for result of self-preservation necessities that ensured the survival of our species. As men we get frustrated by this intrinsic nature; a nature that puts women's imperatives as their primary mental point of origin. As any newly aware Red Pill man will attest, coming to this realization is a very hard truth to accept. It's cruel and contrary to what the *First Set of Books* have taught him he should expect and to build his life around. Furthermore, it's cruel in the respect that this solipsism neither aligns with the romantic, Blue Pill hopes he's been raised to accept, nor the egalitarian, equal and level playing field ideology he's been conditioned to believe he can expect from women. As I stated earlier, coming to terms with men and women's differing concepts of love is a tough disillusionment, but this difference in concept is simply one of many a man must come to terms with in his Red Pill awareness.

When I debunk the myth of women having some supernatural empathy I often get taken to task about women's capacity to feel empathy to a greater degree than do men. It's not that women cannot feel empathetically (a shared experience), my argument was that the idea that women feel a '*greater*' empathy than men is a social convention with the latent purpose of masking women's innate solipsism. That wasn't a very popular idea either. The notion that women are mothers and nurturers was predictably spelled out, but with regards to empathizing and caring for men, the primary concern of women was worry over their own and their children's well being before that of their men should they become injured, incapacitated or killed. Again, this is a cruel truth, but also a pragmatic and survival based one.

Mental Point of Origin

Women's mental point of origin begins with their own self-importance, and the overriding importance of their own and their offspring's survival. I've had women readers lambaste me that they couldn't possibly be so influenced by solipsism because they put their children's wellbeing before their own. However it is just this solipsism that predisposes women to seeing their children as extensions of themselves and their own identities. And the good news is that this dynamic is one reason the human species has been so successful.

Women are bad at reasoning, but good at rationalization.

Let that sink in for a minute. One cannot rationalize without the faculty for reason. So are women really bad at reasoning? No, actually they're great at it. The difference is that women don't place as much value on truth as they do upon self-preservation, and therefore their reasoning processes do not abort when self-contradiction and cognitive dissonance is reached. They'll just rationalize their way out of that too, if exposed.

Ultimately, this rationalization reflects an underlying difference in value systems more than in reasoning ability. Women can and do *learn* to sublimate their solipsism. In fact, cultures and progressive societies have been founded on sublimating female solipsism. Women can and do learn critical thinking quite regularly. Women can learn and function within a society that forces them to compromise their sexual strategies and mitigates the worst abuses that solipsism would visit on men (and themselves). Women can learn to be empathetic towards men as well as live within a social order that looks like mutual justice and fairness.

However, the fact that these civil dynamics should need to be something a woman learns only reinforces the biological and evolved influences of female solipsism as women's mental point of origin. The need for security in a chaotic environment has led to women's solipsism being a selected-for, self-preservation adaptation. This firmware can be overridden by learned behavior. The parallel to this is men's learning to sublimate intrinsic parts of themselves – primarily their sexuality – to reinforce pro-social interaction in society.

Women dislike the idea that their experience is colored by solipsism. It sounds bad, and it runs counter to what they believe are sacrifices on their own part to help others. That may be so, and I'm certainly not going to attempt to discount those investments, but they come from a learned compassion that must overcome an innate solipsism. That '*me and my babies first*' mental point of origin isn't necessarily a bad thing either – it's only when that learned compassion and humility are superseded by it that anti-social behaviors and hubris arise.

I expect the predictable criticism will be that men are also self-important, and / or all humans are intrinsically selfish fucks. I'll elaborate more on this, but for now it's important to grasp that female solipsistic nature is less about selfish individualism and more about pragmatic survival.

Many a male reader of my Hierarchies of Love series (*Preventive Medicine*) grated against the idea that a conventional model of love would progress from men to women, then women to children, and children to puppies, etc. That model is a direct reflection of a uniquely female solipsism that seemingly discards men's reciprocal emotional investment in women. This conflicts with Beta men's investing of themselves in the myth of *Relational Equity*. However, this is also the same dynamic that predisposes women to desire men who can decisively control their environment as well as dominate them sexually and emotionally.

Solipsistic Society

A reader once asked me,

Rollo, it would be great if you could provide some evidence for female solipsism beyond a few examples. From my own experience I could name a few solipsistic women, but I could do the same for men as well, and I'm far from convinced that the trait is universal in women, or even that it's more prevalent in women than in men.

I anticipate criticism of this sort of example-seeking. And to their credit my more vocal female commenters never disappoint me with (sometimes over the top) illustrations. Another reader had a great example I have to quote here:

One of the most eye opening of the solipsistic world of females was when a plate of mine was giving me directions on where to pick her up. It went something like this:

Her: "When you come to that traffic light, turn over to me."

Me: "What do you mean?"

Her: "Just turn here towards me."

Me: "How the hell am I supposed to know which way is that? Left or right?"

Her: "I don't know. Just turn my way"

She eventually gave directions, but it amazed me how hard it is for a woman to put herself in someone else's shoes, even if she wants to.

Women's mental point of origin (solipsism) presumes the entire world outside of her agrees with her imperative and mutually shares the importance and priorities of it.

Just like *The Red Pill Lens*, it takes a sensitivity to it, but you will begin to notice instances of that solipsism all around you if you pay attention. An equalist's feminine-primary acculturation predisposes men to accept the manifestations of this solipsism as something 'normal', so we blow it off or nod in agreement without really considering it. Most plugged-in Blue Pill men simply view this as a standard operating condition for women to such a degree that this solipsistic nature is pushed to the peripheries of their awareness.

It's just how women are and women are more than happy to have men accept their solipsism as intrinsic to their nature. It's excusable in the same sense that women hold a "woman's prerogative" – she always reserves the right to change her mind. When your default is to accept this social imperative any greater inconsistencies fall into line behind it.

Both men and women are conditioned to accept that what best benefits women's sexual strategy is *necessarily* what benefits men. On both a social and personal level women's solipsistic importance presumes, by default, that what best serves themselves automatically best serves men – even when they refuse to acknowledge it. Remember, nothing outside the female existential imperative has any more significance than an individual woman will allow it. So, perceptually to women, if a man suits a purpose in her self-primary requirements she presumes he *must* also mutually share in that awareness of his purpose to her. Thus, she maintains that his imperatives are the same as her own and a society based on blank-slate equalism only serves to reinforce this presumption.

Societal Reinforcement

Social reinforcement of women's solipsistic nature is a self-perpetuating cycle. A feminine-primary social order reflects in itself, and then sustains, female solipsism. For most Red Pill aware men this cycle is apparent in women's exaggerated self-entitlements, but there's far more to it than this.

When men accept and reinforce this socially, we feed and confirm women's solipsistic natures define our social narrative. When men are steeped in a Blue Pill acceptance of what they believe *should* be men's condition, and defend (or 'empower') women's solipsistic behaviors or manifestations of it, that's when the cycle of affirming this solipsism comes full circle.

Solipsism on a societal level will collectively prioritize the self-preservation efforts of the *Sisterhood* on whole. This is what I often refer to as the *Sisterhood Über Alles* – women's needs come before all other concerns or directives. This is another instance of solipsism; that a woman's first directive is to defend her sex's imperatives even above considerations of religious conviction, marriage vows or espoused personal ideology. That's the depth and breadth of feminine solipsism, and again, this reinforces a cycle of affirming it in women. If there is a fundamental principle upon which the Feminine Imperative is founded solipsism is its root.

Communication

One of the easiest ways to identify women's solipsistic nature is manifested in their communication style. Specifically, this is an inherently inward, self-focus to internal conversations. I've outlined many times how women's communication style is covert, reserved and subject to contextual cues and nuanced meanings, while men's is overt, blunt and content, or information driven. Much of women's inward facing existence is manifested in the socialized ideal that women can (should) be islands unto themselves; requiring nothing from an outside agency for self-fulfillment.

I'm not lonely, I enjoy solitude...

I am a whole person who needs no other for my own completion. No man, no woman. The qualities identified by different cultures as male and female...are all mine. Your obsession with division....is absurd.

I've dug into women's communication styles on more occasions than I can account in my essays, and with regard to how women defer to their solipsistic nature there is no better way to identify it than in the priorities they give to communicating with men and other women.

It's endlessly entertaining (and predictable) to see how often women and feminized men's default response to anything they disagree with in regards to gender dynamics is met with a personalization to the contrary. It's always the "not-in-my-case" story about how their personal anecdotal, exceptional experience categorically proves a universal opposite. By order of degrees, women have a natural tendency for solipsism – thus, any dynamic is interpreted in terms of how it applies to themselves first, and then the greater whole of humanity.

Men tend to draw upon the larger, rational, more empirical meta-observations and decide whether they agree or not, but a woman will almost universally rely upon her individual personal experience and cling to it as gospel. If it's true for her, it's true for everyone, and experience and data that contradict her self-estimations? Those have no bearing because '*she's*' not like that. All larger experiences necessarily pass through her filter of self-reference.

This personalization is the first order of any argument proffered by women just coming into an awareness of long standing conversations and debate in the Manosphere. It is so predictable it's now cliché, and each woman's reflexive retort invariably responds with personalized anecdotes they think trumps any objective, observable evidence to the contrary.

It might be entertaining for Red Pill men to count the instances of personalization in a woman's rebuttal comment, but it's not about how many "**I**"s or "**me**"s a woman brings to any counterargument – it's that her first inclination for a counterargument is to use her solipsistic personal experience and expect it to be accepted as a valid, universal truth by whomever she is presenting it to. I's, Me's and Myself's are simply the vehicle and manifestation of women's first directive – a solipsistic mental point of origin; any challenge to that self-importance is invalidated by her personal self-primacy. This mental origin is so automatic and ingrained to such a limbic degree that consideration of it is never an afterthought for her.

This is common to feminine communication preferences (and men who've been conditioned to opt into a feminine-primary communication mode). Women focus primarily on the context of the communication (how it makes them feel while communicating), while men focus primarily on the content (the importance of the information being communicated). This isn't to exclude men from using personal experiences to help illustrate a point, but the intent comes from a different motive. That motive is an attempt to better understand the content and information of that issue, not an exercise in self-affirmation that feminine solipsism requires to preserve a woman's ego-investments (usually her solipsistic mental point of origin). The most visible manifestation of women's rudimentary solipsism is the importance to which they expect their personal, existential, experience to be considered the most valid, legitimate and universal truth apparent in any debate.

Middle of the Story Syndrome

One thing I've been frustrated with by virtually every woman I've ever known in my life is their tendency to begin a conversation in the middle of a story; all the while expecting men to understand every nuance and be familiar with all the minute 'feely' details that made up a back-story that's never forthcoming.

I swear, every woman I've known has done this with me at some time. The presumption is that their story is of such importance that bothering with any pretext, or outlining and describing the events and information that led up to that mid-way vitally important element that made them feel a certain way is all that should matter to a listener. Women have an uncanny way of accepting this when they relate stories among themselves; gleaning incidental details of the back-story as the teller goes on.

There's an ironic feminine-operative social convention that complains that "men aren't good listeners" or "men don't listen" to what women are telling them. This convention is really another manifestation of a solipsistic mindset with regard to communication.

It isn't that men don't listen, it's that our communication styles focus on content information, not the contextual 'feel' of what's being communicated by women. Women, above all else, hate to repeat themselves. Not because of the inconvenience, but because men 'not listening' and requiring a repetition of that information conflicts with her own self-primary solipsism. The want of a 'good listener' is really the want for a man who affirms her self-priority by not needing to be told something that confirms that priority more than once. And this confirmation should never require explanation or an understanding of the back-story of events that made it feel important to her.

Women have an inherent pretext in communication that always begins with themselves. In fact, most are so sure of their solipsistic, personal truth that glaring objectivity never enters their minds; at least not initially. Women are entirely capable of applying reason, rationality and pragmatism, it's just that this isn't their first mental order when confronted with a need for it. Just as a girl can be *taught* to throw an object as well as it comes naturally to a boy, a trained transcendence above her solipsism, one that considers the individuated existences of others' experiences takes a learned effort.

Ladies First

I had reader give me a great illustration as well:

> *I asked my ex if her kids came first or if I did. She paused and said "I really don't know. That's a hard one." I replied "Then it's your kids." I recall my ex-wife reading one of those save your marriage books right after I made it clear I was leaving. She read me a line in it and said she sees how she was wrong. The line went something like this: "If you want to have a strong marriage, you need to understand your husband comes first, even before*

your children. They must be taught by you, their mother, that he is head of the household and respect must be given. The only way they'll see that is by your demonstrating by your actions that this is so."

I still left though.

The irony in this instance is that for all of the humble deference this seemingly good advice promotes, it still presumes a woman is already the primary source of authority who *'allows'* her husband to be "the man". I've heard similar advice espoused by evangelical pastors making Pollyanna attempts at 'granting headship' to husbands and fathers from their reluctant wives. The inherent flaw is that these men already begin from a perspective that women are in a position of unquestioned primacy and require their permission to be 'men'.

In a way they are unwittingly acknowledging women's solipsism (and perpetuating the cycle) as a default source of authority. That a woman would need to be taught to defer authority to her husband belies two things; first, her solipsistic mental point of origin and second, that her man isn't a man who inspires that willing deference.

It's easy to see how a Beta man wouldn't be someone that would naturally prompt a woman to go against her natural solipsism, but in this guy's position (I presume Alpha since he walked) there is a conflict women have to confront in themselves.

In a social order that reinforces the entitlements presumed by women's solipsism there develops an internal conflict between the need for an optimized Hypergamy and the ego-investments a woman's solipsism demands to preserve it. As a woman progresses towards the Wall and a lessened capacity to optimize both sides (Alpha Fucks and Beta Bucks) of Hypergamy this conflict comes to a head. The necessities of long term provisioning war with the self-importance of solipsism at the risk of her losing out on preserving both (and having a guy simply walk away from her).

EMPATHY

Women cannot bear to see a Man experiencing negative emotions such as extreme anger, rage, fear, despair, despondency or depression for extended periods of time. You say you want to "be there" for your Man; but you cannot do it. If it goes on long enough, it kills the attraction; it sets off your hypergamy alarms; and subconsciously causes you to start hunting for a replacement Man.

A woman seeing a Male go through the above will seek to replace that Male immediately.

Women cannot listen to Men talking about or working out their dating/ mating/relationship issues or problems. Women reflexively view a Man discussing such issues as "whining" or "complaining" or "bitterness" or "sour grapes" or "well, you just chose poorly, so sucks to be you" or "suck it up, no one wants to hear you bitching about it".

As to both of the above principles; when a Male is involved, ratchet up by a factor of 5 the disdain and repulsion a woman experiences when seeing a Male do or experience the above.

– Deti

Around the first week of August in 2013 I suffered what's commonly known as a 'dancer's fracture'. For all of the risk taking activities I've engaged in over my life, I'd never had more than a hairline fracture on any bone in my body before this. This fucking hurt. Like edge of the bed, don't turn the wrong way or you're in agony kind of hurt. Forget about putting weight on it for 4-6 weeks, "holy shit I have a two story home" and my bed's upstairs kind of hurt. The Doc explained that there's really no way to set a dancer's break so I'd just have to "tough it out" and take it easy. I refuse to take any kind of narcotic painkiller (Vicodin, etc) so it was ibuprofen and Tylenol for the better part of the first month.

After the first week, the pain went from "holy shit" to "ok, ow, ah fuck, yeah I can do this if I grit my teeth." If a wild animal wanted to eat me, there'd have been no way for me to avoid it; I was literally hobbled for the first time in my life.

Sack up ya big pansy!

Now, do I sound like a big pansy to you? In my time I've squatted well over 400 lbs. I have benched 305 lbs. I've leg pressed the weight of small cars in my younger days. Most of the guys I know who'd broken a bone, or torn a bicep, or slipped a disc knew, and could empathize with, exactly what I was describing to them in great detail. However, my loving wife of 17 years and my fifteen year old daughter's first reaction to my pain was "Oh, men are such babies! They all make such a big noise about how much it hurts. You think that's hurt? That's not hurt." It was as if by their dismissing my injury I would get up and say "yeah, ok it's really not so bad" and go back to mowing the lawn or something.

This has been a pretty consistent theme for Mrs. Tomassi – and every single woman I'd been involved with before her – women don't want to accept that their man could ever be incapacitated. Before I was Game-aware, I took this with a grain of salt. My wife has been a medical professional since she was in her early 20's and she's seen some pretty gnarly shit in various trauma centers so I had to take that into consideration. There's a certain disconnect from human suffering in that line of work that has to be made or you lose it – I get that – but that still didn't account for the default indifference to pain most every other female I know, including my own daughter and mother had ever had with regards to a man in legitimate physical pain.

The Mother-Nurturer Myth

One of the classic perceptions women, and even well-meaning men, perpetuate is the idea that women are the nurturers of humanity. They take care of the children, home and hearth. Theirs is the realm of the private, and men's that of the public – in fact this was one impression that early feminism took as its primary target, they wanted it all, private and public. Despite the statistics about abortion, despite the realities of Hypergamy and the War Brides dynamic, the classic characterization of woman as mother, nurturer, nurse and caregiver have endured, even as a complement to the Strong Independent® characterization feminism would re-imagine for women.

Perhaps it's due to a deeply enrgamatic hard-wiring of the importance of Hypergamy into the feminine's psychological firmware, but women cannot accept that any man, and in particular a Man worth considering as a suitable hypergamic pairing, might ever be incapacitated. The feminine subconscious refuses to acknowledge even the possibility of this. Perpetuating the species and ensuring the nurturing her offspring maybe part of her psyche's hard-code, but ensuring the survival and provisioning of her mate is not. This isn't to say that women can't learn (by necessity) to assist in her mate's wellbeing, it's just not what evolution has programmed her for – it requires effort on her part.

I propose this because women's solipsistic nature (predicated on Hypergamy) necessarily excludes them from empathizing with the male experience – and this extends to men's legitimate pain. The idea that a man, the man her Hypergamy bet its genetic inheritance on for protection and provisioning, could be so incapacitated that she would have to provide *him* with protection and provisioning is so countervailing to the Feminine Imperative that the feminine psyche evolved psychological defenses ("men are just big babies when it comes to pain") against even considering the possibility of it. Thus, due to species-beneficial hypergamy, women fundamentally lack the capacity to empathize with the male experience, and male pain.

Empathy vs. Sympathy

I very specifically used the term *empathize* rather than *sympathize* in my evaluation of women's psychological coping dynamics here. There is a universal and comparative difference between sympathy and empathy:

Empathy is the ability to mutually experience the thoughts, emotions, and direct experience of others. It goes beyond sympathy, which is a feeling of care and understanding for the suffering of others. Both words have similar usage but differ in their emotional meaning.

Sympathy essentially implies a feeling of recognition of another's suffering while empathy is actually sharing another's suffering, if only briefly. Empathy is often characterized as the ability to "put oneself into another's shoes". So empathy is a deeper emotional experience.

Empathy develops into an unspoken understanding and mutual decision making that is unquestioned, and forms the basis of tribal community. Sympathy may be positive or negative, in the sense that it attracts a perceived quality to a perceived self identity, or it gives love and assistance to the unfortunate and needy.

Women do not lack a capacity to sympathize with male hardship or pain, but they categorically lack a capacity to empathize with uniquely male experiences. This needs to be made clear to both sexes. While I have no doubt that many a woman may have experienced the pain of a dancer's fracture they've never experienced that pain as a man, and therefore cannot empathize with that experience. Now, extrapolate this pain to other aspects of a man's life, or his idealizations about how he would want a woman to love him.

I constantly see the term empathy supplant the term sympathy when used by women; as if their feminine character uniquely transcends merely sorrow or compassion for someone in pain, but becomes somehow magically equitable with feeling that person's pain. As an insulation against the cruel realities that their own Hypergamy demands and exacts on men, women convince themselves that their sympathy is really empathy, and their innate solipsism only serves to further insulate them from even having the curiosity to attempt real empathy towards men.

It's the *Just Get It* dynamic I go into in the first book, but on a more subliminal level; if a woman has to put forth the effort to truly attempt to empathize with a man, he just doesn't get it, she marginalizes his experience and continues her hypergamous search for the Alpha who doesn't force her to real empathy.

This fantasy of feminine-specific empathy can be traced back to the Mother-Nurturer myth attributed to the feminine as well as the mysticism of the Feminine Mystique. If women are the unquestionably, unknowable forces of nature that the Mystique constantly batters into popular consciousness, it's not too far a stretch to accept that the mythical feminine intuition might also stretch to their literally experiencing the pain of others in an almost psychic fashion. If women are the "life-givers", (Mother-Goddesses?) how could they *not* have some quasi-psychic connection to that which they've birthed?

That all makes for good fiction, but it hardly squares against the "oh, men are such big babies when it comes to pain" trope, or does it? If women are granted the authority to define what really hurts and what doesn't for men – due to a socially presumed ownership of empathy – then this puts them into a better control of which men can best qualify for feminine Hypergamy. In other words, women own the selective-breeding game if they can convince men that they know, by literal experience, what really hurts a man and what doesn't, or what shouldn't.

APPEALS TO REASON

*"A woman in love can't be reasonable, otherwise she wouldn't
be in love"*— Mae West

The Château Heartiste (formerly known as Roissy) once posted an article
about a Beta male openly asking girls for the reasons why they rejected him.
In the typical deductive logic that most Betas are prone to use, he runs down
a checklist of questions regarding what he thinks killed his chances with the
girls he thought he could get with. He petitions four women with questions
about themselves, which, being women, all are more than eager to answer.

Do you usually figure out if you wanna do more than make out with someone
pretty instantly? Or, is it a slow burn?

Was there anything I did wrong that turned you off?

If you had advice for any guy looking to meet a girl, what would it be?

What makes someone attractive to you? Do you have any types?

Do you feel that you could never date someone shorter than you?

Am I an unattractive person to you?

These are some of the more common questions the guy puts to the girls, and
true to form the girls answer with the standard feminine boilerplate responses
that absolve themselves of their part in his rejection, while trying not to hurt
the feelings of a guy they knew would never see them naked.

Questioning like this is what I've come to expect from most chumps mired
in their Blue Pill bubble of applying logic to their sexlessness, but it's not the
guy's overt grilling of these women that's keeping him trapped in the Matrix
– it's his buildups and follow ups to those questions. He wasn't just interview-
ing them to 'get to the bottom of things' so he could solve his sex problem, he
began leading these women with 'if then' logic in an effort to convince them
that, by their own words, they *should* be attracted to him.

The guy is making the most fundamental error every plugged in chump makes — he makes appeals to women's reason.

Why Women Can't 'Just Get It'

Appealing to women's logic and relying on deductive reasoning to sort it out is the calling card of a Beta mind. There is nothing more anti-seductive for women than appealing to her reason. Arousal, attraction, sexual tension, subcommunication of desire, all happen indirectly and below the social surface for women. It's not that women are incapable of reasoning (hypergamy is one logical bitch) or are crippled by their emotion-based hind-brains, it's that, if you're asking her how to be more attractive you don't *Get It*. It's in the doing, not the asking. The process of attraction isn't something that can be broken down into a logical process for women to deductively follow – the process is men organically knowing how to be attractive and arousing and acting it.

On an intrinsic, subliminal level, women understand that their genuine desire, their genuine arousal and attraction, has to be an organic process. When a guy makes attempts to convince a woman that by her own reasoning (and led by his) she *should* be with him intimately, it offends and then cancels that process for her.

For women, one of the qualities of the Alpha her Hypergamy demands is a guy who *Just Gets It*. An Alpha would intrinsically know what women's arousal and attraction cues are without being told and without even the inclination to ask about them. The guy's issue of overtly confirming for himself 'what women want' is really an abdication of a Beta who doesn't get it. And true to form, for Betas like him, the next logical resort is to rationally convince a woman (preferably using her own words) to be attracted to him by attempting to re-impress her of his status.

Betas like this generally end up as the infamous *emotional tampon*, or the Surrogate Boyfriend to a woman who's banging the most Alpha man her looks can attract. However, this appeal-to-reason rationale filters into other aspects of men's lives. The logical progression for him would be to better identify with the women (really the Feminine Imperative) he hopes to bang in the future – embody the feminine prerequisites, get the intimate approval. For married or monogamous men this appeal-to-reason may come as a mistaken belief that doing more chores around the house will lead to more (or any) sex for him.

The fallacy of *Relational Equity* (*The Rational Male*) is essentially founded on men's dependency on appeals to women's reason. Your doing homework with your children to better their lives (while very ennobling) doesn't make your wife any hotter for you in bed, nor will it be any bargaining tool should she decide to leave you. Women don't fall in love with who you are, they fall in love with what you are, and no appeal to their reason will convince them otherwise.

As always it is better to demonstrate than to explicate with women. You simply wont intellectualize a woman to become sexual with you because women are more interested in playing the game than having it explained to them. Far too many men are conditioned to believe that "open communication is the key to a good relationship", and the guy asking the questions here is a prime example of this mindset. Equalism teaches men that women should be functionally equivalent and equally as reasonable as they are. This leads them to believe that, given the proper reasonable appeals they would use in negotiating other aspects of life, they can be equally effective in attraction.

This is false, but it is also why Game, understanding the female nature and creating rationalizations for why appeals to reason are so counterintuitive for men.

Female Dating Advice

The prey does not teach the hunter how better to catch it.

Why do women give bad dating advice?

I find it ironic that the same guys who whole-heartedly agree with the idiom "believe what she does, not what she says", are often the same men who really want to believe that, select, special women actually do give other men advice that has merit.

The problem is most guys simply parrot the words women have told them over the years when they asked them "What do women want in a guy?" and then think it works since they got it straight from the horse's mouth. Unfortunately, too many guys, especially recently, have bought the same line women have been repeating for ages thinking it's a way to put themselves at an advantage when all it does is disqualify not only them, but the poor suckers who hear 'chick advice' from another guy, repeat it, and the cycle continues.

My take is that the 'chick advice' phenomenon is a socio-evolutionary fail-safe mechanism meant to filter women's selection process of less desirable men from more desirable (competition worthy) men. Think about this – women almost uniquely own "relationship advice" in popular media. There are a few notable feminized male exceptions (i.e. the Dr. Phils), but the ones who don't align their opinions along a feminine-first priority are surreptitiously tagged as misogynists and marginalized or ridiculed.

On some level of consciousness women know they're full of shit when they offer up the 'standard' chick advice. To greater or lesser degrees, they know they're being less than genuine when they see this advice regularly contradicted by their own behaviors. Women (and now men) repeat in article after article how well developed the female capacity is for communication, so it follows that they must know to some, maybe subconscious, degree that they are being less than helpful if not deliberately misleading. Even the mothers with the best interests of their son's at stake still parrot these responses. It's like a female imperative. Why?

For the answer, all you have to do is look at the bios of single women on any on-line dating service. When asked to describe the characteristics they find desirable in a man, the single most common responses are confidence, decisiveness, independence. Traits that would require a man to be a Man and have the foresight and perseverance not to take things at face value. The guy with the capacity to call a woman's bluff with a confidence that implies she is to be worthy of him rather than the other way around is the Man to be competed for. Essentially the 'chick speak', 'chick advice' phenomenon is a shit test writ large on a social scale. And even your own mother and sisters are in on it, expecting you to 'get it'; to get the message and see the challenge for what it really is, without overtly telling you.

Most guys are natural pragmatists, we look for the shortest most efficient way between two points. The deductive reasoning that follows is that if we want sex, and women have the sex we want, we ought to ask them what conditions they require from us in order for us to get it. The problem is that women don't want to tell us this, because in doing so it makes us less independent and more compromising (and lazy) in our own identities in order to get at her sexuality. This is counter to the decisive, independent and masculine Man they really want and is evidenced in their behaviors. He should know what women want without asking because he's observed them often enough, been successful with them often enough, and taken the efforts to make decisions for himself based on their behaviors, especially in the face of a world full of women's conflicting words. This makes him the commodity in the face of a constant, overwhelming contradiction of her own and other women's motives, words and behaviors.

She wants you to 'get it' on your own, without having to be told how. That initiative and the experience needed to have had developed it makes you a Man worth competing for. Women despise a man who needs to be told to be dominant. Overtly relating this to a guy entirely defeats his credibility as a genuinely dominant male. The guy she wants to fuck is dominant because that's 'the way he is' instead of who she had to tell him to be.

Observing the process will change it. This is the root function of every shit test ever devised by a woman. If masculinity has to be explained to a man, he's not the man for her.

ESTRUS

2014 saw the publication of a paper by Dr. Steven W. Gangestad and Dr. Martie Haselton titled *Human Estrus: Implications for Relationship Science*. Anyone who's read the *Rational Male* for more than a year is probably familiar with my citing Dr. Haselton in various essays (her catalog of research has been part of my sidebar links since I began the blog), but both she and Dr. Gangestad are among the foremost notable researchers in the areas of human sexuality and applied evolutionary psychology. In this section I'll be riffing on what this paper proposes with regard to a condition of estrus in women.

In the introduction section of *The Rational Male* I relate a story of how in my Red Pill formative years I came to be a connector of dots so to speak. While I was studying behavioral psychology and personality studies a great many issues jumped out at me with regards to how many of the principles of behavioral psychology could be (and were already being) applied to intersexual relations. For instance, the basic concepts of intermittent reinforcement and behavioral modification seemed to me an obvious link and learned practice of women in achieving some behavioral effect on men by periodically rewarding (reinforcing) them with sex 'intermittently'. Operant conditioning and establishing operations also dovetailed seamlessly into the Red Pill concepts and awareness I'd been developing for several years prior to finishing my degree.

Since then, the ideas I formed have naturally become more complex than these simple foundations, but what I only learned by error was how thoroughly disconnected both students and my teachers were with what I saw as obvious connections. I met obstinate resistance to flat denial when I wrote papers or gave a dissertation about the interplay between the foundations of behaviorism and interpersonal relationships. It was one thing to propose that men would use various aspects to their own advantage (men being expected to be sexually manipulative and all), but it was offensive to suggest that women would commonly use behavioral modification techniques to achieve their Hypergamous ends.

This peer resistance was especially adamant when I would suggest that women had a subconscious pre-knowledge (based on collective female experience) of these techniques. I never thought I had brass balls for broaching uncomfortable topics like this – I honestly, and probably naively, assumed that what I was proposing had already been considered by academia long before I'd come to it.

I was introduced to the work of Dr. Martie Haselton during this time, and along with Dr. Warren Farrell, she's gone on to become one of my go-to sources in respect to the connection between contemporary behavioral 'dots' with theories of practical, evolved, functions of intersexual dynamics. I owe much of what I propose on *Rational Male* to this interplay, and while I doubt Haselton would agree with all of what I or the manosphere propose, I have to credit her and her colleague's work for providing me many of the dots I connect.

I understand that there are still evo-psych skeptics in the manosphere, but I find that much of what passes for their piecemeal "skepticism" is generally rooted in a desire to stubbornly cling to comforting Blue Pill idealisms. That said, I'd never ask any reader to take what I propose here on faith, but personally I've found that the questions proposed by evo-psych reflect many of the observations I had in my college days.

Hypergamous Duplicity

For the social theater of the Feminine Imperative, one of the more galling developments in psychological studies to come out of the past fifteen years has been the rise of evolutionary psychology. The natural pivot for the Imperative in dealing with evo-psych has been to write off any concept that's unflattering to the feminine as being "speculative" or proving a biased positive (by "misogynistic" researchers of course), while gladly endorsing and cherry-picking any and all evo-psych premises that reinforce the feminine or confirm a positive, flattering, feminine-primacy.

Up until the past two years or so, there was a staunch resistance to the concept of Hypergamy (know as sexual pluralism in evo-psych) and the dual natures of women's sexual strategy. Before then the idea of Alpha Fucks / Beta Bucks was dismissed as biased, sociologically based and any biological implications or incentives for Hypergamy were downplayed as inconclusive by feminine-centric media.

However, the recent embrace of *Open Hypergamy* over the last four years has set this narrative on its head; the empowered women who found the idea of their own sexual pluralism so distasteful are now openly endorsing, if not proudly relishing, their roles in a new empowerment of Hypergamous duplicity.

Your Beta qualities are officially worthless to today's women

The following question was from a female reader on the Red Pill Reddit forum:

For those of you that aren't aware, women now are often out earning men and more of them receive college degrees than men. As of now there aren't really any programs to help guys out. Assuming this trend continues what do you think will happen to dating? I think that attractive women, will have their pick regardless.

However, for a lot of women, trying to lock down a guy in college will be more of a big deal. I don't think hook up culture will disappear, but it will definitely decrease.

With the exception with my current boyfriend, I have always earned more than any guy I have dated. It has never been an issue. I just don't have to think about their financials, my attraction is based on their looks and personality. I am guessing the future will be more of that.

I thought this quote was an interesting contrast to the Estrus theory proposed in the Gangestad-Haselton paper. This woman is more than a bit gender-egotistical, and yes, her triumphalism about the state of women in college and their earning is built on a foundation of sand, but lets strip this away for a moment. The greater importance to her in relating this, and every woman embracing open Hypergamy, is the prospect of better optimizing the dual nature of her sexual strategy.

In many a prior essay I've detailed the rationales women will apply to their sexual pluralism and the social conventions they rely upon to keep men ignorant of them until such a time (or not) that they can best consolidate on their dual-purpose sexual strategy. Where before that strategy was one of subtle manipulation and pretty lies to keep *Betas-In-Waiting* ready to be providers after more Alpha men decline her at 30, the strategy now is one of such utter ego-confidence in feminine social primacy that women gleefully declare "*I'm not just gonna have my cake and eat it too, I'm getting mine with sprinkles and chocolate syrup*" with regard to Alpha Fucks and Beta Bucks.

The Estrus Connection

For all of the ubiquitous hand-wringing the Manosphere imparts to the social implications of today's *Open Hypergamy*, it's important to consider the biological underpinnings that motivate this self-interested conceit.

From *Human Estrus: Implications for Relationship Science*:

In the vast majority of mammalian species, females experience classic estrus or heat: a discrete period of sexual receptivity – welcoming male advances – and proceptivity – actively seeking sex – confined to a few days just prior to ovulation, the fertile window. Only at this time, after all, do females require sex to conceive offspring. The primate order is exceptional. Although prosimians (e.g., lemurs, tarsiers) exhibit classic estrus, the vast majority of simian primates (monkeys and apes) are sexually active for at least several days outside of the fertile period. Humans are an extreme case: Women may be sexually receptive or proceptive any time of the cycle, as well as other nonconceptive periods (e.g., pregnancy).

Do Women Retain a Functionally Distinct Fertile Phase?

Graded sexuality: Women's sexual activity is not confined to an estrous period. But are women's sexual interests truly constant across the cycle? Many female primates (e.g., rhesus macaques and marmosets) are often receptive to sexual advances by males outside of the fertile phase, but they initiate sex less.

In fact, women's sexual interests do appear to change across the cycle. Women exhibit greater genital arousal in response to erotica and sexually condition to stimuli more readily during the follicular phase.

A recent study identified hormonal correlates of these changes by tracking 43 women over time and performing salivary hormone assays. Women's sexual desire was greater during the fertile window, and was positively related to estradiol levels (which peak just before ovulation), but negatively related to progesterone levels (which rise markedly during the luteal phase).

*Changes in the male features that evoke sexual interest: Since the late 1990s, some researchers have argued that what changes most notably across the cycle is not sexual desire per se but, rather, the extent to which women's sexual interests are evoked by particular male features – specifically, male behavioral and physical features associated with **dominance, assertiveness, and developmental robustness**. Over 50 studies have examined changes across the cycle in women's attraction to these male features.*

The importance of behavioral features? Whereas preference shifts of major interest early on concerned male physical features (e.g., facial masculinity; scent), several recent studies have focused on women's reactions to men's behavior and dispositions. Previous research had found that women find male confidence, even a degree of arrogance, more sexually appealing during the fertile phase. Recent studies replicate and extend that work, finding not only that fertile-phase women are more sexually attracted to "sexy cad" or behaviorally masculine men (relative to "good dad" or less masculine men), but also that, during the fertile phase, women are more likely to flirt or engage with such men. Females of a variety of species, including primates, prefer dominant or high ranking males during the fertile phase of their cycles. These males may pass genetic benefits to offspring, as well as, potentially, offer material benefits (e.g., protect offspring). Women's fertile-phase sexual attraction to behavioral dominance appears to have deep evolutionary roots.

Much of what's explored here I laid out in Game terms in *Your Friend Menstruation (Preventive Medicine)* over four years ago, but the implications of the behaviors prompted by women's menstrual cycle and biochemistry strongly imply an estrus-like predictability. This estrous state is a foundational keystone, not just to developing Game techniques based on Red Pill awareness, but a keystone to understanding the dynamics behind Hypergamy, women's dualistic sexual strategy, Alpha Fucks / Beta Bucks, and can even be extrapolated into the drive for ensuring feminine social dominance in both overt and covert contexts.

When women embrace a social order founded upon a feminine state of openly revealed Hypergamy they confirm and expose the reality of this estrous state.

Whereas before, in a social order based on concealed Hypergamy, this state could be dismissed as a social construct (and a masculine biased one at that), or one that had only marginal influence to reasoning women with a "higher" human potential. No longer. The confirmation of a true estrus state in women via open Hypergamy confirms virtually every elementary principle PUAs/Game has asserted for the past 16 years.

Dual Sexuality

Within the dual sexuality framework (Alpha genetic and Beta provisional imperatives), fertile-phase sexuality and non-fertile-phase sexuality possess potentially overlapping but also distinct functions. In a number of primate species, extended sexuality – female receptivity and proceptivity at times other than the fertile phase – appears to function to confuse paternity by allowing non-dominant males sexual access. These males cannot rule out their own paternity, which might reduce their likelihood of harming a fe-

male's offspring. In humans, by contrast, extended sexuality may function to induce primary pair-bond partners to invest in women and offspring.

I found this part particularly interesting when you contrast this dynamic with the social resistance that standardized DNA paternity testing has been met with recently. In a feminine-primary social order based on *Open Hypergamy*, the Feminine Imperative can't afford not to legislate a mandated cuckoldry. If Beta provider males will not comply with the insurance of a woman's long-term security (as a result of being made aware of his role in *Open Hypergamy*) then he must be forced to comply either legally, socially or both. The old order exchange of resources for sexual access and a reasonable assurance of his paternity is replaced by a socialized form of normalized cuckoldry. Thus, we get high social praise for the heroic men who will 'Man up' and assume the responsibilities of parental investment by marrying a single-mother and raising a child he didn't sire. Feminine-primary society attempts to make retroactive cuckoldry something of a social reward.

Some studies have found that women's sexual interests in men other than partners are strikingly rare during the luteal phase (the down-cycle 'Beta Phase'), *relative to the fertile phase. Other research has found moderating effects; for example, women who perceive their partners to lack sex appeal experience increased attraction to men other than partners, less satisfaction, and a more critical attitude toward partners, **but only when fertile**. Fertile-phase women in one study were more assertive and focused on their own, as opposed to their partner's, needs, especially when attracted to men other than partners during that phase.*

Most research on cycle shifts has been inspired by theory concerning women's distinctive sexual interests during the fertile phase. One study explicitly sought to understand factors influencing women's sexual interests during the luteal phase, finding that, at that time, but not during the fertile phase, women initiated sex more with primary partners when they were invested in their relationship more than were male partners. This pattern is consistent with the proposal that extended sexuality functions, in part, to encourage interest from valued male partners. Others have proposed that women's estrus phase has been modified by pair-bonding.

Initiating sex or being receptive to a primary partner's sexual interest during the luteal phase (the Beta swing of the ovulatory cycle) follows when we consider that a woman being sexual during this phase poses the least potential of becoming pregnant while simultaneously (rewarding) reinforcing that primary partner's continued investment in the pairing with sex (intermittent reinforcement).

This is a very important dynamic because it mirrors a larger theme in women's socio-sexual pluralism – it's Alpha Fucks/Beta Bucks on a biological scale.

Compare this intra-relationship predisposition for Beta sex and contrast it with the larger dynamic of a socially accepted, open, Hypergamy, Alpha Fucks during a woman's prime fertility window in her peak sexual market value years, and her post *Epiphany Phase* necessity to retain a comforting (but decidedly less sexually exciting) Beta provider. When we look at an estrus phase extrapolated to a sexual strategy for women in the long term it comes very close to the "Sandbergian" sexual strategy promoted by Sheryl Sandberg, CEO of Facebook:

"When looking for a life partner, my advice to women is date all of them: the bad boys, the cool boys, the commitment-phobic boys, the crazy boys. But do not marry them. The things that make the bad boys sexy do not make them good husbands. When it comes time to settle down, find someone who wants an equal partner. Someone who thinks women should be smart, opinionated and ambitious. Someone who values fairness and expects or, even better, wants to do his share in the home. These men exist and, trust me, over time, nothing is sexier."

— *Sheryl Sandberg, Lean In: Women, Work, and the Will to Lead*

Women's sexual strategy on a social scale, mirrors her instinctual, estrous sexual strategy on an individual scale.

Cues of Fertility Status

Females across diverse species undergo physical and behavioral changes during estrus that males find attractive: changes in body scents in carnivores, rodents, and some primates; changes in appearance, such as sexual swellings, in baboons and chimpanzees; changes in solicitous behavior in rodents and many primates. Because women lack obvious cyclic changes, it was widely assumed that cycle shifts in attractiveness were eliminated in humans, perhaps with the evolution of pair bonding.

In 1975, a pioneering study documented increased attractiveness of women's vaginal odors midcycle. A quarter century later, research revealing other detectable fertile-phase changes began to accumulate, including increased attractiveness of women's upper torso odors, increased vocal pitch and attractiveness, and changes in women's style of dress and solicitous behaviors. Meta-analysis of this literature confirms that changes across the cycle in women's attractiveness are often subtle, but robust).

A notable recent study demonstrated that hormones implicated in attractiveness shifts in non-humans also predict attractiveness shifts in humans. Photos, audio clips, and salivary estrogen and progesterone were collected from 202 women at two cycle points. Men rated women's facial and vocal attractiveness highest when women's progesterone levels were low and estrogen levels high (characteristic of the follicular phase, and especially the fertile window).

Emerging evidence suggests that these changes affect interactions between males and females. During the fertile window, women report increased jealous behavior by male partners. A possible mediator of such changes – testosterone – is higher in men after they smell t-shirts collected from women on high- than on low-fertility days of the cycle. A recent study examined related phenomena in established relationships by bringing couples into the lab for a close interaction task (e.g., slow dancing). Following the interaction, male partners viewed images of men who were attractive and described as competitive or unattractive and noncompetitive. Only men in the competitive condition showed increases in testosterone from baseline – and only when tested during their partner's fertile phase.

What remains less clear is how we can understand shifts in attractiveness from a theoretical perspective. It is unlikely that women evolved to signal their fertility within the cycle to men. In fact, the opposite may have occurred – active selection on women to conceal cues of ovulation, which could help to explain weak shifts in attractiveness relative to many species. Concealment might have promoted extended sexuality with its attendant benefits from investing males, or facilitated women's extra-pair mating. Possibly, the subtle physical changes that occur are merely "leaky cues" that persist because fully concealing them suppresses hormone levels in ways that compromise fertility. Behavioral shifts, by contrast, may be tied to increases in women's sexual interests or motivation to compete with other women for desirable mates.

Usually after first-time readers have a chance to digest the material I proposed in my essay *Your Friend Menstruation* the first frustration they have is figuring out just how they can ever reliably detect when a woman is in this estrous state. On an instinctual level, most men are already sensitive to these socio-sexual cues, but this presumptuousness of sexual availability is rigorously conditioned out of men by social influence. In other words, most guys are Beta-taught to be ashamed of presuming a woman might be down to fuck as the result of picking up on visual, vocal or body posture cues.

Beyond this perceptiveness, there are also pheromone triggers as well as behavioral cues during estrus that prompt a mate guarding response in men.

I would however propose that the evolved concealment of an estrus-like state and all of the attendant behaviors that coincide with it are a behavioral mechanic with the purpose of filtering for men with a dominant Alpha capacity to "*Just Get It*" that a woman is in an estrus state and thus qualify for her sexual access either proceptively or receptively. Women's concealed estrus is an evolved aspect of filtering for Alpha breeding potential.

In addition, this concealment also aids in determining Beta provisioning investment for the men she needs (needed) to exchange her sexual access for. A guy who "*doesn't get it*" is still useful (or used to be) precisely because he doesn't understand the dynamics of her cyclic and dualistic sexual strategy. Her seemingly erratic, but self-controlled, sexual availability becomes the Beta provisioning interest's intermittent reinforcement for the desired behavior of his parental investment in children that are only indeterminately of his genetic heritage.

Evidence of this intermittent reinforcement can also be observed in what *Athol Kay* from *Married Man Sex Life* has described as wives "drip feeding" sex to their husbands. The confines of a committed monogamy in no way preclude the psycho-sexual influences of estrus. Thus, the placating of a less 'sexy', but parentally invested man with the reinforcer of infrequent (but not entirely absent) sex becomes a necessity to facilitate the prospect of a future sexual experience with an Alpha while ensuring the present security of her Beta provider. Thus, the dual nature of her Hypergamous sexual strategy is, at least perceptually, satisfied for her.

I think the importance of how this estrous state influences women on both an individual and social level can't be stressed enough in contrast to the social embrace of *Open Hypergamy*. The Hypergamy genie is not only out of the bottle, but women are, perhaps against their own interests, embracing the genie with gusto.

Blogger and author *Vox Day* once posted an article about how men are discovering that pornography is now preferable to relating with the average woman. In an era of *Open Hypergamy* I don't believe this is a rationalized preference so much as it's simply a pragmatic one. Men are rapidly awakening to a Red Pill awareness, even without a formal Red Pill education, and seeing the rewards (the intermittent reinforcement) simply aren't worth the investment with women who blithely express their expectations of them to assume the role they would have them play in their sexual strategies.

Lastly, I think it's important for Red Pill aware men to understand that the biological aspects of women's estrus and Hypergamy is not something a Game savvy man should ever think is insurmountable. It's not an uncommon occurrence for women to have sex with men in the middle of having their period. For the most part, women generally would prefer to get after it with men while they're in their proliferative (ovulating) phase of their cycle, but when presented with an overwhelming prospect of locking down a high SMV Alpha man women cannot afford not to have sex with him expediently.

It's my belief that women's Hypergamy can be overridden by a man who triggers a woman's cues for Alpha acceptance. From an evolutionary perspective, if a man represents a high enough Alpha perception, a woman will ignore the lessened libido that the luteal phase predisposes her to and have urgent sex with that man in order to establish a (hopefully) future sexual availability to him.

There are also studies which indicate that women have a tendency to fake orgasms with more sexually dominant, Alpha men. Beta men love to interpret this phenomenon as some proof that these men "don't know how to sexually please a woman", but the likely truth is that more Beta men are simply not worth the effort of having to fake an orgasm for. Just as Hypergamous proclivities can be bypassed by a worthwhile Alpha man, so too will women fake their own pleasure in order to foster the perception that she is sexually available to that man.

The take-home lesson here for Red Pill aware men is the necessity to understand the particulars of how women's estrus can work in his favor rather than perceiving it as something deterministic for him. Understanding women's menstrual cycle, their estrus phase, the behaviors it prompts, the larger sexual strategy it manifests, etc. should all be considered tools with which a man might better improve his Game as well as his relations with women.

THE EPIPHANY PHASE REVISITED

One of the best things about the Red Pill being a praxeology is that nothing is set in stone. Like any good science there's always room for reinterpretation and updating ideas per new information, or sometimes it's simply something or some observation that seemingly went overlooked that adjust an old interpretation. One of my readers, *Playdontpay* brought something to light in an old essay I'd written:

> *I agree with the 3 Strike rule for younger chicks of 30 and under but once she hits about 32 something seems to flip in their heads, women of this age and up seem determined to hold out longer even if they want to fuck.*

> *It's probably because at this age her clock is ticking and she doesn't have time to "waste" on flings that would won't lead to commitment, so she re-invents herself as a "quality woman" in the hope of convincing you that she is LTR/ marriage material.*

> *It's up to you to decide if you can push the envelope to 5-6 dates max, but I would only do this if I was sure it was her ASD* (anti-slut defense) *holding her back and not down to a low interest level.*

> *If you wait to date 5-6 and the sex is sub par, don't stick around waiting for it to improve as you've been sold a lemon and the juice ain't worth the squeeze!*

This seemingly innocuous comment made me think a lot about some of my older material and how newer readers might interpret it. There's actually quite a bit to unpack in this short response, so with the benefit of over a decade of hindsight I thought I might riff on it.

> *"...once she hits about 32 something seems to flip in their heads, women of this age and up seem determined to hold out longer even if they want to fuck."*

Any long time reader will immediately associate this phenomenon with the *Epiphany Phase* (*Preventive Medicine*) women enter when the reality of their lessened capacity to compete intrasexually with their younger sisters becomes unignorable. Generally this phase comes at or around the ages of 29-31, however, depending on circumstance this may come sooner for some women (those whose attractiveness is already understood to be suboptimal), and sometimes much later for others (women who bought into the lie that their attractiveness is subjective, nonperishable and indefinite). I've written many essays about this phase and dedicated two sections in *Preventive Medicine* to it. It's very recognizable, and very understandable when you have a good grasp of how women prioritize the 'needs' of their sexual strategy as they mature.

The *Epiphany Phase* is really a woman's subconscious knowledge of *The Wall* coming into her cognitive acknowledgment. However, what's not so easy to grasp is why a woman who's come to this phase would actually make it *more* difficult for a prospective long-term, parentally invested, hopefully idealized, mate to become intimate with her?

On several occasions I've proposed just the opposite; that Hypergamy cannot afford to wait for 100% perfect confirmation of a man's Alpha status before she has sex with him. This Hypergamic bypass is actually one vulnerability women have with respect to well calibrated Game. Even for women in the luteal phase of ovulatory shift, (when by all means she ought to be seeking the provisioning, comforting and rapport of more Beta men's attentions) women will be prompted to sexual immediacy and urgency when presented with the prospects of fucking – and hopefully locking down – what she sees as an Alpha man. As I mentioned in the previous section, it is entirely possible to bypass women's natural, ovulation-induced, Hypergamy when you present yourself as the right Alpha incentive to her (I've done this myself). This is the prioritization women's natural sexual strategy has, and in reality, a woman faking an orgasm for a perceived Alpha, or having proceptive sex with him in her luteal phase only confirms the urgency women's natural Hypergamy has with regard to locking down an optimal man.

But why would a woman, who for all intents, knows her capacity to attract men is waning, be so insistent on delaying her becoming intimate with him? This seems counterintuitive, particularly in light of the fact that most women in their younger, *Party Years* eagerly had sex with men for whom they made little or no 'rules' for in order to become sexual with them. It's a common enough idea in the manosphere that women will ride the '*cock carousel*' in their 20s until they realize a lessened capacity to attract guys and then seek to cash out of the sexual marketplace before or around 30. Usually this ends up with a girl settling for a Beta in waiting. Still, why would the rules and prerequisites be something she insists on now but didn't while she was in her sexual peak years?

Vaginas and Moral Compasses

In 2017 there was article on the *Huffington Post* quoting actress Cate Blanchett saying "*My moral compass is in my vagina*", and while this might be the red meat clickbait the HuffPo relies upon for revenue, it adequately sums up how Hypergamy, a woman's sexual agency and a woman's capacity to utilize it throughout her life directs women's intrinsic and extrinsic priorities throughout their lives. I realize this wasn't how Cate intended her comment to be taken; she wanted to express some inherent guiding principle for women in an era she believes women are still repressed in, but in doing so she illustrates the real compass women have with regard to moral interpretations of their ideas and behaviors. If something gratifies, optimizes or otherwise benefits a woman's driving impulse of Hypergamy, it sets a rationale for moral interpretation by her. Or in other words, if it's good for what optimizes Hypergamy, it's good for women.

As men, we want the easy answer to be the best answer. So it seems obvious to us that a woman making arbitrarily 'new' rules of intimacy for her prospectively long-term suitors would follow some epiphany where she comes to her senses, realizes the error of her ways and strives for being some new '*quality woman*' to represent herself as. As such, her quality should symmetrically be matched by a man's quality. And that quality should logically take some time to determine. This is, in fact, most women's self and public rationale for making a 'quality' man wait for her sexually when in the past she had no such obstacles for the *hawt* guy she met on spring break in the Cancun foam cannon party.

Women will break their 'rules' for Alpha men, but create more rules for Beta men, more hoops to jump through, in order to receive the (usually lessened) sexuality that an Alpha never had to make an effort to qualify for.

We want to believe in this ambiguous 'quality' woman because we're taught to expect such reasonings from a girl who now, at 29, wants to "get right with God" or "start doing things the right way" with guys. She's 'learned from all the bad boys' and now wants to settle down with the 'Good Guy' or so the rationale goes. Social conventions abound that condition us to expect that once women, "get it out of their systems" (by following the Sandbergian sexual strategy) she'll realize the errors of her youthful indiscretion and magically transform into a "*Quality Woman*". We want to believe it, and it's in women's best interests that we do believe it.

Most Beta men (and not a few self-described Red Pill men) want to believe in a woman's *Epiphany* about herself. They love nothing better than the idea of the reformed porn star who's finally "grown up" and come to her senses about the error of her youth's indiscretions with the guys they grew up to hate as an archetypal enemy. Better still, they'll feed that rationale/fantasy in the hope that her *Epiphany* will include her saving her best sex for him since now she's come to understand that it's been the 'nice guys' all along she ought to have been getting with if not for a superficial 'society' convincing her otherwise.

The reformed-slut-with-epiphany archetype is a trope Beta men *want* to forgive because it represents a vindication of their self-image, Blue Pill conviction and perseverance (they never gave up on her). Women with the pasts that make them good candidates for eliciting this rationale know men well enough to see the utility it has in securing Blue Pill men's resources and long term security.

Socially, she's got countless sources of 'go grrrl' moral reinforcement from both men and women. In fact, as a Man, just my bringing this to light makes me guilty of being "judgmental" in popular female-defined culture. And that's the insurance women will always have in their Epiphany Phase – whether it's a reformed slut coming to terms with the Wall at 29, or the ex-wife who frivorced her dutiful (but unexciting) Beta to have her own epiphany and discover herself a la Eat, Prey, Love, the social net of feminine-primacy is there with easy rationalizations to catch any and every woman's Hypergamous fall.

Holding Out

Yet *still* that woman hesitates in giving herself to that Beta provisioner.

We excuse this hesitation by claiming it's because, now, she wants to be *extra sure* about him. The Alpha men she so effortlessly gave herself to were all, of course, wolves in sheep's clothing (e.g. men are evil) and in her epiphany she must exercise caution. And if you think it's because of anything else, well, you're a misogynist, so shut up.

A woman holding out on a guy during this phase of her life really isn't about any moral epiphany, it's about her hind-brain coming to terms with having to make herself become sexual with a type of guy whom previously she would never have naturally flowed into having sex with. We like to think a now '*quality woman*' is deserving of putting a man through a set of qualifying tests, that seems like appropriate prudence, but in fact her reservation about fucking him comes from a deep seated, subconscious understanding that, while the guy might make for an excellent parental investment, he's not going to be someone she feels a sexual urgency to fuck.

Later she'll bemoan that she'd rather cry over an asshole than date a guy who bores her, but in the *Epiphany* she has to force this understanding down into her subconscious in order to better insure her Hypergamous security into the future.

This latent, limbic, sexual uncertainty has nothing to do with vetting the 'perfect guy' for the 'quality woman' it's about a woman, who likely for the first time in her life, is presented with the challenge of having to bypass her hind-brain Hypergamy in order to secure her long term security. Thus, we see this demographic of women make even more rules for a Beta to deserve her intimacy, while for a more Alpha tingle-generating man she was more than willing to break rules to get to bed with.

It's important that we focus on the idea that a man, any man, ought to be deserving of a woman's sexual *'gift'*. We get this rationale from the affirmations of even the most well meaning of men. Even though the concept of Hypergamy is regularly proven through her Alpha Fucks / Beta Bucks strategy prior to her epiphany, the Beta mindset is always ready to do more and expect more from men who would get with his idealized 'quality woman'. A woman bordering on the expiration of her sexual market value likes nothing more than to be told, and to encourage the idea in men, that "she deserves better" in spite of her past decisions. Still she hesitates having sex with the 'perfect' guy who is ready to overlook all of it.

This is an internal conflict between what her psyche knows she needs to do to ensure her security, and what her hind-brain wants in an exciting Alpha lover. What *"flips"* in a woman's head is her inability to resolve her sexuality with her self-consciousness in having to force it to be with a man who likely doesn't merit it for her – but this meriting her sex, up to now, has always been a process she left to her hind-brain to decide. In a sense it is quality control, but not for the self-righteous rationales we're supposed to believe it is.

There is a lot of inner negotiation on the part of women entering their *Epiphany Phase*, trying to reconcile the long term security needs of her Super Ego and the visceral short term sexual needs of her Id. At some point, what sexualized qualities satisfies a woman's Id she no longer has the capacity to maintain so there comes an inner negotiation over what available man represents the best compromise depending on her need and her acknowledgment of it – and her true capacity to satisfy her long term security with or without him.

Now introduce a Beta man into this inner negotiation; one who's been preparing his whole life to be the best, most dependable provisioner that his conditioning would make of him. His influence enters the negotiation process, but her Id can never find satisfaction. Thus, the negotiation becomes one of her Ego negotiating with her Id trying to convince it to re-figure its visceral Alpha Fucks needs to accommodate this guy since he represents just such long term security as the Super Ego needs.

There's a bit more to this reevaluation of the *Epiphany Phase*, however, I think I should add here that a lot of not-so-genuine confusion on the part of well-meaning guys about why a woman would so easily break her own rules to fuck an Alpha guy while requiring them to jump through hoops to get to a mitigated sexuality with her is primarily due to a woman's hind-brain expectation about what sex should be like with either type of guy.

I've related in the past how women will gladly engage in a same night lay with a guy they see as a hot Alpha sex opportunity, but would never consider if she saw the guy as "relationship material". This situation is a clichéd joke now – we laugh at it as "chick logic", but the more Blue Pill men become aware of the *Myth of the Good Guy* the more these quandaries will give them pause to think about the women whose pasts they're ready to excuse and the women they're simply never going to consider "*relationship material*" themselves. Hopefully they'll think twice about the social order that's encouraging them to "man up and marry those sluts".

PLAN B

Non-Exclusive Exclusives

I've been writing in the Manosphere for so long now that the same predictable straw men arguments and out of context quotes have become *de rigueur*. Any objective observation of women's sexual strategy by a man is always synonymous with misogyny.

What I've always found entertaining about Blue Pill critics of *Plate Theory (The Rational Male)* is that the concept of non-exclusivity always borders on the criminal when a man suggests men ought to pursue a non-exclusive dating (and sex), yet we hold women up as empowered, prudent and/or exemplary of bucking the repression of an imaginary patriarchy when they suggest the same.

Of course the quick retort to this is that women are '*slut shamed*' for being non-exclusive, but this is simply an old, convenient, sidestep to shame men while distracting from women's practical sexual strategy.

As *Open Hypergamy* becomes more embraced among women the usefulness of drawing attention to 'slut shaming' actually becomes a hindrance to justifying women's Hypergamous priorities. When a high profile woman like Sheryl Sandberg suggests,...

> *"When looking for a life partner, my advice to women is date all of them: the bad boys, the cool boys, the commitment-phobic boys, the crazy boys. But do not marry them. The things that make the bad boys sexy do not make them good husbands. When it comes time to settle down, find someone who wants an equal partner. Someone who thinks women should be smart, opinionated and ambitious. Someone who values fairness and expects or, even better, wants to do his share in the home. These men exist and, trust me, over time, nothing is sexier."*

Sandberg's epitaph here is every bit as "objectifying" as anything you'll find in the 'sphere, but the difference is we are expected to find her advice for assuming a state of sexual abundance practical as well as refreshingly progressive. I've stated this before, but it bears repeating that as women more proudly, openly, embrace the uglier aspects of Hypergamy it will be women who will prove the validity of Red Pill awareness far better than men could. Sample from the largest available pool of prospective sexual experience (Alpha Fucks) and presume that an 'equal partner' (Beta Bucks) provisioner will make himself readily available to you when can no longer reliably attract the men who represent your sexual priorities.

I covered this in *Plate Theory V: Lady's Game*; the natural extension of women's sexual strategy is, at least practically, best served from a presumption of abundance. And as such we also find that the vast majority of feminine-primary social conventions center on facilitating this presumption of abundance for women. Pop culture, social media and a feminine-primary social narrative fosters an over-inflated SMV and an exaggerated sense of self-worth for women, but functionally it convinces women that they can perpetuate a condition of abundance with regard to their sexual viability almost indefinitely.

Even in a condition of committed monogamy that background sense of sexual abundance simmers in women's subconscious. We laud women with the guts to pursue that abundance after divorce or even reward them with popularity and movie opportunities when they write books about pursuing it while married (i.e. *Eat Pray Love*). Either that or we pat them on the back for their ability to continually move the goalposts and convince themselves and others that spinsterhood is a goal state they sought to achieve their entire lives.

In all of these instances, whether legitimate or not, there is an impression that women can perpetuate a condition of abundance for themselves – and often far past their true sexual market viability. One reason I draw the ire of many a Blue Pill male and women is because my breakdown of the predictable schedule women follow throughout their lives with regards to their sexual market value (SMV) and their dualistic sexual strategy is that it directly confronts the doubt that they can perpetuate a condition of abundance in spite of their personal choices in life.

And that is the crux of women's self-affirming social and psychological conventions; to avoid any accountability for the fallout that may be caused by the choices Hypergamy has led them to make. Blogger *Roissy* came up with the maxim that the end goal of feminism is to maximally enable women's sexuality while maximally restricting men's – and of course the consolidation of that enabling of women's sexual strategy must also account for absolving them of misgivings and mistakes made in enacting it.

Failsafes

A majority of boys have, for several generations now, been conditioned to be serviceable providers for women once they enter a phase of life once women find themselves becoming less able to compete intrasexually. Anyone familiar with my second book, *Preventive Medicine,* understands this period as the point during which a woman's Hypergamous priorities shift from short term Alpha Fucks to long term Beta Bucks.

I also outlined the underlying plan involved in ensuring this strategy in *This is now*:

That was then. Now, at 30, and (hopefully) with a learned and earned degree of merit, success, developed judgment, character and a reasonably well kept physique, a man finds himself in a position like no other – his options and agency to enjoy the attentions of women seem to suddenly be at an apex.

The planning women had at 19 when they told him to "wait for me at 30" now becomes more urgent as she becomes more viscerally aware of the Wall. She knew this day would come when she was just entering into her peak SMV years.

For men entertaining women embroiled in their Epiphany Phase inner conflicts, not only is this a very confusing phase for the uninitiated Beta, but it is also an equally precarious period with regard (once again) to the consequences of his life's decisions with her. Most men find themselves players in women's meta-sexual strategy at this time because they believe that their perseverance has finally paid off. All of that sacrifice and personal achievement has finally merited him the genuine interest of a "quality woman".

For the men who never learn a Red Pill awareness what they fail to understand is that it's at this point they're are expected to abandon their own sexual strategy in order to complete that of the (now Epiphany Phase) woman they're considering a pairing with. Whether they were literally asked to wait for a woman until she was 30, the effect is the same, they have waited their turn, they have waited to be of service, they have waited to fulfill a feminine primary sexual imperative.

Now, I'll ask you to draw your attention to the statistics in the picture at the beginning of this section. There are actually several more studies just like this, but what it illustrates is an example of how women's subconscious will prepare failsafe contingencies in the event that the Alpha lover they hope to convert to a Beta provider doesn't comply with her sexual strategy.

Whether he's the one that got away, the office husband, or a gym partner, chances are he is the "Plan B" man she fantasizes about running away with. Like an insurance policy, this man is the handpicked boyfriend or husband replacement women have on standby once "Plan A" starts to break down. According to a survey conducted by OnePoll.com, an online market research company, half of women who are married or in relationships have a Plan B man on standby who is "ready and waiting" because of "unfinished business."

It's important to pick this apart from the get go here because, like most female written articles that describe unflattering facts about female nature, the narrative must be shifted to be the burden of men. The presumption here is that the 'Plan A' lover is always a woman's preferred choice – thus pre-confirming women's blamelessness from the outset – and that a 'Plan B' should only ever be considered if the 'Plan A' man somehow screws up in contenting to fulfill a woman's sexual strategy.

This dynamic is founded on the principle of Dread – remember, the sort that when men use it they're considered evil manipulators? However it should be noted that dread is always an element of any relationship, it's just that since women's imperatives are the socially correct ones today, only women can be held blameless in instituting it.

When there's trouble in paradise, and eventually a break-up, women are left at the starting line again. This means there's more ladies' nights, late-night rom-com marathons, and wine — lots of wine. However, to avoid playing the field and going through all the bases, women have taken a shortcut to get back to the finish line with a Plan B man.

"The saying that 'the grass isn't always greener' clearly isn't deterring women of today. They understand that anything can happen and are ensuring they have a solid back-up plan should things go sour with their current man," a spokesman for OnePoll.com told the Daily Mail.

As I outlined in *Preventive Medicine*, the makings of an Alpha Widow generally begin in a woman's *Party Years*; during the period in which she is at her SMV peak. Hypergamy is always pragmatic. This Plan B insurance policy strategy is only further evidence of Hypergamy, but it is also pragmatic. Women's hindbrains know that their SMV is a perishable asset, so yes, that back up plan makes sense. What's not so obvious in this study is that women also cling to the hope that the Plan B man with whom they consolidated long term security with might someday be replaced by the fantasy of an Alpha she's widowed herself over. Whether that happens with his Red Pill awakening and going more Alpha or her eventual divorce from him later in life remains to be seen.

I think the latter is not only a far more practical reasoning, but since it's unflattering and exposing of the machinations of Hypergamy, the far more likely use of a 'Plan B' alternate.

The narrative behind these studies is always a blatantly entitled male-qualification perspective and a bit more "you better not fuck things up" dread signaling, however, I think the last three stats are the most salient here. **At least half of the men involved knew of the Plan B man,** 1 in 5 was a friend of his, and 1 in 10 of the Plan B's had already made an attempt to jump attraction ladders to be intimate with her.

A couple of things make themselves apparent here: in a social order that is made of at least 80% Beta men women can get an ego boost in real time from the default dread they can inspire without really trying. And second, in generation Beta a default form of soft Beta cuckolding is not just known to them, but apparently it's become normalized for them.

All of this really comes back to, once again, quelling the constant state of internal doubt that Hypergamy instills in women. The Plan B dynamic, and the normalization of it in a feminine centric social order, is yet another play for assurances of security in both the sexual and provisioning aspects of Hypergamy.

Now, so as not to leave you hanging here, I have to end this with a bit of actionable advice. As always, your first order of business is to be aware that this dynamic is in play. Understand that this Plan B insurance tactic is not just reserved for married men with dead bedrooms. You will likely see variations of it in your dealings with women while you're single. Any man who's sexed a girl who depends on a bevy of male orbiters to bolster her self-esteem knows the utility of them. There are many ways you can leverage the Beta-ness of most men to elevate your own SMV.

Finally, if you are a married man experiencing this Plan B dynamic, you need to do some serious reassessing of your relationship and the status your wife holds you in. Are you one of the 50% of men who know who their wife's Plan B is? Is he even a friend of yours?

What can you do to reinforce your Alpha dominance in this situation? Or maybe a better question is, is it worth your effort to do so? There will undoubtedly be the predictable comments about how marriage is never worth the effort, and I'll acknowledge that here first, but are you a victim of endlessly rooting through garbage to reestablish an Alpha impression for your wife that she's reserved for her Plan B alternate?

Ghosts of Epiphanies Past

In *Preventive Medicine* I go into a bit of detail about men in this increasingly common Plan B circumstance. There is a subconscious expectation on the part of Beta men who find themselves at or just past women's *Epiphany Phase*, that predisposes them to believing that what they've become as a result of their perseverance throughout their 20's has now come to fruition and the women who ignored them then have now matured to a point where he's the '*sexy*' one at last.

Unless men have a moment of clarity or a Red Pill initiation of their own prior to this, what they don't accept is that this expectation is a calculated conditioning of the Feminine Imperative to prepare him for women like this; women who can no longer sexually compete for the Alpha Fucks they enjoyed in their *Party Years*. The Feminine Imperative teaches him that he can expect a woman's "real" sexual best from the "real" her – why else would she agree to a lifelong marriage if he weren't the optimal choice to settle down with? Why wouldn't she be even more sexual than in her past with the man she's chosen to spend her life with and have children with?

That is the message the Feminine Imperative has used to subtly and indirectly imply to *Betas-in-waiting*. Now with the comfort of *Open Hypergamy* this message is published in best selling books by influential women.

"...in time, nothing's sexier."

Not to belabor Sandberg yet again, but this is essentially the outline of the script we're reading for Plan B men today. The problem for him is that he took the *"nothing's sexier"* part of her *Open Hypergamy* Schedule of Mating to heart only to find that someone else was *sexier* long before she'd convinced him otherwise. For what it's worth, gynocentrism has far less to fear from the Manosphere revealing the ugly Red Pill truths about Hypergamy and more to worry about from pridefully self-indulgent women gleefully explaining it to the general populace themselves.

The more common *Open Hypergamy* becomes and the more proudly it's embraced by the whole of women the less effective shaming men into acceptance of it will be. I think it's much more prevalent than most men would like to admit; far more common for a majority of men who've tacitly accepted that the woman they married (or paired with) gave her best to her prior lovers and are too personally or family invested to extricate themselves from her after they've realized it. That investment necessitates them convincing themselves of the pre-planned memes the Feminine Imperative has prepared for them – that they are doing the right thing by forcing that dissonance out of their minds.

A lot of *Betas-in-waiting* like to claim a personal sense of vindication about their successfully pairing and breeding with women who they believe are (and were) their SMV evaluated equals once those women have "got it out of their system" with regards to self-discovery and Alpha indiscretions. In a sense they're correct; often enough these are the men who gratefully embrace a woman's intimate acceptance of him precisely at the point when his SMV has matured to match this woman's declining SMV. I call this crossover the comparative SMV point in my SMV graph.

Even women on the down-slide of their SMV like to encourage the idea that their post-Epiphany decision to marry the Plan B Beta provider (long term orbiter) is evidence of their newly self-discovered maturity. How could they have been so foolish and not seen how the perfect guy for her had been there all along? That consideration gratifies the ego of a Beta who's been hammered flat by rejection or mediocre experiences with women up to that point.

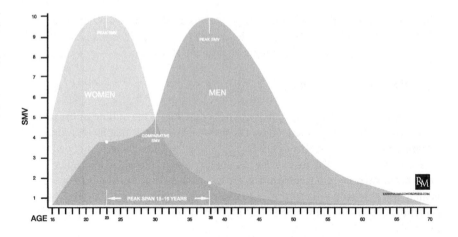

The primary reason I wrote *Preventive Medicine* was to help men see past the compartmentalization of women's phases of maturity, but also to help them see past their own immediate interpretations of those phases as they're experiencing them. Long term sexual and intimate deprivation (i.e. *Thirst*) will predispose men to convincing themselves of the part they believe they should play in the social conventions of the Feminine Imperative. Their own cognitive dissonance is a small, subliminal price to pay when they believe they're finally being rewarded with a woman who's now ready to give him her best.

What inspired me to write this essay was reading a cutesy photo-meme on Facebook. The syrupy message was *"My only regret was not meeting you sooner so we could spend more of our lives together"* superimposed over some kids in black & white holding a rose. Then it hit me, this was a message a guy was posting to his girlfriend; the one he'd met after his second divorce was finalized. What he didn't want to think about was that if he'd met her sooner she'd have been too busy "discovering herself" to have anything to do with him.

CHAPTER 2

Social Imperatives

ADAPTATIONS

Prior to the post-Sexual Revolution era men adapted to their socio-sexual and relational realities based on a pre-acknowledged burden of performance. Later I'll outline the expectations of this period in *The Second Set of Books*:

> *[...] when men transition from their comfortable Blue Pill perspective into the harsh reality that the Red Pill represents, the experience is a lot like Ball discovering that the set of books (the set of rules) he'd believed everyone was using wasn't so. Likewise, men who've been conditioned since birth to believe that women were using a common set of rules – a set where certain expectations and mutual exchange were understood – were in fact using their own set. Furthermore these men 'just didn't get it' that they should've known all along that women, as well as men's feminization conditioning, were founded in a second set of books.*

During the eras prior to the Sexual Revolution that first set of books was more or less an established ideal. Men were every bit as idealistic as they are today, but the plan towards achieving that ideal (if it was in fact achievable) was preset for them. Even the worst of fathers (or parents) still had the expectations that their sons and daughters would follow that old-order rule set as they had done.

For men, a greater provisioning was expected, but that provisioning was an integral aspect of a man's Alpha appeal. The burden of performance was part of a man's Alpha mindset or was at least partly associated with it.

The danger in that mindset was that a man's identity tended to be caught up with what he did (usually a career) in order to satisfy that performance burden. Thus, when a man lost his job, not only was he unable to provide and meet his performance expectations in his marriage, he also lost a part of his identity. Needless to say this dynamic helped incentivize men to get back on the horse and get back to his identity and his wife's esteem (even if it was really her necessity that kept her involved with him).

A lot of romanticizations revolves around the times prior to the Sexual Revolution; as if they were some golden eras when men and women knew their roles and the influence of Hypergamy was marginalized to the point that society was a better place than the place we find ourselves in today. And while it's undeniable that cultural shifts since the sexual revolution have feminized and bastardized those old-order social contracts, men will always adapt to those new conditions in order to effect their sexual strategies.

There's a lot of nostalgia for these idealized periods in the Manosphere as of this writing; seemingly more so as its members mature past their "Gaming" years and begin to feel a want for something more substantial in their lives. Men are the true romantics of the sexes so it's no great surprise that their romantic / idealistic concept of love would run towards romanticizing a hopeful return to what they imagine these eras were like.

It's kind of an interesting counter to how feminism and the Feminine Imperative paints these eras – rather than some idyllic place where women appreciated men, feminists exaggerate and deride these times as oppressive; the Sexual Revolution akin to the Jews exodus from Egypt. What both fail to grasp is the realities of these eras were still just as susceptible to human nature – the human nature described by what we call Red Pill awareness – and both sexes adapted to the social environments of the times to effect their natures.

Condoms were widely available in the 1940's and men painstakingly painted half-nude pinup girls on the noses of their war-time bombers. Women also adapted to that environment. These quotes come from two books by John Costello; 'Virtue Under Fire' and 'Love, Sex, and War' in which all too much of the female psychology manifested itself:

> "Of the 5.3 million British infants delivered between 1939 and 1945, over a third were illegitimate – and this wartime phenomenon was not confined to any one section of society. The babies that were born out-of-wedlock belonged to every age group of mother, concluded one social researcher:
>
> Some were adolescent girls who had drifted away from homes which offered neither guidance nor warmth and security. Still others were women with husbands on war service, who had been unable to bear the loneliness of separation. There were decent and serious, superficial and flighty, irresponsible and incorrigible girls among them. There were some who had formed serious attachments and hoped to marry. There were others who had a single lapse, often under the influence of drink. There were, too, the 'good-time girls' who thrived on the presence of well-paid servicemen from overseas, and semi-prostitutes with little moral restraint. But for the war many of these girls, whatever their type, would never have had illegitimate children. (pp. 276-277)"

"Neither British nor American statistics, which indicate that wartime promiscuity reached its peak in the final stages of the war, take account of the number of irregularly conceived pregnancies that were terminated illegally. Abortionists appear to have been in great demand during the war. One official British estimate suggests that one in five of all pregnancies was ended in this way, and the equivalent rate for the United States indicates that the total number of abortions for the war years could well have been over a million.

These projections are at best merely a hypothetical barometer of World War II's tremendous stimulus to extra-marital sexual activity. The highest recorded rate of illegitimate births was not among teenage girls, as might have been expected. Both British and American records indicate that women between twenty and thirty gave birth to nearly double the number of pre-war illegitimate children. Since it appears that the more mature women were the ones most encouraged by the relaxed morals of wartime to 'enjoy' themselves, it may be surmised that considerations of fidelity were no great restraint on the urge of the older married woman to participate in the general rise in wartime sexual promiscuity. (pp. 277-278)"

Women of the *"greatest generation"* were still women, and Hypergamy, just like today, didn't care about the social environment then either. My fellow blogger Dalrock made a fantastic observation in a post once, but paraphrasing he said:

"Every generation in bygone eras dated differently than the ones before it. Your parents dated in a social condition that was very different than your grandparent or their parents. No one in this generation is going to date like they did on Happy Days."

I think it's important we don't lose sight of this, but it's also important to consider that in all those eras men and women's sexual strategies remained an underlying influence for them. All that changed was both sexes adapted to the conditions of the times to effect them.

Post-Sexual Revolution Adaptation – The 'Free Love' Era

While there's a lot to criticize about the Baby Boomer generation, one needs to consider the societal conditions that produced them. Egalitarian equalism combined with ubiquitous (female controlled) hormonal birth control and then mixed with blank-slate social constructivism made for a very effective environment in which both sexes sexual strategies could, theoretically, flourish.

Women's control of their Hypergamous influences, not to mention the opportunities to fully optimize it, was unfettered by moral or social constraints for the first time in history. For men the idea of a '*Free Love*' social order was appealing because it promised optimization of their own sexual strategy – unlimited access to unlimited sexuality.

The new Free Love paradigm was based on a presumption of non-exclusivity, but more so it was based on an implied condition of non-possessiveness. Men adapted to this paradigm as might have been expected, but what they didn't consider is that in this state their eventual cuckoldry (either proactively or retroactively) amounted to women's facilitating the optimization of their own Hypergamous impulses.

The social contract of Free Love played to the base sexual wants of permissive variety for men, or at least it implied a promised potential for it. Furthermore, and more importantly, Free Love implied this promise free from the burden of performance. It was "free" love, tenuously based, ostensibly, on intrinsic personal qualities. It was what's on the inside that would make him lovable – not the visceral physical realities that inspired arousal nor the rigorous status and provisioning performance burdens that had characterized the old-books intersexual landscape prior.

It should be mentioned that 'free love' also played to men's idealistic concept of love in that freedom from a performance-based love. The equalist, all's-the-same, environment was predicated on the idea that love was a mutually agreed dynamic, free from the foundational, sexual strategy realities both sexes applied to love. Thus men's idealism predisposed them to being hopeful of a performance-free love-for-love's-sake being reciprocated by the women of the age of Aquarius.

That's how the social contract looked in the advertising, so it's hardly surprising that (Beta) men eagerly adapted to this new sexual landscape; going along to get along (or along to get laid) in a way that would seem too good to be true to prior generations. And thus, their belief set adapted to the sexual strategy that, hopefully, would pay off sexual dividends for them in this new social condition.

For women, though not fully realized at the time, this Free Love social restructuring represented a license for optimizing Hypergamy unimpeded by moral or social restraint, and later, unlimited (or at least marginalized) by men's provisional support. For the first time in history women could largely explore a

Sandbergian plan for Alpha Fucks and Beta Bucks and, at least figuratively, they could do so at their leisure.

The problem inherent in the Free Love paradigm was that it was based on a mutual understanding that men and women were functional equals, and as such a mutual trust that either sex would hold the other's best interests as their own. That basis of trust that either sex was rationally on the same page with regard to their sexual strategies is what set the conditions for the consecutive generations to come. This trust, on the part of men, was that these "equal" women would honor the presumption that it was "*who*" they were rather than "*what*" they represented to their sexual strategy at the various phases of their maturity that would be the basis for women's sexual selection of them.

Into the 70s

When I first published the comparative sexual market value (SMV) graph a few years ago (*see The Rational Male*) one of the first criticisms was that the age comparisons between men and women seemed too concrete and too specific to contemporary times. I tried to make concessions for this then, but when I was writing that essay it was at first meant to be a bit tongue-in-cheek. Still, I try to write with the presupposition that critics will take things either too literally or too figuratively. I knew that the literati then and now would think, "*...well, yes it's a good outline, but you're looking at the SMV from the perspective of 2012 and society was much different 50, 70, 100, 2,000 years ago so this graph is flawed...*"

My SMV (sexual market value) graph was never meant to be some canonical tablet handed to me from the Almighty. I thought of it then, and still think of it now, as a very good workable outline for how men and women's comparative SMV relates to the other. This has been borne out in many other statistics from individual studies sent to me by readers or just my coming across them since I created that graph. That said, those critics aren't wrong to suggest that this outline would be subject to the social environments and simple physical realities of earlier times, and likely some times yet to come.

Take what I'm about to delve into here with a bit of salt; I'm not a historian. One of my favorite figures from the civil war era was *Colonel Robert Gould Shaw*. If you've seen the movie *Glory* you know who I'm referencing here. This young man was 23 when he enlisted and 25 when he was promoted to Major and then Colonel. In that time Shaw saw some pretty grisly shit, including the battle of Antietam.

I'd seen the movie when it first came out in 1989, but after watching it again for a class assignment I had a new appreciation for the real man who was Robert Shaw. I saw the film using what was just becoming my *Red Pill Lens*. It struck me that the realities of that era forced men to become *Men* much sooner than men do today. The realities of our times give us a leisure the men of Shaw's age simple couldn't imagine. The realities of that time necessitated a quick maturation to bear the burden of heavy responsibilities. Those burdens were much more imperative then, but a 23 year old is still, biologically, a 23 year old.

I thought about how I'd spent my own years between the ages of 23-25 when I was at the peak of my semi-rock star tail chasing in the late 80s - early 90s Hollywood scene. I began to really think about the differences in the social and physical environments of the 1860s and the 1980s-90s. I've always joked that men don't become Men until they're 30. Even on the SMV graph the point at which I attribute men's real ascendancy to their peak SMV at around age 30, but this wasn't always the case in the past.

Men (comparatively) live longer lives as a result of health and medical advances, but (at least in westernizing culture) it takes much more time and personal investment, as well as acculturation for men to realize their personal potential. Men's burden of performance wasn't much different in prior eras, but the time frame necessary to reach a man's peak potential was much more accelerated.

So to address the concerns of the temporal critics of the SMV graph, yes, that graph might look a bit different to the men and women of the 19th century. Considering lifespans of the era and the social conditions then, the ages during which a woman would reach her own peak might be around 17, and a man's may be 25, however the same curves of the bell wouldn't change drastically. Men adapted to the conditions their environment dictated to them then in much the same way they did before and after the sexual revolution. And this adaptation came as the result of what was expected of them as their burden of performance of the time, as well as what their social leisures would permit them.

Love American Style

Into the 70s the new social contract of the Free Love generation began to take a new shape. Bear in mind that this new equalitarian contract was based on the hopeful presumption that both sexes would mutually honor the "what's on the inside is what counts" normalization of attraction. Under this contract women's Hypergamous natures could flourish, while men's unlimited access sexual strategy could ostensibly be realized.

Of course these lofty, higher-consciousness, presumptions were meant to supersede human nature and an evolved sexual arousal function based on human biology. One thing that still thwarts ideological feminism today is that its perceived goal states contradict human beings' natural, evolved states. This contradiction gets narratively blamed on men not wanting to cooperate with feminism, but even the most ardent feminist is still guilty of her own biology and arousal triggers contradicting herself.

Biology trumps conviction. People get fidgety when I apply this in a religious context, but it's equally applicable to feminism and really any ideology that under-appreciates human nature and the realities of its conditions.

As the new sexual landscape began to solidify, men began to adapt their own sexual strategies to the conditions of this fast and loose environment. Just prior to the Disco Generation hardcore pornography began its path to the ubiquitous free porn we know today. The sexual restraint necessitated by the realities of prior generations loosened in light of widespread hormonal birth control and safe(er) legal abortion.

While Hypergamy was effectively unleashed, the women of this era hadn't fully grasped the scope of it being so or what it could become. Socially acceptable premarital sex, abortion, sperm banks and unilaterally feminine controlled birth control meant that women had an unprecedented degree of control over their Hypergamous decision making. I doubt many women of the time understood this, but the only real control men had (and still have now) over women's breeding and birthing outcomes was now grounded in the psychological (Game) or the physical (arousal). Provisioning was still a consideration for women, but the division between short-term and long-term pairing became more pronounced.

As I mentioned here in the beginning, a slowing of the maturation process was the inevitable result of women's freedom of Hypergamous choice. Short-term Alpha Fucks no longer posed the same societal and personal risks of a pre-birth control generation, thus, long-term pairing choices (Beta bucks) began to be delayed. The ideological cover story was one of women expecting men to "love their insides" despite their age, psychological baggage or their increasingly more overweight physical condition.

Women's preoccupation with *The Wall* was ostensibly mitigated by the Free Love social contract that men would honor their end of the higher-consciousness equalitarian dream of a mutually agreed attraction based on intrinsic qualities. The biological realities for both sexes was much different.

Women trusted they could be sexually 'free' without social stigmatization, but the reality was that the long-term needs of Hypergamy could be postponed in what would eventually become an *Open Hypergamy* sexual strategy. The more Alpha men of the time – ones in touch with the visceral nature of women and themselves – understood the incredible boon this represented for them. It's important to bear in mind that Hypergamy was not the openly embraced dynamic it's come into today. Thus, the unspoken, secretive nature of Hypergamy was something a man who '*just got it*' instinctively understood and women were aroused by it.

Machismo

During the 70s 'Macho' men began to adapt to a new paradigm. They adapted to the reality that women were conflicted by the Free Love paradigm. These men embraced both the sexual openness expected of women, but they also understood that in spite of the social contract of love being based on intrinsic qualities, women still wanted to fuck (with abandon) the men with extrinsic arousal triggering qualities. Evolved physical attributes began to take priority above the emotional pretentiousness.

The Macho quality could take different forms. Whether it was the good ole' boy of the south or the Tony Manero at Studio 54, understanding the mindset is what's important here. Conventional masculinity was what was driving the sexual marketplace underneath the Free Love veneer.

Macho men in the discos and key parties of the 70s figured out they could 'Game' the old paradigm of non-exclusivity paired with birth control by re-embracing (with disco era gusto) a masculinity that had been abandoned just a decade earlier with the Hippies. Unlimited access to unlimited sexuality was for men who overtly challenged the Free Love preconditions. They enjoyed the rewards of its expectations of women while rebounding off the self-expectations of the Beta men who were still cooperating with the Free Love social contract.

This era is an interesting parallel to our own. I think much of the Red Pill resentment coming from men still plugged into a Blue Pill mindset is rooted in a similar perception that they're playing by an acceptable set of rules that "men with Game" are exploiting for their own selfish ends. What they don't realize is that their Blue Pill interpretations are a designed part of a social paradigm that supports feminine primacy. Game works because, like the macho men of the 70s, it's primarily based on women's inborn psychology, innate arousal triggers and the visceral realities of women's biological impulses.

Beta men in the 70s still believed that the Free Love mindset was equally and mutually beneficial for both sexes since it was supposedly based on a freedom from performance for themselves while freeing women from "sexual repression" and (covertly) from the reality of the Wall. In reality, the Free Love paradigm put men at a disadvantage by giving women almost total control of Hypergamy and the time in which to realize short term mating and long term provisioning.

So these Beta men's resentment of the Alphas of the era is understandable when you consider that their visceral attractiveness was observably and behaviorally arousing to women who were *supposed* to idealistically love them for who they were not what they were. These Macho men represented a return to that burden of performance Betas had hoped to avoid in the Free Love contract.

These Alpha men understood women's base impulses then, and that understanding became an integral part of their "*just getting it*" attraction. However, these men would eventually become the butt of their own joke as the Feminine Imperative fluidly transitioned into a new social paradigm of *Fempowerment* developing in the 80s and reaching its apex in the 90s.

The arousing 'Macho' men, the Alphas of the era, would systematically become the most ridiculed parodies and caricatures of masculinity as women came into a better understanding of the power they were only beginning to realize and the Beta men took their perceived revenge. And likewise, men adapted to this new paradigm based on the same visceral reality that women's sexuality is fundamentally based on.

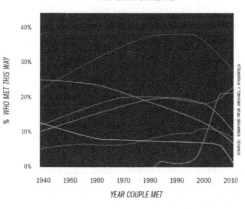

HOW *HETEROSEXUAL* AMERICANS MET THEIR SPOUSES & ROMANTIC PARTNERS
*MULTIPLE ANSWERS ALLOWED

This chart comes courtesy of *Time's* 2014 analysis of how Americans met their spouses. Blogger Heartiste (Roissy) provides the most obvious reasoning for these stats:

> *Every inception source of romance is down over the past 70 years except for bars and online. What happens in bars and online that doesn't happen in the normal course of events when couples meet through the more traditional routes? That's right: Intense, relentless, and usually charmless come-ons by drunk and socially clumsy men, that pump girls full of themselves. We've entered the age of the narcissistically-charged woman who houses in the well-marbled fat of her skull ham a steroid-injected, Facebook-fed hamster spinning its distaff vessel's place in the world as the center of existence.*

Not to be outdone, but what he doesn't address here is the adaptive strategies men are pragmatically employing in order to facilitate their own sexual strategy. What this chart illustrates is a graphic representation of the adaptive sexual strategies of the sexes over the course of 70 years.

Granted, in contemporary society women's attention and indignation needs, via social media, are as ubiquitously satisfied as men's need for sexual release (i.e. internet porn) is . This of course leads the mass of women to perceive their social and SMV status to be far greater than it actually is – and when that inflated SMV is challenged by the real world there are countless social conventions established to insulate women, and simultaneously convince men, that their perceived status should be the fantasy they believe it is.

It's important to keep this in mind because men's adaptive strategies key on women's self-impressions of their of their own SMV (and often personal worth). The intergender conditions we're experiencing today were seeded by the adaptive strategies men used in the past and the contingent counter-adaptations of women employed then too.

The Abdication Imperative

Hypergamy is rooted in doubt. Hypergamy is an inherently insecure system that constantly tests, assesses, retests and reassesses for optimal reproductive options, long-term provisioning, parental investment, and offspring, and personal protection viability in a potential mate. Even under the most secure of prospects Hypergamy still doubts. The evolutionary function of this incessant doubt would be a selected-for survival instinct, but the process of Hypergamy's assessment requires too much mental effort to be entirely relegated to women's subconscious. Social imperatives had to be instituted, not only to better facilitate the hypergamous process, but also to reassure the feminine that men were already socially preprogrammed to align with that process.

In an era when women's sexual selection has been given exclusive control to the feminine, in an age when Hypergamy has been loosed upon the world en force, social conventions had to be established to better silence the doubt that Hypergamy makes women even more acutely aware of today. And nowhere is this doubt more pronounced than in the confines of a monogamous commitment intended to last a lifetime. Thus, we have the preconception of "Happy Wife equals Happy Life" preprogrammed into both gender's collective social consciousness. It's as if to say *"It's OK Hypergamy, everything is gonna be alright because we all believe that women should be the default authority in any relationship."*

When you disassemble any operative feminine social convention, on its most base, instinctive level the convention's latent purpose is to facilitate and pacify Hypergamy.

Heirs of Free Love

Earlier I mentioned the "Free Love" movement. When most people hear that term their first mental impression is usually something like the picture of hippies at Woodstock smoking pot. Later it quickly morphed into the 70's adaptation of socially permissive promiscuity. However, it's very important to understand that this most recent Free Love social push was by no means the first in human history.

Our impression of Free Love today was colored by the Baby Boom generation, but there have been many Free Love "movements" in the past. This was a fascinating read in light of the recent legislative ruling on gay marriage. The following is a quote from Wikipedia's research on Free Love:

A number of Utopian social movements throughout history have shared a vision of free love. The all-male Essenes, who lived in the Middle East from the 1st century BC to the 1st century AD apparently shunned sex, marriage, and slavery. They also renounced wealth, lived communally, and were pacifist vegetarians. An Early Christian sect known as the Adamites existed in North Africa in the 2nd, 3rd and 4th centuries and rejected marriage. They practiced nudism and believed themselves to be without original sin.

In the 6th century, adherents of Mazdakism in pre-Muslim Persia apparently supported a kind of free love in the place of marriage,[15] and like many other free-love movements, also favored vegetarianism, pacificism, and communalism. Some writers have posited a conceptual link between the rejection of private property and the rejection of marriage as a form of ownership

[...] The challenges to traditional morality and religion brought by the Age of Enlightenment and the emancipatory politics of the French Revolution created an environment where ideas such as free love could flourish. A group of radical intellectuals in England (sometimes known as the English Jacobins), who supported the French Revolution developed early ideas about feminism and free love.

Notable among them was the Romantic poet William Blake, who explicitly compared the sexual oppression of marriage to slavery in works such as Visions of the Daughters of Albion (1793). Blake was critical of the marriage laws of his day, and generally railed against traditional Christian notions of chastity as a virtue. At a time of tremendous strain in his marriage, in part due to Catherine's apparent inability to bear children, he directly advocated bringing a second wife into the house.[19] His poetry suggests that external demands for marital fidelity reduce love to mere duty rather than authentic affection, and decries jealousy and egotism as a motive for marriage laws. Poems such as "Why should I be bound to thee, O my lovely Myrtle-tree?" and "Earth's Answer" seem to advocate multiple sexual partners. In his poem "London" he speaks of "the Marriage-Hearse" plagued by "the youthful Harlot's curse", the result alternately of false Prudence and/or Harlotry. Visions of the Daughters of Albion is widely (though not universally) read as a tribute to free love since the relationship between Bromion and Oothoon is held together only by laws and not by love. For Blake, law and love are opposed, and he castigates the "frozen marriage-bed".

There are certain Manosphere writers of note who believe that our current state of "social degeneracy" is unprecedented in human history. And while it's certain that no prior generation did it in the same manner as the one before it, ours is simply one more chapter in a Free Love flareup that's punctuated history for many cultures, not just the west – all prompted by the underlying bio-evolutionary / psychological impulses our race has always been subject to.

That said, it's important to consider the residual social after effects of our most recent Free Love incidence. I can't speak to the era in the past, but the Free Love ideology is very much an evident part of the egalitarian equalism ideology that's rooted itself in our contemporary culture. As western culture spreads, so too does that equalism rooted in Free Love.

The Rise of Fempowerment

By the time the 80s had begun the redefinition of conventional masculinity – masculinity adapted to capitalize on women's short-term, Alpha Fucks, sexual strategy – was beginning to take shape. By the mid 80s, gone were the Captain Kirk and Han Solo archetypal machismo characters. They were systematically replaced by sensitive, supportive, asexual and thoroughly nonthreatening Dr. Huxtable and increasingly contrasted with laughable parodies of conventional masculinity; these roles redefined to fit into shaming and obfuscating any former idea of masculinity and any men who might attempt to embrace it. The action heroes of the era abounded, but the expectation to accept a new archetype, the Strong Independent Ass Kicking Woman® was coming into its own.

Granted, the feminization process was gradual. Throughout the 80s this feminization was primarily reinforced by men (or men like them) who'd borne the brunt of the 'Macho men' of the 70s sexual opportunism; a substantial number of which were increasingly raising their children for them. Beta men of the post Disco Generation and the men who identified with them adapted their own Beta Game of increased identification with the feminine, and thus began the rise of the era of feminine empowerment, or *Fempowerment*.

A new paradigm was evolving; a social environment founded on the same 'higher selves', faux-equalism, of the Free Love generation(s), but one predicated on Beta men's enthusiastic supportiveness of women's imperatives. Gradually, the Free Love narrative was sublimated by a one-sided expectation of male supportive sacrifices and self-identification with women.

From *Identity Crisis*:

Far too many young men maintain the notion that for them to receive the female intimacy they desire they should necessarily become more like the target of their affection in their own personality. In essence, to mold their own identify to better match the girl they think will best satisfy this need. So we see examples of men compromising their self-interests to better accommodate the interests of the woman they desire to facilitate this need for intimacy (i.e. sex). We all know the old adage women are all too aware of, "Guys will do anything to get laid" and this is certainly not limited to altering their individual identities and even conditions to better facilitate this. It's all too common an example to see men select a college based on the available women at that college rather than academic merit to fit their own ambitions or even choose a college to better maintain a preexisting relationship that a woman has chosen and the young man follows. In order to justify these choices he will alter his identity and personality by creating rationales and new mental schema to validate this 'decision' for himself. It becomes an ego protection for a decision he, on some level, knows was made for him.

Beta Game is predicated upon this effort to become more alike, more in touch with a calculating feminine ideal men they were being conditioned to believe was equitable to their concept of love and would be reciprocated with appreciation and intimacy. Into the 90s, men built their lives around the 'high self' hope that if they could just relate more to the feminine – supporting their girlfriends and wives in equalist endeavors women of the past never had access to – they could out-support the 'ridiculous cad' parody straw men they'd created for themselves.

The burden of performance that the men of the Free Love eras had hoped to avoid with higher self conditions of love were replaced with a burden of more accessible Beta supportiveness. Thus, into the 90s we had more and more characterization of masculine competition become associated with men *out-supporting* one another. Stay-at-home Dad became a socially lauded life choice to be proud of. *Tootsie, Mr. Mom, Friends*, and the culmination of total abdication to feminine identification, *Mrs. Doubtfire*, became apex examples of men adapting to a socio-sexual environment they'd been conditioned for – a burden of support.

Mrs. Doubtfire was a particularly egregious depiction of this male to female transition. The apex Beta Father Provider versus the social and sexual Alpha 'great guy' in a battle for the genetic rights to the Beta's children (which he eventually concedes and accepts). This story epitomizes the subtle undercurrent of socially acceptable cuckoldry that would define men's adaptations during this era. The Beta must *become* a woman to have any relationship with his kids.

By assuming the female role, by identifying with the feminine they'd been convinced was so lacking in themselves, men reinforced, aided and abetted the rise of contemporary women's default entitlements; not just to support, but to conventional masculinity when convenient, and equalist independence when convenient.

There's a presumption in the manosphere that women have become more masculinized today, and while this is true, the Hypergamy that's defined every era for women is more dominant now than in any other age. There is nothing that defines the feminine more than the Feminine Imperative's want for the security of provisioning and sexual optimization that the masculine provides for women.

As men, we're prone to believe that if we've become more feminine women have become more masculinized, but is it this or is it the expectation that women need to adapt a masculinized outlook to counter men's conditioned Beta passivity? Even staunch feminists get tingles from conventionally masculine, unapologetically Alpha men.

MALE SPACE

There's an interesting discussion that's been belabored in the manosphere for a while now, that of traditionally "male spaces" being infiltrated by women and / or being redefined by feminized restructuring. The modern, western, workplace is the easiest example of this, but whether it's the recent inclusion of women in the formerly all-male membership of the Augusta Golf Club, or the lifting of the ban on women (and accommodating their prevalent physical deficits) being in combat roles in the military, the message ought to be clearer to Red Pill men; the feminine imperative has a vested interest in inserting itself into every social and personal condition of male exclusivity.

Whether this condition is an all male club or cohort (gender segregated team sports for example) or a personal state that is typically attributed only to the masculine – characteristic strength, rationality, decisiveness, risk taking, even brashness and vulgarity – the Feminine Imperative encourages women to insert themselves, and by association the Feminine Imperative itself, into masculine exclusivity. Scout Willis' (Bruce Willis' daughter) 'activism' to encourage female equality by going topless in public is a more extreme example of this female-to-male parity – in an equalist utopia, if men can do it, women *should* be able to as well.

The First Woman

This push into male space is rarely due to a genuine desire to belong to a traditionally all-male institution or condition, but women are encouraged to believe they'll make some dent in the universe simply by being the first to push past a "*gender barrier*." It's not about making a true contribution to that male institution or endeavor, but rather a goal of being '*the first woman to do it too*'.

The social presumption is always one of men holding women back, or some institutionalized sexism that conflicts with the equalist ideal that men and women are exactly the same except for the plumbing. Needless to say this ideology more often than not conflicts with physical realities of both sexes, but women's default victimhood status requires that 'common sense' says it's sexist men keeping girls out of the tree house.

For all of the misdirections of a hoped for equalism, it's not about becoming an astronaut for a woman, but rather becoming the first *woman–astronaut* – then moving on to being the first woman assigned to a combat role in the military, then the first woman to play at Augusta. If equalism were the real intent, we could expect the desire of, and passion for, the endeavor itself would supersede this. But the Feminine Imperative motivates women (and socially demotivates men's resistance) to the *first-woman* goal, not the actual accomplishment or excellence in that accomplishment or endeavor. The trail being blazed is less important than being the first woman trailblazer – in fact, the goal can simply be the same trail men blazed centuries before and it will still be recognized as a significant accomplishment for the first woman to do it too.

The goal *is* to be a woman in traditionally male space. No thought is given as to why it's been a traditionally male space beyond the default presumption of male sexism.

The cover story is the same trope the Feminine Imperative (and its social arm, feminism) always finds useful; the never ending push towards gender equalism. The practice however reveals the push into male space serves two purposes – social control and female oversight of a previously male space.

Social control is the easier of the two to grasp. Even when changing the rules of an all-male game to accommodate a lack of genuine female interest in a conventionally male endeavor, it fundamentally alters the nature of that game. When the WNBA first formed there was a push to lower the height of the net since very few women could get above it.

The first woman allowed to participate in that male-game is novelty enough to extend the Feminine Imperative's social control into that male space (i.e. "nowadays women do it too"). An easy example of this would be NASCAR's embracing a driver like Danica Patrick. It's not that she's an exceptional driver, and while I can't vouch for her genuine passion for NASCAR, the social control she represents is that she is the first woman to (dubiously) be taken seriously in the nominally all-male space of NASCAR drivers. Once the goal has been achieved, all that's left now is female oversight of this male space.

Overseers in the Locker Room

The second purpose in the goal of female inclusion into male space is really a policing of the thought dynamics and attitudes of the men in that space. When women are allowed access to the 'locker room' the dynamic of the locker room changes. The locker room can take many different shapes: the workplace environment, the sports team, the group of all-male coders, the primarily male scientific community, the 'boys club', the group of gamer nerds at the local game store, even strip clubs and the sanctuary you think your 'man cave' is – the context is one of women inserting themselves into male space in order to enforce the dictates of feminine social primacy.

When the influence of feminine-primacy is introduced into social settings made up mainly by men and male-interests, the dynamics and purpose of that group changes. The purpose becomes less about the endeavor itself and more about adherence to the feminine-inclusionary aspect of that endeavor. It starts to become less about being the best or most passionate at what they do, and more about being acceptable to the influence of the Feminine Imperative while attempting to maintain the former level of interest in the endeavor.

Men unaccustomed to having women in their midst generally react in two ways; most men being Betas, they act according to their proper feminized conditioning. They embrace the opportunity to impress these 'trailblazing' women (hoping to be found worthy of intimacy) with their enthusiastic acceptance of, and identification with, their new feminine overseer(s), or for the less socially savvy, they become easy foils of an "outmoded" way of thinking that the new 'in-group' happily labels them with.

Once the feminine-primary in-group dynamic is established a 'feminine correct' social frame follows. This feminine correction restructures the priorities of goals, and validates any accomplishments, in terms of how they reflect upon the feminine as a whole. Thus any in-group success is perceived as a feminine success in male space. However, in-group failures or simple mediocrity is either dismissed entirely or blamed on the out-group men's failure to comply with the Feminine Imperative's 'correcting' influence on the in-group.

'Bro Culture'

Bro Culture is an epithet created by the social justice warrior mindset to easily identify men who follow conventional masculinity despite the efforts to cull it by feminism and its failed dictates. It seems that a constantly self-reinventing feminism loves to attach "culture" to the end of anything it sees as threatening – *Rape Culture, Male Culture of Privilege*, and of course *Bro Culture*. Make no mistake, the concept of Bro Culture is an operative feminine social convention. It may be convenient to think of the stereotype of Bro Culture as a male creation, but this convention is the direct result of the Feminine Imperative's controlling need to insert itself into male spaces. Thus, any conventionally masculine endeavor always smacks of the jocks they hated in high school.

There are other feminine social conventions with the same latent purpose, but the 'Bro Culture' meme is really a dual purpose shaming tactic intended to restrict and control traditional male bonding while also fostering infighting amongst in-group and out-group men once feminine influence has been established in a formerly all-male space.

One of the most threatening aspects of conventional masculinity for the Feminine Imperative is the cooperative potential of male bonding. When only men comprise an in-group, team building, common purpose and a masculine-primary environment tend to define that group. I would argue that the modern insertion of feminine influence into all-male spaces is a concerted effort to limit this bonding and unity in favor of a feminine-primary 'correctness'. The purpose *is* to isolate and confuse men's understanding of masculinity.

This limitation may not be directly influenced by a present female; often all that's needed to foster feminine-primary correctness is a feminine-identifying male in the in-group (anonymous White Knight), or even just a prevailing attitude of not wanting to offend the sexism suspicions, or other in-group men may subscribe to this feminine-identifying influence for fear it may get back to a woman they perceive may have authority over them.

Infighting

This is the hallmark of a feminized Beta mindset – to believe that "guys being guys" is inherently aberrant. It's something *other* guys, *typical guys* do. I could go into detail about how men giving each other shit is an evolutionary (and useful) vestige of tribalism and how men would use this "challenging" to ensure the strength and survivability of the collective, but this will only grate against a Beta's '*gender-as-social-construct*' belief.

This discomfort with 'being a guy' is the root disposition of many high-functioning Betas, and particularly those seeking to better identify with the feminine in the hopes it will pay off in sexual dividends. These are the guys who never '*got it*' that shit talking and locker room jibes (the same male space invaded by the feminine) are intended not just to determine masculine fitness, but to foster living, building and measuring up to a better masculine standard that benefits both the individual man and the collective tribe.

The fact that 'Bro Culture' is even a term, or the go-to archetypal examples of it begins with stereotypical jocks, "douchebags" and team sport locker rooms, illustrates the threat that male-exclusive forms of communication pose to the

Feminine Imperative. If male space can be co-opted in the name of gender equalism, it's far easier to restrict that male communication and influence it to encourage a sense of responsibility towards feminine-primary security needs. In other words, it's a much easier task to create future Beta providers if a feminine influence can pervade all male spaces – this is facilitated all the better when it is men themselves who hold other men accountable to the dictates of the Feminine Imperative and feminine sexual strategies.

I think it's important that we don't lose sight of the way men communicate, test each other, hone each other, give each other shit, etc. being primarily defined in the context of Bro Culture, douchebaggery, team sports, etc. That intra-male dynamic crosses so many social, racial and cultural strata it becomes an overarching threat to the Feminine Imperative.

This is the "*let's you and him fight*" dynamic women will employ with their own power rivals. While a certain element of intersexual competition is a part of this, the purpose of this social convention is one of occupying men with an infighting that suppresses their power over her.

It's an easy task to set men against each other when they perceive sexual rivals to be part of an out-group, and feminine influence in male space fosters this passive (sometimes active) infighting amongst men. Disrupting male bonding, or even the potential for it, limits men's potential to unify in their own interests and their own imperatives. There are many in-group examples of all male space where this infighting and resentment plays out, but it's important to understand that male-exclusive forms of communication, testing, encouragement and shit talking, are in no way limited to just the locker room. Even guys in the chess club will give each other shit – at least until the Feminine Imperative inserts itself there too.

Resisting the Influence

I can't end this section without drawing attention to the all male meta-space that has become the collective gestalt of the Manosphere. The manosphere is male space writ large and a testament to what men can do when they come together, share experiences and put their minds to a common purpose. The methods may vary, but the desire to collectivize male experience for the benefit of other men is a meta-scale form of male bonding.

And, as should be expected, there will be resistance to that communication and bonding on a comparative meta-scale by the Feminine Imperative and the men and women who subscribe to it. I should also add that a very obvious attempt on women's inclusion into Red Pill praxeology, theory and practice is also a move by the feminine into a male space with much of the same purpose I've outlined here – social control and female oversight of it.

Even the most well meaning of women involved (however peripherally) in the Manosphere are still motivated by their innate security needs – and those hypergamous security needs imply a want for certainty and control. As such the psychological influence of the Feminine Imperative will always be a predominant motivator in their participation in this all male space. This leads women to a want to sanitize Game to fit the purposes of the imperative, as well as oversee the thought processes of the men who come to participate in it.

Just like any other male space, the Manosphere is subject to all the sanitizing efforts of the Feminine Imperative I've outlined here – by both women and men who still subscribe to feminine-primacy.

FEMPOWERMENT

I'm often asked by *'fempowered'* women critics whether I 'believe' in some of the more socially acceptable tenets of feminism. It's usually something like, "Do you or do you not think women ought to have the right to vote?" Or it's the ever-reliable "Shouldn't women have the right to do with their bodies what they choose?" These questions are always binary ("yes or no will do") and usually couched in a context that implies that if you even slightly disagree or have a slight caveat to answering 'appropriately' you'll be dismissed with a name tag that has "misogynist" printed on it. Say 'no' and you're a despicable misogynist. Say 'yes' and you're tar-pitted in "yes, but" caveats – *mansplaining* – that are disqualified because you're a man. Until recently, it's been a very effective means of silencing uncomfortable truths about the Feminine Imperative.

I've always found it ironic that a movement (feminism) that predicates itself on an egalitarian notion that rational, reasonable considerations of issues should lead us to ideals of equality is the first to reduce itself to unquestioned, blind faith binaries at the first sign of that rational reasonable truth being unflattering to women. If you want to know who holds power over you, look at whom you aren't allowed to criticize – or even hint at criticism.

My position on these and many other questions of the sort is usually met with simple observational analysis (as you'd probably expect). I don't necessarily have a problem with women voting or even having access to legal (relatively safe) abortions. What I have a problem with is the latent purpose behind the reasons that led to women's decisions to vote a particular way or the latent purposes that brought them to having that abortion. For the greater part, any dubious 'right' women feel they were somehow denied in the past usually comes at the expense of men being liable for decisions they had nothing to do with today.

What I have a problem with is an expectation of lowering the standards of the game and thus fundamentally altering the game, to better accommodate the variable strengths and weaknesses of women – up to, and including changing the nature of women's realities that would endanger the wellbeing of both sexes. What I take issue with is the expectation of making men liable for the decisions and consequences of the rights and freedom of choices we've reserved for only women to make (almost unilaterally Hypergamous choices) that are not in men's best interests.

Men today find themselves in a very precarious position with regard to entertaining women's perceived wrongs of the past. Men are expected, by default, to be held accountable for past injuries to the ever-changing Feminine Imperative for no other reason than they were born men. Your existence as a man today, your failed understanding to accommodate women's social primacy, your lack of catering to the ambiguous nature of what conveniently passes for masculinity, is a constant affront and obstacle to the "advancement" of women. The Feminine Imperative has known how to manipulate men's *Burden of Performance* for millennia, and at not other time in history has it had the unfettered leisure to do so than now.

Thus, we get socially acceptable default presumptions of 'male privilege' without qualifying what it even means, or we get catchy jingoisms like '*mansplaining*' to give a name to women's need for silencing men's inconvenient observations of women's 'presumed-correct' perceptions, their decisions and the reasons they came to them. We get default presumptions of male guilt for sexual assault and lack of sexual consent as fluidly defined in as convenient a way that serves women's imperatives. The true intent of feminism has never been about establishing a mutually agreed 'gender equality', rather it's always been about retribution and restitution for perceived past wrongs to the *Sisterhood*.

There has always been a subtext, a cover story, of equality mentioned in the same breath as feminism. Only the most antagonistic asshole, only the most anti-social prick, would be against "equality between the sexes". Thus, to be against feminism is to be against a simplistic concept of baseline equality. However, taken out of the propagandizing efforts to shame and 'correct' men's imperatives, it's easy to demonstrate that the true intent of feminism is female '*fempowerment*' in the guise of an equality that no man (or woman) wants to appear to be against.

Yellowed Pearls

I found an interesting example of this *Catch 22* in the *Economist*:

Pick and choose: Why women's rights in China are regressing.

In 2007 China's official Xinhua news agency published a commentary about women who were still unmarried at the age of 27 under the title, "Eight Simple Moves to Escape the Leftover Woman Trap". The Communist Party had concluded that young Chinese women were becoming too picky and were over-focused on attaining the "three highs": high education, profes-

sional status and income. Newspapers have since reprinted similar editorials. In 2011 one said: "The tragedy is they don't realize that as women age they are worth less and less, so by the time they get their MA or PhD, they are already old, like yellowed pearls."

This is illustrative of the expansion that the Feminine Imperative has taken on a global scale. One of the old missives of the Manosphere has always been about how American women are too far gone to be worth entertaining anything beyond a pump-and-dump consideration. They are too damaged. Too self-absorbed beyond all redemption, and men ought to expatriate to another country where women are more feminine, pleasing, or at least necessitous enough to appreciate a conventionally masculine man.

I get that. I understand the want for a *Pussy Paradise* or some promised land where women are still raised to respect and love men by being conventionally feminine. I also get that there exist certain cultures where this is still true, but for all of that, I think it's important to recognize the social undercurrent that the Feminine Imperative exercises in these cultures. *'Feminism is Cancer'* is a popular meme on Twitter, but there's a kernel of truth to the humor of this. The spread of the westernizing social primacy of the Feminine Imperative is spreading, not unlike cancer, into what we would otherwise believe were societies and cultures still oppressed by the mythical Patriarchy – a belief necessary to perpetuate the narrative of default female victimhood.

It may not be now, but at some stage, the Feminine Imperative will exercise its presumptive control over even the societies we think ought to be immune from that cancer. Even in underdeveloped countries where we would expect to find the horrible oppression of girls and women, we make a triumphant example of the incidents of where girls (not boys) are taught to read and "think for themselves". Westernized culture, founded on the Feminine Imperative, celebrates every time a woman in Saudi Arabia is allowed to drive a car, much less run a business on her own as if it were some blow against the tyranny of men.

Little by little, or in leaps and bounds, your second or third world Pussy Paradise will eventually be assimilated by the Feminine Imperative.

I bring this up because China is also experiencing the long-term results of having adopted feminine social primacy in its own culture. From women's popular consciousness, we're still, to this day, told of how horrible "communist" China has been in mandating its one-child policy and how its draconian 'sons live, daughters die' social structure has been the result. However, once we reasonably investigate it, we find that China now has a problem with "Yellowed Pearls" as a result of a cultural shift that placed women's interests as preeminent in that culture. And it should be noted that this shift came about as the direct result of the men who adopted and accommodated the Feminine Imperative as their own.

Now the problem for women in China is not unlike the plight of American women bemoaning the lack of men with "equal" marriageability as themselves. And likewise, the self-same social authorities responsible for institutionalizing the fempowerment of women are now the horrible misogynist villains for suggesting that women ought to lower their unrealistic standards.

The tone of these Yellowed Pearls articles is surprising, given the Communist Party's past support for women's advancement. Mao Zedong destroyed China, but he succeeded in raising the status of women. Almost the first legislation enacted by the Communist Party in 1950 was the Marriage Law under which women were given many new rights, including the right to divorce and the right to own property.

This sounds a far cry different from the pictures women, even women in this century, have painted of China's institutionalized, one-child sexism doesn't it? Remember, this advancement in women's rights took place before the Cultural Revolution in China.

Though collectivization made the latter largely irrelevant, women played an active role in Mao's China, and still do today. By 2010, 26% of urban women had university degrees, double the proportion ten years earlier. Women now regularly outperform men at Chinese universities, which has led to gender-based quotas favoring men in some entrance exams. However, many of the earlier advances have been eroded in recent years by the gradual re-emergence of traditional patriarchal attitudes.

Consider this part in contrast to other industrialized nations and how women have increased their socio-political standing as the result of having the Feminine Imperative adopted as the primary social order of those cultures. Even in cultures that are still popularly deemed "*repressive*" to women we still see educational and socioeconomic parallels to western(ized) cultures. We also see the same resulting consequences and the shifting of blame for them to men. The downside consequences of Yellowed Pearls is placed at the feet of men for not living up to the convenient, feminine-primary definition of what their *Burden of Performance* ought to mean in promoting and forgiving women's decisions.

The party has joined an alliance of property companies and dating websites to confront the issue. Government surveys on marriage and property are often sponsored by matchmaking agencies, and perpetuate the perception that being "leftover" is the worst thing that can happen to a woman. They also promote other myths, such as the idea that a man must have a house before he can marry.

As you may expect, the tone of the article is written to emphasize the egalitarian perspective that conflicts with a reality that the Feminine Imperative would have men change or be responsible for not having changed. It's men's fault that women might feel bad for not having married by a post-wall age. It's men's fault for promoting myths that women would expect that a man must be successfully established in his life and career before any considerations of marriage occur to him. It's also a man's fault for clinging to the "myth" that women don't want him to be established.

The law is reflecting the shift away from women's empowerment too. An interpretation by the Supreme Court in 2011 of the 1950 Marriage Law stated that, when a couple divorces, property should not be shared equally, but each side should keep what is in his or her own name. This ruling, says Ms. Fincher, has serious implications. In the big cities a third of marriages now end in divorce but, based on hundreds of interviews, she finds that only about 30% of married women have their name on the deeds of the marital flat. Women believe the party hype about becoming a "leftover" woman so strongly, she says, that many rush into unhappy marriages with unsuitable men, made on condition that the brides agree not to put their name on the property deeds.

Feminism Would be a Success if Men Would Only Cooperate More

Several years ago fellow blogger and friend, Dalrock, had a post detailing the sentiment of feminists that feminism would be a success if only men would cooperate with the ideology by abandoning their own interests and sublimating their own biological impulses. The fact remains that feminism and egalitarianism are failed ideologies because at the root level those ideologies ask men to participate in their own extinction. Not only this, but they ask men to raise successive generations to accommodate and participate in their own degradation.

This narrative expects Yellowed Pearls to be prized by men, or respected as Spinsters, or pandered to as 'Cougars' while still maintaining that men sublimate their own imperatives by willfully ignoring the fact that abandoning their own sexual strategy is what is being asked of them.

As I stated in the *Cardinal Rule of Sexual Strategies*, for one sex's strategy to succeed the other must either be compromised or abandoned – and what better way is there to assure this for women than to socially mandate through shame, persecution or financial liabilities that men abandon their own strategy in favor of women?

For some time now, I've detailed how, for the past 4 or 5 generations, there has been a popular social re-engineering effort to raise and condition boys to become the 'better betas' – boys designed to become the supportive, male-reinforcement of empowering women's interests and imperatives. For a greater part this effort has been primarily focused on boys and men in western society, and while it's still open for debate, I'd say that westernizing cultures are really the only cultural environments that can afford to entertain this '*fempowerment*' social initiative. This is changing radically now, if it was ever really the case to begin with.

In the Manosphere we like to highlight the '*pussification*' of modern men through various efforts on the part of a nebulous 'society' aligned against masculinity. However, the flip side to this is the *fempowerment* agenda; a feminine-primary social structure that disallows any criticism of inherently female nature while promoting the empowerment of women on every level of social strata.

We coddle and cater to the feminine in every aspect of social interaction, every aspect of academic achievement, every socioeconomic advantage thinkable, every story we tell in every form of media and we do so under the threat of not being supportive or misogynistic for suggesting anything marginally pro-masculine. This is the other side of the demasculinization imperative of boys & men – the total consolidation of handicapping men and empowering women into unrealistic effigies of feminine triumphalism.

How do you counter this?

I'm always lauded for describing these social dynamics, but I'm run up the flagpole for not offering concrete ways of dealing with and pushing back on these imperatives. Many a MGTOW (men going their own way) will simply suggest men no longer play the Game; that isolationism is the way to go, but this only serves to eventually concede power to the Feminine Imperative. You don't get to check out of the Game even if you refuse to play it.

For all the guys who left for parts unknown to find their quasi-utopia of feminine women in a foreign country, even they will explain that the tide of feminism is changing those seemingly idyllic places. And for every guy to voluntarily go celibate and "refuse to deal with women" I'll show you a man whose tax dollars go to fund the consequences of women's legislated rights to Hypergamous choice.

Sooner or later Men will have to confront and push back against both men and women who are convinced of their purpose in idealizing the dictates of the Feminine Imperative. A lot of men in the 'sphere believe they're being clever when they refer to people with this world-view as 'SJWs', social justice warriors, but for every hair dyed, gender-confused man-woman you see on Twitter there are hundreds of 'normal' people who all share similar perspectives – some are just subconscious generalization they're oblivious to – sitting next to you at church, or working in the cubicle next to you.

As I've mentioned countless times, the change needs to take place by appealing to the hearts and minds of Men by making them Red Pill aware from the bottom up, but moreover, we need to live out that awareness in our own lives and lead by Red Pill example. Our decisions in life, our aspiration in parenting, family and career, in our business dealings, in the women we Game and the people we hire, all of these aspects need to take on the perspective of how they fit into pushing back against a feminine-primary world that demands we surrender any thought of individuated male power.

As Men, we need to unapologetically exercise what little power we're left with to inform this, and successive, generation of Red Pill truths tactfully, but with strength of conviction in the face of a feminine-primary society bent on our surrender.

Life finds a way. Feminism and the consolidation of the Feminine Imperative have failed because Men were not evolved to acquiesce their dominant spirit. On the same evolutionary level women also evolved to requiring that conventionally masculine dominance. This is why feminism and egalitarianism will ultimately fail – nature simply will not cooperate with it's own stagnation. As men, we can use this truth to our Red Pill aware advantage.

THE POLITICAL IS PERSONAL

My friend Dalrock had an interesting post titled *Black Fathers Don't Matter*. I'll be quoting from this here, emphasis mine:

> *While HHS (Health and Human Services) says any man currently shacking up with mom counts as the father,* **the Census says any man currently shacking up with mom counts as the father so long as mom says so.** *Either way, fathers clearly can't matter that much to the US government if distinguishing between the actual father and the man currently banging mom isn't important.*
>
> *There are other ways we can tell that fathers don't matter (and therefore Black fathers don't matter). Under our current family system fathers are a sort of deputy parent. Just like a sheriff's deputy serves at the pleasure of the sheriff,* **a father in an intact family serves at the pleasure of the mother.** *Our entire family court structure is designed to facilitate the removal of the father should the mother decide she no longer wants him to be part of the family unit. How important can fathers really be, when we have a massive and brutal bureaucracy devoted to helping mothers kick them out of the house?*

What Dal is pointing out here has a far broader implication than simply how various governments define fatherhood. Many critics of how I define the Feminine Imperative like to think it's a work in conspiracy. However, as I've explained before, there really is no need for a conspiracy; the Feminine Imperative has no centralized power base because feminine-primacy is so ensaturated into our collective social consciousness. It needs no centralization because feminine social primacy is literally part of women's self-understanding – and by extension men's understanding of women and what women expect of them.

Thus, on a Hypergamous social scale we see that male objectification is ignored while female objectification is railed against. The message is clear – It is Men who must perform, Men who need to change themselves, optimize themselves and strive for the highest physical ideal to be granted female approval. Women should be accepted, respected and expected to inspire genuine desire irrespective of men's ideals, physical or otherwise.

On more than a few occasions I've made the connection that what we see in a feminine-primary societal order is really a reflection of the female sexual strategy writ large. When we see a culture of obesity, a culture of body fat acceptance and a culture that presumes a natural evolved order of innate differences between the sexes should be trumped by self-impressions of female personal worth, we're viewing a society beholden to the insecurities inherent in women's Hypergamy.

A feminized, feminist, ordered social structure is one founded on ensuring the most undeserving women, by virtue of being women, are entitled to, and assured of, the best Hypergamous options by conscripting and conditioning men to comply with Hypergamy's dictates.

It's important for men to really understand that the power struggle women claim to be engaged in with men has already been settled on a meta, social scale. When a father is *whomever* a woman says he is, that's a very powerful tool of social power leveraging.

- A father is anyone a woman/mother claims he is

- A father is legally bound to children he didn't sire

- A father is prevented at great legal and social effort from access to DNA testing of children he suspects aren't his own

- A father is legally responsible for the children resulting from his wife/girlfriend cuckolding him

- A father is financially obligated to the support of children that he didn't sire or he had no power in deciding to sire

These aren't just examples relating to men's lack of power in parenting; these are examples of determining the degree of control a man can exercise over the direction of his entire life.

Real Power is the degree to which a person has control over their own circumstances. Real Power is the degree to which we control the directions of our lives.

The inherent insecurity that optimizing Hypergamy poses to women is so imperative, so all-consuming, to their psychological wellbeing that establishing complex social orders to facilitate that optimization were the first things women collectively constructed when they were (nominally) emancipated from men's provisioning and granted social acceptability for exercising their control of Hypergamy around the time of the sexual revolution. Ensuring the optimization of women's biologically prompted Hypergamy is literally the basis of our current social order. On a socio-political scale what we're experiencing is legislation and cultural mandates that better facilitate Alpha Fucks and Beta Bucks.

A commenter, *Driver,* had a good comment that illustrates another aspect of this feminine-power consolidation:

"All the "feeling good about your body" that a fat woman can muster is NEVER going to be an aphrodisiac or a substitute for having a great body that men are aroused by."

It's funny how women are very attracted to a guy who works out, eats right and takes care of his body but they fully expect men to love them (or be attracted to them) for "who they are" – thin or big. You would think that these overweight women would get the memo by now but women (and more of them) keep getting bigger each year.

Feminine-Primary Social Doctrine is the Extension of Women's Hypergamy

In a feminine-primary social order women presume, without an afterthought, that they are entitled to an attractive guy who works out and meets or exceeds women's very stringent and static physical ideal. At the same time they expect an entitlement to absolute control of that attraction/arousal process regardless of, and to the exception of, any influence or difference in men's control of that process. And they expect this without any thought to meriting it beyond appeals to a nebulous and inflated concept of their personal self-worth.

When we consider the present, ambiguous state of sexual consent laws we begin to understand the latent Hypergamous purpose those laws serve – absolute consolidation of women's Hypergamous strategies as the motivator of any sexual encounter.

Furthermore, they expect an entitlement, either directly or indirectly, to the material support and provisioning of men for no other reason than they were born female. Any deviation from this is on the part of men is met with a cultural reprisal designed to convince or coerce men to accept their inevitable role in providing those entitlements to women. When those social contingencies fail, or become played out, the Feminine Imperative then appeals to legal legislation to mandate men's compliance to what amounts to women's social entitlement to optimized Hypergamy.

Legislating Hypergamy

From the Alpha Fucks side of Hypergamy this amounts to socially shaming men's sexual imperatives while simultaneously empowering women's short-term sexual strategies and fomenting men's societal acceptance of it (i.e. the Sandberg plan for Open Hypergamy). This is further enforced from a legal perspective through consent laws and vague "anti-harassment" legislation to, ideally, optimize women's hypergamous prospects.

When we read about instances of the conveniently fluid definitions of rape and harassment (not to mention women's pseudo-victimhood of not being harassed and feeling deprived of it), this then turns into proposed "rape-by fraud" legislation. Hypergamy wants absolute certainty, absolute veracity, that it will be secured in its optimization. And in an era when the only restraint on Hypergamy depends on an individual woman's capacity for being self-aware of it, that Hypergamy necessitates men be held legally responsible for optimizing it.

Even the right for women to have safe and legal abortions finds its root in women's want to mandate an insurance of their Hypergamous impulses. Nothing says "he wasn't the right guy" like the unilateral power to abort a man's genetic legacy in utero.

Feminist boilerplate would have us convinced that expanding definitions of rape is an effort to limit men's control of women's bodies – however, the latent purpose of expanding the definition is to consolidate on the insecurity all women experience with regard to optimizing Hypergamy.

The Beta Bucks insurance aspect of Hypergamy is evidenced by cultural expectations of male deference to wives' authority in all decision making aspects of a marriage or relationship. And, once again, this expectation of deference is a grasping for assurances of control should a woman's Hypergamous choosing of a man not meet her shifting, long-term expectations. This is actualized covertly under the auspices of egalitarian equalism and the dubious presumptions of support and feminine identification on the part of men.

Beyond this there are of course the ubiquitous divorce, financial support, child support and domestic violence legalities that grossly favor women's interests – which should be pointed out, are rooted in exactly the same Hypergamous insecurity that her short-term Alpha Fucks mating strategies demand legislation for.

As Open Hypergamy becomes more institutionalized and made a societal norm by the Feminine Imperative, and as more men become Red Pill aware (by effort or consequences) because of it, the more necessary it will become for a feminine-primary social order to legislate and mandate men comply with it.

The Sisterhood Über Alles

I've never done politics on The Rational Male. I will never do screeds on race or multi-culturalism or religion for a very good reason – it pollutes the message.

We now are seeing the results of this pollution as the Manosphere is attacked from both sides of the political spectrum.

I've given this example before, but if you put Gretchen Carlson and Rachel Maddow on the same show and confronted them with Red Pill truths about women and Game-awareness they would readily close ranks, reserve their political differences and cooperatively fight for the Feminine Imperative.

This is the degree to which the Feminine Imperative has been saturated into our western social fabric. Catholic women in the Vatican may have very little in common with Mormon women in Utah, but let a Mormon woman insist the church alter its foundational articles of faith with regard to women in favor of a doctrine substituted by the Feminine Imperative and those disparate women have a common purpose.

That is the depth of the Feminine Imperative – that female primacy should rewrite articles of faith to prioritize women's interests.

Religious doctrine, legal and political legislation, cultural norms, labor and economic issues; all are trumped by the Feminine Imperative. All have been subverted to defer to the Feminine Imperative while maintaining a default status of victimhood and oppression of women and women's interests necessary to perpetuate that covert decentralized power base.

It doesn't matter what world view, ideology, conviction or political stripe the opposition holds; men, masculinity and anything contrary to the feminine-primary social narrative will always be a common enemy of the Feminine Imperative, and both liberal and conservative will climb over one another to throw the first punch if it means defending women and defending the feminine social order by proxy.

This is why anything even marginally pro-masculine is vilified in mainstream society. Anything pro-masculine is always an easy, preferred target because it's so hated, so incorrect, in a feminine-primary context that it can unite people of hostilely opposed political and ideological differences.

It's my opinion that Red Pill awareness needs to remain fundamentally apolitical, non-racial and non-religious because the moment the Red Pill is associated with any social or religious movement, you co-brand it with an ideology, and the validity of it will be written off along with any preconceptions associated with that specific ideology.

Furthermore, any co-branding will still be violently disowned by whatever ideology it's paired with because the Feminine Imperative has already co-opted and trumps the fundamentals of that ideology. The fundamental truth is that the Manosphere, pro-masculine thought, Red Pill awareness or its related issues are an entity of its own.

This is what scares the shit out of critics who attempt to define, contain and compartmentalize the Manosphere / Red Pill awareness; it's bigger than social, racial, political or religious strictures can contain. It crosses all of those constructs just as the Feminine Imperative has co-opted all of those cultural constructs. The feminized infrastructure of the mainstream media that's just beginning to take the Manosphere seriously enough to be critical are now discovering this and trying to put the genie back into a bottle defined by their feminine-primary conditioning.

The idea that one of their own, whether in a liberal or conservative context, is genuinely Red Pill aware and educating others of that awareness is unnerving for the Feminine Imperative that's already established strong footholds in either ideology.

OPEN CUCKOLDRY

During the Q&A section of the Man in Demand talk I gave back in September of 2015 I was asked about where I believed the social dynamic of *Open Hypergamy* would lead. In specific, the idea was proposed, and I agree, that the logical next step for a social order founded on Hypergamy, and one that prioritizes the female sexual strategy as preeminent, would lead to a state of openly accepted cuckoldry.

Although I can't say it's an accepted social dynamic as yet, there are many social indicators that are revealing this push towards a normalized cuckoldry. I'll explore these for a bit in here, but for now these indicators are about a move away from conventional monogamy in the hopes that a 'soft cuckoldry' might be a precursor to instituting a more accepted open cuckoldry.

I think it's also important to keep in mind a couple of primary principles about this shift. First is the fact that, initially, an openly accepted state of feminine-controlled cuckoldry will never be called '*cuckoldry*' proper. If we use the example of a socially accepted (if not celebrated) open Hypergamy as a model, open cuckoldry will be sold as a more logical, more *humane* sexual strategy for men and women in light of divorce statistics, romantic boredom and other sexual studies that indicate men and women never evolved for monogamous commitment. We're already seeing this in the attempt to normalize polyamorous relationships today.

The second is that open cuckoldry is the extension of a unilaterally feminine controlled Hypergamy. That is to say that as Hypergamy becomes more normalized as a social imperative that sexual strategy will extend to optimizing Hypergamy across genders. If that optimization is taken to its logical conclusion it will require men not just to accept cuckoldry as a norm, but to socially reward men for advocating it among their own sex.

Cuckoldry By Any Other Name

As I said, it wont be called '*cuckoldry*'; the connotations are negative, so a redefinition will be made in order to make the practice more socially palatable. The Feminine Imperative wont recruit the very men it needs to perpetuate cuckoldry as their own sexual strategy if the term is derogatory. Thus, we'll get euphemisms for alternative lifestyles, 'open marriages' a "Designer Relationship" or "polyamory", all of which will be the advertising to promote what amounts to open cuckoldry. The following is from *Salon.com, This is how we remake monogamy: More choices, better sex, better marriages:*

> *We live in an era when everything is customizable. Relationships are no exception. Some people will continue to practice their grandparents' form of monogamy, and others, probably the majority, will be serially exclusive and pair-bonded. Still others will explore some form of non-monogamous expression that encompasses one or more of the facets we've discussed or may flow in and out of being exclusive based on what the relationship requires. (We've done this ourselves.) Having the ability to customize a relationship means having the freedom to respond to life's vicissitudes.*

The first time I came across the concept of 'soft polygamy' I was in a behavioral psychology class exploring the practices of modern marriage and contrasting them with the long term sexual behaviors of men and women. As you might imagine the context of the study focused entirely on the 'bad behaviors' of men who essentially transitioned from serial monogamy to serial marriage. The idea was that in the process of moving from one long term relationship (LTR) to another men were establishing a soft form of polygamy.

In a social and financial respect, men have far more to lose from serial marriages than do women. The financial liabilities of divorce are well known to the Manosphere, but so too are the emotional and familial accountabilities. So, from a strictly male perspective, serial LTRs are a dicey proposition, but from a female perspective institutionalized Hypergamy and the soft polygamy that results from the *Sandbergian* sexual strategy, soft cuckoldry becomes pragmatic in optimizing Hypergamy for women.

At this point we should consider the Heartiste maxim about feminism again:

> *The feminist goal is removing all constraints on female sexuality while maximally restricting male sexuality*

Institutionalized, normalized cuckoldry is the logical means to restricting male sexuality, but we have to consider what function that restriction serves for women. From an Alpha Fucks / Beta Bucks perspective the plan is simple; restrict that sexuality as women find need for a particular man's service. The selling of polyamory to men will of course appeal to men's want for sexual variety, but in truth single men can indulge in this without marriage. What polyamory really represents is a Hypergamous insurance plan for wives who want to breed with the 'best genes' man and live with the 'best provider' man.

Diamonds and Rust

While I'm reluctant to prognosticate, my guess is that future generations of men will be conditioned to accept their role in this cuckoldry as part of their socialization. *Open Hypergamy* and its acceptance has already made its popular debut in mainstream media and advertising, and likewise open cuckoldry is just now finding a social foothold.

It takes the *Red Pill Lens* to appreciate the efforts as they're being made by a larger society. Popular commercial advertising of *Open Hypergamy* is intended to be funny or cute, but it belies a deeper, more poignant truth about Alpha Widows, Hypergamy and the long term sexual strategy *Plan* and roles women expect men to play in it.

I was made aware of a Forevermark diamonds ad being circulated from a reader on Twitter and at first thought it was a reworded joke.

She'll forget every Fireman, Sailor and Rockstar of her dreams,...

The subcommunication being that if you buy her a Forevermark diamond she forget all the Alphas she's been widowed by. Without the benefit of a *Red Pill Lens* I can see how most men would laugh it off or women might giggle sardonically about it, but the fact remains that a clever copywriter is aware of the sexual dynamics that make it funny.

I pulled the following quote from commenter *Deti*:

"I think what we will continue to see is growing disengagement."

I think that what will happen is that things will continue sliding in the same direction they're going now, until a critical mass is reached. I don't know what that critical mass is, what will trigger it, or when it will be reached.

We live in a mostly free society with a hybrid of capitalism and socialism. We have maximum freedom and autonomy right now, with both sexes being free to pursue pretty much whatever they want, however they want to. That is the prime characteristic driving the current circumstance — that, and up to now, there's been enough money taxed, borrowed and stolen to pay for it.

A growing number of men are not getting as much sex as they want.

A growing number of women aren't getting commitments in the form they want — when they want or from the men they want.

So things are going to keep sliding that way. More and more men will walk away and direct what energies they have left elsewhere — into work, or beer/bros/X-Box/porn, or travel/leisure. (Oddly enough, this might make many of them more attractive to women, since they're spending less time directing their attentions to women.) More and more men will earn just enough to support themselves, since they don't plan on marriage, and fatherhood is out of the question. They will lack the skills to improve their lives. They will not get nearly as much sex as they want, but they will learn to live with it — mostly through porn, the occasional hookup, and the even more occasional prostitute. The price of prostitutes will skyrocket as demand increases; and a few more women will go into high-end call girl work to earn side money.

More and more women will direct their attentions into their work, travel/ leisure, and having children without men. (This will definitely make more of them less attractive to men except as on again, off again sex partners.) They will not get the commitments from men they want, but they will learn to live with it. They will complain about it with increasing volume and shrillness, but they'll learn to live with it.

Until something happens to cause the tides to turn. Again – don't know what, or when, or how. But something will happen to cause a hard reset. And it will be exquisitely painful for everyone. I don't want it to happen, nor do I relish it. It's not something to desire or look forward to because of the pain it will bring. But I do think it will happen. I don't think it will happen in my lifetime or my kids' lifetimes. We could easily slide like this for another 50 to 100 years.

I think one consequence of this separation of the genders will include a socially normalized institution of cuckoldry. To take hold it will need to be termed something different, but in effect the process of women conceiving with one man and then expecting another man to parentally invest himself in that child will be a casual expectation of women. With so many men effectively (if not intentionally) 'going their own way', the idea that any man could be expected to serve as a surrogate parent will become commonplace.

As it stands today popular culture and sociologists alike always define cuckoldry from the perspective of a duplicitous wife engaging in an extramarital affair, becoming pregnant and deliberately deceiving her unaware husband that the child is not his. When we define cuckoldry in these terms, and we look at the DNA data that indicate 'rates of cuckoldry' we get a fairly low incidence of *actual* cuckoldry. Any writer in the *Femosphere* will gleefully wave these stats around to prove that women aren't committing birth-fraud, but when we look at the out of wedlock birth rates (41%), when we look at the extents to which we will arbitrarily assign legal fatherhood to whomever a woman says is a father, when we look at the resistance to allowing men access to DNA testing, and when we look at how the legal system will hold non-biological fathers liable for children they didn't sire, then we see that cuckoldry deserves a much broader definition.

There are proactive and retroactive forms of cuckoldry and it's time we start addressing these aspects as Red Pill aware men. Genders divided by feminism or feminine social primacy will need a 'customized' form of cuckoldry that allows for the Alpha Fucks side of Hypergamy to be reconciled with the Beta Bucks side by enlisting different men for either purpose. What this amounts to is a socially engineered, socially acceptable, subversion of men's evolved need to verify paternity.

The Pink Pill

I want to end here with an essay I read on the fallout of the new female form of Viagra, the 'pink' pill, from *Aeon.com, The Libido Crash*:

In an infamous cartoon in The New Yorker in 2001, one woman confides to a friend over drinks: 'I was on hormone replacement for two years before I realized what I really needed was Steve replacement.' Medicine has been reluctant to engage the question of just how much monogamy and long-term togetherness affect sexual function and desire, and the 'Steve' problem remains an issue that is tacitly acknowledged and yet under-discussed. To return to Julie's growing pile of self-help titles, the books all promise to return, revive, restore without really getting down to the brass tacks of why desire extinguished in the first place. As Julie notes, the honeymoon grinds to an end, but the issues leading there are complex. In short supply is attention to the way mind and body react to social structures such as popular media, faith and marriage.

To develop drugs to boost libido is like 'giving antibiotics to pigs because of the shit they're standing in'

The American psychologist Christopher Ryan argues that the institution of modern marriage – meaning an exclusive couple bound by romantic love – is antithetical to long-term excitement. Ryan is best known for Sex at Dawn (2010), a book authored with his wife Cacilda Jethá, that makes the case that sexual monogamy is deeply at odds with human nature.

He is among a growing number of researchers suggesting that the rift between women's purportedly limitless sexual potential and their dulled actuality might owe to the circumstances of intimacy. Accordingly, the conjugal bed is not only the scene of dwindling desire, but its fundamental cause. The elements that strengthen love – reciprocity, closeness, emotional security – can be the very things that smother lust. While love angles toward intimacy, desire flourishes across a distance.

The entire article is very insightful if not a bit depressing, but with the *Red Pill Lens* we can begin to understand the latent purpose behind the message. I've gone on record about the push back against clearing the pink pill for use as being a direct threat to women's control of their own Hypergamy. The concern, ostensibly, is that a libido stimulating drug might be used to induce a woman into having sex that her otherwise sober sensibilities would prevent; effectively it could be a 'rape' drug.

What's finally being addressed now is what I've been saying since I was aware of the drug's trials – a chemical that induces libido in women removes an element of their control in sexual selection and compromises Hypergamy. I'm not entirely sure the author here was aware of the points she was revealing in this, but she succinctly makes the case for both institutionalized cuckoldry (or certainly a 'designer' polygamy for women) and advocates for women maintaining control of their Hypergamy unclouded by a drug that would remove that control by chemically inducing them into sex that isn't of their own natural choosing.

The 'cure' to women's low libido is holistic, not biological. Women's sexual deficiencies are presumed not to be the result of a 'broken' biology, but rather a lack of proper motivation. I should point out that all of this validates all the points I've ever made about Dread being a utility for men in marriage – maintaining a condition of proper motivation (i.e. Dread), the holistic cure, is exactly what even *femosphere* authors are tacitly advocating for.

The elements that strengthen love – reciprocity, closeness, emotional security – can be the very things that smother lust.

Yet, even when a pharmaceutical solution to the lust problem is made available the 'cure' is rejected. Why? Because on a root, limbic level women's hindbrains know that Hypergamy cannot be optimized with a drug that removes Hypergamous choice. Women do not want the pink pill and a stable, but passionless, marriage. They want an open form of cuckoldry to be a socially acceptable standard.

The real solution has never changed and women are now put into a position of having to openly acknowledge that for all of the pretense of "mismatched libidos" or "sex just declines after marriage" social conventions, men's eventual cuckoldry is the real plan for Hypergamy. When presented with a pill that will make them sexual, when given a *cure* to their low sex drives with the men who've made lifetime commitments to them, women will still refuse to take it because it's about the guy, not her low sex drive.

Hypergamous doubt can't be quelled with a pill.

POSITIVE MASCULINITY

TRIBES

Rollo — You've been a major help to my understanding the underlying dynamics between men and women. I've observed them in bits and pieces over the years but never really understood the whys behind them or how to turn them in our favor.

It seems like one mid-term focus you have is on male-male dynamics, specifically fathers and sons. But I also wonder whether you'd consider writing more about bonding and support between men and how those relationships can anchor men's lives at a time when male relationships are regarded with skepticism by larger society. Lately it's struck me that men tend to innately trust the men they know and distrust those they don't (and that it's often the reverse for women). This inclines us to believe women when they decry the "assholes" who have mistreated them in the past while women are empathetic and credulous toward women whose character they don't know and whom they've never met.

Many of us out here are lacking strong male relationships, and our small social circles translate to fewer men we innately trust and more men we innately don't. Women seem to regard male friendships as a luxury at best – we should be focusing on career, family, and her needs – while women's friendships are seen as a lifeline in their crazy, have-it-all world. Indeed, a man discouraging his wife/girlfriend's friendships is widely seen as a sign of emotional abuse, whereas the reverse is "working on the relationship."

This strikes me as a deep but largely untapped Red Pill well and could provide essential guidance for men looking to live a proud, constructive Red Pill life however women and children might fit into it. I'd definitely welcome your insights in future entries.

Back in February of 2016 blogger *Roosh* proposed (and attempted to initiate) a worldwide event that would be a sort of 'gathering of the tribes' with the intent of having men get together in small local gatherings to "just have a beer and talk amongst like-minded men." My impression of the real intent behind putting this together notwithstanding, I didn't think it was a bad idea. However, the problem this kind of 'tribes meeting' suffers from is that it's entirely contrived to put unfamiliar men together for no other purpose than to "have a beer and talk." The problem with unfamiliar men coming together simply to meet and relate is a noble goal, however, the fundamental ways men communicate naturally makes the function of this gathering seem strange to men.

Women Talk, Men Do

The best male friends I have share one or more common interests with me – a sport, a hobby, music, art, fishing, lifting, golf, snowmobiling, etc. – and the best conversations I can remember with these friends occurred while we were engaged in some particular activity or event. Even when it's just moving a friend into his new house it's about accomplishing something together and in that time relating about whatever is relevant. When I lived in Florida some of the best conversations I had with my studio guys were during some project we had to collaborate on for a week or two.

Women, on the other hand, make time for, and with the expressed purpose of, talking between girlfriends. Over coffee perhaps, but the *act* of communication is more important than the event or activity. Even a 'stitch-and-bitch' where women get together socially to knit, is simply an organized excuse to get together and relate. For women, communication is about context. They are intrinsically rewarded by how that communication makes them feel. For men communication is about content and they are rewarded by the exchange of information, solutions to problems and ideas.

From an evolutionary perspective, it's likely that our hunter-gatherer tribal roles had a hand in men and women's communication differences. Men went to hunt together and practiced the coordinated actions for a cooperative goal. Bringing down a prey animal or building a communal shelter would likely have been a very information-crucial effort. In fact, the earliest cave paintings were essentially records of a successful hunt and instructions on how other men might do it too. Early men's communication would necessarily have been a content driven discourse or the tribe didn't eat.

Similarly women's communications would've been during gathering efforts and childcare. It would stand to reason that due to women's more collectivist roles they would evolve to be more intuitive, and context oriented, rather than object oriented. A common recognition in the manosphere is women's predisposition toward collectivism and/or a more socialist bent to thinking about resource distribution. Whereas men tend to distribute rewards and resources primarily based on merit, women have a tendency to spread resources collectively irrespective of merit. Again this predisposition is likely due to how women's psychological 'hard-wiring' evolved as part of the circumstances of their tribal roles.

From this perspective it's a fairly easy follow to see how the tendency of men to distrust unfamiliar (out-group) men might be a response to a survival threat whereas women's implicit trust of any member of the 'Sisterhood' would be a species-survival benefit for the sex that requires the most parental investment and mutual support. There is also a notion that early men's predisposition towards the infanticide of his rivals children, and the uncertainty of paternity within a tribal collective made covert communication and collusion among women a survival necessity.

Divide & Conquer

In our post-masculine, feminine-primary, social order it doesn't take a *Red Pill Lens* to observe the many examples of how the Feminine Imperative goes to great lengths to destroy the intrasexual 'tribalism' of men. Since the time of the *Sexual Revolution* the social press of equalism has attempted to force a commonly accepted unisex expectation upon men to socialize and interact among themselves in the same, socially 'correct' way that women do.

The duplicity in this striving towards "equality" is, of course, the same we find in all of the socialization efforts of egalitarian equalism – the emasculation of men in the name of equality. A recent (2015), rather glaring, example of this social push can be found at Harvard University where more than 200 female students demonstrated against a new policy to discourage participation in single-gender clubs at the school. Women were very supportive of the breaking of gender barriers when it meant that men could no longer discriminate in male-exclusive (typically male-space) organizations, but when that same equalist metric was applied to women's exclusive organizations, then, the cries were accusations of insensitivity and the banners read "Women's Groups Keep Women Safe."

That's a pretty fresh incident that outlines the dynamic, but it's important to understand the underlying intent of the "fine for me, but not for thee" duplicity here. That intent is to divide and control men's communication by expecting them to communicate as women do, and ideally to do so of their own accord by conditioning them to accept women's communication methods as the normatively correct way to communicate. The most effective social conventions are the ones in which the participants willingly take part in and willingly encourage others to believe is correct.

Tribes vs. The Sisterhood

Because men have such varied interests, passions and endeavors based on them it's easy to see how men compartmentalize themselves into various sub-tribes. Whether it's team sports (almost always a male-oriented endeavor), cooperative enterprises, cooperative forms of art or just hobbies men share, it is a natural progression for men to form sub-tribes within the larger whole of conventional masculinity.

"Four experiments confirmed that women's automatic in-group bias is remarkably stronger than men's and investigated explanations for this sex difference, derived from potential sources of implicit attitudes"

This quote sums up the results of Rudman, L. A., & Goodwin, S. A. (2004). *Gender differences in automatic in-group bias: Why do women like women more than men like men?* Journal of personality and social psychology, 87(4), 494.

Because of a man's' outward reaching approach to interacting with the world around him, there's really no unitary male tribe in the same fashion that the collective 'Sisterhood' of women represents. One of the primary strengths of the Feminine Imperative has been its unitary tribalism among women. We can see this evidenced in how saturated the Feminine Imperative has become into mainstream society and how it's embedded itself into what would otherwise be diametrically opposed factions among women. Political, socioeconomic and religious affiliations of women (various sub-tribes) all become secondary to the interests of 'womankind' when embracing the collective benefits of just being women and leveraging both their default victimhood and protected statuses.

Thus, we see no internal disconnect when women simultaneously embrace a hostile opposition to one social faction while still enjoying the benefits that faction might offer to the larger whole of the 'Sisterhood'. The Sisterhood is unitary first and then it is broken down into sub-tribes. Family, work, interests, political / religious compartmentalizations become sublimated to fostering the collective benefits of womankind.

Speculatively, I can understand the evolutionary benefits of how this psychological dynamic came to be, but I'd be remiss if I didn't point out just how effective this collectivity has been in shaping society towards a social ideal that supports an unfettered drive towards women's need to optimize Hypergamy. This unitary, women-first, tribalism has been (and still is) the key to women's social power – and even in social environments where women genuinely do suffer oppression, the Sisterhood will exercise this gender-tribalism.

Given this collectivist, female gender tribe vs. atomized male tribes we begin to see why men organizing what might be a 'Brotherhood' is so difficult and discouraged.

Threat Assessments

Asserting any semblance of a unitary male tribalism is a direct threat to the Feminine Imperative.

Nothing is more threatening yet simultaneously attractive to a woman than a man who is aware of his own value to women.

That quote is from a section called *The Threat* in my first book, *The Rational Male*. When I wrote this essay I did so from the perspective of women feeling vulnerable about interacting intimately with men who understood their own value to women, but also understood how to leverage it. One of the reasons Game is so vilified, ridiculed and disqualified by the Sisterhood is because it puts this understanding and awareness into practice with women and, in theory, removes some degree of control from women in the optimization of Hypergamy. Red Pill awareness and Game lessens women's control in that equation and makes intersexual dynamics adversarial. Men who *just get it* is sexy from the standpoint of dealing with a self-aware, high SMV man, but also threatening from the perspective that her long-term security depends on him acquiescing to her *Frame* and control. Women are conditioned to expect men to be ridiculous, untrustworthy and lacking any capacity to provide them with the long-term security they need, so it follows that the Sisterhood would balk at the idea of men coming into an awareness of their value to women and using it on his terms.

Up to this point, Game has represented an individualized threat to women's Hypergamous control, but there has always been a larger majority of men (Betas) who've been easily kept ignorant of their true potential for control. However, on a larger social landscape, the Feminine Imperative understands the risks involved in men forming a unitary tribe – a Brotherhood – based solely on benefiting and empowering men. The manosphere, while still effectively a collection of sub-tribes, represents a threat to the imperative because its base purpose is making men aware of their true state in a feminine-centric social order.

As such, any attempt to create exclusively male-specific, male-empowering organizations (such as the Men's Rights Movement) is made socially synonymous with either misogyny (hate) or homosexuality (shame). Ironically, the shame associated with homosexuality, that a fem-centric society would otherwise rail against, becomes an effective form of intra-gender shame when it's applied to heterosexual collectives of men. Even suggestions of male-centered tribalism are attached with homosexual suspicions, and these come from within the collectives of men themselves.

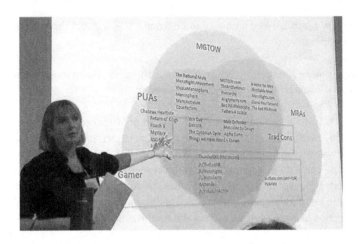

This picture is from an "academic" conference (class?) called *Mediated Feminisms: Activism and Resistance to Gender and Sexual Violence in the Digital Age* held at UCL in London. There's quite a bit more to this than just collecting and codifying the sub-tribes of the manosphere.

Now, granted, this conference was replete with all of the uninformed (not to mention willfully ignorant) concern to be expected of contemporary feminists, but this does serve as an example of how men organizing for the exclusive benefit of men is not just equated with misogyny, but potential violence. As a unitary collective of men, a growing manosphere terrifies the Feminine Imperative. That fear, however, doesn't stem from any real prospect of violence, but the potential for a larger 'awareness' in men of their own conditions and the roles they are expected to play to perpetuate a feminine-centric social order. They fear to lose the control that the 'socially responsible' ignorance of men provides them with.

Men's predisposition to form sub-tribes and intrasexual competition ("lets you and him fight") have always been a means of covert control by women, but even still the Feminine Imperative must insert its influence and oversight into those male spaces to make use of them. Thus, by assuring that feminine primacy is equated with the idea of inclusive equalism, all *Male Space* is effectively required to be "unisex space" while all-female sub-tribes must remain exclusively female. For an easy example of this, compare and contrast the reactions to Harvard's unisex institution of campus club equalism I mentioned earlier to the worldwide reactions to, and preemption of, the "Tribe" meetings only just attempted to be organized by Roosh in February, 2016.

Making Men

By controlling men's intrasexual communications with each other the Feminine Imperative can limit men's unified, collective, understanding of masculinity and male experiences. Feminine-primary society hates, and is terrified of, men defining and asserting masculinity for themselves (to the point of typifying it as "toxic"), but as connectivity progresses we will see a more concentrated effort to lock down the narrative and the means of men communicating male experiences.

I've detailed in many essays how the imperative has deliberately misdirected and confused men about a unified definition of masculinity. That confusion is designed to keep men guessing and doubting about their "security in their manhood" while asserting that the feminine-correct definition is the only legitimate definition of healthy, 'non-toxic', masculinity. This deliberate obfuscation and ambiguity about what amounts to 'authentic masculinity' is another means of controlling men's awareness of their true masculine potential. This potential they rightly fear will mean deferring to men's power over their Hypergamous social and personal control. Anything less than a definition of masculinity that fosters female primacy and 'fempowerment' is labeled "toxic masculinity" – literally and figuratively, poisonous.

This is the operative reason behind the obsessive, often self-contradicting, need for control of traditionally male spaces by the Feminine Imperative. Oversight and infiltration of male sub-tribes and instituting a culture of men who will self-police the narrative within those sub-tribes maintains a feminine-primary social order.

Building Better Betas

Since the time in which western(izing) societies shifted to unfettered Hypergamy on a social scale there have been various efforts to de-masculinize – if not outright feminize – the larger majority of men. Today we're seeing the results, and still persistent efforts, of this in much starker contrast as transgenderism and the social embrace of foisting gender-loathing on boys becomes institutionalized. A deliberate promotion of a social constructionist narrative about gender identity and the very early age at which children can "choose" a gender for themselves is beginning to be more and more reinforced in our present feminine-primary social order.

As a result of this, and likely into our near future, today's men are conditioned to feel uncomfortable being "men". That discomfort is a direct result of the ambiguity and misguidance about conventional masculinity the imperative has fostered in men when they were boys. This feminization creates a gender loathing, but that loathing comes as the result of an internal conflict between the feminine-correct, "non-toxic", understanding of what masculinity ought to be and the conventional aspects of masculinity that men need to express as a result of their biology and birthright.

Effectively, this confusion has the purpose of creating discomfort in men among all-male sub-tribes. These masculine-confused men have difficulty with interso-cial communication within the male sub-tribes they're supposed to have some sort of kin or in-group affiliation with. Even the concept of "male bonding" has become a point of ridicule (something typical of male buffoons) or something suspiciously homosexual. Thus, combined with the feminine identification most of these men default to, today's "mangina" typically has more female friends and feels more comfortable communicating as women communicate. These men have been effectively conditioned to believe or feel that uniquely male inter-action or organization is inherently wrong. It feels uncomfortable or contrived, possibly even threatening if the organizing requires physical effort. Consequent-ly, interacting 'as a male' becomes ridiculous or superficial. For the past 60 years of social feminization, all-male connection has been effectively suppressed.

Pushing Back

What then is to be done about this conditioning? For all the efforts to destroy or regulate male tribalism, the Feminine Imperative still runs up against men's evolved predispositions to interact with the extrinsic world instead of fixating on the intrinsic world of women. I've pieced together some actionable ideas here that might help men come to a better, unitary, way of fostering a male tribalism the Feminine Imperative would see destroyed or used as a tool of socio-sexual control:

•   While it is vitally important to maintain a male-specific mental point of origin, together men need a center point of action. Women talk, men do.

Men need a common purpose in which the tribe can focus its efforts on. Men need to build, coordinate, win, compete and problem solve amongst themselves. The 'purpose' of a tribe can't simply be one of getting together as like-minded men; in fact, groups with such a declared purpose are often designed to be the most conciliatory and accommodating of the Feminine Imperative. Men require a common, passionate purpose to unite for.

• Understand and accept that men will naturally form male hierarchies in virtually every context if that tribe is truly male-exclusive. There will be a reflexive resistance to this, but understand that the discomfort in acknowledging male hierarchies stems from the Feminine Imperative's want to make any semblance of male authority a toxic form of masculinity. Contrary to feminine conditioning male hierarchies are not necessarily based on Dark Triad manipulations. That is the 'fem-think' – any male created hierarchy of authority is by definition evil Patriarchy.

• Recognize existing male sub-tribes for what they are, but do so without labeling them as such. Don't talk about Fight Club, do Fight Club. As with most other aspects of Red Pill aware Game, it is always better to demonstrate rather than explicate. There will always be an observer effect in place when you call a male group a "male group". That tribe must exist for a mutual goal other than the expressed idea that it exists to be about men meeting up. Every sub-tribe I belong to, every collective interest I share with other men, even the instantly forming ones that arise from an immediate common need or function, all exist apart from "being" about men coming together. Worldwide "tribe" day failed much for the same reasons an organization like the *Good Men Project* fails – they are publicized as a gathering of men just "being" men.

• Push back on women's invasion of male space by being uncompromising in what you do and organize with passion. Make no concessions for women in any all-male space you create or join. There will always be a want to accommodate women and/or the fear of not being accommodating of feminine-primary mindsets within that all-male purview. Often this will come in subtle forms of anonymous White Knighting or reservations about particular passions due to other men's Blue Pill conditioning to always consider the feminine before considerations of themselves or the tribe. It is vitally important to the tribe to quash those sympathies and compromising attitudes as these are exactly the designs of the Feminine Imperative to destroy a tribe from within. Make no concessions for competency of women within the tribe if you find yourself in a unisex tribal situation. Even the U.S. military is guilty of reducing combat service requirements for women as recently as the time of this writing. If you are a father or you find yourself in a role of mentoring boys or young men, it is imperative that you instill this no-compromise attitude in them and the organizations that they create themselves.

• The primary Red Pill awareness and Game tenets that you've learned with respect to women are entirely applicable in a larger scope when it comes to resisting the influences of the Feminine Imperative. *Frame* control and a return to a collectively male-exclusive Mental Point of Origin are two of the primary tenets to apply to non-intimate applications of resistance. Objective observations and an internalized Red Pill perspective should inform your interactions with women and men on a social scale.

My approach to resisting the influences of the Feminine Imperative on a meta social scale is the same bottom-up approach I would use with unplugging men from their Blue Pill conditioning. Once men have taken the first steps in Red Pill awareness this new perspective has a tendency to expand into greater social understandings and a want for applications that go beyond hooking up with desirable women. Red Pill awareness becomes a way of life, but moreover, it should inform us as men, as tribes, about how best to maintain ourselves as masculine-primary individuals and organizations.

Individually men are competitive. It's part of our survival instinct to desire to win. Studies prove we get a rush of testosterone when we are the victors over some adversary or adversity – a fact that coincides with women's sensitivity to, and arousal for the winners. However, we are also cooperative in our victories. Men banding together to overcome adversity or to create magnificent achievements of humanity are also characteristic of conventional masculinity.

As the social influences of feminine-primacy has spread over the last 60 years the effort to separate and isolate men from this conventional cooperation has become more and more evident. There's no shortage of concerned bloggers lamenting the 'drop out' generation of young men who've become so disenfranchised from conventional masculinity that they content themselves with video games and online porn. What they fail to consider is that these young men have been deliberately isolated in order to contain their masculine potentials. As a result these young men have no male-only purpose or endeavor to apply themselves to. With a lack of purpose comes a lack of male communication and engagement, and with that comes the atrophy of understanding masculine ways of interacting with each other.

RITES OF PASSAGE

In the past I've discussed the hesitancy of young men to refer to themselves as 'men' or to really even embrace what might be considered a 'conventional' idea of masculinity. You've probably read me using that word before. I use the word *conventional* because I feel it conveys a better understanding of a naturalized expression of masculinity in a way that men evolved into. Occasionally I have a reader ask me why I don't use the term '*traditional*' with respect to masculinity, but I'm not sure they really mean the same thing.

It's easy to think of masculinity in terms of tradition, but whose tradition are we really referring to? 'Traditional Masculinity' as a term has assumed a derogatory meaning in a feminine-primary social order. It's become one of those catch-terms that we're all supposed to understand as being characteristic of backward mindsets. It's part of the social convention that seeks to ridicule, shame and confuse boys who later become men about what masculinity ought to mean to them. So, it's for this reason I use the word '*conventional*'. It conveys the idea that masculinity in a binary sense has evolved aspects that are inherent and unique to men. So while certain cultures may have had different traditions and traditional roles for men, there is a unifying conventionality of masculinity that relates to all men and maleness in general.

Feminine-centrism doesn't like this idea. It doesn't like the idea that masculine characteristics or behaviors are the sole propriety of men. The reflex then is to paint any conventionally masculine attribute, way of thinking, aggression, passion or aspiration as either representative of 'toxic' harmful or anti-social, or, depending on its usefulness in securing power, it's cast as something "not necessarily masculine" (i.e. strength) since some women can lay claim to that trait.

I've outlined before how boys are taught from a very early age to gender-loathe their maleness. It's part of Blue Pill conditioning, but more so, I think it's important for Blue Pill or unplugging adult men to understand the mechanics and reasoning behind why it's in the Feminine Imperative's interests to keep conventional masculinity something ambiguous, arbitrary or something men ought to be able to fluidly define for themselves. That last part there is important, because what most men of today think is their own self-generated definition of masculinity is generally founded in what the Feminine Imperative has conditioned him to believe is healthy and correct.

Latent Purposes

In a social order that's ostensibly founded upon a baseline equalism (in principle) among men and women we have to look at why it might be necessary for boys to be taught that 'traditional' masculinity is toxic. The easy answer is that it stems from a want for control, but not so much in the terms of convincing boys to become men who will loathe their maleness. Remember, there are many aspects of conventional masculinity that are conveniently useful to further the interests of women and Hypergamy – but the conditioning becomes one of selectively classifying the useful aspects as 'healthy' and the non-useful ones as 'toxic'.

The most important thing to consider here is that, for future men, egalitarian equalism's (the Village's) purpose in boy's upbringing is to prevent them from ever internalizing the idea that they should be their own mental point of origin. This, I think, is one of the fundamental issues most Blue Pill men struggle with in their own unplugging; unlearning the deeply embedded idea that his wellbeing must always come after that of women's.

One of the *Old Books*, traditional, understandings is that men, by virtue of being male, can expect a degree of authority in their lives and in their families. A man may not be the boss at work, but the traditional understanding was that he could expect to be the head-of-household in his own home. Feminine primacy, under the auspices of equalism, has effectively conditioned this idea out of men over the course of generations. If men and women are blank-slate functional equals, ideally, there will never be a default authority in an intersexual relationship.

From a conventional, evolutionary perspective we know this baseline equalism is not just false, but we also understand that it serves as a control over the masculine nature men are born into. Men and women are different; cognitively, neurologically, biologically and psychologically, but our feminine-socialized presumptions with regard to how boys are raised to be men deliberately conditions them to believe we are the same – or at least functionally so.

The Crime of Being Male

There's been some push-back to this in our Red Pill awakening, and not all of it is the result of the manosphere. As Hypergamy becomes more openly embraced in a larger social respect, more men are made aware of their deliberate conditioning to accommodate it. What men choose to do with that awareness is up to them, but the response from the Feminine Imperative to this awareness is to criminalize or make 'toxic' the embrace of conventional masculinity on the part of men. It becomes a hate-crime to express any conventionally male attribute, but moreover it's a hate-crime to foster those attributes in boys/men.

This is a potential danger for Blue Pill men in that the expressions of maleness that they display are on one hand desired by women, but also a risk to their reputation or livelihoods if that expression is offensive to womankind. Red Pill aware men may have the advantage of knowing women's nature well enough to mitigate the risks, but Blue Pill men will be stuck in a paradigm that puts them at risk for wanting to be conventionally masculine men.

Again, equalist Blue Pill conditioning's purpose is to prevent men from assuming themselves as their mental point of origin, but once a man's disabused himself from putting the feminine as his primary internal concern there must be an opposite, contingent, reaction on the part of the Feminine Imperative to put him back into compliance. Thus, we see the criminalization of maleness.

Pedestals

For some time it's been a manosphere staple to tell guys to take the girl off the pedestal if he wants to be successful with women. We call it *pedestalization*, but one reason that dynamic, to put a woman on a higher order than oneself, is so pervasive among men is due exactly to this "equalist" conditioning. The internalization is one of making that girl, that woman, that mother, that female boss, the centerpiece of a man's headspace. This becomes *who* he is and it's the result of a childhood that taught him he must place the concerns of girls above his own on many different psychological levels. Ostensibly this is sold to men as being 'honorable' in putting others before himself, however the latent purpose of 'being a good servant' has been bastardized by the Feminine Imperative to be defined as being 'supportive' of women. And men are to be supportive of women's interests at the risk of being considered a misogynist.

Once that guy becomes Red Pill aware, no matter who does his unplugging, not only does he remove girls from the *pedestal* personally, but also in a larger, sociological scope. And this scope is what the Feminine Imperative must push-back against.

Blue Pill conditioning teaches boys/men to cast doubt on their own masculinity. What constitutes masculinity? Is it a mask or a performance they put on? Is it something to be proud of, or some problem/privilege to keep in check? Should boys/men feel insecure or secure about it? These are the consistent ambiguities the Feminine Imperative wants to invest into the next generations of men because it keeps women on the pedestal. In this social paradigm only women possess the solution to men's *problem* of maleness.

But the Blue Pill also conditions boys/men to never presume to consider themselves as a "*man*". The joke is that men are never really men, but rather they become 'bigger boys'. This is a social convention that attempts to keep men in a juvenilized state and thus ensuring women are the only 'adults' to make the judgment call. This ridicule has the purpose of denying men their status of 'manhood'. If men are perpetual boys, they can never assume the default 'headship' of being men. It is a control for authority.

This is another reason men are conditioned to keep women on the pedestal; only women can confirm 'manhood' from a superior (mental) position in that man's mind. When a woman is at the top of a man's mental point of origin – and not even a specific woman, but womankind – *she* decides and confers his status of being a man. So it follows that men ought to be raised to internalize the doubt of understanding manhood or conventional masculinity.

The struggle men have in coming to a Red Pill awareness is one of removing women from this pedestal, but also one of giving oneself permission to be a man. This may seem kind of simplistic, but to a guy who's been conditioned to put women before himself in his own internal, mental, conversations it's a very tough challenge. Blue Pill conditioning invests a doubt into boys and then men. They are conditioned to self-regulate on many levels, but to generally put their own concerns beneath those of others and largely the feminine. They are taught to self-sublimate by never giving themselves permission to be "men" in a conventional sense.

Iron Rule of Tomassi #9

Never Self-Deprecate under any circumstance. This is a Kiss of Death that you self-initiate and is the antithesis of the Prize Mentality. Once you've accepted yourself and presented yourself as a "complete douche" there's no going back to confidence with a woman. Never appeal to a woman's sympathies. Her sympathies are given by her own volition, never when they are begged for – women despise the obligation of sympathy. Nothing kills arousal like pity. Even if you don't seriously consider yourself pathetic, it never serves your best interest to paint yourself as pathetic. Self-Depreciation is a misguided tool for the AFC, and not something that would even occur to an Alpha mindset.

One important reason I made this an Iron Rule (see *The Rational Male*) was because it is almost a default response of men to presume the validity of their own ridiculousness. The reflexive response is, of course, "not to take yourself so seriously" and have an ability to laugh at yourself when it's merited. That's all fine and well, a necessity for a healthy sense of self, but few men realize their ease with self-deprecation is a result of their conditioning to find themselves ridiculous as men. The concept of "Men" is associated with "ridiculous".

It's very easy for Red Pill aware men to lose sight of what the Blue Pill conditions men for and how this conditioning has evolved over the course of generations. The latent purpose remains the same (preventing men from adopting their own mental point of origin), but the methods and social mores change fluidly with what the Feminine Imperative finds most efficient for the time. For the past 20 years there's been a concentrated effort to remove men from deciding their own manhood for themselves.

Remove the Man

In 2013, Washington state Governor Jay Inslee signed off on the final installment of a six-year effort to make language in the state's copious laws gender-neutral. The sponsor of the bill, Senator Jeannie Kohl-Welles' reasoning for initiating the six-year endeavor was,

> *"It brings us to modern times, to contemporary times, why should we have in statute anything that could be viewed as biased or stereotypical or reflecting any discrimination?"*

Thus, words such as 'freshmen', 'fireman', 'fisherman' and even 'penmanship' are neutralized to 'first year student', 'fire-person', 'fisher' and 'writing skill'. Perhaps the easiest way to grasp the process the committee used in their six-year effort is to presume that any noun or verb with the successive letters of 'm-a-n' in its syntax was replaced with 'person' or a substitution for a term that excluded the offending 'm-a-n' letters.

This hasn't been the only effort to geld the English language under the guise of a want for avoiding legal repercussions. The University of North Carolina has initiated a similar effort in their school's by-laws. Kent Law, Marquette and virtually every state college in the union, while not mandating the 'manless' language, has made efforts to encourage linguistic androgyny.

The Washington state initiative is really just the next predictable progression in this gelding, however the six-year effort represents something more endemically hostile; the Feminine Imperative, in its inconsolable insecurity, would re-engineer the very language society uses in order to feel more secure.

Now granted, this is English, the second most commonly spoken language in the world, but in order to fully appreciate the scope of the Feminine Imperative and the lengths to which it will go unhindered to assuage the need for feminine-security, a Red Pill man has to recognize the importance language represents to the human race as well as the removal of male, not masculine, influence from that language.

In all Latin-based languages there are gender associations with definitive articles. Nouns (and many adjectives) are specifically feminine or masculine as part of their intrinsic qualities. In Spanish 'La Casa', the home, is a feminine association. 'El Toro', the bull, is a masculine association. Anyone with even a rudimentary grasp of a Latin-based language understands that millennia ago the Latin culture found gender differentiation so important that it attached gender associations to the words, written and spoken, that represented the ideas and articles each word meant.

This might seem like a remedial review of language and society, but it's important to understand what it is the Feminine Imperative hopes to undo, and the magnitude of its insecurities. The six-year effort of gender-abridgment in the Washington state law is really an illustration of the lengths to which the Feminine Imperative would re-engineer society; from the very foundations of human communication, language, by eliminating masculine associations with any article or quality. The Feminine Imperative, that is dependent upon men being Men when convenient, simultaneously makes herculean efforts to remove men from its idealized environment and society.

> *"But if thought can corrupt language, language can also corrupt thought.*
> *Bad usage can spread by tradition and imitation, even among people who*
> *should and do know better." – George Orwell*

Be a Man

There used to be a time when some cultures had a rite of passage into manhood or a passing into adult responsibility and masculine respect. In Latin cultures a young woman becomes a woman on here quinceñera – her fifteenth birthday. Jewish boys have a Bar Mitzvah, certain Native American tribes had similar traditions, etc. I think that if there's a modern social complaint about men remaining perpetually juvenile this is the root of it – we don't respect Manhood enough to define what's expected and when that adult, masculine respect is due.

A lot has been written on my blog and many others about the ceaseless efforts of the feminine to marginalize and ridicule anything masculine. It's easy to find consistent examples of this in the past 50 years of popular media, movies, TV sitcoms, music, etc. While masculinity is ridiculed, there's more to it than this. It's not simple masculine ridicule, because the same masculine attributes and qualities that make women 'strong' are the same that make men strong. The difference is in the application – it wasn't enough to implant the seeds of masculine self-doubt into men, the Feminine Imperative had to make men, not necessarily masculinity, the *problem* to be solved.

In all of the examples of masculine gender reversal in popular culture, men are the unique problem, to which only women have the resources, wisdom and intuition to correct. The men of today are characterized as the Lucy Ricardos of the 50's, requiring women's guidance to avoid, often mutually destructive, disasters. However, the key to solving those problems, characterized as uniquely male, still require masculine-associated, mindsets, skills and applications.

Guys vs. Men

I was participating in a conversation with a young woman of 26 and a young man of 18. The conversation itself wasn't important, but at one point the young man referred to himself as a 'Man'. He said something to the effect of, "Well I'm a man, and men do,.." At the word 'man' she cut him off with the unconscious snigger that's resulted from years of feminine ridicule conditioning. Just the mention of a man self-referencing as a "man" is enough to inspire feminine ridicule. It's laughable for a man to consider himself a man.

This exchange got me to wondering about the turning point at which I began to self-reference as a "Man". In the face of a constant conditioned ridicule, it's almost an uncomfortable recognition to distinguish yourself as a Man. It's too easy to just think of yourself as a 'guy' and never be so presumptuous as to insist upon your manhood. In girl-world, to claim to be a Man is to accept one's own arrogance – it's to embrace a flawed nature.

It's important to note here that in embracing your status as a Man, instead of 'just a guy', you are passing a meta-shit test. By embracing self-referenced manhood, you are rejecting what a world aligned against you would like you to believe about yourself. You're endorsing yourself as a Man with self-assurance despite the self-doubt the Feminine Imperative relies upon men believing about themselves – masculinity and the dubious state of manhood as a whole.

By flagrantly referring to yourself as a Man you are passing the meta-shit test, you're overtly declaring you're a Man, but you you're covertly stating "I Just Get It."

The Man Removed

The Feminine Imperative perceives your Manhood as a Threat. By endorsing yourself as a Man, on some level, whether you're cognizant of it or not, you're alluding that you have an inkling of your own personal value as a Man. You're expressing a self-awareness that is attractive and terrorizing for women, but due to the constant influence of feminine primacy you're perceived as arrogant, self-serving and prideful. Even in the most innocuous context, insisting upon your status as a Man is inherently sexist to a world defined by the Feminine Imperative.

But the imperative needs masculinity. To insure its (temporary) satisfaction of security a masculine element is required. Strength, confidence, determination, a capacity for risk taking, dominance and the comfort in security that women naturally derive from those masculine attributes are necessities of a healthy, secure, existence for women and the feminine. However, brutish, ridiculous and stupid men can't be trusted to universally provide this masculine security that every woman has been taught she deserves irrespective of attractiveness or merit by the Feminine Imperative. So Men must be *removed* from masculinity.

No longer are Men allowed a monopoly on masculinity. Domineering, "Alpha Women" as a default status in heterosexual relationships pushes masculinity into her domain. Dominant masculine partners in Sexually Fluid lesbian relationships are similarly, unironically, re-characterized.

These are the easy examples. Volumes have been written in the Manosphere about how feminine-primary government assumes the masculine providership role in modern relationships, thus freeing an already unhindered Hypergamy even more so, but the effort to remove the Man goes far beyond this obvious institution. The fundamental restructuring of gender reference in our very language – in the way we are to communicate appropriate thoughts – attempts to, literally, remove the Man from the equation.

Masculine Security

I can remember an instance at a former workplace where some coworkers were organizing a team to run in a Breast Cancer awareness walk/run. At one point a particularly 'mangina' coworker suggested we all wear the prerequisite pink color at the event, and needless to say I arrived in a black T-Shirt amongst a sea of pink. The predictable accusation of my sexual security came up: "What, aren't you secure enough in your manhood to wear pink?" to which I answered "I'm secure enough in my Manhood not to wear pink."

What the guy was obliviously parroting back is the same social tool that's been used by the Feminine Imperative for the past 60 years; inspire self-doubt in male-specific masculinity. By making compliance with the Feminine Imperative a qualification of masculinity, men assign the power to define masculinity to the Feminine Imperative. My answer to him was simply taking that power of definition back into a male-controlled frame – "I'll tell you what manhood is, your conditioned grasp of manhood doesn't qualify you to tell me."

This power of defining the masculine isn't limited just to snarky, subconscious referencing; it's simply one aspect of a greater effort to remove men from masculinity. While the efforts of certain women bloggers and psychologists (both within and without the Manosphere) to build better betas seems ennobling to White Knights, the unifying purpose behind their efforts is really one of apportioning masculine authority to men in as convenient a way as would satisfy their immediate needs for those masculine aspects. Be Alpha as needed, but Beta for the greater part so as to allow for feminine-masculine dominance and primacy.

I've explained this previously as the Male Catch 22 in my first book (*The Honor System*), but it's important to understand that this Catch isn't some unfortunate byproduct of male inheritance; it's a careful, calculated feminine social dynamic with the latent purpose of making men accountable for masculine responsibilities while simultaneously making them shamed and guilty of 'male privilege' when that masculinity conflicts with the dictates of the Feminine Imperative. That's the crux of the dynamic, but the mechanics of it are still rooted in specifically male masculine self-doubt.

For the Feminine Imperative to sustain itself men can never be trusted with masculinity. Solution: remove men from being the definers of masculinity and apportion them only enough authority of it that would benefit the Feminine Imperative as necessary.

Rites of Passage

One of the key elements to unplugging is changing your mind about yourself. This is one of the biggest obstacle to guys coming to accept a Red Pill aware reality. This self-denial of their own 'manhood', which becomes a resistance to embracing anything conventionally masculine as being positive, is a foreign thought.

There used to be a time when boys would go through some rite of passage and be considered a 'man' by his family and peers. It's important for Red Pill men to realize how this passage into a state of manhood has been deliberately confused or shamed out of significance to all but the most traditional of cultures.

Most male rites of passage are painted as cruel and barbaric hazing rituals in a fem-centric society. That's a popularized and easy connection to make, but what underlies this effort to disqualify manhood as legitimate is a push to force men into compliance with the Feminine Imperative and feminine-primacy.

I would suggest that men coming into a Red Pill awareness need to embrace being a "man". Red Pill men need a rite of passage of some sort. In the Mano-sphere we sometimes ask about when a guy finally came into his Red Pill awareness. We compare stories about what we were like when we were still living in a Blue Pill paradigm and then what form of trauma (or not) triggered that Blue Pill disillusionment. We discuss the various stages of grief for our past Blue Pill idealism, the nihilism, the anger, the disbelief, then the acceptance and the new enthusiasm of being Red Pill aware and the potential it proposes.

But there needs to be a rite of passage for passing from that Blue Pill state to a new Red Pill awareness and part of this should be a conscious acknowledgment of giving yourself permission to be a man. This needs to be part of changing your mind about yourself as you become more aware of the agency you have in a conventionally male respect. You need a baptism of sorts; a point at which you set yourself apart from Blue Pill men and a feminine-primary social order.

Most (Beta) guys have a difficult time embracing the authority and due defer-ence that being a conventional man conveys to him. They're uncomfortable on an ego-personality level with accepting this dominant male role because it goes against everything their feminine-centric upbringing has taught them.

However, with that authority comes responsibility. I would argue that many a Blue Pill guy is comforted by the lies of equalism because he believes that egalitarianism and the expectations that men and women are functional equals in some way exempts him from his uniquely male burden of performance. On some level of consciousness, even the Beta men who are comforted by equalism still realize that their maleness will only ever be merited and judged by his per-formance. And that performance is firmly grounded in conventionally male tests.

THE SECOND SET OF BOOKS

One of the cornerstones of Red Pill truth lies in men coming to terms with what amounts to (in most cases) half a lifetime of feminine conditioning. It's interesting to consider that there was a time (pre-Sexual Revolution) when a man wasn't in someway socialized and acculturated in his upbringing to give deference to the feminine or to become more feminine-identifying. There are plenty of other manosphere bloggers who'll run down in detail all of the many ways boys are now raised and educated to be what a feminine-primary world would like them to be, but at the heart of it is a presumption that boys should be raised and conditioned to be more like girls; conditioned from their earliest memories to be better providers for what women believe they will eventually want them to be as adult 'men'.

For men who've become aware of this conditioning through some trauma or personal crisis that prompted him to seek answers for his condition, we call this period our Blue Pill days. I think it's important to make a distinction about this time – whether or not a man is Alpha or Beta doesn't necessarily exclude him from the consequences of a Blue Pill conditioning. That isn't to say that a more natural Alpha Man can't see the world in a Red Pill perspective by his own means, but rather that his feminine-primary upbringing doesn't necessarily make a man Alpha or Beta.

I'm making this distinction because there is school of thought that being Blue Pill (unaware of one's conditioning) necessitates him being more Beta. To be sure, feminine-primary conditioning would raise a boy into a more feminine-pliable man – ready to serve as the good Beta provider when a woman's sexual market value declines and she's less able to compete with her younger sexual competitors.

However, there also exist more Alpha Men conditioned to be servants of the Feminine Imperative. These men make for some of the most self-evincing White Knights you'll ever meet and are usually the first men to "defend the honor" of the feminine and women for whom they lack a real awareness of. Binary absolutism and an upbringing steeped in feminization makes for a potent sense of self-righteousness. Blue pill Alphas live for the opportunity to defend everything their conditioning has taught them. To the Blue Pill Alpha, all women are victims by default, all women share a common historic suffering and any

239

man (a White Knight's sexual competitors) critical of the feminine are simply an opportunity to prove his worth to any woman in earshot he believes might at all find his zealousness for feminine identification attractive.

The Second Set of Books

On June 15th, 2011, a man by the name of *Thomas Ball* set himself on fire in front of Cheshire Superior Court in New Hampshire after a particularly ugly divorce proceeding. Prior to his suicide, Ball left a lengthy manifesto outlining his disillusionment with the government process, but more importantly it outlined his eyes being opened to a great deal of the more discomforting aspects of Red Pill awareness. I'd encourage readers to look up his last testament online. Unfortunately, Ball's manifesto is a bit too long to include in its entirety here, but I will quote the operative point here:

Any one swept up into this legal mess is usually astonished at what they see. They cannot believe what the police, prosecutors and judges are doing. It is so blatantly wrong. Well, I can assure you that everything they do is logical and by the book. The confusion you have with them is you both are using different sets of books. You are using the old First Set of Books - the Constitution, the general laws or statutes and the court ruling sometime call Common Law. They are using the newer Second Set of Books. That is the collection of the policy, procedures and protocols. Once you know what set of books everyone is using, then everything they do looks logical and upright. And do not bother trying to argue with me that there is no Second Set of Books. I have my own copies at home. Or at least a good hunk of the important part of it.

While I strongly disagree with his decision to self-immolate, I do understand his sentiment. I've had many a Red Pill critic attempt to call me to the carpet over how a man might come to the conclusion of suicide or murder once he'd become confronted with a total loss of all his personal and emotional investment in life:

But Rollo, you just justified murder as "logical", by illustrating that insecurity is the prime motivator for this man's life. The decision may have be understandable in an empathetic sense, and he might have seen it as logical at the time, but there is nothing logical about it. You are making extreme beta-ism seem more and more like a mental disorder.

Just for the record, I've argued in the past that ONEitis, or a life founded on the idea of the Soul-Mate Myth, however extreme, *is* in fact a mental disorder.

However, I haven't justified anything, murder or suicide, I've simply outlined the deductive process men use when confronting the actualized loss of their most important investment (or perceptually so) in life. They are convinced and conditioned to believe that women are playing by a set of rules, and will honor the terms of those rules; but only after ego-investing themselves for a lifetime in the correctness and appropriateness of those rules do they discover women are playing by another set of rules. They then wonder at how stupid they could've been to have ever believed in the rules they were conditioned to expect everyone would abide by. When critics label Red Pill men as characteristically 'angry' or bitter, this is the source of that sentiment – their anger isn't directed at women, but rather themselves for having been so blind.

Suicide or murder certainly *is* a deductive and pragmatic end for some men, but by no means is it justified nor would I advocate for it. Thomas Ball, for all of his due diligence in uncovering the ugly processes of the American divorce industry, was far more useful alive than dead in some symbolic suicide. Now, in passing, he wasn't the martyr he probably expected he'd be, he's just another footnote. A casualty of the Feminine Imperative.

For all of that, Thomas Ball and his last message to humanity serves as an excellent illustration of a man coming to terms with his own conditioning. In his message Ball makes a very important observation about his legal ordeals. He comes to understand that there are two sets of books rather than the one he'd been led to believe that everyone understood as 'the rules' everyone should play by.

Ball was largely making a political statement in his account of going through the legal system and the cruel education he got in the process, but when men transition from their comfortable Blue Pill perspective into the harsh reality that the Red Pill represents, the experience is a lot like Ball discovering that the set of books (the set of rules) he'd believed everyone was using wasn't so. Likewise, men who've been conditioned since birth to believe that women were using a common set of rules – a set where certain expectations and mutual exchange were understood – were in fact using their own set. Furthermore, these men 'just didn't get it' that they should've known all along that women, as well as men's feminization conditioning, were founded in a second set of books.

In my estimate, that first set of books – the *Old Books* – represents the social contract of an era before the Sexual Revolution. It was an old set of rules men were taught they could expect women and other men would honor in exchange for accepting a burden of performance that was itself an extension of those rules.

The second set of books, the new set, represent the true rules a man is playing by whether he's aware of it or not. These are the post-Sexual Revolution rules that serve the Feminine Imperative and unfettered Hypergamy; the rules that are extensions of the social re-engineering necessary for a feminine-primary social order.

Coming to terms with this separation of rule sets is an integral part of a man's unplugging himself and becoming Red Pill aware. Men are expected to abide by the second set of books, while still being held accountable for the liabilities of the first set. Much of men's disillusionment with notions of Chivalry comes from this serving of two masters. The old social contracts are an anachronism, but men are still taught to respect them while at the same time are persecuted according to the second set of books if they step over a line they may not ever be aware of.

This is a difficult lesson for young men to learn and then disabuse themselves of before they've invested their most productive years into what their Blue Pill conditioning has convinced them they can expect from life and women. However, when a mature man, who's based the better part of his life, and invested his future, into the hope in the first set of books is disenfranchised by the second set of books, that's when all of the equity he believed he'd established under the first set of books counts for nothing. Literally his life (up to that point) counted for nothing. This is the foundation of what I termed the *Fallacy of Relational Equity* in my first book.

When a man is faced with the prospect of rebuilding himself after living so long under false pretenses, after having all he believed he was building turn up to be a lifetime of wasted effort, he's faced with two real options; recreate himself or destroy himself. Needless to say suicide statistics among men (5:1 over women) are a strong indication that the majority of men (Betas) more commonly don't have the personal strength to recreate themselves. Thomas Ball didn't.

There's usually a lot of disillusionment that comes with making the transition to Red Pill awareness. Guys get upset that what they now see was really there all along, but it's not so much the harshness of seeing Red Pill dynamics in women or a feminized society play out with such predictability, it's the loss of investment that causes the real sense of nihilism.

The overarching reason most men experienced what they called a righteous anger, isn't directed at how the second set of books had been directing their lives behind the scenes for so long, but rather it was anger at having invested so much of themselves in the first set of books and losing that very long term investment.

The good news is you can rebuild yourself. A lot gets written about how nihilistic the Red Pill is, but this is due to a lack of understanding that you can recreate yourself for the positive with the knowledge of both sets of rules. One common thread I see come up often on the Red Pill Reddit forum is how Game-awareness has completely destroyed a guy's world view. I get it, I realize it's a hard realization, but their depression is only for a lack of understanding that they can become even better in this new understanding than they were in their Blue Pill ignorance.

A foundation of internalizing a new definition of positive masculinity for yourself begins in coming to terms with the reality of your situation. And this is in respect to how these conflicting sets of rules have influenced the course of your life up to this point. Rebuilding sucks. I've done it enough times myself to feel exactly this sense of loss at many points in my life. And the older a man gets the more grave that loss will seem. Any sense of equity we believe we've merited must be valued by us first, but that value will always have a context.

The value of what we make of ourselves in an old books context has to be set and compared against what that value is in a second books context. Much of what we believed would be valuable in our Blue Pill existence, the equity we believed would get us closer to Blue Pill idealist goals, is expected or taken for granted. Yet we think it's some kind of insurance against the worst of what those operating in the new social contract (if it can be called that) would use it for.

Understand now that you're living on the cusp of deciding what aspects of conventional masculinity are valuable to you, and yet you must still operate in the knowledge of the second set of rules being used all around you. I use this comparison of the old and new sets of books in many of my essays, but this is really a convenience, a tool, to set a contrast in the ideas I'm exploring. Just like Alpha, Beta, Red Pill, Blue Pill, etc. the old and new sets of books are abstracts to describe an idea of two states.

I don't think men ought to pine for some return to the good ole' days – most of which are simply romanticizations of times that never really existed – but rather to accept the nature of how the Blue Pill conditions us, emancipate ourselves from it, and use the second set of books to our own best advantage. Once we become aware of our misguidance in basing our masculinity on the false terms of a social contract, a rule set, no one is playing by, then we can begin to effectively direct ourselves towards a positive, new conventional masculinity.

THE RED PILL BALANCE

I had a reader hit me with this meta-scale Red Pill question that dovetails very nicely into what I proposed in the *Second Set of Books.*

A lot of what you've said echoes my own thinking to such a degree that it's as if you read my mind. I agree 100%.

What you're talking about here, I think, is the inherent value of goodness or justice. I think Plato took up this question in the Republic and nailed it better than most.

In the beginning of the dialogue the question is "what is justice?" But it quickly transforms into "what is the value of justice?" In other words, if goodness wins us no reward, then what value does it have? Is it valuable in its own right? Would it have value even if it cost us something, or indeed cost us everything?

Glaucon puts the question like this (paraphrasing): "What if the perfectly just man is seen by everyone as perfectly unjust, while the perfectly unjust man is seen as perfectly just?" He then puts it on Socrates to effectively prove that, even in this scenario, justice would be worth it.

We could gender this question and simply ask "what if the perfectly good man is seen as perfectly unattractive to women, while the perfectly evil man is seen as perfectly attractive?"

Is goodness worth it even if it isn't profitable sexually or socially? It's the same question.

Why be a 'good' man when what we consider good by both personal and social measures isn't rewarded (or only grudgingly rewarded), while what we consider 'bad' is what is enthusiastically rewarded with women's genuine desire and intimacy? In other words, Hypergamy doesn't care about what men consider to be good or bad.

It seems like this is the predicament Red Pill awareness puts us in when we have to consider the value of our formerly Beta self. What makes the Beta the Beta is his weakness, of course, but it is simultaneously his civility. We're not defective people for wanting or even needing the possibility of love, empathy, truth, friendship, kindness, and – above all else – trust in our lives. It just makes us human. If we project our deeply rooted desires for these things and treat others the way we want to be treated, wouldn't society be better off for it? And isn't this what the supplicating, loyal Beta does when latches on to a woman he believes to be "the One?"

No Quarter Given

In my post (and book chapter) *Of Love and War* I quote a reader who summed up this want for relief from men's inherent Burden of Performance:

We want to relax. We want to be open and honest. We want to have a safe haven in which struggle has no place, where we gain strength and rest instead of having it pulled from us. We want to stop being on guard all the time, and have a chance to simply be with someone who can understand our basic humanity without begrudging it. To stop fighting, to stop playing the game, just for a while.

We want to, so badly.

If we do, we soon are no longer able to.

When I consider this perspective I begin to see a stark paradox; mens' want for a relief or a respite from that performance burden tends to be their undoing. I wont get too deep into this, but one reason I see the MGTOW (Men Going Their Own Way) sphere being so seductive is the hopeful promise of that same relief from performance. Simply give up. Refuse to play along and reject the burden altogether. The culture of Japan's herbivorous men crisis is a graphic example of the long term effects of this.

However, this is the same mistake men make in their Blue Pill, Beta conditioning. They believe that if they meet the right girl, if they align correctly with that special ONE, then they too can give up and not worry about their performance burden – or relax and only make the base effort necessary to keep his ONE happy. The Beta buys the advertising that his Blue Pill conditioning has presented to him for a lifetime. Find the right girl who accepts you, independent of your performance, and you can let down your guard, be *vulnerable*, forget any notion of Red Pill truths because your girl is a special specimen who places no conditions on her love, empathy, intimate acceptance or genuine desire for you.

This is also very seductive and inuring for the Beta who's been conditioned to believe there can realistically be a respite from his burden. My reader continues:

That's how it seemed to work in my own life. Looking back on it, I was so grateful to my ex, who was easily the most attractive girl I'd ever been with, that I would have taken a bullet for her. I didn't want anybody else. I didn't even think about other girls – the first time that had ever happened to me in a relationship. I can remember thinking that even if she gained weight, lost her looks, and got old, I'd still want her. I would have "loved" her forever. I was good and ready to cash in my chips, exit the sexual marketplace, and retire. I would have arranged my whole life around making her happy and would have felt lucky to have had the privilege.

At the time, all of that felt noble and brave, but looking back on it now, it just seems pathetic and pathological; the result of my neediness. But the thing is, what if she had reciprocated it? Wouldn't it have been a relationship worth having? Had she reciprocated it – if any woman was capable of reciprocating that – it wouldn't have been Disney movie bullshit, but the real thing. We're supposed to think such a thing is possible and that's what keeps us playing along. The Red Pill is really about recognizing its impossibility, I think. There is no possible equity. To be sure, a woman can be loyal and dedicated to you, in theory, but she'll only give that loyalty to the guy who needs it least. It's like a cruel, cosmic joke.

Such as it is, that girl lied to me, ran for the hills the moment I showed weakness and needed her the most, and cheated on me. Big surprise, right? With a red pill awareness now I can see how predictable that result was, but at the time I was blindsided by it. I never saw it coming. I couldn't understand how she could do such a thing when I'd invested so much in her, when I was so willing to give her all the things I'd always wanted most. I assumed she wanted the same things – men and women are the same, right? That's what the egalitarians tell us. I couldn't understand how those things could be so valueless to her that she would just throw it all away like that. She didn't value them at all.

On occasion I've suggested that men watch the movie *Blue Valentine*. You can check out the plot summary on IMDB, but you really need to watch the movie (on Netflix) to appreciate what I'm going to relate here. The main character suffers from the same romantic idealism and want for a perfected, mutually shared concept of love between himself and the single mother he eventually marries.

It follows along the same familiar theme of Alpha while single / Beta after marriage that most men experience in what they believe is their lot. More often than not the Alpha they believed their wives or LTR girlfriends perceived they were was really just a guy *who'd do* for their needs of whatever phase of maturity she found herself in.

By itself this would be enough for me to endorse the movie, but the story teaches a much more valuable lesson. What Dean (Ryan Gosling) represents is a man who idealistically buys the Blue Pill promise that men and women share a mutual love concept, independent of what their sexual strategies and innate dispositions prompt them to. Because of this misbelief Dean gives up on the burden of his performance. He drops his ambitions and relaxes with his Soul Mate girl, contenting himself in mediocrity, low ambitions and his idealistic belief in a woman sharing and sustaining his romanticized Blue Pill love ideal – in a word, "performancelessness."

He relaxes, lets his guard down and becomes the vulnerable man he was taught since birth that women would not only desire, but require for their false, performanceless notions of mutual intimacy. The men of this stripe who don't find themselves divorced from their progressively bored wives are often the ones who trade their ambitions and passions for a life of mediocrity and routine,… so long as the security blanket of what they believe is a sustainable, passable semblance of that love (but not desire) exists in their wives or girlfriends.

Their burden of performance is sedated so long as their women are reasonably comfortable or sedate themselves. That false sense of contentment is only temporary and leads to their own ruin or decay.

No Quarter Expected

I've since watched something similar happen to a friend not once but twice. It's textbook, standard shit.

Cultivating these unrequited beta aspects of somebody's character, if we did it on a mass scale, creates a society worth living in. It's a civilized society where these things are most possible and it's a truly worthwhile relationship where both parties regard each other this way and can full expect it to be reciprocated. It requires faith and trust, but we all know better. Our survival depends on knowing better, post sexual revolution. Women were never worthy of such trust and they're entirely incapable of it. They were never capable of it. We were just supposed to think they were and cultivate the better aspects of our natures in order to be worthy of them.

The ugly truth of it is that women were never worthy of us.

Women's sexuality doesn't reward justice or goodness – if it did, reciprocity would be the norm and none of us would be confused about relational equity. Women reward not goodness, but strength. And strength is amoral, meaning it can be either just or unjust, good or bad. The guy with strength can either be the villain or the hero – it makes no difference to women. They can't tell the difference and in truth don't care anyway.

There is a set of the Red Pill that subscribe to what I'd call a 'scorched earth' policy. It's very difficult to reconcile the opportunistic basis of women's Hypergamous natures with men's hopeful, idealistic want for a love that's independent from their performance burden. So the idea is again one of giving up. They say fuck it, women only respond to the most base selfishly individualistic, socio or psychopathic of men, so the personality they adopt is one that hammers his idealism flat and exaggerates his 'Dark Triad' traits beyond all believability. This assumes those traits aren't some act he's adopted to present the appearance.

It's almost a vengeful embrace of the most painful truths Red Pill awareness presents to us, and again I see why the scorched earth PUA (pickup artist) attitude would seem attractive. Women do in fact observably and predictably reward assholes and excessively dominant Alpha men with genuine desire and sexual enthusiasm. Agreeableness and humility in men has been associated with a negative predictor of sex partners.

The problem inherent in applying reciprocal solutions to gender relations is the belief that those relations are in any way improved by an equilibrium between both sexes' interests. Solution: turn hard toward the asshole energy. Once men understand the rules of engagement with women and they know Game well enough to capitalize on it, why *not* capitalize on that mastery of it?

The dangers of this are twofold. First, it lacks real sustainability and eventually becomes a more sexualized version of MGTOW. Secondly, "accidents" happen. MGTOWs will warn us that any interaction with a woman bears a risk of sexual harassment or false rape claims, but for the scorched earth guy a planned unplanned-pregnancy on the part of a woman attempting to lock down the guy she's sure is Alpha is far more likely to be his long term downfall. Emotional and provisioning liabilities for a child tends to pour cold water on the scorched earth guy.

It wouldn't be inaccurate to say that women are philosophically, spiritu-
ally, and morally stunted. They have a limited capacity for adherence to
higher ideals and this is why they don't know or care what actual justice
or goodness is. Like Schopenhauer said, they "mistake knowledge for its
appearance."

It took me a long time to be able to accept this. That is women's true
inferiority – and women are profoundly inferior. And I take no pleasure in
recognizing that, as if I'm somehow touting the superiority of team-men. It's
awful, in fact. Dealing with it is the ultimate burden of performance for us
as individual men, but also as a society. At some point we're simply going to
have to confront women's moral inferiority. If we look at our institutions, the
very same that are crumbling now all around us, we can see that previous
generations of men already figured this out. We just forgot what they knew.

So what's the answer? Is justice valuable for its own sake? All of us would
probably on some level want to be able to say yes and argue the case, but I
don't know if I can do so convincingly.

I'm with you on this, part of me thinks "Fuck this. It can't be like this." But
it is. I wish I had the answer.

There are men who attempt to redress the assumption that men feel some
necessity to be someone they really aren't. The Feminine Imperative is only
too willing to exploit this self-doubt by labeling men as existential posers and
their conventional masculinity is a 'mask' – a false charade – they put on to hide
the real vulnerability that lies beneath. Unfortunately many men accept this as
gospel. It's part of their Blue Pill upbringing and is an essential aspect of their
feminine 'sensitivity training' and gender loathing conditioning. When masculinity is only ever a mask men wear the only thing *real* about them is what *real*
women tell them it should be.

What we don't consider is the legitimacy of our need for strength, independence,
stoicism, and yes, emotional restraint. That need to be bulwark against women's
emotionality, that need to wear psychological armor against the Red Pill realities
of women's visceral natures is legitimate and necessary. If a man's vulnerability
is ever valuable it's because his display of it is so uncharacteristic of his normal
impenetrability. Women's contempt is palpable for the weak, vulnerability they
expect from lesser child-men – and a commensurate expectation of him to just
get that he needs to be strong. Women hate to have to explain to men how to be
masculine.

That's the inconsistency in women's Hypergamous nature and the narrative of the Feminine Imperative's messaging. Be sweet, open, vulnerable; it's OK to cry, ask for help, be sick and weakened, we're all equal and empathetic – all new books rules – but, Man Up, "what, you need your mommy?", assert yourself, the asshole is sexier than you, where's your self-discipline? – all old books expectations – but, your masculine identity is a mask you wear to hide the real you,......

I play many roles in the male life I lead today, and I've played many others in my past. I'm Rollo Tomassi in the manosphere, I'm a father to my daughter, a husband and lover to my wife, a brilliant artist and pragmatic builder of brands in my job, an adventure seeker when I'm on my snowmobile and a quiet contemplator of life and God when I'm fishing. All of those roles and more are as legitimate as I choose to make them. Do I have moments of uncertainty? Do I waiver in my resolve sometimes? Of course, but I don't let that define me because I know there is no real strength in relating that. And strength is all that matters.

The Red Pill Balance

Red Pill awareness is both a blessing and a curse. The trick is balancing your Red Pill expectations with your previous Blue Pill idealism. It's not a sin for you to want for an idealistic reality – that's what sets us apart from women's opportunism. You do yourself no favors in killing you idealistic, creative sense of wonderment of what could be. The trick is acknowledging that aspect of your male self.

If men did not hold heroism as a higher ideal, we wouldn't be here. If women did not hold survival as a higher ideal, we wouldn't be here.

Men's idealism and idealistic concepts of love are the natural counterbalance to women's pragmatic, Hypergamously rooted opportunism and opportunistic concepts of love and vice versa. Those differing concepts can be applied very unjustly and very cruelly, or very judiciously and honorably, but they are the reality of our existence.

Red Pill awareness isn't just about understanding women's innate natures and behaviors, it's also understanding your own male nature and learning how it fits in to that new awareness and living in a new paradigm.

Is something like justice valuable for its own sake? I'd say so, but that concept of justice must be tempered (or enforced) in a Red Pill understanding of what to expect from women and men. Red Pill awareness doesn't mean we should abandon our idealism or higher order aspirations, and it certainly doesn't mean we should just accept our lot in women's social frame because of it. It does mean we need to balance that idealism in as pragmatic a way with the realities of what the Red Pill shows us.

Idealism

When Neil Strauss was writing *The Game* there was an interesting side topic he explored towards the end of the book. He became concerned that the guys who were learning PUA skills and experiencing such success with women of a caliber they'd never experienced before would turn into what he called "Social Robots." The idea was one that these formerly Game-less guys would become Game automatons; mouthing the scripts, acting out the behaviors and meeting any countermanding behaviors or scripts from women with calculated and planned "if then" calibration contingencies.

The fear was that these Social Robots "weren't themselves", they were what Mystery Method, Real Social Dynamics, etc. were programing them to be and the relative success they experienced only reinforces that "robot-ness". My experience with guys from this blog, SoSuave and other forums has been entirely different. If anything most men transitioning to a Red Pill mindset tenaciously cling to the 'Just Be Yourself and the right girl will come along' mentality.

A strong resistance guys have to Red Pill awareness will always be the "faking it" and keeping it up effort they believe is necessary to perpetuate some nominal success with women. They don't want to indefinitely be someone they're not. It's not genuine to them and either they feel slighted for having to be an acceptable character for women's intimate attention or they come to the conclusion that it's impossible to maintain 'the act' indefinitely. Either way there's a resentment that stems from needing to change themselves for a woman's acceptance – who they truly are should be enough for the right woman.

I've written more than a few essays about this dynamic and the process of internalizing Red Pill awareness and Game, but what I want to explore here is the root idealism men retain and rely on when it comes to their unconditioned Game. A lot of what men invest their egos in with regard to the old set of books is rooted in men's innate idealism. In truth this Game is very much the result of the conditioning of the Feminine Imperative, but the idealistic concept of love that men hold fast to is what makes that conditioning so effective. Thus, men's unplugging becomes a conflict between conviction in old books idealism and new books opportunism that serves the feminine.

What's Your Game?

I've written before that every man has a Game. No matter who the guy is, no matter what his culture or background, every guy has some concept of what he believes is the best, most appropriate, most effective way to approach, interact with and progress to intimacy with a woman. How effective that "Game" really is is subjective, but if you asked any guy you know how best to go about getting a girlfriend he'll explain his Game to you.

Men in a Blue Pill mindset will likely parrot back what their feminine-primary conditioning had them internalize. *Just Be Yourself*, treat her with respect, don't objectify her, don't try to be someone you're not, are just a few of the conventions you'll get from a Blue Pill guy who is oblivious to the influence the Feminine Imperative has had on what he believes are his own ideas about how best to come to intimacy with a woman.

For the most part his beliefs in his methodology are really the deductive conclusions he's made by listening to the advice women have told him about how best to "treat a woman" if he wants to get with her. A Blue Pill mindset is characterized by identifying with the feminine, so being false is equated with anything counter to that identification.

When you dissect it, that conditioned Blue Pill / Beta Game is dictated by the need for accurate evaluation of men's Hypergamous potential for women. Anything that aids in women's evaluating a man's hypergamous potential to her is a tool for optimizing Hypergamy. The dynamics of social proof and preselection are essentially shortcuts women's subconscious uses to consider men's value to her. Likewise the emphasis Blue Pill Game places on men's 'genuineness' is a feminine conditioning that serves much the same purpose – better hypergamous evaluation. If men can be conditioned to be up front about who they are and what they are, if they internalize a mental point of origin that defers by default to feminine primacy, and if they can be socially expected to default to full and honest disclosure with women by just being themselves, this then makes a woman's hypergamous evaluation of him that much more efficient.

This is where most Blue Pill men fail in their Game; who they are is no mystery, their deference and respect is worthless because it's common and unmerited, and just who he is isn't the character she wants him to play with her. So even in the best of Blue Pill circumstances, a man is still playing at who he believes will be acceptable to the feminine. His genuineness is what best identifies with the feminine. Blue Pill / Beta Game is really an even more insidious version of social robotics; the script is internalized, the act *is* who he is. However, it's important to consider that this genuineness is still rooted in his idealistic concept of a mutual and reciprocal love.

What we need to consider here is that Beta Game stems from old books idealism being repurposed by the Feminine Imperative for its own usefulness. The message to men is this; hold fast to your idealism, but only express it in ways that are useful in terms of Hypergamous opportunism.

As with the opportunism that Hypergamy predisposes women to, men's idealistic concept of love stems from his want for genuineness and a want for what *could* be. I'd suggest that men's idealism is a natural extension of the burden of performance. From a Beta perspective, one where women are his mental point of origin, that burden is an unfair yoke; one to be borne out of necessity and ideally cast off if he could change the game. To the Alpha who makes himself his mental point of origin, that burden is a challenge to be overcome and to strengthen oneself by. In either respect, both seek an idealistically better outcome than what that burden represents to them.

In and of itself, a man's idealism can be a source of strength or his greatest weakness. And while unfettered Hypergamic opportunism has been responsible for many of women's worst atrocities with men, in and of itself Hypergamy is the framework in which the human species has evolved. Neither is good nor bad, but become so in how they are considered and how they are applied.

Men's idealistic concept of love is a buffer against women's opportunistic concept of love. When that idealism is expressed from a Beta mindset, women's opportunism dominates him and it's debilitating. When it's expressed from an Alpha mindset it supersedes her opportunism to the relationship's benefit.

Conditioned Idealism

If you want to use *Blue Valentine* (the movie) as an example again, the guy in the relationship abdicates all authority and ambition over to his wife's opportunism. He idealistically believes "love is all that matters" and has no greater ambition than to please her and 'just be himself', because his conditioning has taught him *that* should be enough. His Beta conditioning convinced his idealism that his wife would share in that idealistic concept of love despite his absence of performance. Consequently, she despises him for it. She's the defacto authority in the relationship and he slips into the subdominant (another child to care for) role rather than his ambitious Alpha idealism caring for her.

Now if a man's mindset is Alpha, willful idealism propels him to greater ambition, and to prioritize his concept of love as the dominant, and places himself as his mental point of origin. When a woman accepts it, you can see how this leads to the conventional model of masculinity. His idealism is enforced by how he considers it and how he applies it – irrespective of his woman's direct interests.

Men's idealistic concept of love can be the worst debilitation in a man's life when that idealistic nature is expressed from a supplicating Beta mentality. It will crush him when that idealism is all about a bill of goods he idealistically hopes a woman shares and will reciprocate with. This is predominantly how we experience idealism in our present cultural environment of feminized social primacy.

From an Alpha perspective that idealism is a necessary buffer against that same feminine opportunistic concept of love that would otherwise tear a Beta apart There was a time when men's idealistic concept of love was respected above the opportunistic (Hypergamy based) concept of love.

Under the old set of books, when a man's attractiveness (if not arousal) was based on his primary provisioning role, his love-idealism defined the intergender relationship. Thus, we still cling to notions of chivalry, traditional romance, conventional models of a love hierarchy, etc. These are old books ideals. The main reason I've always asserted that men are the True Romantics is due exactly to men's idealism as it translates to their concept of love.

There was a time when men's idealistic love concept pushed him to achievements that had social merit and were appreciated. Ovid, Shakespeare and the Beatles would not be the humanist icons they are if that idealism weren't a driving force in men and society. Likewise, women's, hypergamy-based concept of love, while cruel in its extremes, has nonetheless been a driving motivation for men's idealistic love as well as a filter for sexual selection.

Under the new set of books, in a feminine-centric social order, the strengths of that male idealism, love honor and integrity are made to serve the purpose of the Feminine Imperative. Men's idealistic love becomes a liability when he's conditioned to believe that women share their same idealism, rather than hold to an opportunistic standard.

Men believe that love matters for the sake of it. Women love opportunistically. The Red Pill aware man realizes that men are the "romantics pretending to be realists" and women; vice versa.

What we have today is generations of men conditioned and feminized for identifying with the feminine. These are the generations of men who were conditioned to internalize the equalist lie that men and women are the same and all is relative.

From that equalist perspective it *should* follow that both sexes would share a mutual concept of love – this is the misunderstanding that leads men to expect their idealism to be reciprocated and thus leads to their exploitation and self-abuse.

A man's idealism becomes his liability when he enters a woman's opportunistic frame still believing they both share a mutual concept of love. Men and women are different. Both sexes are incentivized to differing concepts of love by way of differentiated experiences, outlooks, in-looks and necessities. This isn't to say that both sexes cannot find a mutual, symbiotic reference for love between them, it's that both begin from differing concepts. The problem arises when men are conditioned to believe women share that concept and that women's conditions and experiences are the only valid definition of love.

And this then brings us back full circle to the confusion men experience when they attempt to balance the old books expectations of love with the new books, feminine-primary definition of love based on their own concepts of it. And all of this in the context of an equalism that neither acknowledges men's experience as individuated from women, nor that love could be anything but what a woman's experience necessitates it begin as and culminates as.

COMPLEMENTARITY

Over the years I've done my best to explain the differences between equalism and complementarity in *Equalism and Masculinity* (*Preventive Medicine*) and *Positive Masculinity vs. Equalism* (*The Rational Male*) My detailing the social dynamics and psychological influences men face in an equalist headspace has been a recurrent theme in many of my essays as well. On occasion I've made contrasting comparisons to Complementarity, but until the Red Pill Parenting series I hadn't gone into the detail I'd like to.

As many readers have already mentioned in the stories they've shared, it is usually the father who pushes their children towards a higher standard of success. This is critical for the child to develop into a successful adult that excels in society.

It is usually the mother who coos and coddles their children. This is also necessary, as it's vitally important for children to feel loved and accepted by their parents. This shows the necessity of the roles of both mothers and fathers in the development of children. If a child faces only criticism, it may have lasting effects on their self esteem. If a child is never criticized, they may never grow up into an adult.

The negative effects of too much coddling are so widespread, that we actually have sayings that illustrates it. "A ____ only a mother could love"

To understand the dynamic of complementarity first it's important to consider the theology behind egalitarianism. I tend to use the term *egalitarianism* and *equalism* interchangeably, but I do so because I see them both as stemming from the same tree of blank-slate humanism. In the first *Red Pill Parent* section I made the following case against of a single parent, single gender upbringing of children:

> *Parenting should be as collaborative and as complementary a partnership as is reflected in the complementary relationship between a mother and father.*

It's the height of gender-supremacism to be so arrogantly self-convinced as to deliberately choose to birth a child and attempt to raise it into the contrived ideal of what that "parent" believes the other gender's role ought to be.

This should put the institutionalized social engineering agenda of the Feminine Imperative into stark contrast for anyone considering intentional single parenthood. Now consider that sperm banks and feminine-specific fertility institutions have been part of normalized society for over 60 years and you can see that Hypergamy has dictated the course of parenting for some time now. This is the definition of social engineering.

The idea that a single mother is as co-effective as a father stems from the blank-slate belief that gender is a social construct rather than the physical and psychological manifestation of humans' evolved mental firmware. While the foundations of this blank-slate theory originated with John Locke in in the 17th century it would take the anima/animus theories of Carl Jung to cement egalitarian equalism into the popular conscious with regard to gender relations.

Tabula Rasa (blank-slate) refers to the epistemological idea that individuals are born without built-in mental content and that therefore all knowledge comes from experience or perception. With the scientific and technical advancements of the 20th and 21st centuries we now have a better understanding of how the human brains of men and women operate from a far more advanced perspective than Jung or Locke ever had knowledge of. To be fair, Jung's presupposition was one that humans possess innate potentials for both the masculine and feminine (thus the *"get in touch with your feminine side"* feminist trope for men), but those potentials derive from a presumed-accepted egalitarian base.

Yet still, from a larger social perspective, western(izing) culture still clings to the blank-slate models from Jung inspired by Locke and other tabula rasa thinkers of old.

Why is that? Why should it be that for all of our greater understanding of the biomechanics of the human body and its influences on behavior that the greater whole of society persists in the belief that men and women possess co-equal gender proficiencies based on an outdated, largely disproved Tabula Rasa model?

I would argue that the more obvious and practical model of evolved gender differences presents an uncomfortable proposition of biological determinism to people conditioned to believe gender is a nurture, not nature, proposition.

One of the key elements Jung introduced into western culture's popular consciousness is the theory of anima and animus; that each individual, irrespective of sex, possesses greater or lesser degrees of association and manifested behavior of masculine and feminine psychological affiliations. In 2017, when you hear a 6 year old girl tell a 6 year old boy "you need to get in touch with your feminine side" in order to get him to comply with her wishes for him, you can begin to understand the scope to which this idea has been internalized into society's collective consciousness.

So long and so thoroughly has this theory been repeated and perpetuated that we can scarcely trace back its origins – it's simply taken as fact that men and women possess varying degrees of masculine and feminine energies. First and second wave feminism founded their psychological premises of gender on Jung's ideas and so evolved the reasonings for a push towards the social feminization we know today. The seeds for the feminine-centrism we take for granted today were planted by a Swiss psychiatrist in the early 1900's who really wanted to nail his female patients.

It's important to consider Jung's bi-gender individualities within the individual person in context with Locke's Tabula Rasa theory because in tandem they constitute the basis of the egalitarian equalism which feminism and our present feminine-primary conditioning rely upon. To the modern egalitarian mind, inequalities in social dynamics, gender conflicts and economic disparities are the result of a deliberate (if not malicious) intent on the part of individuals to limit the presumably 'equal' potentials of others. Social ills are the conflict between the selfish need of the one versus the equalized needs of the many.

There is very little headspace given to the material, innate, mechanics that make up the condition of the individual. Natural talent, innate ability, in-born predispositions, and physical and adaptive advantages stemming from evolved differences – whether a boon or a burden – are either disqualified or marginalized in an egalitarian mindset. The egalitarian, while very humanistic, leans almost entirely on the *learned* behavior model of human development. It's Tabula Rasa, social constructivism, and the zeroed-out-at-birth content of the individual is filled by the influence of a society that is corrupted by those who don't agree with an idealized egalitarian imperative.

Complementarity

However, a second model exists, that of Complementarity. Complementarity acknowledges the importance of the inborn differences between the sexes that egalitarianism marginalizes or outright denies exist while recognizing and embracing the strengths and weaknesses those differences represent.

There are many well documented, peer reviewed, scientific studies on the neurological differences between men and women's brain structure. The easiest evidence of these differences is the cyclic nature of women's sexuality (versus men's always-on sexuality) and the neurological/hormonal influences on beliefs, behaviors and the rationalizations for those behaviors prompted by the innate drive to optimize Hypergamy.

Women experience negative emotions differently from men. The male brain evolved to seek out sex before food. And while our feminine-centric social order insists that, in the name of equalism, boys should be forced to learn in the same modality as that of girls, the science shows that boys brains are fundamentally wired to learn differently.

Yet, stark differences exist in the wiring of male and female brains. In a 2013 PNAC brain study, maps of neural circuitry show that on average women's brains are highly connected across the left and right hemispheres, in contrast to men's brains, where the connections were typically stronger between the front and back regions.

Ragini Verma, a neurological researcher at the University of Pennsylvania, said the greatest surprise was how much the findings supported old stereotypes, with men's brains apparently wired more for perception and co-ordinated actions, and women's for social skills and memory, making them better equipped for multitasking.

"If you look at functional studies, the left of the brain is more for logical thinking, the right of the brain is for more intuitive thinking. So if there's a task that involves doing both of those things, it would seem that women are hardwired to do those better," Verma said. "Women are better at intuitive thinking. Women are better at remembering things. When you talk, women are more emotionally involved – they will listen more."

"I was surprised that it matched a lot of the stereotypes that we think we have in our heads. If I wanted to go to a chef or a hairstylist, they are mainly men."

Ironically, in an egalitarian gender-neutral social order, a college professor publicly suggesting that men are more adept at mathematical thinking gets him fired from a lengthy tenure, but when a female researcher suggests the same she's rewarded with professional accolades and grant money.

As you might expect, this study focuses primarily on the triumphant advantages of the female brain structure, but the studies themselves are revealing of the empirical evidence that men and women are not the functional equals that egalitarianism would insist we are.

The scans showed greater connectivity between the left and right sides of the brain in women, while the connections in men were mostly confined to individual hemispheres. The only region where men had more connections between the left and right sides of the brain was in the cerebellum, which plays a vital role in motor control. "If you want to learn how to ski, it's the cerebellum that has to be strong," Verma said. Details of the study are published in the journal Proceedings of the National Academy of Sciences.

"It's quite striking how complementary the brains of women and men really are," Ruben Gur, a co-author on the study, said in a statement. "Detailed connection maps of the brain will not only help us better understand the differences between how men and women think, but it will also give us more insight into the roots of neurological disorders, which are often sex-related."

These distinct neurological differences between men and women are evidence of a an evolved intersexual complementarity that has manifested in both the personal and social dynamic of intergender relations for millennia. Conventional gender roles where there is a defined interdependence between the sexes is reflective of precisely the hardwired "stereotypes" researchers were so shocked to discover in men and women's neural wiring.

Talents and Deficits

I'm often asked what the complementarian model looks like and it's all too easy to not want to fall into the perceived trap in defining gender roles for men and women as they've been for centuries before our own era. Conventionally feminine women and masculine men are 'shocking' stereotypes to a society steeped and conditioned to accept the egalitarian model as the norm. The simple fact is that equality is only defined by the conditions and environmental circumstance that make something equal or unequal. It is the task, the challenge, presented to either sex that makes inherent ability an advantage or a disadvantage.

Men and women are biologically, physiologically, psychologically, hormonally and sexually different. This presents a very difficult proposition to an egalitarian mindset – men and women are simply better suited for, better wired, better enabled and more physically capable of succeeding in different tasks, different environments, different socialization, different mental or emotional demands as those circumstances dictate.

We simply evolved for a symbiosis between the sexes; the strengths of one compensate for the weakness of the other. Depending on the challenge presented, yes, this means that in our complementarity the differences between a man and a woman are going to be *unequal*. Much of the gender discord our present society suffers is due primarily to the intentional rejection of this evolved, symbiotic complementarity and its replacement with the fantasy of a blank-slate, uninfluenced, independently sustaining equalism. From the egalitarian mindset, the genders are presumed to be self-sustaining and independent, thus men and women simply have no need for the other. Or, in a feminine-primary social order, men become superfluous to women – the prime agent in society.

Though egalitarians will argue it does, complementarity doesn't imply a universal superiority of one gender above the other. Rather, depending on the task at hand, one sex will be better predisposed to accomplishing it. Furthermore, this isn't to say that the gender-specific deficiencies of one gender cannot be overcome by learning, practice and brain plasticity to achieve the same ends – it is to say that men and women's brains, and the task-specific adaptations in them, predispose them to being better capable of achieving them.

Fighting Nature

I've outlined the process of how the Feminine Imperative conditions men to embrace their "feminine sides" and create generations of ready-made Betas. Most Blue Pill men will fail to identify with the more masculine specificity I've outlined above. It's important to remember that learning to be better at non-gender specificity in an attempt to override this natural gender-wiring is not always a voluntary effort on the part of a person – especially when egalitarian Mom and Dad are in on the conditioning of their offspring.

When we see the recent popular social effort to embrace transsexual acceptance what we're being asked to do is accept a learning process that countermands a male or female's evolved neural architecture by presuming that gender is strictly a social construct. Brain plasticity is a marvel of evolution, but it is subject to external manipulation and the ideologies of those doing the manipulating.

Natural proclivities can be overridden by learning. There's been a criticism of western public education's push to force boys to learn like girls – we treat boys like they are defective girls. This is a prime example of not just a social engineering effort, but an effort in reprogramming boys to override their natural, neurological maleness. Thus, they become less effective girls because they are required to think, emote and react in way their brains never predisposed them to.

Likewise there is a popular push to encourage girls to adopt male modalities of thinking – thus, masculinizing women. In the hopes to make mathematics and technology fields more gender-equal egalitarian society will make special compensation and establish exclusive academic rewards for girls who teach themselves to override their intrinsic mental proficiencies and find intrinsic reward in adopting the proclivities of boys. Male sexism is always the presumed foil for women's natural disinterest in conventionally male proclivities.

The egalitarian mindset simply denies the foundational truths that decades of evolutionary psychology, evolutionary biology and anthropological research indicate about our present state of intersexual relations. In so doing, they reject a natural complementary model and embrace an ideologically egalitarian one. Their mistake is presuming that evo-psych necessitates a biological determinism and thereby absolves an individual of personal responsibility for their behavior. It does not, but it does provide a framework that more accurately describes the natural mental state, sexual strategies and social environment in which men find themselves with women.

When you hear or read the trope that "women are just as sexual as men" what's being related to you is founded in the same egalitarian root that teaches us to believe that "women are just as good at fathering as any man". All are equal, but men's sexuality seems like a boon that egalitarian women would like to adopt. Thus, if a conventionally male proclivity seems like an advantage, egalitarianism will fluidly redefine what is equal and what is not according to what benefits the Feminine Imperative best – or at least perceptively so.

One reason egalitarianism is an appealing cover story for feminism is because its primary goal is leveling the sexual competition playing field for all women to optimize Hypergamy at the expense of men's own sexual strategy interests. If all is equal, if men's basic biological impulses are reduced to shamed criminality or an illness, if women can expect men to be aroused by their perceived value of their self-defined self-worth, then all material and physiological deficits can be effectively dismissed.

Under the guise of egalitarianism, feminism has effected feminine social dominance for over half a century now.

Likewise egalitarianism is appealing to evo-psych detractors because a belief in egalitarianism should mean that men can escape their burden of performance.

The presumption is that if the more intrinsic, ephemeral aspects of men's higher-order thinking and personal worth is appreciated as a sexual attraction, then all deficiencies in meeting his naturalistic burden of performance can be rescinded. Game, physique, personality, status, success, achievement, essentially all of the most conventional aspects of masculinity that make a man an attractive mate choice are superseded by his equalist belief system. And this is sold to him as the new order upon which women should find him attractive. Men adopt equalism because it presumably excuses him from having to perform for a woman's intimate acceptance.

Complementarity is the evolved interdependence between the sexes and it's been a responsible element of how the human race has risen to be the apex species on this planet, but it doesn't ensure an optimal breeding schedule for either sex. So long as men and women are mired in a denial of the evolved psychological differences between the sexes, their only alternative is to embrace egalitarianism.

The reason feminism hates the Red Pill – in its concrete sense – is because it more accurately predicts human behavior than feminism and equalism have ever been capable of. A return to a true complementarity model for the sexes is part of a Red Pill awareness. Adopting this model is key to Game and successful interacting with the opposite sex.

THE RED PILL LENS

One of the results of becoming Red Pill aware is a larger, meta "awareness" of the feminine centric social order we live in today. On this side of the Red Pill, and a bigger understanding of intersexual dynamics, it's almost routine for me now to filter what's presented to me in popular media, social doctrine or even casual conversation through a *Red Pill Lens*.

Whether it's the latest pop hit lyrics of a song my daughter is listening to in the bathroom, the latest movie or book, or just listening to someone rattle off an old Blue Pill trope in casual conversation, my sensitivity to how thoroughly immersed in feminine-centric narratives our (western) society has become is overwhelming.

I've had guys in the manosphere joke with me that having this 'lens' is like having the special glasses that let you see the alien/zombies and propaganda in the campy 80s movie *They Live*. While I get a laugh out of this I also have to think that those glasses never really come off. So when the holiday season comes around this awareness manifests itself more for me since I'm generally reacquainting myself with family and friends who are themselves immersed in this Matrix and don't realize they're mouthing the meme's and social focus of a feminine centric order.

I think it's kind of ironic that during the holidays we're expected to lock horns with our relatives over the latest social generational, political or ideological differences, yet these all take place in a common, feminized social narrative. Your uncle may not agree with you politically, but he'll slap you on the back while you both drink a beer and say, "Women 'eh? I guess we'll never figure 'em out" and expect you to have some common agreement with him in spite of those differences.

I bring this up here because it was due to this seasonal Red Pill awareness that I was better prepared to appreciate the holiday classic, *It's a Wonderful Life* from a Red Pill perspective.

I'd just returned from a work trip the week before Christmas and my daughter informed me that the movie was being shown in our local metroplex theater on Christmas eve. Of course, I'd seen it before on TV with all the intermittent commercials, and remembered how tedious I thought it was (it's a pretty long movie for 1946), but she insisted and I wanted to do something Christmas-ish with the family. I've never watched the movie start to finish, and when I did pick up scenes on TV during Christmas time back in the day, it was long before I had any Red Pill inclination.

Needless to say I was shocked (pleasantly) by how thoroughly 'Red Pill' I found it. If you want to see what a pre-sexual revolution gender dynamic is like, this is your movie. Yes, it's idyllic, but its idealism is founded in a social order, an '*old books*' social order, that reveals what our new feminine-primary social order is today. It shows you what we've become, but unfortunately the greater whole of our contemporary society lack the special glasses to really appreciate this distinction.

Some notable scenes were:

- George Bailey, the cab driver Ernie and the cop Bert ogle the sexy Violet Bick after she flirts with George and just flows down a busy street to be checked out all the more by every man on the street. In modern terms these men are all guilty of sexual harassment, but in 1928 (the film's beginning) and viewed from a 1946 perspective of that time, there is nothing harassing about it. It's *de rigueur*, and she enjoys the attention. Had this scene been considered in our era the catcalls would be nothing short of sexual harassment worthy of protesting the movie.

- The family interaction between George, his brother Harry, and their father with Ma Bailey just prior to Harry's graduation party; there is matronly deference to their mother, but both of the boys are being boys and there is no expectation for them to 'settle down'. Both the brothers are naturally and effortlessly, cocky & funny with the maid and their mother. This isn't a forced attitude, it comes off as both positively masculine and fun at the same time. Also, their father is the respected head of the household, both by virtue of his social status and integrity as well as his position as 'father'. Needless to say, he's never ridiculed as the buffoon he'd be portrayed as on a post-sexual revolution social order, and in fact dispenses a wisdom that benefits George later in life.

- After the graduation party George and Mary walk home in the odd dry clothes they were able to find after having fallen into the school pool. Mary is in a bathrobe and George in a football outfit. This flirtation and interaction is perhaps one of the best examples I can think of as an old order form of

Game. George is cocky, funny, confident, ambitious, playfully teasing and yet still conscious of Mary's perception of him as he effortlessly delivers a positive masculine vibe. Again, it's idyllic, and men being the true romantics will want to believe such receptivity could actually take place without any confusion of mixed signals with an idealized, *Quality Woman* woman like Mary, but it's the atmosphere and the attitude of expecting Mary to respond to George's delivery that belies the era this scene and story was written in. Nothing seems forced at all, and we don't expect Mary to match George's masculine Game with one of her own feminine-empowered forms of Game. She doesn't try to 'one-up' George or prove her moxie by acting like a man herself as we'd expect from a feminized Hollywood script today. There is no thought of making Mary into the *Strong Independent Woman®* trope, but she exemplifies strength in her role as a woman in deferring to her man and a devoted mother. From a Red Pill perspective, we want a gal like Mary to exist, but you wont find her in 2017.

These were just a few scenes I thought stood out, but this film is an essay in the old order social structure a lot of well meaning Red Pill advocates would like to believe is still a possibility today.

I'm often asked the question whether an Alpha man could also be a provider. A lot of criticism of the manosphere is that Alpha men are being painted as caricatures of cads, assholes and bad boy players women want to bang as part of their Hypergamous mating protocol. Betas are the opposite of this; good for provisioning only – cuckolds to be used for parental investment with only a perfunctory servicing of mediocre 'duty' sex as an intermittent reward to keep him pulling the cart. Thus, *'Beta Provider'* becomes an easy label for those men.

If there are caricatures of Alpha and Beta being drawn I'd suggest this is due more to women and their comfort with an embrace of *Open Hypergamy* and men deductively modeling their gender expectations as a result. That said, the criticism is not wrong. It is entirely possible for an archetypal Alpha Man to be an upstanding member of society, provide for his family and be well respected both by his peers and his wife (or the women in his life). The character of George Bailey is an old order example of exactly this kind of man.

In our era women have an unprecedented facility for providing for their own security needs, but that doesn't eliminate the root level, emotional need for optimizing Hypergamy with a man who is an Alpha provider. For the most part women simply don't expect to find this optimization in the same man. There are men they want to fuck and men they want to consolidate monogamy with, and finding this satisfaction in the same man is so rare, so unexpected and so unlooked for that his character becomes unbelievable. The George Bailey of 1928 is an unbelievable character in 2017.

As I've illustrated in many a prior essay, Alpha is a state of mind, not a demographic. Just because the Alpha energy of an older order scoundrel will get him laid without trying doesn't preempt a woman from being aroused by, and attracted to a George Bailey archetype. Context is king of course, but what matters is that self-interested Alpha mindset. The dialog between George and Mary when they're first getting together is textbook pickup artist Cocky & Funny Game, with a natural, unforced Amused Mastery on George's part.

While many a convicted felon possesses an Alpha mindset, and receives women's sexual interests as a result of it, I'd still encourage men to use that Alpha energy to a positive, self-benefiting effect. It is entirely possible to direct an Alpha energy in a pro-social manner. In this era, the natural default is to play the Sigma, Lone Wolf role with respect to how we apply our Red Pill awareness. Adopting the role of the anti-hero is easy when we see how effective Dark Triad personality traits trigger women's arousal and attraction.

That said, I would also offer that a positive Alpha mindset can still be effective insofar as a man is diligent in maintaining himself as his mental point of origin.

So now the questions I'll put to you is what Red Pill observations do you find unignorable in contemporary society? It's always going to be dangerous to attempt to make others aware of this perception, but do you try anyway?

Do you see examples of the old order as I have in *It's a Wonderful Life*? Understanding the idealisms inherent in it, what other examples of this old order to you know? What media or aspects of popular culture do you see your old Blue Pill conditioning manifested in? Popular music is an easy example, but are you sensitive to more the more subtle way this condition still persists even after you're become Red Pill aware?

Alpha providers, while being an idealistic character, can exist, but are they realistic? I'd propose that embodying this role has become one of being seen too readily as a Beta by women due to the unbelievability of it. Does men's romantic nature predispose them to thinking they can adequately fulfill this role? Does that romanticism expect women to be receptive and appreciative of it? Is that expectation based on investing in Relational Equity?

MYTH OF THE 'GOOD' GUY

For as often as I've made my best attempts to define what I believe constitutes feminine Hypergamy in all my writing, it seems that critics of the Red Pill, and even newer, well-meaning Red Pill advocates, are beginning to think of Hypergamy as some convenient trope that *manosphereans* refer to when they want to explain away some annoyingly female trait.

Is she shit testing you? Must be Hypergamy.
She broke a nail? Must be Hypergamy.

There is a very real want for understanding things in as simplistic a solution as possible, but feminine Hypergamy isn't a dynamic that lends itself to a simple definitions. One of the reasons the early proponents of PUA ran into issues with legitimizing their ideas was due to so many of their 'students' seeking out easily digestible answers to solve their *'girl problems'*. As I laid out in *Dream Girls and Children with Dynamite* from the first book, these guys wanted the TL;DR (too long; didn't read) footnote version of what to do in order to get to the silver bullet, magic formula part of the lesson to either get with their dream girl or *"start fucking hot bitches"*.

It is exactly this mentality that's now causing such frustration in understanding Hypergamy and seeing how it works, not just in individual women's personal decisions, but as a societally influencing force of the Feminine Imperative. Hypergamy is not a *"math is hard"* dynamic, but because it requires a comprehensive (and evolving) understanding it seems like the go-to throwaway answer to women's behaviors and mental schema to men (usually new to the Red Pill) without the patience to really invest themselves into grasping it.

I've defined Hypergamy so often on my blog that if you search the term "hypergamy" in Google, the *Rational Male* blog is the number two return below the Wikipedia definition. As I wrote my way through the second volume of the *Rational Male* book I found that a concise understanding of feminine Hypergamy is vital to grasping so much of the social and psychological dynamics that are a result of it. Every PUA technique, every common frustration MGTOW experience, and every gender-biased social injustice MRAs set themselves against, all find their roots in feminine Hypergamy, women's pluralistic sexual strategy and the social and legal efforts employed to ensure maximal feminine social primacy in optimizing Hypergamy.

Looks vs. Character (Game)

In many of my blog posts, the topic of discussion in the comment threads eventually finds its way back to the basics of Looks versus Character (or Game, depending on your perspective of how learning affects character). Only the discussions over what constitutes 'Alpha' in a man are so contentious as the importance with which women prioritize physical arousal in men.

First and foremost it's important to understand the part that women's biologies play in influencing Hypergamy and how women's biology is more or less the point of origin for how they conduct their sexual strategy. To review, I'll ask that readers refer to the first chapter in my second book, *Preventive Medicine. Your Friend Menstruation*, but the basis of women's sexual pluralism is found in the natural attraction predispositions that women experience as a result of (healthy) ovulation. Also known as *ovulatory shift*.

In her up cycle (proliferative) phase of ovulation, women are psychologically and behaviorally motivated to prioritize physical arousal with more masculinized men above all other breeding considerations. In her down cycle (post-ovulation, luteal phase) women are similarly motivated to prioritize comfort, rapport, and long term security to ensure parental investment and benefit survival.

What I've described here, in as brief a fashion, is the foundation of Ovulatory Shift. There exists over a decade's worth of experimental psychological and biological evidence supporting this theory. Due to biological and psychological influence, women become subliminally predisposed to behaviors which maximize fertility odds with the best available breeding opportunity, and maximize the best potential for long term provisioning and parental investment.

Whether this behavior is manifested in a preference for more masculinized male faces and body type, greater ornamentation and lower vocal intonation for women during ovulation, or a predisposition for more comforting, nurturing and supportive male characteristics during her luteal phase, the end result is optimizing Hypergamy, and ultimately reproduction. From an evolutionary standpoint this is the basis of women's dualistic sexual strategy euphemistically referred to as Alpha Fucks and Beta Bucks in the manosphere.

For further reading on Ovulatory Shift, see the research of *Martie Haselton*.

Arousal vs. Attraction

Females only receive two quantities of evolutionary value from males – direct benefits (observed in long-term mating, with implications for the survival of offspring), and genetic benefits (observed through indications of physical attractiveness in her mate). And since females can receive genetic benefits outside of a monogamous social contract or marriage (i.e. through extra-paired sexual encounters), and no longer need rely upon mates for the survival of their offspring, there is no pressure for them to compromise on holding out for an unlikely (long-term) fantasy partner.

This current social pattern increases male variance in mating success, because female sexual choices always tend towards small male breeding populations (narrow range of male phenotypes), while male 'preferences' are inclusive of a broad range in female variance.

One of the main contentions this understanding kind of needles with is that, as described, modern conveniences of female social empowerment (actual or imagined) discounts the need for Hypergamic assurances of long term security. I'm not so willing to accept an overall disregard for the provisioning aspect (Beta Bucks) – you're not going to reprogram millennia of psychologically evolved firmware overnight – but in discounting this need, the characteristics for which women would seek out a male exemplifying the best long-term security are deemphasized if not unconsidered entirely.

If you read through any woman's online dating profile you undoubtedly come across some variation of what's described as the "483 bullet point checklist" of stated prerequisites a man must possess in order for her to consider him a viable candidate for her intimacy. While I don't think there are quite that many items on the checklist, you'll find a host of common-theme personal qualities a guy has to have in order to "be her boyfriend" – confident (above all), humorous, kind, intelligent, creative, decisive, sensitive, respectful, spiritual, patient,..

The point is that all of these characteristics that women list as being 'attractive' have absolutely no bearing on how sexually, physically, 'arousing' a woman finds a man. While Game and personality can certainly accentuate arousal, all of these esoteric personal qualities have no intrinsic "'vagina tingle" value if a man isn't an arousal prospect to begin with.

The confusion that most Beta men make is presuming that what women list as being necessarily 'attractive' *is* what makes him 'arousing'. So when he models himself (often over the course of a lifetime) to personally identify with this checklist of attractive prerequisites he's often frustrated and angered when all of that personal development makes for little difference when a woman opts to regularly fuck men of a better physical standard. It's duplicity of a sort, but it is also a strategy of deliberate confusion.

It may not be a woman's conscious plan, but this deliberate confusion makes the best pragmatic sense to effect an optimized Hypergamy. Remember that Hypergamy is not just Alpha Fucks, it's also Beta Bucks ... if a bit delayed in her life in order to maximize Alpha Fucks. So when a woman describes what she finds "attractive" in a man this list will include all of the above bullet point characteristics because they *"sound right"* – because they shine her in the best light, yes, but also because in being so concerned she imputes the idea that she's following the 'right' plan of looking for a *good* man to have a future with, and raise kids with. That is the impression we are supposed to be left with in spite of all the behavioral evidence that tells us the real, evolved, reasons for those behaviors.

Then and Now

This is going to sound like I'm glossing myself, but bear with me – I can remember how effortless sex used to be for me when I was in my 20's. I had sex outdoors, in cars, hotel rooms, in hot tubs, in the steam room of an all women's gym (after hours), I even got after it with a girlfriend in the balcony of a church in Los Angeles once (again after hours, no one around, only for convenience I assure you). Mostly I didn't have a dime to my name, but I still had one of two fuck-buddies who would literally come to the bedroom window of my studio to fuck me in the morning once or twice a week before I went off to the community college I was going to.

The point is there was no pretense of 'attraction' being anything other than a girl and I enjoying ourselves then. There was no 'checklist' of acceptable prequalifications for intimacy. The providership necessity that dictates a need for long-term consideration wasn't even an afterthought; in other words, the Beta Bucks / Character / Integrity aspect of Hypergamy that women publicly claim is a deal breaker for real intimacy was prioritized far below Alpha Fucks sexual urgency.

You can say these were just the types of girls I was getting with at the time, but courtesy of social media, I assure you, you would think these women would never have had that capacity now. They were all "sooo different when they were in college."

It's not until after a woman's *Epiphany Phase* at around the time she becomes aware of her SMV decline that she begins to consider making that Beta Bucks checklist any kind of prerequisite for sex and intimate partnering. However, this epiphany isn't the sudden revelation women would like men to believe it is.

For the life of me I can't remember where I read the link, but I was reading a 'Dear Abby' sort of advice seeking article from a young girl (early 20's) who was exasperated over finding the "perfect guy" only she couldn't 'get with him now'. Her words were something like "He's so great, awesome personality, funny, in love with me, supportive, etc., but I wish I could freeze him in time so he'd be the same guy and waiting for me when I turn 29 or 30."

On some level of consciousness, like most women, she knows the dictates of what her own Hypergamy is predisposing her to. She knows she'll eventually need that 'perfect' supportive, in-love guy to live out the long-term aspect of her Hypergamy with,...after she's exhausted her short term breeding potential with men who better embody the Alpha Fucks dictates of her Hypergamy.

Arousal Preparation vs. Provisioning Preparation

The balance between women's short term breeding impulse and the long term provisioning needs Hypergamy predisposes them to now strongly favors the Alpha sex side of that optimization. We see this realization in otherwise high status, high functioning men today. The emphasis on becoming an attractive mate is no longer the old books preoccupation with status and success, but men pursuing an optimal physique.

In *Open Hypergamy* I made a case for the aspect of an 'old order' of Beta Provisioning being a previously 'attractive' element for women's determining long term suitability with a man, and that this old order was being replaced with other, extrinsic means of ensuring a woman's security needs. Whether by social funding, or by indenturing men to provide for women's wellbeing through other social conventions (alimony, child support) the effect is an imbalance between the dual nature of women's sexual strategy.

However, I also feel it goes beyond just the social element now. Men are still confused by a feminine conditioning that wants to 'freeze' him in time in order to be the dutiful 'perfect' guy, ready to be thawed out and ready to serve the Feminine Imperative at a woman's convenience.

While it's still convenient, a man must be conditioned to confuse him that 'attraction' qualities *are* 'arousal' qualities in order to have him ready to be 'perfect' at his appointed time – and it is women who need to believe for themselves that this is what they think should be true.

The Myth of the 'Good' Guy

In the beginning of one of my earliest essays, *Schedules of Mating*, I briefly refer to the ideally balanced guy who would satisfy the optimization purpose of women's Hypergamy:

> *There are methods and social contrivances women have used for centuries to ensure that the best male's genes are selected and secured with the best male provisioning she's capable of attracting. Ideally the best Man should exemplify both, but rarely do the two exist in the same male (particularly these days) so in the interest of achieving her biological imperative, and prompted by an innate need for security, the feminine as a whole had to develop social conventions and methodologies (which change as her environment and personal conditions do) to effect this.*

> *There is a dichotomy that exists for men in this respect, which really has no parallel for women.*

I am aware of certain (formerly Red Pill) writers who promote the archetype of a 'Good' guy as some role for men to ideally aspire to. The 'Alpha Cad' archetype must necessarily become the 'douchebag' caricature of an overtly distasteful hyper-masculinity (for men less able to embody it) and yet, the opposite caricature of the doormat, supplicating 'Beta Dad' is equally distasteful and certainly untenable when we consider that 'attractive' qualities are never necessarily 'arousing' qualities.

So the archetype of the 'Good' guy is offered up as some sort of livable, compromised ideal. If men could aspire to embody the best of the Alpha and temper that with what they define themselves as the best of the Beta, well then he'd be the 'perfect' catch for any woman of course.

The problem with this 'Good Guy', best of both men, myth is not because men can't or wouldn't want to try to balance those halves to accommodate women's Hypergamy for them, but simply because women neither want nor expect that balance in the same man to begin with. We've reached a point in our socio-sexual environment where not only do women not need, or need less, the old order 'good provider' they also compartmentalize men into sets of Alpha and Beta. The guy they want to fuck and the guy they see as "relationship material".

The man who rides the cusp of both influences isn't believable.

It comes back to the *Just Get It* principle for women – any guy who needs to make a concerned effort to become what he expects women will want from him to be 'the perfect guy' doesn't *get it*. They want Mr. Perfect because that is who he already is, without having to be told, without making a conscious effort.

I mentioned above that there really is no parallel for this in women (the Madonna / Whore dichotomy not withstanding), but allow me to point out that there is no concerted parallel social effort on the part of women in which women prompt each other to become a 'Good Girl' in order to satisfy the ideals of men. If anything a hostile opposite resistance to this is most true – women are conditioned never to do anything to better please a man. Yes, they do so anyway, but this is in spite of that conditioning.

Women neither expect nor want a 'Good Guy' because he's not believable, and his genuineness is always doubtable. That may sound jaded, but throw away any idea of being a 'Good Guy' balance of Alpha and Beta, because the Beta side of 'good' is so reinforced and common in men that it's become the default template for women's perception of you.

There is no mid point that is sustainable, there is only the man whose genuine concern is first for himself, the man who prepares and provisions for himself, the man who maintains *Frame* to the point of arrogance because that's who he is and what he genuinely merits. There is only the Man who improves his circumstance for his own benefit, and then, by association and merit, the benefit of those whom he loves and befriends. That's the Man who Just Gets It.

Up the Alpha

I've been taken to task about this assertion in the past. The idea that the 'Good Guy', the guy who is the perfect balance of Alpha Fucks and Beta Bucks is an unsustainable myth always rubs guys the wrong way. Particularly the guys who've taken to heart that they can mold themselves into this feminine-fantasy ideal.

Do you disagree that the best option for a woman is a man with both alpha and beta traits?

That is to say, wouldn't a man with great genes/physicality/confidence as well as financial stability and kindness be the "perfect man" for a woman?

Wouldn't that satisfy both her short term and long term mating strategies?

I get the sense that it is in absence of men that have both traits that women seek out these different qualities in separate men under short and long term circumstances.

This want for the perfect amalgam of hot Alpha and parentally invested Beta is literally hard-coded into women's brains and endocrine system. From the most rudimentary level, the conflict that Hypergamy instills in women is due to this *want* of fusing together the arousing Alpha with the attractive Beta in the same man. Thus was women's pluralistic sexual strategy evolved.

The problem that confounds Hypergamy is that the arousing Alpha and the attractive Beta rarely exist in the same male, at the same time, yet also at the most opportune time for women to appreciate and capitalize on it. By this I mean that as women proceed through their peak SMV years, they place higher priorities and higher mating value upon predominately Alpha traits. These are the *'fuck me now'* Party Years, and Alpha seed far out-values Beta need.

As I wrote in *Schedules of Mating*, on a macro level this translates into a proactive form of cuckoldry. Even if it doesn't result in a pregnancy, the latent urgency in a woman's peak is to *'get the seed first, find the provider later'* (i.e. protracted cuckoldry).

The fantasy for women of course is to 'tame the savage Alpha' and convert him into a parentally invested partner by encouraging Beta traits in him as he matures, and hopefully prospers. This is a prime fantasy in most romance literature; the otherwise unmemorable woman becomes the object of an untamed Alpha wild-man for whom she is his only source of civilizing.

Many a thwarted single mommy knows the unfortunate outcome of attempting to 'fix' their Bad Boy Alpha into the Good Dad Father, but this is the emphasis, assuming a woman pauses long enough to invest in one particular Alpha during her peak years. The base strategy is to maintain that hot Alpha arousal, while developing him into a more attractive Beta provider while still sustaining that Alpha sexual urgency.

As a woman approaches the downturn of her SMV, that hypergamic urgency shifts to favor Beta providership traits as the prospect of long term security alters the priorities of her Hypergamy. Now the script changes to one favoring the nice, dependable, and necessarily resourceful man with all the attractive features she needs for a commitment to long term security. It's not that she doesn't still become aroused by the physicality and charisma of a predominately Alpha male (particularly in her proliferate menstrual phase), but she is more aware of the balance between her lessened ability to attract that man (post-Wall) and the need to pair-bond with a man who can provide for her and her offspring. Women will mitigate this arousal-attraction imbalance with their own forms of pornography or self-initialized rationalization about their 'deeper maturity', but in essence the doubt that Hypergamy seeds in them has to be held in check either through self-repression or by dread of loss.

There is also the fantasy for women in this instance to hope that their predominately Beta partner will "Man Up", *Just Get It* on his own and develop more arousing Alpha traits as he matures. The base strategy here is to maintain the sweet Beta provider attraction, while developing him into a more arousing Alpha as her needs demand.

Beta with a Side of Alpha

To compound this confusion we also have to bear in mind that women themselves believe, or want to believe that this perfect balance of man is something within the real of possibility for them.

They want to believe that the true '*Manicorn*' can exist. A "greater Beta with fries" seem like something that might quell a woman's innate doubt about her optimizing Hypergamy with a man.

Women say they want this balance, in spite of the unbelievability of it, but they don't know what they're praying for. Women who endlessly kvetch about the 'overly sensitive men' they committed to probably wished for the same thing once. In fact I'd argue that the majority of married men now looking to the manosphere for insight also believed once that they were Greater Betas with a side of Alpha.

These are women in a stage of life when the Beta providership male makes far better practical sense to pair off with. Around her *Epiphany Phase*, women's definition of attraction and 'a good relationship' is biased by the personal conditions of her present SMP valuation. She understands this from her age, SMV and necessity perspective, but this undoubtedly wasn't her perspective when she was in the prime of her SMV years.

This then is the 'build-a-better-beta' paradox. The overarching point is to create a more acceptable man for a female defined goal, *not* to truly empower any man. There is no feminine opposite to this; there is no counter effort to make women more acceptable to men – in fact this is actively resisted and cast as a form of slavish subservience. This is the extent of the feminine reality; it's so instaurating that men, with the aid of "concerned women", will spend lifetimes seeking ways to better qualify themselves for feminine approval. That's the better Beta they hope to create. One who will Man-Up and be the Alpha as situations and use would warrant, but Beta enough to be subservient to the Feminine Imperative. They seek a man to be proud of, one who's association reflects a statement of their own quality, yet one they still have implicit control over.

Whether their reasonings are based on morals, entitlements or some ideal of being 'honor bound' in nature, the end result is still feminine primacy. The sales pitch is one of manning up to benefit yourself, but the latent purpose is one of better qualifying for normalized feminine acceptance. What they cannot reconcile is that the same benefits that are inherent in becoming more Alpha (however you choose to define that) are the same traits that threaten his necessary position of subservience as a Beta.

This is precisely why 'real' Game, and truly unplugging, cannot be sanitized. In its truest sense Game cannot serve men and women. This social element wants to keep you plugged in; more Alpha, more confidence, more awareness, is a threat to fem-centrism. "It's great that all this Game stuff has finally got you standing up for yourself, but remember who's got the vagina. Remember who makes the rules."

The problem I see with the approaches in balancing Alpha with Beta is that they begin from a fem-centric origin. By and large, the men seeking advice about how to better their lot with women are Beta men who've been red-pill enlightened to the fact that they need to up the Alpha – presuming they had an Alpha element to start.

Women who still want a degree of control simply want a Beta, who's an Alpha at a woman's convenience. But there is no 'side of Alpha'.

The conflict most women don't grasp is that Alpha demands dominance, and this doesn't fit very well with the Feminine Imperative's false religion of equalism. In any relationship one partner is the dominant personality, the other the submissive. Even homosexual couples recognize this order, but the women and men of the feminine Matrix resist this with the delusion of an equalist utopia amongst the genders.

So when I read about a desire for achieving some balance of Alpha to Beta traits in the 'perfect man' I realize that this is an extension of this feminine-primary equalist want for balance amongst the genders; which really equates to women wanting a perfected security.

In their need for control (dominance) they want hypergamy definitively settled in the perfect man, for the perfect occasion, and at every stage of their SMV maturation. Men, mangina sympathizers or otherwise, are simply the means to that end. That end may be with the perfect husband, or via cuckolding or through fem-side pornography (romance or divorce porn), or any other methodology women's sexual pluralism will help her invent.

I've written this before, but it bears repeating: for men wanting to change their lives and relationships, working up from Beta to Alpha is a far tougher row to hoe than tempering Alpha dominance with a personalized touch of Beta. How many of the simpering, socially conditioned, Betatized men that women seethe about would make for believable Alphas once they had a Red Pill epiphany? It is precisely because of this impressionistic, binary solipsism that women will never be happy with 'fixing' their Beta. This is why he has to *Just Get It* on his own.

It is a far better proposition to impress a woman with an organic Alpha dominance – Alpha can only be a man's dominant personality of origin. There is no Beta with a side of Alpha because that side of Alpha is *never* believable when your overall perception is one of being Beta to begin with.

This is why I stress Alpha mindset above all else. It's easy and endearing to 'reveal' a flash of Beta sensitivity when a woman perceives you as predominantly Alpha. If your personality is predominantly Beta, any sporadic flashes of Alpha will seem like emotional tantrums at best, character flaws at worst.

Women may love the Beta, but they only respect the Alpha.

THE PERFECT MAN

When we consider the biological and behavioral influences of women's Ovulatory Shift dynamic we begin to see how this manifests itself on an individual and societal level as Hypergamy – or simply put in the vernacular of the Manosphere, the Alpha Fucks and Beta Bucks sexual strategies of women. For more information on this topic I'll again suggest my second book *The Rational Male, Preventive Medicine* wherein I detail this more fully.

With both an individual and social grasp of how Hypergamy influences women, the most deductive solution to men's breeding and long term relationship strategy (presuming you go that route) is a want to embody both of these disparate aspects of women's sexual strategy. Deductively it seem like the best plan; become the best of either side of Hypergamy and women will think you're the perfect guy, right? This is really a fool's errand, but it's important that we explore this foolish errand in order to better understand why it is so.

So, then how would someone reconcile the two characteristics... Is there some sort of balance of Alpha and Beta traits? Should we show Alpha and Beta traits on different times of the month according to the influence of women's Ovulatory Shift needs? In strict Game terms as well as in a marriage or long-term relationship it's always an advantage to calibrate for a woman's behavioral fluctuation per their ovulatory shift cycle, even if it's only with a woman you happen to work with. But in a larger scope, the key to answering this question is found in how women perceive attraction versus how they feel when sexually aroused. I think where most Beta men lose the trail is in the belief that Beta attraction *is* (or should be) synonymous with Alpha arousal. Each of these concepts is representative of a different facet of women's pluralistic sexual strategy – Alpha seed, Beta need. Women's sexual imperatives can be defined by the degree to which her short term mating strategy can be justified, or offset, by her long term mating strategy. And even this is modified by what her most pressing needs may be at the various stages of her maturity and how she prioritizes them.

For women, and most plugged-in men, what I'm illuminating here probably seems like an effort in semantics, but it's important to make a separation between what conditions and cues a woman is sexually aroused by and what traits make for her overall attraction for a man.

Attraction is not Arousal

Women love to be asked about what they look for in a man. It's kind of like imagining what you'll do with all your lottery winnings after you buy a quick-pick – you want the mansion and the yacht, but, of course, you'll also give some to charity so as not to seem like money could fundamentally change you into a greedy prick. Women's hind-brains understand the necessity to rationalize that their most self-indulgent wants need to be tempered with some measured appearance of prudence. This is a kind of meta-scale Anti-Slut Defense. But while ASD is an individual private dynamic, on a socialized, public scale this translates into women presenting a perception of judiciousness in explaining what they find *"attractive"* in a man – without being burdened with the perception of 'shallowness' for what they find *arousing* in a man.

You also have to consider that when women list their prerequisites for their ideal man, they are approaching this question from the perspective of whom they would like to pair off with for committed long-term security and provisioning – entirely sidestepping women's innate pluralistic sexual strategy and what really turns them on for a short-term sexual experience. This is how women's subconscious reconciles Alpha Fucks with Beta Bucks. On a limbic level women know there is a dichotomy between their dualistic sexual strategy, thus, they opt for the more socially acceptable of the two, provisioning/attraction, while their behaviors reveal the visceral side of sexuality/arousal.

Most of what a woman will list as redeeming attributes on her 'attraction list' are what Red Pill men would describe as Beta traits. In fact, most of these attraction cues would be best expressed while a woman is in her luteal phase. In this frame of mind she says she wants comfort and trust endearing qualities – sensitivity, empathy, familiarity, humor, charm, compliments, caring, etc. – in other words, the Beta traits the average chump has in spades as the result of his constant immersion in a fem-centric acculturation.

While an open embrace of Hypergamy continues in our present-day social context, women will always default to attraction cues as being paramount to their sexual selection process because they know in the long term they will need provisioning longer than they will need breeding opportunities.

Generation AFC

One of the most resounding themes in the manosphere is that the vast majority of guys are Beta chumps. A lot of men and women outside the 'sphere bristle at this Pareto Principle (80/20 rule) estimation because it sounds callous and accusatory – all coming at them from the end of a pointed arrogant Alpha's finger.

But the root of their anger really comes from being made to understand that the overwhelming mass of average frustrated chumps are actually the direct result of the feminization they thought would benefit humanity. The idea was simple enough. Let's level the playing field and play by women's standards for a change, lets see what *they'd* like men to be, lets identify with the feminine more and the world will, of course, be a better place.

Only it turned out not to be a better place. It turns out women didn't know what was best for men as based on their own inadequate (really solipsistically indifferent) understanding of masculine nature and the results are summed up in articles written by feminized men bemoaning the feminization of men. All as a proxy for women complaining about how the feminized men they created are now too feminine for them to be attracted to, much less be aroused by.

As you can see, the world is actually awash in Beta men; and all so well conditioned to be in touch with their feminine sides that they seek out the guiding dominance of masculinized women (by choice or by perception) to do the providing for them with a direction in their life. Beta Game is a dead end (sometimes literally), so unsurprisingly it's a painful realization for the majority of men to have this spelled out for them in no uncertain terms. At the same time it comes as a stinging retribution for women who see what's become of the men they created – they got the docile men they deserved.

More Beta is not a Sexual Strategy

There are certain *femosphere* bloggers who'd advocate the building of a better Beta. Their presumptions are based on the same misguided feminization that resulted in the greater feminization of the men they themselves complain about. They fear a push back towards masculine Alpha dominance will result in a new generation of arrogant assholes, devoid of the nurturing Beta qualities they thought women could identify with more, and mistakenly believed should be a source of physical arousal (not necessarily attraction). Yet, they simultaneously bemoan the absence of dominant, arousal inspiring, Alpha aspects of masculinity in men today. We can go on and on about how most women **love** good Beta traits, but they simply are not turned on by them.

This encapsulates the conflict between *Attraction* and *Arousal* for women. When women say "they want the whole package" they enumerate the qualities of what makes for their best long term provisioning, however, this conflicts with what arouses women sexually. The guy who exemplifies the best Beta male character-istics isn't getting the same play as the guy exemplifying the best Alpha arousal cues. This is precisely the duplicity men experience when women mislead them to believe that Beta provisioning traits are equatable with Alpha arousal cues. This is the '*just get it*' part of intersexual dynamics that women hope men will come to, yet they continue to mislead men because their innate solipsism pre-sumes men should already know this about women.

A stay at home Dad might have himself convinced that he's more fulfilled in his new mothering role, but he's gravely mistaken in convincing himself that women find his fatherly efforts sexually arousing. They may find it attractive in the "whole package" sense, but ultimately Hypergamy doesn't care how great a father you are.

For the better part of the last 70 years men have been conditioned to think that more Beta equals more pussy, and the results of this social experiment are now manifest in the pathetic feminized men women themselves complain of. The greater problem women face now is accepting the genuineness of an Alpha transformation of so many men.

Women love the concept of tempering the dominant asshole Alpha. It's a com-mon romance novel fantasy for women to be the uniquely soothing influence over the rebellious jerk who wets her panties with her arousal. It's self-affirming for women to think their Alpha superhero would only show his Beta side to her. Unfortunately the reverse of this situation is the reality – the vast majority of men must fight an uphill battle from Beta origins to Alpha transformation. It is Game and Red Pill awareness that aid in upping the Alpha, but for women conditioned to expect Beta male frailty from men, for women whose lives have been defined by male submissiveness, this transformation will largely continue to seem disingenuous.

Women would rather share a high value Man than be saddled with a faithful loser. The easier path for women is to ditch the primarily Beta man in favor of holding out for and taming an arousing, primarily Alpha man.

Mr. Perfect

I've had guys ask me why would a woman stay with a guy she knows is a chump? How is it women will stay with their boyfriend's/husband's regardless of how Beta they are. There will be those guys who will say they get with these men for their money, or stay with them for financial security. They'll say, "come on, we all know women will generally only give their intimacy to men who have their game down tight and fit the profile – doesn't matter how much they make. We know you don't need to make a lot of money to get laid or to develop relationship with a woman. There are plenty of guys who have had shit for resources develop long term relationships with hot women. So how do these mostly Beta men get with these women in the first place if they're Betas to begin with?

Why would a woman stay with a guy she acknowledges as an overall Beta? A lot of reasons actually, but there are some commonalities. First, there's the guy that was once the Jerk, who had been attractive enough, or played the role well enough, to get involved with a woman who successfully "changed" him. And in an effort to better identify with what she's convinced him (and herself) that he ought to be living up to, he reverts to being the Beta he always was in the relationship. She can't complain because he's changed into what she thought she was supposed to want in a guy, but he's turned into the kind of guy she'd never have been attracted to if she were to meet him while single. So she stays with him up until the point that she meets another Jerk who she wants to fuck and eventually 'fixes' him too.

Second, lets not forget that some of the most wealthy and physically attractive men also happen to be the worst cases of Blue Pill conditioning you'll ever meet. I realize that sounds odd, but the wealthy man and the attractive man have little to prompt them to re-think their own behaviors. Because they are more readily rewarded with female intimacy, there's less reason to question the framework of intergender relations, and / or their own predispositions and conditionings that would make them Beta.

I once worked with this guy named Jake who was model tier good looking. He had no trouble with attracting women, and most would regularly approach him, but Jake was probably the worst Blue Pill tool I'd ever met. He used to complain that he couldn't get a girlfriend or keep a girl interested in him, even though he was tapping beautiful women every other weekend. Once he opened his mouth and spilled his life story out on the restaurant table on the first date these girls would treat him with pity and gradually fade away on him. He literally had ONEitis for *any* girl he was dating at the time and swallowed hook, line and sinker the soul-mate mythology. He tried to be friends, tried to be sensitive, tried to be funny, tried to be a savior and every other Beta Game technique in the book, but all this did was push these women away from him. They enjoyed being fucked by the guy, but when he started up the ice cream cones and puppy dogs, cuddle-bitch mentality, they moved on to other guys.

In other words, Beta men aren't all dorks and geeks, and being attractive doesn't insulate you from internalizing stupid, feminized romanticisms. Nice Guys may finish last, but that doesn't mean they don't finish at all, and some manage to get laid occasionally along the way.

Mr. Perfect

The problem with guys like Jake is that they strive to fit a feminine-centric idealization. They want to be 'perfect' for her. But Mr. Perfect is neither realistic or expected. A *Telegraph* poll in 2015 showed that three in four women believe there is no such thing as the perfect man, with most seeing their own long-term partner as only 69% perfect. The poll of 2,000 women also showed more than 75% believed the perfect man did not exist. Women are actually quite realistic on what they look for from their partner.

"While they might happily overlook a few common flaws from their guys, there are certain behaviors that men just won't get away with." The results showed one in five women think their partner only pretends to listen to them while leaving clothes on the bedroom floor and snoring were among other gripes. The perfect man would be expected to make an effort with his partner's friends, avoid using her toothbrush, stay clean-shaven and not be lazy.

Perfect is Boring.

Say that again, Perfect is boring. It seems counterintuitive, but it's your imperfection that makes you attractive. There's an implied, ambient confidence that's radiated from a Man who knows what a woman's stated ideal of perfection would be and yet refuses to embody it for her. That underlying message to her is "I know you hate having the toilet seat left up, but I'm supremely confident enough in your attraction, and other women's attraction, to me that I'll ignore your silly pet peeves rather than pander to them." It's the guy who engages in this pandering by attempting to be a woman's stated ideal who sends the message that he is really optionless. It's essentially a failed meta-shit test. It says to her that he'll be a willing participant in his own manipulation.

As I've written in many an essay, women will never substantively appreciate the efforts a man makes to facilitate her reality. A feminine-centric reality means that any extraneous attempt he makes to appease her will be interpreted as the new normative. It's just expected that he'll do her bidding, because that's just what guys are supposed to do. Yet, it is the Man who refuses, either consciously or as a matter of course, to engage in trying to appease her who holds women's attentions the most. If there is a categoric Alpha trait it's just this obliviousness to the wants of a feminine-centric norm.

Mr. Perfect doesn't get extra points for being perfect because the aspects of that "perfection" *is* the expected norm. It's boring because it's mundane. The problem of a feminized norm is that it makes feminine similarities between the genders the ideal state.

Androgyny is homogeny. It ignores, willfully or otherwise, that biomechanics have evolved an appreciation for the differences in the genders to be primarily attractive to one another. The more like we become – men becoming feminine, women becoming masculine – the more we lose that innate attraction. This goes for the aspects we both love and hate about the other gender.

In defying this inborn attraction, and making attempts to socialize it to better fit the feminine sensibility, we grate against what is really characteristic of each gender. In the natural world Men will be Men and despite the protestations, women really don't want it any other way.

ALPHA TELLS

For as long as I've been writing in the Manosphere, the definition of 'what is Alpha?' has been the number one point of contention I've had to state and re-state most often. I'm not going to rehash this here as I have several essays on the nature of Alpha on my blog and in the first volume of *The Rational Male*, so if you're looking for my take on Alpha that's where you'll find it.

However, for now I need to address the basis of what I believe are the most common misunderstandings about the term *Alpha*.

Well before the inception of my blog, in the early beginnings of what would evolve into the Manosphere, there was a need of terminology to describe the more abstract concepts developing in the Red Pill '*community*'. Some of these analogies and terms are still with the Manosphere today, others have morphed into more useful abstractions; Alpha Widows, Hypergamy (in its expanded definition), the Feminine Imperative, even Red Pill awareness are all examples of established terms or analogies for understood abstractions. Among these are also the concepts of a man being Alpha and Beta.

One of the most common disconnects men encounter with the Red Pill for the first time is equating the term Alpha with its usage in describing the mating habits of Lions, Wolves or Silver Back Gorillas. It's easy to ridicule or simply dismiss a valid, but uncomfortable, Red Pill truth when you're simplistically comfortable in only ever defining 'Alpha Male' in literal, etymological, terms.

This is the first resistance Blue Pill men claim they have with the Red Pill. They have no problem understanding and using abstractions for Blue Pill concepts they themselves are ego-invested in, but challenge that belief-set with uncomfortable Red Pill truths and their first resort is to obstinately define Alpha (as well as Hypergamy) in as narrow, binary and literal a sense as they can muster.

"Get in Touch with Your Feminine Beta Side"

The next most common misunderstanding comes from conflating the abstractions of Alpha and Beta with masculine and feminine traits. In this (often deliberate) misdirection, the concepts of being Alpha or Beta become synonymous with being masculine or feminine. This is the personal basis of Alpha and Beta many Purple Pill 'life coaches' (really Blue Pill apologists) comfortably redefine for themselves, to suit themselves.

This Purple Pill conflation is really just a comforting return the curse of Jung – Anima & Animus – if the complete man is an even mix of Alpha and Beta, masculine and feminine, then all the worst aspects of his "betaness" can't be all bad, and he reinterprets what really amounts to a complete androgyny as "being the best balance".

Unfortunately, and as Blue Pill chumps will later attest, the feminine expects to find its paired balance in the masculine, not an equalist idealization of both in the same man. Thus, women, on a limbic level, expect men to be Men.

This one of the missives of an equalitarian mindset; that an individualized, egalitarian balance of masculine and feminine aspects in two independent people should replace the natural complementary interdependence of conventional masculine and feminine attributes in a paired balance that humans evolved into.

What Purple Pill temperance really equates to is a 21st century return to the 20th century feminized meme "men need to get in touch with their feminine sides"… or else risk feminine rejection. Sixty-plus years of post sexual revolution social engineering has put the lie to what an abject failure this concept has been.

What they failed to grasp is that an Alpha mindset is not definitively associated with masculine attributes. There are plenty of high-functioning, masculine men we would characterize as Alpha based on our perception of them in many aspects of life, who nonetheless are abject supplicating Betas with regard to how they interact with, and defer to women. Whether that disconnect is due to a learned, Beta deference to the feminine (White Knighting), some internalized fear of rejection, or just a natural predisposition to be so with women, isn't the issue. What matters is that the abstraction of Alpha isn't an absolute definitive association with the masculine.

Likewise, Beta attributes are neither inherently feminine. As has been discussed ad infinitum in the Manosphere, 80%+ of modern men have been conditioned (or otherwise) to exemplify and promote a feminine-primary, supportive Beta life-role for themselves and as many other men they can convince to identify more with the feminine. The Beta mindset isn't so much one of adopting a feminine mindset as it is a deference to, and the support of, a feminine-primary world view.

The reason Purple Pill (watered down Red Pill) ideology wants to make the association of Alpha = Masculine, Beta = Feminine is because the "get in touch with your feminine side" Beta attributes they possess in spades can be more easily characterized as "really" being Alpha if it helps make him the more androgynously acceptable male he mistakenly believes women are attracted to (if not directly aroused by).

Alpha Tells

The sexual *alphaness* of a male towards a female is exhibited by her wanting to please him, and the sexual *betaness* of a male is exhibited by him needing to please her. A man's *alphaness* obviously, and by definition, does not cause her to more require him to please her (i.e. *alphaness* does not rub off like that). And also, *betaness* is not transferable, no matter how much Betas wish that their women-pleasing caused women to want to please them.

Moreover, the social dominance of a male in a male dominance hierarchy is barely correlated with his sexual *alphaness*, and certainly not causal. There are far too many counterexamples, such as Bill Gates, Napoleon Bonaparte, Horatio Nelson, and the list is very long.

However, and this is a key empirical point, the social dominance of a female human in a female human hierarchy is correlated, in this precise way: A woman to whom women cater to will 99% of the time demand to be catered to by her man. This is why women believe man-pleasing women are "lesser" women. It is also why men who have tended to be mated to females who are socially dominant in a female hierarchy are invariably Betas. It's simply false that female-dominant women tend to choose men who demand pleasing. What critics of an Alpha/Beta dichotomy conveniently sweep under the carpet is that the dichotomy they want to debate only exists in what their convenient, personal interpretations of Alpha or Beta mean to them.

From a male perspective we can endlessly debate (from our own personal biases) what we believe constitutes an Alpha state (remember, Alpha is an abstract term, stay with me here) and the expectations of which we think women should respond to according to those expectation. But it's women's instinctive behaviors around Alpha men (or men they contextually perceive to be Alpha) that provide us with the tells as to how she perceives a man's Alpha or Beta status.

For as much as we believe women should respond to our definition of Alpha – and despite how women will explain they agree with those self-prescribed definitions – as always, it is their behaviors when in the presence of, or in a relationship with men they perceive as being Alpha (or of higher sexual market value than themselves if you prefer) that they bely their true, instinctual recognitions of Alpha.

In a social environment where men are conditioned to believe that women are as equal, rational agents as men, the belief men put their faith into is that women will appreciate their intrinsic qualities and base their sexual selectivity upon a man's virtue, bearing, intelligence, humor, and any number of attractive intrinsic qualities. However, the truth of what women base their sexual selectivity upon (arousal) is far more evident in their instinctual, unconditioned behavior when around Alpha men – as well as men's instinctual sensitivity to that behavior.

There are many examples of this Alpha reflexive behavior. I'll make an attempt to illustrate a few of them here, but I expect there'll be many more offered by my readers. I encourage a discussion among men about the behaviors that serve as Alpha tells. Long time Red Pill blogger, *Roissy/Heartiste*, has made a kind of sport with his ongoing "spot the Alpha" series of posts in which he analyzes a picture or video of a woman's reaction to a man whom she obviously has an Alpha interest in as her body language and subcommunications suggest. The common criticism of these images is that Red Pill men would read too much into these displays, but the underlying message in that criticism is rooted in understanding and willfully ignoring what our instinctual perceptions of them are. We know Alpha when we see it, but need an explanation to protect our own ego's Alpha assessment of ourselves.

The Real Selection

For all the delighted ego 'empowerment' of women boasting they are the sexual selectors in this life, there is still a nervous uncertainty about being found acceptable themselves to an Alpha lover of higher SMV status than they might otherwise merit. This is where the illusions of an assortive mating model break down for women. If feminine-primary sexual selection were the only element to mating there would be no need for the behaviors women are subject to in seeking the approval from men they perceive as Alpha.

There's a look, an attitude and a presence women will give off to Men for whom they have a natural deference to. I don't just mean blatant sexual subcommunications like casually biting her lower lip, or the hair twirling that's almost cliché now. It goes beyond the sexual into a kind of meta-attraction/arousal. While the sexual urgency for an Alpha is strong and manifests in a woman's forwardness toward him, the meta-attraction is both one of submission and a subconscious desire for his approval of her.

Men predisposed to a Beta mindset also display many of these same behavioral cues with the women they hope will appreciate them in the same fashion a woman does for a Man that her hind-brain instinctually knows is of a higher SMV. In Beta men we see these behaviors as evidence of "clinginess" or "neediness" and is an identifiable Beta tell; but in women this natural and unprovoked *leaning in* to a Man, this desire to submit for his approval, is a positive indicator of Alpha attraction.

As third party observers, we instinctually find such behavior in men distasteful; we subliminally sense a complementary imbalance between the man and woman. When a woman makes an unforced effort to please a man with subtle words, unintentional wide-eyed contact, and body positioning / posture you're dealing with a woman who is compelled to defer to you as Alpha.

That isn't to say this can't be faked. In fact strippers, good ones at least, are not just physically arousing, or more sexualized, but are in tune with the deficit most men feel when it comes to this Alpha deference. Beyond just the sexual aspect, one thing that makes strippers so enticing and seductive is that the majority of men are simply unused to the fawning affections and Alpha interest (albeit feigned) of any woman, much less an attractive one.

This is also one reason men become so prone to ONEitis both inside and outside this contrived, transactional, sort of attraction. Men are the *True Romantics*, they want to believe a woman's sincerity in her Alpha deference to him.

Does the girl you're interested in come to you, or do you go to her?

I've emphasized the importance of establishing and maintaining *Frame* for years now, but I sometimes wonder if the importance of holding *Frame* isn't lost on most men. To an equalist mindset, this *Frame* establishment seems like I'm advocating men be domineering in their relationships and a man rely on some dark manipulative psychology to enforce his will in that relationship. That's not what I'm suggesting for the simple reason that it's too effort consuming, and genuine desire is unsustainable within that constant effort. Maintaining *Frame* demands a voluntary, uncoerced, desired compliance on the part of a woman.

What I'm suggesting is that men simply not invest themselves in women whose Alpha interest in them is mitigated by doubt or any obvious SMV imbalance. This is difficult for most men as it conflicts with our want for an idealized romance with a woman – a want for a love that requires a mutual definition with a woman lacking the capacity to realize this with him, or at least in the way he believes should be possible for her. And it's within that idealized desire men lose *Frame* and excuse the lack of Alpha deference on her part.

The Medium IS the Message

In *The Rational Male* you'll find a section called, the Medium *is* the Message. It would be good to review it if you have the book. On some level of conscious-ness men instinctually understand their relative status with a woman based on the medium of women – the behaviors she directs toward him.

- Is she affectionate without being prompted or only when circumstance makes your comfort needed for her?

- Is *Amused Mastery* an easy default conversational technique for you, or does she resist even your playful attempts at it?

- Does she initiate sex with you, or is your initiating it only ever the precursor to sex?

- Is sex even a priority for her (with you)?

- Does she make efforts to make things special for you or is your relationship one of her grading your efforts in qualifying for her Alpha approval of you?

What most guys think are 'mixed messages' or confusing behavior coming from a woman is simply due to their inability (for whatever reason) to make an ac-curate interpretation of why she's behaving in such a manner. Usually this boils down to a guy getting so wrapped up in a girl that he'd rather make concessions for her behavior than see it for what it really is. In other words, it's far easier to call it 'mixed messages' or fall back on the old chestnut of how fickle and ran-dom women are, when in fact it's simply a rationale to keep themselves on the hook, so to speak, because they lack any real, viable, options with other women in their lives. A woman that has a high interest level (IL) in a guy has no need to engage in behaviors that would compromise her status with him. Women of all ILs will shit test, and men will pass or fail accordingly, but a test is more easily recognizable when you consider the context in which they're delivered.

Are you making psychological concessions with a woman who's never dis-played an Alpha deference to you? What would change in your relationship if she did?

BETA TELLS

Knowing your woman's menstrual cycle can be extremely powerful.

During the fertile stage of her cycle, thousands of years of evolution means her body is screaming at her to get knocked up by an alpha male. A simple test to determine is she sees you as her alpha fucks is to not initiate during the fertile period of her cycle and observe her behavior: does she come to you to get fucked? Does her body language or physical behavior change when she's fertile. Maybe she touches you more often or more intimately or plays the role of the seductress: things like coming to bed wearing lingerie where she usually wouldn't? Even if she's relatively low-sex drive and doesn't initiate, does she at least respond more passionately to your sexual advances or orgasm more easily or intensely when she's fertile?

You obviously can't draw conclusions from a single cycle but you should eventually see a pattern – and the more she values you sexually during her fertile period the better. If she isn't doing anything differently or reacting to you differently when she's fertile, something's up.

This test can have false negatives but not false positives. There's no false positive case where she suddenly starts riding you while you're watching the Packers game but she doesn't see you as her alpha. But it can have false negatives where she doesn't initiate but still sees you as her alpha. If she isn't initiating when she's fertile (and you aren't initiating in order to test her reaction), it could be due to stress, lack of time, being too used to you doing the initiation, etc. But at the very least she should be demonstrating increased passion and sexual ecstasy during her fertile period.

The best case: She initiates during her fertile period if you don't. She gets cravings for your dick.

The OK case: She responds more passionately and orgasms more easily during her fertile period.

The uh-oh, something might be wrong case: No observable change during her fertile period.

The beta case: Dead bedroom, what the fuck are you even doing (sorry if you got married and you can't get out).

Of course if she's an extremely sexual being and all of the above describes your sex life 24/7, then none of this should even concern you.

Disclaimer: Once again, this test is a tool that works best for women with higher sex drives (who really wanna get fucked when they're fertile). If your 37 year old wife of 15 years fucks you when you want and isn't cheating, you're fine. I don't think test applies to all women (LOL, broke /trp/ rules oops) but it's useful nonetheless.

This quote was from a guy on the Red Pill Reddit forum. It provides a good, if somewhat raw, perspective of indicators of a woman's hind-brain perception of a man she's paired herself with. For the moment remember this, marriage, monogamy, commitment, etc. will never be any insulation from the sexual marketplace and no insurance against a woman's innate Hypergamy, no matter how reassuring your pastor, life coach or dating guru sounds when they tell you it is.

Lets presume for a moment that neither a controlled experiment nor an uncontrolled, but documented, sociological field study has ever been performed to test the principle of feminine Hypergamy. For a moment, as a man, imagine yourself living in a period of time prior to any formalized school of psychology; before the turn of the 20th century. There is no Pavlov, there is no Skinner, there is no Freud, there is no Jung.

Using only personal observations – that is observations of learned behaviors related by your father and brothers, male friends and the intergender experiences of a very socially isolated (by today's standards) group of people who make up your peers, and a restrictively limited access to any classic philosophical literature beyond the Christian Bible – what would you presume would be the nature inimical to women and the feminine?

Would your observations, intuition and the education proffered by your father, brothers and other influential male friends and relations lead to an insight to know what Hypergamy is, how it motivates women and how to control for, or capitalize on it?

Not only do I believe it would, but I would argue that, up until the sexual revolution and the past 60 or so years, men have had both an innate and learned understanding of Hypergamy, how it functions, and how to control for it.

To be sure, it didn't have the formal name of 'Hypergamy' – in fact that term was until recently, strictly defined and reserved for "women with the tendency to marry above their socioeconomic level" in polite, pop-psychology circles – but men *knew* Hypergamy before the Manosphere (re)exposed its true definition.

Waging Hypergamy

Resistance to the uncomfortable truths innate to the female experience is to be expected from women – until the advent of *Open Hypergamy*, the Feminine Imperative needed the Sisterhood to be united and its secrets jealously guarded to the point of cognitive dissonance. My guess is that most of my female critics would still agree with the basic parameters of Hypergamy, but what I doubt they're aware of is that in denying the inherent biological nature of female Hypergamy women must also reject the sociological, psychological and (observably) behavioral aspects of Hypergamy inherent (and largely subconscious) in women.

> *"As women approach the Epiphany Phase (later the Wall) and realize the decay of their SMV (in comparison to younger women), they become progressively more incentivized towards attraction to the qualities a man possesses that will best satisfy the long-term security of the Beta Bucks side of her Hypergamy demands."*

> *Did your woman say, "you're (so much) different than the guys I used to date." Or, "I finally got smart and found a good guy." If so, this is clear evidence that you are her Beta Bucks guy. Maybe she used to date DJs, NFL players, drug dealers, whatever. If these guys are different types of guys than you, do NOT continue the relationship. She has no clue, but she is rationalizing her choice in her mind. You will pay a severe price later, as in cheating, nonstop bitchiness, or sudden divorce. Find a girl that always dated guys like you. She may have swooned for the lead guitarist, but if she didn't devote her early 20s to chasing him, you're okay.*

Beta Tells

One of the more common questions I'm asked in consults is whether something a guy did was 'Beta' or not. Usually it was a situation wherein the guy was instinctually sensitive to his own behavior in context to his *Frame* and how the woman he was dealing with perceived him. In most cases a man knows when he's slipped in his perception of dominance with a woman, they just look for a third party confirmation of it – which is then followed by more rationalizations for why his behavior shouldn't be considered Beta because they believe women are equally rational, equally forgiving, agents as men (really he is) are.

Whenever you feel something isn't quite right in your gut, this is your subconscious awareness alerting you to inconsistencies going on around you. We tend to ignore these signs in the thinking that our rational mind 'knows better' and things really aren't what they seem. It's not as bad as you're imagining, and you can even feel shame or guilt with yourself for acknowledging that lack of trust. However, it's just this internal rationalization that keeps us blind to the obvious that our subconscious is trying to warn us about. Humans are creatures of habit with an insatiable need to see familiarity in other people's actions. So when that predictable behavior changes even marginally, our instinctual perceptions fire off all kinds of warnings. Some of which can actually effect us physically.

It's at this point most guys make the mistake of acting on the "good communication solves everything" feminized meme and go the full disclosure truth route, which only really leads to more rationalizations and repression of what's really going on. What they don't realize is that the medium is the message; her behavior, her nuances, the incongruousness in her words and demeanor (and how your gut perceives them) is the real message. There is an irregularity in her behavior that your subconscious is alerting you to which your consciousness either cannot or will not recognize.

I began Alpha Tells with the intent of recognizing how a woman behaves when she's in the presence of a Man she perceives to be Alpha. A lot of men get hung up on trying to 'act' Alpha; wanting to ape (and later hopefully internalize) the behavioral tells a more confident Alpha displays.

Consequently there's a lot of debate about how men posture and how they naturally display these Alpha cues, but I think the best gauge of what defines those cues is not in men's displays, but women's behaviors and attitudes that are prompted by a perception of Alpha-ness.

And, just as women will respond viscerally to an Alpha perception, they will also manifest behaviors which indicate her subconscious knows she's dealing with a Beta aligned male.

It's easy to pick apart what a guy thinks are his own Alpha tells, but it's far more uncomfortable to dissect women's Beta tells when they're in the presence of men they perceive to be Beta. Much of what I'll outline that follows will be hard to read for many guys, and as always you're free to disagree.

My purpose here isn't to bash Betas, rather it's to increase awareness of women's reflexive behaviors toward them. Try to put these behaviors into a Hypergamous context and how they would be perceived by women who've evolved to have an instinctual sensitivity to these Beta behaviors, as well as expressions of Beta attitudes in your words and emotional emphasis.

I could very easily compile a list of behaviors that are simply the reverse of the Alpha Tells I noted in the previous section, but it's much more important to address the root reasons for these Beta Tells:

• Does she initiate sex or affection spontaneously?

• Does she entertain a large pool of "male friend" orbiters with the expectation of you being 'mature enough' to accept it?

• Does she keep a core peer group of 'girlfriends' she insists on prioritizing over being with you? Does she make frequent habit of Girl's Night Out?

• Has she explained to you how she was so different in college and how she's glad those days are behind her now?

• Is she experiencing her *Epiphany Phase*?

• Does she cite "mismatched libidos" as a reason for her lack of sexual interest in you now that you're married or living together (even after she's had better sex with you or a former lover when single)?

• Is she averse or repulsed by your ejaculate being on her skin, in her mouth or overly concerned with soiling a bed sheet?

• Will she have sex with you anywhere besides the bed?

• Do you perform oral on her to get her off more than you have intercourse?

• Is she a wide-eyed lover or does she squint her eyes closed while having sex? Is sex a chore for her to perform?

• If you're married, did she take your last name, or did she insist on a hyphenated surname for herself?

• When you're together does her regular, unpracticed body posture indicate an openness or are you always having to break into her intimate space?

- Is she preoccupied with her side of the family or a certain pet in preference to being concerned with your well-being?

- Is she consciously aware of being 1-2 points above your own relative SMV? Is she overt about it?

- Does she presume authority in your relationship? Do you concede this authority as a matter of (equalist) belief?

There are many more tells of course, but it's important to understand that these behaviors and attitudes are manifestations of a woman who on some level of consciousness understands that she's dealing with a Beta man.

I should also mention that, there are particular phases of a woman's life when she becomes more attuned to dealing with Beta men due to perceived necessities on her part. A clear understanding of how these phases predispose women to convince themselves to be more accepting of Beta behaviors and a Beta mind-set is imperative to avoiding the common pitfalls men encounter with regard to issues of holding *Frame* in their relationships.

Beta men are all too eager to believe they've matured into being a self-defined Alpha when a semi-attractive 29 year old in the midst of her *Epiphany Phase* is giving him wide-eyed indicators of interest in him. Only after she's consolidated on that long-term security does he realize the plans her sexual strategy had for him.

Predisposition for Mate Guarding

One of the best Beta tells is how defensive a guy gets about the subject of mate guarding. An Alpha has little preoccupation with mate guarding because subconsciously he knows he has sexual options. That applies both within and without monogamy. I'm presenting this here because the majority of what motivates Beta tells (and really a Beta mindset) is rooted in how men deal with a scarcity mentality. Beta tells are almost always indicators that a man believes he needs to guard his paired-with woman and thus telegraphs a Beta status to that woman as well as other women in her peer clutch.

Mate guarding, and its intrinsic set of subconscious suspicions and behaviors, is an evolved adaptation of ensuring paternity for a Beta-provider. These men must rely upon exchanging resources and external benefits for women's sexual fidelity. In essence, it's an unspoken awareness that Beta men must negotiate for what they hope will be a woman's genuine desire in exchange for his provisioning, parental investment support and emotional involvement. Beta men are aware on a limbic level that Hypergamy dictates an Alpha Fucks / Beta Bucks trade-off in women's sexual strategy – thus, a subconscious 'mate guarding' mindset evolved from Beta men's heightened awareness of women's preference for Alpha Fucks, particularly around the proliferative phase of women's ovulation.

Paradoxically, the best assurance you have of fidelity with a woman is simply not to allow yourself to become exclusively monogamous with a woman and rather, have her make the efforts to pair with you under her own auspices of you being Alpha. Romance is not required from a lover a woman perceives as Alpha, only his sexual interest – this represents a confirmation of Hypergamous optimization for a woman. The fuck-buddy dynamic – all sexual interests with no reciprocal expectation of emotional investment – is a strong Alpha tell for a man.

The best gauge for determining a woman's perception of you as either an Alpha or Beta type is examining yourself and your feeling a 'need' to mate guard her, to appease her, or an impulse to correct yourself in order to align with her terms for intimacy. A scarcity mentality is the mental point of origin for a Beta mindset – and that internalized mental model will manifest itself in a predisposition for Beta behaviors.

There's a common belief that even the most Alpha of men will at times slip into a Beta behaviorism. You can't be 'on' your game all of the time, and while that's true it doesn't invalidate that women have a mental model of your overall, predominant condition being either Alpha or Beta. A predominantly Alpha frame and mindset (and yes, looks), plus an acknowledged (real or perceived) SMV primacy above her own will cover a multitude of Beta sins, but the predominant Beta has the Sisyphean task of convincing a woman he's more Alpha than she pegs him for.

So, to answer the man asking whether or not something he did was Beta, your answer really lies in your motivation for behaving 'Beta' as you did in comparison to how a woman perceives your predominant character.

THE RECONSTRUCTION

One of the most common misconceptions of guys coming into a Red Pill awareness experience is an expectation of being able to use that awareness and Game to reconstruct an old relationship. Most often this hope is about a guy wanting to 'fix' his broken relationship with a girl who dumped him. This is easily the most common reason Blue Pill guys make themselves open to what the Red Pill has to reveal to him. They are desperate, not so much for the intergender truths that the Red Pill presents, but rather for a solution to their hearts being crushed by a girl.

This is understandable when you consider that these men are still very steeped in the Blue Pill idealism they've yet to unlearn (or understand why they need to unlearn it) and haven't made the connection that their idealism *is* part of the reason why they were dumped. All they feel is a desperate longing to reconnect to a girl who was their '*One*', and only now they are desperate enough to seek answers from the Red Pill.

It's funny how some of the most ardent Red Pill deniers will be open to listening to its truths about men and women if it presents the possibility of them getting back with a former lover they invested themselves in. This is a good illustration of the degree of control Blue Pill idealism has over guys; that they would be open to amending their beliefs if it means reconnecting to those feelings they've been cut away from.

Unfortunately, the Red Pill is not a salve for Blue Pill disillusionment. It's a cure, not a band-aid. I tried to succinctly address this in the 7th Iron Rule of Tomassi:

Iron Rule of Tomassi #7
It is always time and effort better spent developing new, fresh, prospective women than it will ever be in attempting to reconstruct a failed relationship. Never root through the trash once the garbage has been dragged to the curb. You get messy, your neighbors see you do it, and what you thought was worth digging for is never as valuable as you thought it was.

Another Red Pill reconstruction attempt is men who make it their goal to 're-seduce' a woman they failed to effectively Game while still wrapped up in their Blue Pill mindset. The first presumption is that revenge might motivate a guy to want to pump and dump a girl who once blew him off back when he was locked into his Blue Pill mentality. Women like this idea because they think it confirms men's egos being easily bruised, but I don't think this is always the case.

It's entirely possible that some past coquette has taken an organic liking to "the new him" now that his Red Pill transition and better grasp of Game has made him attractive to her. I've had several guys relate to me about how they have turned a former ONEitis into a plate they were spinning along with others. The experience of doing so will often solidify Red Pill/Game principles for him – the act of cycling an old 'soul mate' into a guy's roster of non-exclusive lovers is a lesson in taking women off a formerly idealistic pedestal and helps humanize women for him in the process.

I should also add that there's usually a period of time necessary to effect this. Too many men will see Red Pill awareness and just the loosest form of Game as some magic formula for pulling this off too soon. A sudden incongruent shift in his demeanor only puts her off more and leaves him discouraged.

Doing Everything Right

The third type of Red Pill reconstructionist is the married man – or the guy in a multi-year LTR – seeking to find the secret to remedy his dead bedroom. There was a time (pre-internet, pre-Red Pill) when these men were reluctant to even voice the problem they were having with their sexually indifferent wives. Generally, this was due to a couple of specific fears.

The first is that most Blue Pill men are conditioned from a very early age to always find fault in themselves before they would ever imply that it would be a woman's. This was especially true if it was about sex. If you can't satisfy a woman, it's your fault. If a woman isn't aroused or attracted by you, it's your fault, so the presumption used to be that a man could only better himself as a means to reestablish an attraction that (presumably) he had with his wife before they were married.

Back in the day this 'improvement' could be defined in various *old books* ways. He might get a promotion at work, a shift up in status and pay. He might lose weight or find some form of competition he might possibly do well in. He might change his beliefs or accede to better identifying with his wife, or do more chores around the home, help with the kids, arrange more 'date nights'.

He might go to marriage counseling or participate in his church's "men's spiritual retreats" in order to show that he's *growing.*

All of these ways of "rekindling the old flame" are essentially a man's effort in acquiescing to his woman's *Frame* while keeping him in a perpetual state of negotiating for her genuine desire. From a Red Pill perspective we understand this, but there was a time, not so long ago, when men's preoccupation was all about doing everything right in order to get his wife to fuck him like she used to, or with something resembling genuine enthusiasm.

The second fear men of that time had was admitting to their inability to satisfy their wife (LTR) sexually. Again, this was all about a female-dominant *Frame*, and his qualifying for her pleasure, but we're talking about a time when men's interpretation of their own masculinity was always being questioned. It's interesting to see how times have changed with communication technology. I can remember a time when it would've been taboo to be too direct about sex in church. Now it's unavoidable and we have pastors encouraging sex quota months in order to spur the sexually indifferent wives in the congregation.

In a Blue Pill social order, men learn to always qualify for women. So the natural, male-deductive response has always been to 'do everything right' in order to keep the sex faucet flowing. Sacrifice dreams, belay ambitions, get the right job with the right status and become a person who a woman would want to bang. These are all *old books* presumptions based on the Beta Female-Identifying Provider archetype, but it's important to keep this in mind today because this same 'do everything right' presumption still persists for men today.

The following is a post from the Married Red Pill Reddit:

Story time....

I moved out a few months ago in exasperation after following my married Red Pill path to a T and seeing little to no improvement in our relationship. I've "fixed" myself in ways I never thought I could and moving out was me punting the final decision for a bit before I blow my beautiful children's lives to pieces.

Things are calm, peaceful, friendly and kinda fun at "home" but the sexual dynamic hasn't changed at all despite all odds. I've finally reached the point that I give 0 fucks either way and every day that goes by makes me a bit more ambivalent to the whole deal.

It's taken a long time to get here but something happened last week that opened my eyes to how shitty my life has been for a looooong time and how at this point she is the only "problem" left in my life and I can't "fix" her.

The quick back story is that I was a fat, beta fuck for a long time and have been on this journey for about 2 years. I am fairly ripped now and have "fixed" myself to the point that I feel comfortable saying I'm a top 5-10% guy in my metro. Good looking, successful business, dress well...etc.

Last week I initiated with the wife while I was over at our house helping get the kids to bed. She shot me down like she has been for months. We still fuck here and there but the quality has been shitty for a while.

I laughed, told her goodnight and went back to my house. I actually prefer being there now. I've come to love the solitude too as the loneliness and missing the kids has worn off a little.

I worked out and read for a while and got bored so I decided to download Bumble and Tinder to get a no risk gauge of where I'm at if I end up nexting her. I've been getting plenty of IOI's in public but I live in a small town so pursuing them would eventually lead to big problems. I also downloaded a GPS location faker and put myself in a state far, far away to make sure I don't get doxxed by one of her shitty, single friends...

Gentlemen...It's been 4 days and I currently have over 60 unsolicited messages from all kinds of women. My inbox is full of unsolicited titty and pussy shots from women waayyy hotter than my wife. I've got 5 women literally begging me to come fuck them and another 5 or so I'm confident I could fuck within a week if I wanted.

It's a good thing I put myself so far away or the temptation would probably be way too much to handle. I deleted the apps this morning as I'm not ready to blow everything up yet and I want to give the marriage every last chance for my kids sake. I know myself well enough to know that once I taste some strange there will no turning back. The constant buzzing of the burner phone was also killing my productivity.

The end result is that this whole experiment has killed off any last shred of oneitis I had and opened my eyes to what my life will look like going forward if this goes the way it's heading. My wife is a good woman and is fairly hot but it appears that she may not be able to see past all those years of beta shittiness from me and that's ok.

I didn't tell you my story to brag but to re-affirm that only you can change and determine the quality of your life. I can tell you that 2 years ago I was a mess trying to hang on to the shreds of my marriage while my wife was pretty much repulsed by me. My wife will or will not change into the sexy woman I want over the next few months but now I really don't care because I have painfully built myself into a man that the world will treat very well either way.

Today the hope for bettering a man's sexual prospects in marriage is found primarily in Red Pill awareness. I would daresay that the Red Pill, Game and the Manosphere have done more in improving men's sexual access in marriage than contemporary marriage counseling for about 10 years now. That's to be lauded I think, but it also has to come with the understanding that no man's experience, no man's situation with his wife/woman, is ever the same, nor is it ideal.

There is a set of Red Pill men (usually married) who also attempt to do every-thing right – according to Red Pill awareness and applied Game – and, as per this man's story, the situation is such that it is still 'not enough'.

These men become Red Pill aware, they unplug, they struggle to accept it while disenfranchising themselves from their Blue Pill conditioning. They put in the time for insight and soul-searching, they deal with the uncomfortable truths of what they've been all their lives. They deal with the anger that inspires and they come out on the other side and begin to remake themselves. They self-improve.

Roosh once had some Dali Lama moment in a video about how he believes self-improvement is some Zen preset channel for men, and they ought not worry about bettering themselves. I say bullshit. Self-improvement itself is a state of being. Once a man applies himself, invests more in himself than he ever has, changes his mind about himself, etc. he becomes his own mental point of origin.

These men begin to see the results of their efforts; efforts often unbeknownst to his woman. She may witness the outward changes, but only he knows the experience of his inward changes. Now he's got to deal with new experiences that were previously foreign to him in his old, Blue Pill self-identity. Some are uncomfortable and require him to use judgment he's never had to before. Others are temptations or opportunities he's never had access to before.

All of what's led to this transition required a lot of personal investment on his part, and by his Red Pill awareness he's 'done everything right'. This trans-formative experience becomes a kind of *Relational Equity* for him; equity he believes his wife, his ex, the old high school girl who ignored him, should have some appreciation for. Just like the *old books* men who believed that building themselves up in their careers or getting more in touch with their feminine sides would be the key to doing everything right, the Red Pill aware guy finds that it's not him, it's her.

Why Men Are The Way They Are

One of the most influential books I've ever read I picked up from my father's home library when I was about 24. That book was *Dr. Warren Farrell's Why Men Are The Way They Are*. At the time it didn't strike me as odd that my father would have this book in his collection – my clinically depressed, 3rd wave feminist, aging hippy of a step-mother had eventually roped him into reading it for some Unitarian book club they belonged to in the early 90s. I still have it. It's even got her penciled-in liner notes scribbled in the margins with all the feminist outrage I imagine it must've inspired in her. It's sort of a cosmic irony that the book she raged over would be instrumental for my own writing and online persona.

People always ask me when my point of unplugging came about, but if I'm honest, it was a gradual process that required a lot of bad experiences to learn my way out of the Matrix. However, Farrell's book was a turning point for me. Unfortunately, I've since had to reassess my opinion of Dr. Farrell – he's still very much Blue Pill and will likely go to his grave never making the connection that a belief in egalitarian equalism (as taught to him by early feminism) is what's kept him blind to really accepting Red Pill awareness. But if I had a moment of unplugging I'd say it was directly attributable to this book.

I think what got me the most about it at the time were the many stories of the men Farrell had done 'men's group' sessions with while doing his research for the book. It was published 1986 (about 7 or 8 years before I read it) so it was already kind of dated when I read it, but for the most part these men sort of had these sit-ins with other men to relate with each other. If you've read the *Tribes* section at the beginning of this chapter you'll understand why these new-agey get together seem very contrived to me, but the stories these guys were relating in the early to mid 80s were about what I'd expect coming from my own Dad.

They all did everything right. Some were the products of the free love generation or the hedonistic 70s, but overall these guys were caught in the perfect storm of still clinging to the *old books* Beta-provisioning social contract and the expectation of 3rd wave feminists that they be 'evolved males'. More than a few were attending these men's groups at the behest of their empowered wives in the hopes that they'd learn to get in touch with their feminine sides or at least find some better way to meet their "needs". I could see my father as one of these men. Papa Tomassi was a very confused man with regard to women as it was, but to be caught on the cusp of an era when feminine social primacy coming into its own and still being part of the 'do everything right' social contract and the belief system that was doomed to fail in the decades to come, I can understand a lot of that confusion. One man in the book described it thusly:

"I feel like I've spent 40 years of my life working as hard as I could to become somebody I don't even like."

Each one of these guys related a similar frustration. They busted their asses for decades to fulfill the *old books* social contract, the one that had been the way you did the right thing in order to have a life with a woman, a family, kids, maybe grandchildren, and all of that was no longer working for men. The 24 year old Rollo Tomassi reading this book didn't know what Hypergamy really was back then, but as I recount these men's confusion today I can see that it was a result of being the first men to realize that institutionalized Hypergamy was erasing that old social paradigm for them.

Bad Investments

I've covered the fallacy of *Relational Equity* in my first book, but I think it's necessary to revisit the idea here to understand how it still undermines men in an era of *Open Hypergamy* and feminine social primacy. These men, most of whom are likely into their 70s now, had a preconception of what it meant to 'do everything right'; to play by an understood rule set that women were supposed to find attractive, to acknowledge and honor. Furthermore, they were taught to expect a degree of mutual equalitarian reason from these new, empowered and evolving women. If needs weren't being met, well, then all that was necessary was a heart to heart and *open communication* and negotiation would set things back on track because women could be expected to be the functional equivalents of men. This was the golden, egalitarian, sexual equality, future that feminism promised the guys in the 70s and 80s.

Relational Equity is the misguided belief that 'doing everything right' would necessarily be what ultimately attracts a woman, kept a woman, a wife, an LTR, from both infidelity, and was an assurance of her continued happiness with her man. Needless to say, the collected experiences of men that's led to the praxeology of what we know as Red Pill awareness puts the lie to this – but as men, we expect some kind of acknowledgment for our accomplishments. Rationally, in a male context, we expect that what we do will at least be recognized as valuable, if not honored, by other men. So by extension of our equalist social contract, women, whom we are told we should expect to be co-equal agents with men, should also be expected to see past their emotional Hypergamous natures and make a *logical* conclusion to be attracted to men who are good fits in a mutually understood sense.

This, of course, is nonsense for the same reason that expecting that genuine desire can be negotiated is nonsense, but essentially this is the idea the shifting social contract of the time was trying to convince men of. And as you might expect, those men, the ones with the insight to recognize it, saw it for the opportunism it really was. Even if they ended up at 40 hating who they'd become.

From *Relational Equity*:

> *This is a really tough truth for guys to swallow, because knowing how Hypergamy works necessarily devalues their concept of Relational Equity with the woman they're committed to, or considering commitment with. Men's concept of relational equity stems from a mindset that accepts negotiated desire (not genuine desire) as a valid means of relationship security. This is precisely why most couples counseling fails – its operative origin begins from the misconception that genuine desire (Hypergamy) can be negotiated indefinitely.*

When we become Red Pill aware there is also a kind of *Relational Equity* we need to acknowledge and manage. Once we've unplugged it's easy to get caught up in thinking that because we know the game, because we've gone through the trials, because we know we're higher value men – if for no other reason than that we no longer subscribe to the misgivings of our Blue Pill conditioning – because of that awareness we tend to think that this should be consciously or tacitly appreciated by a wife, a girlfriend or the women we're *sarging* in the club.

This can be kind of tough for a Red Pill aware man because it's often something we need to keep latent in ourselves. Being overt about Red Pill awareness with women is almost always self-defeating because it exposes the Game. Women want to play the game, they don't want to be told how it operates. In our everyday lives it's necessary to reserve and observe or we risk changing the process.

Openly acknowledging the value a man believes he ought to inspire in a woman will alter her perception of that value. Most men who resort to forcing a woman's hand by laying bare all the qualities of himself (real or imagined) he believes she should recognize and appreciate are only exposing their belief that

Relational Equity and an old paradigm mindset is his mental point of origin. In truth, guys who attempt to set themselves apart by listing all the ways they're valuable for playing by the rules generally get shamed by women in the end because those qualities have become so common place and expected that they've become debased.

So, you're a great father to your kids and a devoted husband who built himself into the guy that any woman should be attracted to, who should be a great catch?

That's great, but that's what you're supposed to do. And all those things you're supposed to do, those aren't what engender a woman's genuine desire. In a feminine-primary social order – the same order that deliberately misinterprets masculinity for men – all men need to do, endlessly, is just a bit more to 'do everything right'.

The Awakening

On both the Married Red Pill and MGTOW Reddit forums there's been discussed the concept of being 'awakened while married'. Hopefully I wont butcher that concept too badly here, but I think one aspect of becoming Red Pill aware, whether you're a young single guy or an older, mature, married one is that there comes a point when you are awake and aware of the conditioning and the intersexual paradigm you truly live in. Honestly, I envy the younger men who come into this awareness early in life, but I also recognize that theirs is a greater responsibility to the truth for the rest of their unplugged lives. Men awakened while married at least have the excuse of having been deluded by Blue Pill conditioning for most of their lives to that point.

For younger men the Red Pill presents challenges with each new prospective woman a man applies himself with. For the awakened married man, his challenge is reinventing himself in a Red Pill aware paradigm with a woman who is already intimately aware of his persona, possibly for decades. We always say that once you've become Red Pill aware there is no going back. Even for men who go into total denial and choose to live with the cognitive dissonance of what they know about their own Blue Pill conditioning and the socio-sexual game going on around them there will always be reminders of Red Pill awareness he'll notice on his peripheries.

For a man awakened to his condition while married, his state is a never ending reminder of what his Blue Pill indenturement has made of him. Like the guy in Dr. Farrell's men's group, the Blue Pill husband has spent most of his life trying to become someone he may or may not like, but that process of becoming was prompted by his Blue Pill conditioned existence. Once that man becomes Red Pill aware he's now faced with two problems – how will he remake himself and how will his wife accept that remaking?

From the earliest posts of my blog I've always stressed that a man's dominant *Frame* in his relationship is vital to the function of that relationship. Unfortunately, most men who were awakened while married began their relationships with a strong Beta perception for their wives. We can debate as to whether just the commitment of marriage itself makes for a predominantly Beta perception of a man, but in an era of masculine ridicule, *Open Hypergamy* and Alpha Widows it's a good bet that women's impression of their husbands is rarely one of reserved Alpha confidence.

This is a tough position for a Red Pill aware husband to confront. Sometimes a wife's impression of his Beta-ness is too embedded, or she's built a relational framework around expecting him to be a hapless Beta. Humans are creatures of habit with an insatiable need to see familiarity in other people's actions. Your predictability gives them a sense of control. I should add that this expectation of predictability isn't just limited to a wife's perception of her Beta husband. That can, and often does, extend to a man's family or friends who also expect him to be the Beta he's always been. This then presents another challenge in remaking himself into something new, dominant and respectable in his Red Pill awareness.

Many of the men I used to do peer counseling with back in the early 2000s only wanted one thing; they wanted their wives to have a genuine desire to fuck them with either an enthusiasm they'd never known (but believed was possible) or they hoped to re-experience (and hopefully sustain) a genuine sexual desire they'd enjoyed with their wives while they were dating. None of them wanted (at least at first) to abandon their marriages, they just wanted to do thing right so their wives would fuck them, love them, respect them. They really wanted things to work, and so much so that they would overtly ask their wives "what do I have to do to get you to love/fuck/respect me and I'LL DO IT!" Which of course was precisely the thing that turned their wives off even more.

Their overtness and desperation was only more reinforcement and confirmation of these men's wives perception of their Beta statuses. However, these men are the descendants of the generations that convinced them that 'open communication' solves all relationship problems, but here they were, being open, direct, expecting a rational, negotiable solution to their problem only to have it drive their disgusted wives further from them.

Hypergamy doesn't care when a woman's lasting impression of a man is his

Beta status. How a man's Red Pill awareness and the changes it brings in him will be accepted depends largely on his predominant condition. What husbands want is a sea change in their wives' impression of them once they adopt a Red Pill / Game aware way of life. Most husbands have to weigh their emotional and personal investments in their wives with the reality that their wives' impressions of them may simply never change. Becoming Red Pill aware forces husbands into a position of having to judge whether their marriages are even worth the considerable effort of trying to improve.

The Sexiest Man Alive?

When we consider that western cultures have consolidated on feminine social primacy, and a women's-needs-first way of interpreting any social dynamic, things get a bit easier when you distill the intent down from a social scale to a personal scale. What's being related is the desire to socially, culturally, change the definition of what should be considered "sexy" by women in spite of all evolved arousal and attraction cues they're subject to. The presumption this is based upon is that attraction is a social construct and therefor something that can be changed.

This is the paradox men find themselves in; they are trapped in trying to appease deliberately manipulative, but deliberately conflicting social paradigms to be 'successful' with women. As the narrative goes, if a man does everything by the book, if he does everything right, if he accepts the responsibilities feminine-primacy expects of him, he can be considered to be an adult, and he can assume his chances of being considered 'sexy' by women and certainly his own wife. In so accepting this definition of his burden of performance he is taught that women will necessarily appreciate the equity he accrues in the relationship by investing himself in it. If he holds to the *old books* paradigm, eventually, once a woman has got her *Party Years* indiscretions 'out of her system' he can expect to be found "sexy" by women.

From a Red Pill perspective we see this for what it is, the *old books* social contract that is still being sold to a generation of men who increasingly are seeing it for the life-changing lie it is. Men are encouraged to see adulthood as getting married, becoming a father and working hard to buy a home. I could argue that there are no June Cleavers left in the world or that getting married is a high-risk, low yield gamble. I could argue that becoming a father only makes a man fall in line with the ridiculous or hated caricature popular culture has made of them. I won't even start on the risks of the housing market.

For all of this, the desire is still a return to a social contract wherein men are conditioned to believe that they will be rewarded for doing everything right. That old school notion has become the Beta bait of the past three generations.

Most men who are 'awakened while married' want to apply their Red Pill awareness in such a way that they might achieve this idyllic state that we're assured is possible if we'd all just Man Up. Most married Red Pill (MRP) men are looking to save their marriages. They see it as a key to getting a woman to appreciate his investment in her, in their kids, in his marriage, his dedication to 'doing everything the right way',

Much in the same way that single Red Pill guys will (initially) focus on Red Pill awareness and Game in order to eventually connect with their ill-fated *Dream Girls*, so too does the MRP guy. The difference being that he's convinced he's already married to his dream girl and the only thing between him and that ideal life with her is finding the formula to achieve the life-plan this paradigm sells us.

As I said before, most married men's first intent when they unplug isn't to divorce their wives, hit the clubs and spin plates. His first thought is "how do I get her to come around to appreciating me?" or "How do I get back to the kind of sex we had (or I think we could)?" I think it's important for men, both Red Pill singles and MRP to disabuse themselves of the Blue Pill goals they think might ever be achievable with Red Pill awareness. I say this because it's put Red Pill awareness into the perception of it being a cure to their problems. While it may seem noble to a newly unplugged guy to want to use his new superpowers of Red Pill awareness for good (not for evil) and valiantly use it to do the right thing for his wife, his desire to do so is still founded in a Blue Pill conditioning that's taught him that she'll be receptive to it and he'll be appreciated for it.

It may be that his new Alpha impression on his wife isn't something she will ever recognize or accept as 'the real him'. And while this frustration plays out in his marriage, he also sees the positive responses from women outside his marriage – women unfamiliar with his Beta past – who readily respond to the Game he applies. That new positive reinforcement with outside women contends with his wife's negative reinforcement inside his marriage.

What man sees a woman as a viable long term option and is eager to please (in fact has pleased on many occasions) but is aware she may never reciprocate in kind? Will he waste his best years coveting something he may never have?

Wouldn't it be better to entertain a slightly lesser, woman and be her top priority?

If a wife can no longer give of herself, does she still see fit to demand the level of investment as when she did? Can a man still appreciate the tacit approval his wife offers him, in not questioning his whereabouts when he's engaged in an extramarital affair. Does she show affection and support in other ways? The truth is most women under the influence of the Feminine Imperative don't support their partners, nor do they cultivate an understanding with them in regards to the limits of their sexual capacity.

Men, for their part, like to think sexual intercourse with their partners, will always be available, given time and circumstance. The reality is, it isn't. Our biologies weren't meant to tolerate these conditions. Especially with a woman who will constantly shit test you and emasculate you, in every conceivable way she can divine.

A woman will invariably condemn you for your weakness, but expect understanding for hers.

Common Experiences

There is a school of thought about being Red Pill and married that believes that getting a wife (or LTR girlfriend) to accept the 'new you' as being impossible. Things may nominally improve due to a Dread dynamic working, but your new Red Pill marriage will never be what you want it to be because you have improved, she hasn't and she never wanted you this way in the first place.

I don't accept this assessment in its entirety, however I do see where this sentiment comes from. Most men who are awakened while married are men who followed the same script as the men I illustrate in *Betas in Waiting*. These are the men who have 'done everything right' for the better part of their lives. They cultivated themselves to be the perfect providers that Sheryl Sandberg would have women believe will be waiting for them when their looks begin to fade and it's time to cash out of the sexual marketplace. These are the men who believe their hard work and perseverance is finally paying off with the women who now find him irresistible because he represents their salvation in long term security and parental investment.

Most women entering their *Epiphany Phase* are expressly looking for a Beta to take care of them now that the *Party Years* are coming to an end for her. They're (ostensibly) done with the Bad Boys (something they had to 'grow out of') and now want to do things 'the right way'. This, of course, suits a *Beta in Waiting* just fine because his Blue Pill conditioning has prepared him by expecting him to 'do things the right way' as well and to believe any woman wanting to do the same must be a mythical *Quality Woman.*

These men believe their ship has finally come in, but because of this these men are often the most difficult to unplug. They have the hardest time with Red Pill awareness because in accepting it they must also accept that what led up to their marriage to that *Quality Woman* was also a result of their Blue Pill conditioning. A lot of their ego is invested in Beta Game and Blue Pill convictions, but also a forced-convincing of themselves that they did everything right and were rewarded for it.

This is why it's a bitter pill to swallow when that guy's wife drip-feeds him sex, or he discovers her sexual best was reserved for another man in her past, or she tells him she loves him, but she's not *in* love with him. Even in the face of outright disrespect or his Beta confirmations of failed shit tests, he'll still refuse to acknowledge his state. Often it's only prolonged sexlessness (and even this is rationalized for a long time) that motivates him to seek the answers of Red Pill awareness.

The *Beta in Waiting* never had Frame before or during his marriage. In fact, it was just that lack of Frame that made him marriage material for his wife. He was never "Alpha" for her, and in his equalist mindset he believed this was what set him apart and made him attractive then. Thus, going from this very strong Beta initial impression to an Alpha position of dominance can be all but impossible – particularly if his self-confirmed status was that of being a proud Beta to begin with.

There are other men who'll report having had an Alpha status prior to their marriage, but they lost it somewhere along the way. They were the Alpha 'backsliders' who, possibly, entered into the marriage with a dominant *Frame*, but this dissolved as his wife's *Frame* or insecurities about him came to dominate their relationship. I think this is likely the scenario that seems the most comfortably believable when a man becomes awakened while married. It is a return to a prior impression (or one his wife had hoped he'd find) and therefor more believable when he does. The 'tamed' Alphas are also the guys with wives who'll try to actively minimize his Red Pill transformation. Their wives are simultaneously aroused by this rekindling of his Alpha dominance, but fearful that he will come to see her as the failed investment she likely is for him. That may or may not be the actual case for him, but for her it will prompt possessiveness and a control over how he's allowed to 'appropriately' express this dominance – which in turn disqualifies it.

The Red Pill shows you the dark side of women. Not so that you will hate them but so you appreciate them for what they are, not what they're not.

I think one of the harder aspects of the Red Pill for men who get awakened-while-married (or while monogamous) to accept is seeing the disillusionment of their Blue Pill idealism about women confirmed for them in the behavior and mindsets of their wives. Breaking the Blue Pill ego-investments of single men who unplug is a difficult task, but their investment risk in women (real or imagined) they believe might make acceptable long-term mates is far less than a man who's been married for more than 4 or 5 years.

For the single Red Pill guy with the option to simply walk away from a less than optimal situation, his conflict becomes one of potentials and weighing them against his Blue Pill ideals – ideals his unplugging should rid him of. His struggles is one about the "what ifs" and disabusing himself of the scarcity mentality that the Blue Pill has conditioned him for. While Hypergamy inherently instills in women a persistent doubt about a man's quality, the Blue Pill instills in men a doubt about "quality" women's scarcity and his capacity to find and maintain a 'soul mate'.

However for married men, with a considerable amount of emotional, social, financial and familial investment at stake in his marriage, there's a natural resistance that comes in the form of denial. What's tough is that, within this initial state of denial, a husband accepts the Red Pill truths about women and then has those truths confirmed for him by the woman he's been sleeping next to for a number of years. All of the awareness about men and women's differing concepts of love, the truth of women's Hypergamously motivated opportunism, her confirming her open Hypergamy, all of the events that led up to his committing himself in marriage to her while he was still effectively Blue Pill – all of that gets confirmed for him when he puts into practice the concepts he learns from the Red Pill.

For all of the supposed '*anger*' that profiteering critics would like to wipe off on Red Pill thought, that anger finds its base in men's confirming their own role in what was (or would've been) a life-long strategy for him to fulfill the dictates of women's Hypergamy as well as the larger scope of the Feminine Imperative. When we put this into the perspective of a married man who unplugs, you can see why this is such a threat to the imperative. That man must reassess his life from the position of his being an unwitting participant in his Blue Pill conditioning, but furthermore, he becomes a constant caution, a warning, for men who have yet to make the same uneducated decisions he has.

There is nothing more depressing to me than to listen to a married man parrot back all of the tropes the Feminine Imperative has taught him to repeat about why he's in the subservient role in his marriage. These are the guys who'll laughingly tell single men how they must "clear everything with the Boss" before they are allowed (or will allow themselves) to participate in anything remotely masculine or self-entertaining. These are the men who prattle about their 'honey-do' lists, the men who count themselves fortunate to have such a 'great wife' who'll allow him to watch hockey or football on a weekend.

These husbands are depressing to me because, in their Blue Pill ignorance, they represent the summation of their roles according to the strategies of the Feminine Imperative. They'll gladly White Knight for their wives' right to the *Frame* of their marriage (under the pretense of equalism). They'll laugh and commiserate with other husbands sharing their position of powerlessness-but-with-all-accountability. They'll chirp with funny little *Facebook* memes that share their ridiculous, married state, but for all of that acquiescing to their 'fates' what they really represent is the goal-state of men in the Feminine Imperative's plan for their lives.

Men generally come to the realization of their appointed role at some point in their lives. Whether it's Red Pill awareness or coming to a mid life crisis epiphany, men get '*woke*' in some respect. The few who don't are men whose existence literally depends on their not coming to terms with how the Blue Pill has made them what/who they are. The most common way for men to come into this awareness has been that mid-life epiphany, but in order for men to reconcile that awareness with maintaining a comfortable sense of self they become men who readily abdicate *Frame*. They really don't know anything else but what the Blue Pill has created them to be, so they go into denial and add some self-deprecating humor to it to cope with the dissonance of knowing they've been played by the Feminine Imperative for the better part of their lives. So you get the 'Yes Dear' husbands; the men who realize the truth too late, but that same scarcity mentality forces them to go along to get along.

The rise of Red Pill awareness of intersexual dynamics on the internet has made for a community of men who find this denial distasteful. Rather than abdicate to the imperative and their wife's Frame they look to the Red Pill and Game for a remedy to that state. Sometimes that's getting their wives to have sex with them more frequently or they're looking to better themselves in a Red Pill context to gain women's (their wives') respect. As I've mentioned many times before, the Red Pill represents a threat to the Feminine Imperative keeping men ignorant of their roles in women's Hypergamous plans. Now that threat comes to fruition in the context of men's marriages.

One way or another, men will become aware of their role, how that man goes about dealing with it is another story. Most (being Blue Pill) abdicate and accept their powerlessness in their relationships. It's the other men who choose not to just cope, but to reconstruct themselves that the Red Pill will have answers for.

Break Up with Your Wife

In various comment threads on my blog and on the Red Pill Reddit forums readers had a discussion about how *any* marriage (at least in the contemporary sense) is always founded on a Beta status for the husband. I don't entirely agree with that assessment, but considering how the large majority of marriages are the culmination of Blue Pill conditioned men fulfilling their role as semi-cuckolded provider for women cashing out of the sexual marketplace it's certainly an understandable presumption. I won't elaborate too much on the particulars, but the very act of committing to a woman monogamously implies a man (even one with an Alpha persona) is leaning towards a predominantly Beta perception. As the logic goes, Alpha's don't commit to anyone but themselves, Betas are eager to commit from necessity and scarcity. The act becomes the confirmation.

If we follow this binary logic, the only solution to a man's condition within his marriage – the only way to institute a real change – is to reject and break that commitment. Personally, I have lived out what most men would envy in my marriage for over 21 years now, so the idea of leaving Mrs. Tomassi would only seem like a good idea if I weren't satisfied sexually, psychologically and life-wise with her. But, as I always repeat, don't use my marriage as a benchmark. There was a point where I needed to break up with her, if only by adopting my own mental point of origin above that of hers or women in general as my own Blue Pill conditioning would expect of me.

I mentioned in the beginning of this section that married (committed) men seeking to reconstruct themselves within that context ought to read the post for the Iron Rule of Tomassi #7:

Iron Rule of Tomassi #7
It is always time and effort better spent developing new, fresh, prospective women than it will ever be in attempting to reconstruct a failed relationship. Never root through the trash once the garbage has been dragged to the curb. You get messy, your neighbors see you do it, and what you thought was worth digging for is never as valuable as you thought it was.

I mention this as a starting point because when you're making the decision to reconstruct yourself you must 'do it for you'. Once again, any real change always beggars the question about who you're really changing for. Nothing is an act of unguided, unbiased, self-initiated change – there is always some ancillary influences as well as consequences. This is the crisis of motive – who are we really doing something for?

However, if you find yourself awakened-while-married and you want to remake yourself, know that this change must be for *yourself* and not for your *wife*. This decision to reconstruct your life, your persona, your belief set, etc., and reject what the Blue Pill has made of you must come as a result of making yourself your mental point of origin. This 'new you' precludes any consideration of your wife's interests. It must be in order for your transformation to be genuine to both yourself and those who know the 'old' you. As I mentioned earlier, the likelihood of your wife accepting your new persona is dependent upon whose dominant *Frame* you entered that relationship with as well as what you've surrendered of your self-respect to her.

This is the most difficult part for Blue Pill men wanting to reconstruct themselves. Their mental point of origin doesn't change. They want to change because they want to be "more Alpha" for their wives, not themselves. The Purple Pill hope is to adopt just enough Alpha that their wives turn the sex spigot back on for them, but never really internalize the Red Pill to the point that is fundamentally changes who they are. Thus, it becomes an act not unlike newbie Pickup Artists (PUAs) aping the behaviors of their mentors, but never internalizing the deeper meanings of why they work or making them part of 'who' they are as a person.

This is what kills a man's reconstruction before it ever starts. That change must be a self-first proposition. Your Red Pill self-work must be intrinsically rewarding because there is absolutely no guarantee that a man's wife / girlfriend will ever reimagine him from a different perspective. Particularly if that woman entered into that marriage/LTR because she'd hoped to maintain *Frame* indefinitely due to him abdicating it.

You must become Red Pill aware for the sake of knowing the larger truth, internalize it and then apply it without the pretense of believing it can be used to achieve Blue Pill ideals. Those ideals must be replaced with new ideals founded on what a Red Pill aware reality makes possible.

With this in mind, you must presume that you are breaking up with your wife / girlfriend. It is far better to approach your reconstruction from the idea that the new Red Pill *you* would likely have nothing to do with a woman like your wife. If you were a single man, Red Pill aware and Game savvy, would you even approach your wife knowing what you do now about her personally as well as what you know about the Feminine Imperative and how it influences her? Would the juice be worth the squeeze with her knowing what you do about Red Pill truth?

Your reconstruction requires a radical shift that is only possible for you by breaking up with your LTR, at least in a subconscious respect. It is important to assess what, if anything, is worth rooting through garbage for. If you approach your reconstruction by first making yourself your mental point of origin, the next step is to assume you will be breaking up with your wife. In actuality it may never come to that, but this is the gravity which a man must bring to his reconstruction. The same reasoning I mention in *Rooting through Garbage* applies to your reconstruction:

Even if you could go back to where you were, any relationship you might have with an Ex will be colored by all of the issues that led up to the breakup. In other words, you know what the end result of those issues has been. It will always be the 800 pound gorilla in the room in any future relationship. As I elaborated in the Desire Dynamic, healthy relationships are founded on genuine mutual desire, not a list of negotiated terms and obligations, and this is, by definition, exactly what any post-breakup relationship necessitates. You or she may promise to never do something again, you may promise to "rebuild the trust", you may promise to be someone else, but you cannot promise to pretend that the issues leading up to the breakup don't have the potential to dissolve it again. The doubt is there. You may be married for 30 years, but there will always be that one time when you two broke up, or she fucked that other guy, and everything you think you've built with her over the years will always be compromised by that doubt of her desire.

You will never escape her impression that you were so optionless you had to beg her to rekindle her intimacy with you.

It is always time and effort better spent developing new, fresh, prospective women than it will ever be in attempting to reconstruct a failed relationship. This is the same rationale you will need to adopt when you transition into a new Red Pill aware persona. This is necessary because once you've become aware there is no going back to that previous state of ignorance. You will know what can be possible with or without your wife/LTR.

Thus, it is important to zero everything out in your own head and treat your old wife as a new prospective woman. This perspective may mean she becomes someone not worth your effort, but it might also mean she likes the prospect of a new husband. This may mean she too will have to undertake some kind of transformation in relating to a Red Pill aware husband, or it might be that this is something she never foresaw. Dread works best when a man understands the Cardinal Rule of Relationships: *In any relationship, the person with the most power is the one who needs the other the least.*

By adopting the mindset that you are breaking up with her you reclaim this power. You have nothing to lose and have no way of going back to unknowing the Red Pill awareness you have now.

For single men I often point out that breaking up with a girl is one of the best ways to demonstrate higher value (DHV). The downside to that is that by the time you get to the point of leaving demonstrating higher value isn't what you really care about. For the reconstructing man, adopting the position that you are breaking up (or have broken up) harnesses some of this DHV.

Most women (wives) will interpret your new self-importance as some kind of phase or your reclaiming your independence (rather than her co-dependence) as some childish sulking behavior. Anticipate this. She will presume you're 'going your own way' within the marriage to force her to fuck you more or to get her to comply with your *Frame*. This is to be expected, but watch what her initial reactions to your takeaway are. This will give you an insight into how she perceives you.

If you're predominantly Beta her response will be that you're pouting or sulking by removing your attention. She'll roll her eyes and reflexively respond with Beta Tells. If she sees you as Alpha her response will be much more serious and you'll get the "what's wrong baby?" reaction. This is a good starting point in determining her genuine perception of you.

You will effectively be NEXTing your wife so be prepared for her post-NEX-Ting behavior-set (extinction burst behavior) in the same way you would if you dropped a Plate you were spinning. This will be a tough transition for men who have invested themselves emotionally in their wives (which is to say most men). You'll want to come back to that place of comfort, but always remember that place is one of disrespect and sexlessness.

Most men will go half-way in their reconstruction and this is usually the result of having played a game of relationship 'chicken'. Men have their bluff called because it was always a bluff to begin with them – they never made themselves their mental point of origin so they go back to the safety of their Blue Pill disrespect. Their wives respond to the takeaway of their attention, but never really connect with being attracted to his new self-respect and self-importance. Once that woman even marginally steps up her sexual frequency – motivated by her wanting him to return to her *Frame* – the guy gets comfortable and wants to go back to his comfy wife while feeling validated by thinking he made a genuine change that she responded to.

You must go all the way. If you don't, the next time you attempt to exercise your Red Pill awareness in the hope that she'll accept the new you, you'll be that much more laughable to her. In fact, you'll only further cement her perception of your whiny Beta status. The first time it's Dread, the second time it's you being pissy.

All that said, the real authenticity of your Red Pill transformation is ultimately up to you. I've read the testimonies of men who've completely redirected the course of their lives and their marriages because they stuck to their guns (usually had nothing to lose) and went through the fire of having their wives resist their transformation. These men went from a predominantly Beta perception to at least a lesser Alpha one and were surprised that the lackluster wives they'd been married to for years responded with an eager submission to a dominance they never knew she truly wanted. Their equalist mindset had taught them never to experiment with assuming a dominant Frame with a women who would be their wives, but were surprised that authentic dominance was exactly what she wanted from a husband.

Then there are the men like the one whose story started us off in this section. The men who made an authentic reconstruction of themselves, but their pre-dominantly Beta impression with their wives was to great an obstacle for her to overcome. Even in these instances that Red Pill transformation is always a net positive since that man is much better prepared for the new prospective women he will eventually find himself with. It may be depressing that he was unable to reinvent his relationship with a woman he'd had so much emotional investment in, but in the long term that Red Pill awareness made him a greater man than the Beta husband he'd been before.

THE POWER OF NEXT

The opposite of love is not hate – the opposite of love is indifference.

I think one of the biggest mistakes guys against a Three Strikes rule make is assuming that it means a guy would be so preoccupied with sex that you couldn't wait for 4-6 dates. They assume that a Three Strikes rule (or any rule dependent upon sexual reciprocation) makes them *Players* at best, superficial and overly sex-concerned at worst. Nothing could be further from the truth.

The mistake is to presume that a 3 date policy is some form of punishment for the girl for not having 'put out' soon enough to verify interest. It's not punishment, it's a fail-safe that serves to protect a guy from some protracted personal investment for a very limited return. For example, I play golf and when I want to improve my game I hire a golf pro. I pay him $120 for 3 lessons, so $40 per lesson (very similar to the $40 per date rule). At the end of my 3rd lesson I assess whether or not my game's improved and I can decide to continue with him or, if I see no improvement I can choose to find another pro and do the same. There are a lot of golf pros ready to work with me. I'm not punishing the pro for doing this, I'm simply looking for the best value in an area I wish to improve in. If I think my swing has improved or I notice my average go up, I'll continue with the pro.

The misunderstanding is to see a Three Strikes rule as a threat. "She'd better put out after tonight or I'm outta here". I can see why that would place a burden upon a woman, but you must take into account why a Three Strike rule would even be a necessary concept. Three dates (and I mean real dates, none of this coffee / lunch crap) over the course of three weeks should be ample time to make the assessment as to whether a woman has interest and attraction enough to become intimate. Anything beyond this is indicative of filibustering on a woman's part and usually points to an only lukewarm interest level if at all. In this way a Three Strike rule benefits both men and women; why would either sex want to engage in a relationship that was lackluster from the start? Why would either want to be involved with a person who was settled on or settled for?

It's urgency and anxiety that makes for genuine, chemical-fueled sexual desire – not comfort, not familiarity. This is precisely why I say "any woman who makes you wait for sex, or by her actions implies she is making you wait for sex; the sex is NEVER worth the wait". It's not that you can't have sex with her, it's that the sex is compromised, filibustered, internally debated, choice-of-necessity sex. It becomes mundane before anyone's clothes come off.

The Power of NEXT

I used the above situation as a prelude to illustrate the power of tapping into one of the most elusive and difficult to internalize principles of Game – the power of NEXT. It's very easy to casually type, "just NEXT her man" when you have no personal investment in the advice you give. It's standard male deductive pragmatism, and rightly so, to solve the problem by eliminating the source of it. Likewise when you lack a real understanding of the personal conditions and mental schema the average guy (i.e. Matrix-Beta) is predisposed to, telling him to simply NEXT the only plate he's got spinning is about as useful as telling him to *Just Be Himself* with the next girl he happens into.

Spinning Plates is actually the best starting point for mastering the power of NEXT. When you have other irons in the fire it's much easier to shift the focus of your attention to another woman; at least in theory. There's a certain degree of emotional dissociation that needs to be made and this is usually dependent upon the personal investment a Man puts into any one woman. Far too many men, and even practiced PUAs, have a very hard time with NEXT not only because of this dissociation, but also the doubt that comes from "what might have been." Couple this with a soul-mate myth inspired ONEitis and you can see why most guys will fight to their own bitter end not to NEXT the girl they're with.

It's exactly this doubt that makes men think they'd be throwing the baby out with the bath water by NEXTing a woman. A lot of men think that NEXTing a girl is some knee-jerk response from guys who don't have any other ideas of what to do, when in fact it should be a practiced, default response for the first indication that a woman is insisting on setting the *Frame* in her favor by manipulating a guy using her intimacy as a carrot to pull the cart.

It's men without options that find NEXTing a girl in some way 'wrong', and to a man with only one plate spinning this is entirely counterintuitive, but it's important to remember that **Rejection is better than Regret** – even if you're the one doing the rejecting. It's better err on the side of NEXTing than be dragged into the quicksand of a woman's frame.

Tactical NEXTing

The opposite of love is not hate – the opposite of love is indifference. When your silence inspires more anxiety than any spoken threat, that's when you're approaching Alpha status.

Learning indifference is the key to mastering the power of NEXT. Women are masters of indifference for the same reason Men with options (i.e. Plate Spinners) find it useful; they derive confidence from having options. Since women (in their prime) are the primary sexual selectors, indifference is their natural default state. It's only Men with options who make an impact enough to rattle a woman out of this default indifference and fire her imagination.

NEXTing as a tool is one of the best ways to determine real interest level in a woman. Dumping a woman is one of the highest forms of demonstrating higher value that a man possesses. Nine times out of ten the NEXTed woman will attempt to reconnect with the guy who's got the personal confidence enough to walk away from her. Why is this? Because it shakes up the routine which you slip into by playing in her *Frame*. In behavioral psychology terms she's about to go into what's called an *extinction burst*. You've removed her source of reward (i.e. attention, comfort, familiarity) and now – if it was at all rewarding to her – she will frantically attempt to restore it.

Uncertainty is exciting, particularly after you've set a pattern of behavior that she thinks is secure. Unpredictability is good. The guy who can walk away from a less than optimal situation is a man communicating that he believes he has options and the confidence to be uncompromising (or at least less compromising) in what he's willing to accept. The secret is that pussy is an easily had commodity and it's up to a woman to convince you that her intimacy is in someway uniquely valuable among all others.

The hard truth, that she's well aware of, is that no amount of sex is an equitable trade for a man's complacency and/or compromising his identity. That's always going to be the paradox of walking away from sure-thing pussy; what degree of sexual access is your lowest bidding point with regard to compromising your authentic identity and your own wants and needs?

In fact, a woman wants you to walk away; it communicates that her intimacy has no control over you putting you decisively in control (where she wants you to be), increases her desire by planting a seed of doubt of her estimation of you, proves you to be a man with other irons in the fire, and confirms for her that your attentions are valuable to other (potentially competing) women.

Permanent NEXTing – Going Dark

There will come times when NEXTing a poisonous woman becomes a necessity. For any number of reasons, extracting her from your life may be essential to saving your own life. NEXTing under these conditions (really a break up) takes on much more gravity since the woman you're cutting off will still experience the same extinction burst despite the factors (perhaps her own fault) that led to it. The same basic principles of emotional dissonance apply, but the emotional investment may make it impossible to achieve true indifference. It's during these extinction burst when she opens up sexually to retain a failing interest that prove the most difficult for men to resist. A starving man can't help but want to eat from the most convenient buffet prepared for him, even when arsenic is on the menu.

As I mentioned in *War Brides* in my first book, women have an innate psychological facility in achieving a degree of indifference that men can scarcely believe they're capable of – even after decades of an LTR or marriage. So imagining and enacting a disconnect of this emotional magnitude is kind of a foreign concept for men to embrace themselves. It not only goes against our deductive, problem solving natures, but it also conflicts with our idealistic concept of love that teaches us to stick with her no matter what, "all for love."

Keep that in mind; the intent of your leaving isn't punishment for her misbehavior, nor is it meant to teach her a lesson to learn from –you're not leaving her 'better than you found her' – it's to save your own life from further damage. As I stated earlier, NEXTing a woman is demonstrating higher value of the highest order. True or not, It implies you have other, better options than her. NEXTing her implies you've just gone from a comfortable, familiar Beta to the indifferent Alpha that she never appreciated you had a capacity for. What serves as a benefit in Tactical NEXTing is liability in a Permanent NEXT. You will hear from her again. At first it will be desperate and crying, later it will be casual with feigned nonchalance, then it moves to anger and spite – don't take the bait.

The best thing you can do is go dark. Block her calls / texts, drop her from *Facebook* if you have one, cut off all contact. No messages via friends, no "hey howya doing?", nothing but indifference. You're off the grid for her.

Learning indifference is the key to the power of NEXT. Presuming and cultivating that presence of indifference makes your attention that much more valuable and makes a permanent NEXT a much easier transition.

THE CARDINAL RULE
OF SEXUAL STRATEGIES

When I first began writing on the SoSuave forums well over a decade ago I used to get into what I consider now some fairly predictable arguments about monogamy. It was an interesting time since it was around then I was getting into some heated arguments in my behavioral psychology classes in college.

I had just written what would later become my essay, *There is no One* and a good majority of my classmates and all of my teachers but one were less than accepting of the theory. I anticipated most of the women in the class would be upset – bear in mind this was around 2001-02 and the Red Pill was yet to be a thing – what I was surprised by was how many men became hostile by my having challenged the soul-mate myth.

I got a lot of the same flack from women then that I get from uninitiated women when they read my work now; *"Aren't you married? Isn't she your soul-mate? Don't you believe in love? You must've got burned pretty bad at some time Mr. Hateful."* Those were and are what I expect because they're the easy subroutine responses a Blue Pill ego needs to protect itself with.

There was a time I probably would've mouthed the same. That's how the conditioning works; it provides us with what we think ought to be 'obvious' to anyone. And at the same time, we feel good for 'defying the odds' and believing in what we take for granted, or common sense.

This is how deep the subconscious need for assuring our genetic heritage goes. For women this assurance is about optimal Hypergamy, for men, it's about assurances of paternity. In either case, we need to believe that we will reproduce, and so much so that we will attribute some supernatural influence to the process of doing so. The fulfillment of your own sexuality is nothing less than your battle for existence, and on some level, your subconscious understands this. Thus, for the more religious-minded it gets attributed to fate and faith, whereas for the more secular-minded it's about the romanticized notion of a soul-mate.

Monogamy & ONEitis

I contemplated the idea of ONEitis for a long time back then. I'd most certainly been through it more than once, even with the BPD ex-girlfriend I mention on occasion. By then I understood first hand how the soul-mate belief absorbs a Beta and how it is an essential element, effectively a religion, for a Blue Pill life experience. I didn't realize it then, but I was maturing into a real valuation of myself and I had the benefit of some real-world experiences with the nature of women to interpret and contrast what I was learning then.

Honestly, I had never even encountered the term 'ONEitis' prior to my SoSuave forum days. I referred to the soul-mate myth in my writing as best I could, but it wasn't until (I suppose) PUA *Mystery* had coined the term. Outside the 'sphere people got genuinely upset with me when I defined it for them. Back then I attributed this to having their ego-investment challenged, and while that's part of it, today I believe there's more to it than this.

The old social contracts that constituted what I call the *Old Set of Books* meant a lot in respect to how the social orders prior to the sexual revolution were maintained. That structuring required an upbringing that taught men and women what their respective roles were, and those roles primarily centered on a lifetime arrangement of pair bonding.

It's interesting to note that the popular theory amongst evolutionary anthropologists is that modern monogamous culture has only been around for just 1,000 years. Needless to say, it's a very unpopular opinion that human beings are in fact predisposed to polyamory / polygamy and monogamy is a social adaptation (a necessary one) with the purpose of curbing the worst consequences of that nature. We want to believe that monogamy is our nature and our more feral impulses are spandrels and inconveniences to that nature. We like the sound of humans having evolved past our innate proclivities to the point that they are secondary rather than accepting them as fundamental parts of who we really are.

Women, in particular, are far more invested in promoting the idea of 'natural' monogamy since it is their sex that bears the cost of reproductive investments. Even the hint of men acknowledging their *'selfish gene'* nature gets equated with being a license to cheat on women. This is an interesting conflict for women who are increasingly accepting (if not outright flaunting) of *Open Hypergamy*.

I've attempted in past essays to address exactly this duplicity women have to rationalize with themselves. The *Preventive Medicine* book outlines this conflict and how women internalize the need to be both Hypergamously selective, but also to prioritize long-term security at various stages of their lives. Ultimately a woman's position on monogamy is ruled by how she balances her present Alpha Fucks with her future prospects of Beta Bucks.

Seed and Need

It might be that women would rather share a confirmed Alpha with other women than be saddled with a faithful Beta, but that's not to say that necessity doesn't eventually compel women to settle for monogamy with a dutiful Beta. In either respect, the onus of sustained, faithful monogamy is always a responsibility placed upon men. We're the 'dogs' remember? Our Masculine Imperative distills down to unlimited access to unlimited sexuality, and women innately presuppose this about us.

The indignation that comes from even the suspicions of a man's "straying", a wandering eye, or preplanned infidelity is one of the most delicious sensations a woman can feel. Suspicion and jealousy create a wonderful chemical cocktail women crave. Women will create syndicated talk shows just to commiserate around that indignation for the chemical rush. But in an era when the likes of Sheryl Sandberg encourages women to fully embrace their Hypergamous natures and expects men to be equally accepting of it, it takes a lot of psychological gymnastics to reconcile the visceral feelings of infidelity with the foreknowledge that a less exciting Beta will be the only type of man who will calm her suspicions – suspicion that make her feel alive.

It's important to also contrast this with the socialization efforts to make women both victims and blameless. In a feminine-primary social order men who lack an appreciation of the necessity to prepare for a sustained monogamy with a woman are considered 'kidults' or prolonging their adolescence. They are shamed for not meeting women's definition of being mature; that definition is always one that centers on the idea that men ought to center their lives around being a better-than-deserved, faithful, monogamous potential for women's long-term security and parental investment.

On the other hand, women are never subject to any qualifications like this. In fact, they are held in higher regard for bucking the system and staying faithful to themselves by never marrying or even aborting children along the way to 'empowerment'. So once again, we return to the socialization effort necessary to absolve women of the consequences that the conflict of Hypergamy poses to them – they become both victims and blameless in confronting a monogamy they expect from men, but are somehow exempt from when it's inconvenient.

Pair Bonding

Arguably, pair bonding has been a primary adaptation for us that has been species-beneficial. It's fairly obvious that humans' capacity for both intra- and inter-sexual cooperation has made us the apex species on the planet. However, the Feminine Imperative's primary social impetus of making Hypergamy the defining order of (ideally) all cultures is in direct conflict with this human cooperation. A new order of open Hypergamy, based on female primacy (and the equalist importance of the individual), subverts the need for pair bonding. There is no need for intersexual interdependence (complementarity) when women are socialized and lauded for being self-satisfying, self-sufficient individuals.

Add to this the conditioning of unaccountable victimhood and/or the inherent blamelessness of women and you get an idea of where our social order is heading. Both sex's evolved sexual strategies operate counter to the demands of pair bonded monogamy. For millennia we've adapted social mechanisms to buffer for it (marriage, male protectionism of women, etc.), but the cardinal rule of sexual strategies still informs these institutions and practices:

The Cardinal Rule of Sexual Strategies:

For one gender's sexual strategy to succeed the other gender must compromise or abandon their own.

In this respect, in this era, it is men who are expected to make the greater compromise due to an evolved sense of uncertainty about paternity and the social mandate to accommodate women's sexual strategy. The counter to this is that women have always borne the responsibility of parental investment if they chose a father poorly (or didn't choose at all), but in our post-sexual revolution social order, the consequences of this responsibility, for better or worse, have been virtually eliminated for women. In fact, those consequences are now viewed as evidence of women's independent strength.

In our present social climate even aborting a child is a source of pride for a woman now.

Men bear the greater effect of compromising their sexual strategies to accommodate and resolve the strategy of women. When we account for the normalization of *Open Hypergamy*, soft cuckoldry, and the legal resistance to paternity testing (ostensibly centering on the emotional wellbeing of the child in question) it is much clearer that men bear the most direct consequences for compromising their sexual imperatives.

From *Dr. Warren Farrell's* book. *Why Men are the Way They Are*:

Why are men so afraid of commitment? Chapter 2 explained how most men's primary fantasy is still, unfortunately, access to a number of beautiful women. For a man, commitment means giving up this fantasy. Most women's primary fantasy is a relationship with one man who either provides economic security or is on his way to doing so (he has "potential"). For a woman, commitment to this type of man means achieving this fantasy. So commitment often means that a woman achieves her primary fantasy, while a man gives his up. — P.150

Men who "won't commit" are often condemned for treating women as objects — hopping from one beautiful woman to the next. Many men hop. But the hopping is not necessarily objectifying. Men who "hop from one beautiful woman to another" are usually looking for what they could not find at the last hop: good communication, shared values, good chemistry. — P.153

The meaning of commitment changed for men between the mid-sixties and the mid-eighties. Commitment used to be the certain route to sex and love, and to someone to care for the children and the house and fulfill the "family man image." Now men feel less as if they need to marry for sex; they are more aware that housework can be hired out and that restaurants serve meals; they are less trapped by family-man image motivation, including the feeling that they must have children. Increasingly, that leaves men's main reason to commit the hope of a woman to love. — P.159

Dr. Farrell is still fundamentally trapped in a Blue Pill perspective because he still clings to the validity of the *old order books/rules*, and the willfully ignorant hope that women will rationally consider men's sexual imperatives as being as valid as their own. He also makes the same Apex Fallacy presumption women do in believing 'many men hop'. This is a common misplacement among women; many men would like to hop from woman to woman, but only the upper echelon (top 20%) of SMV men can actually do so.

That said, Farrell's was the germ of the idea I had for the *Cardinal Rule of Sexual Strategies*, he just didn't go far enough because he was (and still is) stuck in Blue Pill idealistic hopes of equalist monogamy. Bear in mind, Farrell's book is based on his intrasexual understandings (inspired by feminism) of everything leading up to its publication in 1986, however, this does give us some insight into how the old order evolved its approach to monogamy then into an open, socially accepted form of Hypergamy now.

He relies on the old trope that men are afraid of commitment by reasoning that men only want to fulfill a fantasy of unlimited access to unlimited sexuality – all shallow, all superficial, while women's priority of commitment is 'correct', selfless, valid and blameless. Farrell also reveals his Blue Pill conditioning by making the presumption that men only Game women in the hope that they'll find a unicorn, and they're endlessly fucking women for no other reason than to find a woman with good communication skills, shared values, good chemistry, etc. – all prerequisites for women's intimacy.

I sincerely doubt that even in the mid 80s this was the case for men not wanting to commit to a woman, or essentially compromise his sexual strategy to accommodate that of women's. Though he brushed on it, Farrell never came to terms with dual nature of women's sexual strategy and how it motivates women over time because he believes men and women have, fundamentally, the same concept of love and mutually shared end-goals.

The presumption of equalist correctness is really an endorsement of feminine correctness. Because equalism presume a baseline, blank-slate equality between the sexes it also presumes an equality among experience for both sexes. Farrell falls into this trap, as most Blue Pill men do, by presuming a unitary long term goal of both sexes is essentially the fulfillment of women's sexual strategy.

Mandates & Responses

In the decades since the publication of *Why Men Are The Way They Are*, the normalization and legal mandates that ensure men will (by legislated force if necessary) comply with this compromise is something I doubt Farrell could've ever predicted. Legal and social aspects that used to be a source of women's stigmatization about this compromise have all been swept away or normalized, if not converted to some redefined source of supposed strength. Abortion rights, single parenting (almost exclusively the domain of women), postponing birth, careerism, freezing women's eggs, sperm banks, never-marrying, body fat acceptance and many more aspects are all accepted in the name of strong independence® for women.

Virtually anything that might've been a source of regret, shame, or stigmatization in the old order is dismissed or repurposed to elevate women, but what most men never grasp (certainly not Dr. Farrell) is that all of these normalizations were and are potential downsides to a woman's Hypergamous decisions. Since the time of the Sexual Revolution all of these downsides have been mitigated or absolved.

MGTOW/PUA/ The Red Pill, are all the deductive responses to this normalization, but also, they're a response to the proposition of the compromise that the
Cardinal Rule of Sexual Strategies presents to men in today's sexual marketplace. In all of these 'movements' the fundamental, central truth is that they all
run counter to the presumption that men must compromise (or abandon) their
sexual imperatives – long or short term. Thus, these ideologies and praxeologies
have the effect of challenging or removing some of the total control of Hypergamy which women now have mandated to them. Even just the concepts of
MGTOW/PUA/TRP are equatable to removing this control.

However, it is still undeniable that there is a necessity for monogamy (even if
it's just temporary) or some iteration of pair bonding that ensures men and wom-
en raise healthier, stronger, better-developed children. We are still social animals
and, despite what equalism espouses, we are different yet complementary and
interdependent with one another. Mutual cooperation, tribalism, monogamy and
even small-scale soft-polygamy have been beneficial social adaptations for us.

Gynocentrism and the respondent efforts against it defeat this complementary
cooperative need. Gynocentrism / egalitarianism defeat this cooperation need in
its insistence that equalism, self-apart independence, and homogeny ought to be
society's collective mental point of origin in place of the application of differing
strengths to differing weaknesses.

I'm often asked by offended critics whether I believe in "equality among the
sexes". Even just the asking in an implied accusation of misogyny, but the
answer is a resounding 'no'. I do believe in complementarity among the sexes,
but equality always implies a belief in a homogeneous capacity for either sex to
meet environmental and situational challenges to equal effect.

Men and women are fundamentally different, but by my sayings so the binary
response is that I must believe that men are the superior sex. This is also untrue.
I believe that for some environmental, situational or adaptive challenges, men's
strengths can make them superior or weaker than women. Likewise, women's
innate natures can make them greater or weaker than men meeting the same
challenges. What egalitarian equalism presumes is that life happens in a vacuum
and functionally equal women are as good as men within that vacuum.

But life is not a level playing field at all times in all ways and men and women
have evolved differently and often cooperatively, to be complementary to the
other in meeting the demands of an ever-changing reality. Either sex's imperatives or life strategies is only superior or inferior insofar as it meets a challenge.

Presuming that men and women are standalone, autonomous, self-sustaining entities is one of the great lies perpetrated by egalitarian equalism. The meme of the *Strong Independent Woman*® is an indictment of an ideology that ostensibly rejects the need for complementary support between the sexes, but at the same time presumes a superiority of women.

So we come to an impasse then. It's likely it will require a traumatic social event to reset or redefine the terms of our present social contract to ever make monogamy a worthwhile compromise for men again. We can also contrast this 'raw deal' compromise against the Cardinal Rule of Relationships: *In any relationship, the person with the most power is the one who needs the other the least.* It's easy to think women simply have no need of men when their long-term security is virtually assured today, but fem-centrism goes beyond just separating the sexes by need. It wasn't enough to just separate male and female cooperation, fem-centrism has made men's compromise so bad that they must be made to despise their sex altogether. Men had to be made not only to accept their downside compromise but to feel ashamed for even thinking not to.

SMV RATIOS AND ATTACHMENT

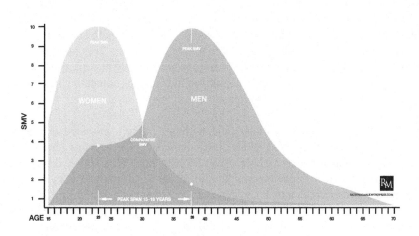

Since I produced the now infamous sexual market value (SMV) graph/time line I have had more than a few earnest readers and irritated critics call me to the carpet about the variables involved in estimating even a rough sketch of the modern, western, sexual marketplace landscape. Before I get in too deep, let me reiterate that my SMV chart is an imperfect tool; sexual market evaluation doesn't happen in a vacuum, I know that, but it is a necessary starting point and framework against which we can better understand social, behavioral and psychological dynamics between the genders.

One of the larger messages this SMV life-overview brings to light is the rise and fall of an individual's sexual market value according to their age and the personal implications that a phase of their life has on affecting that valuation. I originally published the SMV chart with the intent of enlightening men as to what their future SMV (*should*) will be in relation to women's faster burning SMV, and the social conventions women, and the feminine imperative, have established in order to derail that awareness to better service women's sexual priorities and Hypergamy. However, since then I've seen this chart passed around the Manosphere and into outside forums as an example of other related gender dynamics. The chart has other uses than my original idea.

The Ennobled Beta

With this in mind I was debating the idea of secure attachments in relationships with a friend during a summer hiatus. He's what I'll call an *'ennobled Beta'*, not necessarily guilty of outright White Knighting, but he's steeped in his Matrix conditioning enough to conflate a prescribed male role in egalitarian equalism with masculinity. In other words, to him, to be a 'supportive husband' ® is to presume a position of absolute equalism in his relationship. Since he subscribes to the feminized notion of an historic condition of 'male privilege', generally this means he believes that limiting his inborn masculine nature allows his wife to be "more equal". To him, real manhood is repressing his innate masculinity (such as it is) so that his wife will feel less inhibited in becoming something more than what a 'masculine' society will permit.

Yes, it's classic Beta Identification Game; nothing I haven't addressed already in the past decade. And yes, it's also the classic feminist boilerplate that feminism has bred into contemporary males for over 60 years now. What hit me during this conversation is the presumption of an idealized equalism that can in some way be realized between a man and a woman in a long term relationship. The reason the topic came up with us was due to his wanting for his wife to be more aggressive with him sexually. He simply couldn't grasp that his wife didn't want to take the initiative with him in the bedroom. Here he was explaining the virtues of being a 'better male' in his playing fair and even with his wife, yet for all his giving her space to grow, she wouldn't be the sexual instigator with him despite his equalist expectations that she would feel comfortable being that instigator. In a way he subscribes to the Relational Equity fallacy – he believes she ought to appreciate him sexually because he's invested so much of himself in ensuring she feels like his equal.

True Neutral

The problem he's dealing with is the result of his belief in true gender neutrality. Learn this now, taken to its logical extreme, the end result of true gender neutrality is androgyny. No sexual dimorphism, just simple homogeneous androgyny. Fortunately for us, nature abhors homogeny and has always found dynamic ways around the dead ends that the inbreeding of androgyny produces.

My friend's wife's sexual passivity (and general disinterest) is one such dynamic. Try as he may, no amount of social equalization will prompt his wife's biological sexual impulse – in essence he's attempting to negotiate her desire with himself.

For all his frustration and inability to accept Red Pill truths I have to thank him because it was from this conflict that I had a starting point in estimating relationship attachment theory and its relation to SMV.

Blogger *Roissy* once proposed that the strength and security of any relationship rests in the disparity between each person's sexual market value. While I endorse this principle, I'm going to take it a bit further. As a general principle it works well for the guy wanting to maintain his *Frame* in an LTR or marriage, however there's more wrapped up in that SMV disparity than I think has been explored thus far.

As I stated, SMV doesn't happen in a vacuum. Men may have an Alpha dominance established only to have it knocked back down after failing a particularly bad shit test. He may rate lower or higher depending on a social status that's in flux. A woman must find ways to cope with an ever decaying SMV once she reaches her SMV peak and begins her decline towards the Wall. Childbirth and rearing, weight gain, satisfying a security need, and many other factors may also accelerate this process.

What I'm going to do here is propose a general outline for SMV disparity based on the ratio between both sexes. Before you read my outlines, keep in mind the **Cardinal Rule of Relationships:** *In any relationship, the person with the most power is the one who needs the other the least.* The overarching concept here is that the person in the relationship with the superior sexual market value will at least be perceived by the person of lesser value to need them less than the other. If it is established by concrete social proof that one person is of higher SMV than the other, it's usually an accepted reality of that relationship, but bear in mind that it is the fluctuating perception of SMV that has more influence on the attachment and strength of that relationship.

Finally, from a feminine perspective it's important to remember that Hypergamy is a game of perceptions, testing, confirmations and retesting new perceptions. This process has a pronounced effect on SMV evaluation, which is then influenced by a woman's own self-perceptions.

1:1

This is the position of True Neutral I illustrated with my friend's situation above. I'm starting here because this ratio is the mythological ideal every equalist will tell you they're striving for. Be they male or female, what adherents of equal balance fail to consider is that real, sustainable equilibrium in SMV is an impossibility. What every modern woman and gelded male in an LTR will tell you is that they believe they are common examples of that SMV equilibrium. The truth is that their ego investment in that equalist idealism wont allow for the real introspect necessary to accurately evaluate what their true individual SMV really is –both in relation to themselves and the greater whole of society in their demographic. Hypergamy never seeks its own level, but this is what a True Neutral believes is possible.

A 1:1 SMV doesn't exist. I'm sure there will be naysayers who feel they "play it fair" with their wives or girlfriends, but the fact remains that SMV is always in flux and doesn't allow for a true, sustainable equilibrium. Hypergamy is an easy example; fail one too many shit tests and your equitable 1:1 ratio slips to 2:1 in a woman's favor. A man getting to the gym more frequently or getting a promotion in status may be enough to raise that 1:1 balance. There are simply too many variables in a contemporary relationship to take the notion of SMV equilibrium seriously. Furthermore, we must consider the effect that social media plays in women self-evaluations of their own SMV. And this is only one (albeit significant) social distortion that can upset the idealistic equitable balance.

Even in the most stable and SMV balanced pairings, the simple fact that both sexes' SMV peaks occur at differing phases of life makes the notion of a contented balance laughable. However, it is important for a Man to bear in mind that his SMV will eventually exceed that of any woman if he continues to improve himself and grows personally, physically and financially into his SMV peak years. There will eventually come a time when a woman's SMV will decay to the point that her necessitousness will exceed her value. In other words, due to her fast burn-fast decay SMV, and recognized or not, she will eventually need a Man more than he needs her when he enters his peak SMV phase and she's declined to the *Wall* of her own.

It's during this critical phase that a woman must rely on her man's socially expected love, charity, obligation and parental investment to maintain his secure attachment to her in the face of an obvious SMV imbalance. As I've covered before, women fundamentally lack the capacity to appreciate the sacrifices men make to facilitate women's reality – and once those facial wrinkles and cellulite can no longer be disguised by makeup or collagen, women will still persist in the expectation of monogamous obligation, in preference to the genuine desire, love, devotion, etc. a man may legitimately feel about her regardless of her wrinkles.

2:1

This ratio has been defined in the past as the golden mean of SMV between the genders – so long as the man is on the beneficial side of it. The most successful, stable and loving relationships don't result from being 'equally yoked' – they result from a mutually acknowledged SMV superiority and masculine dominance of a positively masculine male and his adoring, yet subconsciously anxious, woman who is up to a point below him in her subjective SMV evaluation.

Some guys get to this position by default. Either aided by genetics, prior hard work or simply being single at the phase of life when his SMV is peaking while hers is in decline, a man can prolong this ratio far longer and far more realistically than the 1:1 idealization. This isn't to say his SMV can't be reduced by failing shit tests or by unfortunate personal circumstances, but the durability and resiliency of his higher SMV affords him more leeway in recovering from these missteps or calamities.

A man doesn't necessarily need to be an Alpha cad to establish this ratio, all that's required is an acknowledged recognition of this SMV imbalance and the appropriate recognition and adoration from the woman involved. There are plenty of Betas who enjoy the benefits of a 2:1 ratio even when they don't (or refuse to) recognize an SMV imbalance that weighs in their favor.

From a female side a 2:1 ratio is generally what most modern women find themselves dealing with; through realized fact or by self-deluded overestimation of their own SMV, most women reflexively presume they are the party with the higher SMV. These are the naggers, the brow beaters, the women who wistfully to resentfully wish their men were more than they are. They crave the SMV imbalance that a dominant Alpha would satisfy, yet through their own ego investments, or due to their inability to lock that Alpha down, they must relegate themselves to being the less necessitous person in their LTR.

3:1

While this is a tenable situation for a Man it borders on the unhealthy. Marginal fame, notoriety or an actualized condition of widely acknowledged social proof can make for a 3:1 SMV ratio. These are the Men who other women can't help but be attracted and aroused by, and other men aspire to be in one way or another. The women they do pair off with are faced with two options: either maturely accept this inequity and rely on feminine wiles (and sexual performance) to create a situation of 'value added' emotional investment and secure his monogamy, or accept that she will only be a short term breeding option for him before a woman who's a better SMV option presents herself to him.

Only the most secure of women in this ratio pairing don't suffer from an state of passive *Dread*. While a 2:1 pairing may force a women to deal with marginal self-doubt and underlying competition anxiety, a woman in a 3:1 pairing will have to confront the dread of loss that accompanies a less stable pairing. From a Hypergamic perspective, she's hit the evolutionary jackpot – sexual pairing with a mate she wouldn't normally have access to. Fat women who garner the drunken attentions of an out-of-options man of higher SMV make for the most common occurrences of a 3:1 pairing. Irrational jealousy and *accidental pregnancies* are not uncommon in this pairing. I should point out that a 3:1 pairing may also be the result of a 2:1 pairing that lasted into a man's peak years and bumped him up a point, or more likely, the woman depreciated down a point or more as she hit the *Wall*.

From the female side, a 3:1 ratio is generally only a temporary condition. Leaving a man who is recognizably a full 2 points beneath her in SMV is really only a formality. Women's Hypergamous attraction floor simply doesn't work like that of men's. Generally this female-side pairing is the result of an extreme circumstance, a particularly materialistic woman or a man who convinced a woman he was more Alpha than he seemed only to backslide into Betaness once he mistakenly thought he could get comfortable with her and expected her to love him for just being himself. It should also be considered that a 3:1 female-side pairing may also be the result of a post *Wall* professional woman pairing off with the only Beta so intently conditioned in feminine-primary psychology that she would consider him preferable to celibacy.

4+:1

We're pushing into the improbable here, but these pairings do exist. Your first thought may be the famous celebrity or musician who marries a 'commoner', but the more likely scenario is one where a previously more equitable pairing was solidified and one partner decayed so dramatically that this extreme imbalance resulted. It's easy to find online before and after examples of women progressively fattening from a trim sexy girl of 19 to a 200lbs+ *Landmonster* of 26. I wish I could say these were outliers, but as all too many bloggers in the Manosphere will attest, it's increasingly common.

Women in the 'before-and-after' demographic who find themselves in a 4+:1 are often the most dependent upon the feminine social convention established to delimit men's sexual selectivity. The *Body Fat* embracers and the 'shallow' men shamers are the most obvious examples.

Other than for the most egregious of gold diggers a sustainable 4:1 balance from the feminine side is a virtual impossibility.

HUMANISM, BEHAVIORISM
AND THE AMORALITY OF GAME

Our great risk in life is not that we aim too high and fail,
but we aim too low and succeed.

I think one of the major hurdles guys new to Game encounter is an inherent discomfort with experiencing just how raw and uncaring the motivators are behind intergender dynamics. I can't entirely blame this on a naive, White Knight dependency on wanting to have things fit into their moral perspective, it's something more than that. For men with some *old books* sense of honor or duty there also comes a need to enforce a perception of morality. Understanding the evolutionary psychology roots that drive what would be considered 'immoral' behavior by their mental frame is often enough to have men reject Game and the Red Pill altogether. They believe that even attempting to understand the roots of that immoral behavior is tantamount to rationalizing a way to excuse it.

For all the accusations of my being a moral relativist, it's still very hard not to see the latent purposes behind the behavior itself – this is cause for a lot of internal conflict for a morally predisposed man newly discovering the foundations of Game. In *War Brides* I made a case for women's propensity to establish new emotional bonds after a breakup or a widowing with far greater ease than men due to a hard-wired psycho-evolutionary sort of Stockholm Syndrome. The implications of that is one of rationalizing a cruel, heartless bitch's actions that could very well be considered amoral, if not immoral. There are plenty of other illustrations that to a newly Game-aware Man seem deplorable and duplicitous behaviors. Why can't women just say what they mean and mean what they say, right? It seems like a horrible inefficiency to have to rely on women's behaviors in order to really see their true motivators. What's ironic is that much of what men have invented as moral considerations were designed to keep these behaviors and their functions in check.

All that said I can't help but see a want for a higher order of self-image in understanding Game and how the visceral world of sexual dynamics operates. It's raw behaviorism clashing with a desire to find a humanistic meaning in the cosmos, all set in the theater of intergender relations. I could simply take the easy way out and advise men to drop the pretense of morality altogether since it's always subjective to whomever's benefit the moralizing is done for. But that doesn't remove the desire to see what we think is justice; the key being the desire for it, not necessarily the application of it. While I can certainly respect the aspirations of the nobler prospects of this approach, overall it's a bit naive to nuts & bolts behaviorists. That's not intended as a statement of fact, it's just an observation.

From the humanist perspective you have to follow a linear, chronological advance in human understanding in many different realms – math, art, cultural ritual, science, societal conditions and any number of other 'advances' we've made from our hunter gatherer, tribalist beginnings to our globally connected present. And while it is very ennobling and self-satisfying to see such achievements as evidence of our high-minded progress, it's far too easy to overlook the root motivations for these advances that are anchored in the very evolution that the humanist perspective would like to claim triumph over.

For example lets consider Pablo Picasso. Not my favorite artist, but one of them and one most people recognize as a considerable personality in art. The humanist would likely hold Pablo up as the banner of human achievement – a fantastic artist as the result of our progress as a race and a tribute to our overcoming our brutish past. To which the behaviorist would ask, "why should it be that art is so highly valued among human beings?" For that answer we have to go back to the root causes for creative expression. Cavemen painted pictures of animals they'd killed on cave walls for millennia before Pablo arrived on the scene. Now you can argue that these drawings were communicative in nature, but the function of them was to convey a message – "Here is how we killed an antelope and you can too thusly." Language then springs from this methodology and we progress, but the base function is communication that benefited the survival of the species.

Then you may ask why would Pablo personally want to be an artist? The humanist replies, "to fulfill his personal need for expression to become a self-actualized being" and the behaviorist answers "to make his life's function easier." I doubt that if any manifestation of creative intelligence wasn't a precursor for sexual selection there wouldn't be so many "artists" throughout history. I could easily make similar arguments for famous inventors, scientists or even Benjamin Franklin. It all returns to root motivations.

The self-actualized man still finds himself aroused by the Playboy Playmate irrespective of how much he convinces himself he should reserve his 'feelings' for his wife or girlfriend to "morally" conform to his higher-order of self-expectations. Powerful establishing operations such as deprivation virtually ensure that he will have an 'inner conflict' and to remedy this he will behaviorally condition himself to act accordingly. Regardless of the method, it's still the biological root that has been hardwired into his mental firmware millennia ago by his hunting ancestors. Whether or not he acts on an opportunity to cheat on his wife, the base desire is still present and an undeniable motivation. A wife can close her eyes and imagine she's fucking Brad Pitt when she's with her husband – the motivation is still the same.

Over two-thirds of the American population is overweight, why do you suppose this is? According to the cognitive-humanist we've solved our hunting/gathering needs and can devote ourselves to 'higher pursuits', but yet statistics confound us here. The behaviorist sees this and notices that our own evolutionary biology predisposes us to over-eat since in our evolutionary past we didn't know whether or not we'd eat at all tomorrow or the next day (thus the 'gathering' was invented I suppose). Our bodies process this food in such a way that we burn fat far slower than carbohydrates and protein is reserved for muscle building. All of this in an evolutionarily efficient manner to preserve us, but now once we've (more or less) mastered our environment and food is convenient and plentiful it becomes a disadvantage. It's not right or wrong, it's just our innate biological mechanisms motivating us to behave in a manner that will benefit us best.

Every vice you can point a negative finger at operates in precisely in this dynamic. Our morality, our intelligence, our sexuality and the behaviors that are manifested by them are all motivated by this base. It would be a pleasant fiction if we could all remove our consciousness from this and be these enlightened, self-actualized beings, constantly operating in a state of peak experience, but this damn testosterone in my body keeps pulling me back down to earth. It may be morally reprehensible for a woman to break her marriage commitment, divorce her husband and remarry a rich entrepreneur, but from a behavioral perspective it makes perfect long term pragmatic sense.

The problem that moral relativism poses to the humanist approach isn't so much in recognizing this primitive base motivation, but an unwillingness to embrace it and live with it and use it. I want to run, I want to fuck and I want to fight. I want to feel the blood, testosterone and adrenaline in my arteries. I also want to write a sonata, paint a masterpiece and be a loving father to my daughter.

Behaviorism is the antithesis of putting angels wings on our backs and claiming we've evolved 'above all of that.' I haven't, you haven't and no one has, and our behaviors will make hypocrites of us whenever condition and opportunity facilitate it for us. It's not that behaviorism would have us all living like animals in the bush as an ideal state, nor does it deny that people have very ennobling qualities; it simply accepts the whole of what prompts us to do what, why & how we do things and explores the reasons why in a far more fundamental way than a romanticized humanism. I'm sure this is akin to atheism for people invested into humanism, but nothing could be further from the truth. It's simply a more pragmatic, efficient and realistic approach for explaining behavior.

Moral to the Manosphere

Putting angel's or devil's wings on observations hinders real understanding.

I say that not because I don't think morality is important in the human experience, but because our interpretations of morality and justice are substantially influenced by the animalistic sides of our natures, and often more than what we're willing to admit to ourselves. Disassociating one's self from an emotional reaction is difficult enough, but adding layers of moralism to an issue only convolutes a better grasp of breaking it down into its constituent parts. That said, I also understand that emotion and, by degree, a sense of moralism is also characteristic of the human experience, so there needs to be an accounting of this into interpretations of issues that are as complex as the ones debated in the Manosphere.

Although I'm aware that observing a process will change it, it's still my practice not to draw moralistic conclusions in any analysis I make because it adds bias where none is necessary. The problem is that what I (and others in the Manosphere) propose is so raw it offends ego-invested sensibilities in people. Offense is really not my intent, but often enough it's the expected result of dissecting cherished beliefs that seem to contribute to the well being of an individual.

Let that sink in for a moment; the reason that what I propose seems nihilistic, cynical and conspiratorial is because it's analytical without the varnish of morality. For example, when I wrote *War Brides*, it was in response to men's common complaint of how deftly and indifferently women could transition into a new relationship after they'd been dumped by a girlfriend or wife. I wanted to explore the reasons of how and why this functioned, but from a moralistic perspective it is pretty fucked up that, due to Hypergamy, women have an innate capacity to feel little compunction about divesting themselves emotionally from one man and move on to another much more fluidly than men. If I approach the topic in a fashion that starts with, "isn't it very unjust and / or fucked up that women can move on more easily than men?" not only is my premise biased, but I'd be analyzing the moral implications of the dynamic and not the dynamic itself.

I always run the risk of coming off as an asshole because in analyzing things it's my practice to strip away that moral veneer. It challenges ego-investments, and when that happens people interpret it as a personal attack because those ego-investments are uniquely attached to our personalities, and often our own well being. Although there's many a critic on 'team woman' shooting venom from the hip as to my emphasis on the feminine, don't think that this iconoclasm is limited to the fem-centric side of the field – I catch as much or more vitriol from the Manosphere when I post something like the importance of looks for men.

If you choose to derive your personal value from some esoteric sense of what sex 'should' mean, more power to you, but I find it's a much healthier position to accept a balance between our carnal natures and our higher aspirations. It's not one or the other. It's okay to want to fuck just for the sake of fucking – it doesn't have to be some source of existential meaning. If you think it means something more, then that's your own subjective perspective – even in marriage there's 'maintenance sex' and there's memorable, significant sex – but it's a mistake to think that the totality of the physical act must be of some cosmic significance.

It is as equally unhealthy to convince oneself that self-repressions are virtues as it is to think that unfettered indulgences are freedoms. There is a balance.

THE PLAN

For the longest time I never had a plan. Oh, I knew what I wanted to do in life; something artistic, publicly recognizable, flamboyant, but the path to get to that reality was never really concrete for my 17-19 year old mind. First and foremost I wanted to get laid. I had aspirations and I did recognize my innate talents, but I really had no plan.

At first I did what most conditioned Betas do at 17 and followed the 'official' script approved by the feminine imperative – nice guy > rapport > comfort > commitment > monogamy > and if magical predestined sex happened to be graced upon me at one of these stages then it was all the confirmation of process any Beta required. But still I had no plan. It felt like a plan, but it never quite played out as a plan once that plan came together.

Serial monogamy with a 'ONEitis' girlfriend seemed like a plan. That's what the imperative had always reinforced and it seemed logical. Man, did I ever hate the guys who had the capacity (ability) to entertain multiple women concurrently. How could women be so enthralled by these 'players' and not see their deviation from the 'official' approved script of the feminine imperative? Didn't they know they were wrong in their deviation? Why did women reward them with sex and intimacy, and why did they do so without the prerequisite steps laid out and approved by the imperative's teachings? The Feminine Imperative had always taught me women were to be treated with default respect – as gender equals, as rationally acting an independent agent as my (equal) self. Could they not rationally conclude, as I did, that they themselves were *rewarding* the very Men who deviated from the plan that the imperative had set before all of us?

I didn't realize it at the time, but what I failed to consider is that women's innate Hypergamy was in conflict with the plan of the Feminine Imperative. Later in life, the male offspring of the Feminine Imperative (Betas) would come to realize the true plan of the imperative, and the supporting, provisioning role it conditions them for in raising other men's genetic legacies, or their own, less than optimal ones. Either by self-realization or self-actualization men, even the most beta men, usually come to realize the plan of the imperative. For some it's a sad realization, too late to really do much of anything but moderate the impact the plan had. For others, it might be freeing in a post-divorce separation from not just their wives but the plan the imperative convinced them of. And still for others, it's the relief of having sidestepped the consequences of a life-impacting ideology.

Making a Plan

There's a clever saying that goes, "Man plans, God laughs." It's kind of endearing in a patrician way, but it really amounts to another saying by the world's most famous Beta, "Life is what happens while you are busy making other plans." Or in other words, 'it is what it is' and you never really had any influence over the circumstances that have led to your present conditions.

I used to believe this. I used to think that having a plan was more or less irrelevant, because ultimately you're really never in control of what happens to you. My Mother used to give me grief about being "obsessed" with bodybuilding and staying in shape. She'd say, "you never know what tomorrow will bring, you could get cancer or hit by a bus, and then all that fussing over your body will be a waste." I remember telling her yes, but this is how I want to look now, I wont care about it in a casket.

Those were always some interesting conversations, but the fact of the matter is I really had no plan for myself of my own creation.

Failing to Plan

Failing to plan is planning to fail. My Marine buddies like this line. In the military I'm sure it was a great mantra, but how many of us allow things to happen to ourselves as the result of not having and sticking to a plan? I'm not saying we ever have a complete control over our circumstances, but when we don't have a plan, the plans of others influence the consequences of our own conditions. As I illustrated above, when a young man has no plan the Feminine Imperative is already there with its own – ready to fill that void for its own purposes, ready to convince that young man that its plan was really his own concept.

One thing I've always advised the high school forum readers on the SoSuave forums is to plan for success when they sarge a girl they like. So many of these young Men get so absorbed in the mechanics and anxieties of asking a girl out, or maneuvering to become intimate with her that they don't plan for success, they only plan to mitigate failure. I tell them to expect success, so plan for that eventuality, and there's a foundational reason for this.

Suddenly a girl agrees to go out with him and he has no plan for a date. What this telegraphs to her is she's agreed to a date, agreed to potential intimacy, agreed to a Hypergamous assessment, with a guy who hasn't thought past the getting a date part. His lack of a plan revealed his Beta essence – he wasn't expecting to succeed, she detects this on a limbic level, and the context, the frame, of the date becomes one of working back from a Beta presupposition.

An Alpha mindset expects success. One of the key tenets of Game is irrational self-confidence, and while this is a core element of Game, its successful application hinges upon follow through – and follow through requires a plan. Whether that plan is about a PUA on an insta-date after a successful 'sarge' or that plan is about banging the wife you reserved your virginity for on your honeymoon night, the conditionality is the same – Alphas already know what they want and have a concrete plan of where they want to go.

Confidence

One of the more frequent questions I'm asked on the SoSuave forums is,

> *"Rollo, I understand confidence is the most attractive aspect about men for women, how do I develop confidence?"*

Confidence is an interesting concept, not just in it's application with women, but in a meta-life sense. Confidence has been elevated to this mystical realm so we read, "The reason you fail is because you don't believe in yourself enough." This is a very similar mechanic to the *'Just Be Yourself'* line of reasoning. It's something people say when they don't know what else to say – "aww man you just need to be confident with her, that's what the bitchez want, just look at any Plenty of Fish profile, confidence, confidence, confidence,..." What they're not explaining is that confidence is derived from past successes and the inherent knowledge that you can repeat those successes again.

I understand the frustration; women say just be yourself, guys say just be confident, both imply some nebulous quality that only those in the know really have a grasp of. I've addressed the *just be yourself* principle in the first book, but how do you get this confidence women declare is so important in their list of demands?

Confidence is derived from options.

When you know you can repeat your past successes, or you have the resources to repeat concurrent successes already available to you, you have confidence.

This is the code women are asking for when they claim to want confidence: "I want a man who has the presence of a man that other men want to be and other women want to fuck." The great irony of this is that the male confidence women want, that exceeds a woman's deserving of that confidence, will always be considered conceit. Why? Because that confidence conflicts with the plan of the feminine imperative. It's sexy as hell, but it represents too great a threat to the Feminine Imperative.

As I stated in my *Plate Theory* series in the first book, it's much easier to have an 'I don't give a fuck' attitude when you really don't give a fuck. If you maintain a presence of non-exclusivity with women, and down to each individual woman, the straight-jacket of the plan of the Feminine Imperative begins to loosen. Included in *your* plan is a sampling, and filtration of, women who have a genuine desire to be with you. Not a mitigated desire, not an obligated desire, but a genuine desire to associate themselves with the potential you represent, confidently, prospectively and sexually. It doesn't seem like filtration or vetting in this sense that you're cognitively looking for the perfect mate – the perfect mate presents herself to you.

Too many guys think they can't spin multiple plates. They think it *must* mean they *must* bang every available woman at their disposal and wanton sex is the ultimate goal. This is the distortion my critics hope to attach to Plate Theory,..

"Rollo says to fuck anything that moves, that's outrageous!"

No, but the concept of non-exclusivity does fundamentally disagree with the plan of the Feminine Imperative, which is why the Feminine Imperative and its agents rely upon those distortions to maintain the imperative's social dominance.

If you have the confidence that comes from having succeeded at a task with predictable regularity in the past, you can say with a reasonable expectation that you are confident to repeat that task in the future. In the context of a career, a sport, a particular social engagement, or maybe a talent or skill we all stand up and applaud that individual's confidence – they make it look easy. Say you're confident with women, say you've had success in the past with them, and you are a Player, even when you are a devoted husband of many supportive years, make this declaration and you are a deluded, typical male.

But confidence is what chicks dig Rollo,...WTF?

It's not the confidence, it's the plan. *Your* plan. It's easy to give illustrations about men having date plans beyond the approaching her, but this is only one example of the overall planning a man must have in his life. Alphas plan, Alphas act. That may be cognitively or not, but their confidence is evolved from a sense of others, of other women recognizing their unspoken, pre-recognized plan.

The reason that *Frame* is the first *Iron Rule of Tomassi* is that it relies so much upon a man having such a concrete plan that he will exclude others, even potential mates from it if situation warrants it. A Man's plan needs to supersede his desire for sex, but also includes using sex to effect it.

"My God Rollo, are you suggesting that sex be an inclusive part of a Man's plan even if he has no intention of long term commitment to her?"

In terms of a plan, yes. That may seem immoral or dehumanizing of me, but stop and think about it. Is it any more immoral or dehumanizing than the plan of the Feminine Imperative on a personal scale? What about a global, legalistic scale?

Is it beyond the pale of hypergamy?

Begin with the Ending in Mind

But we're better than that right? We're the noble, chivalrous, honorable sex. It's our commission to ensure that women fall in line because they know not what is right for themselves. (insert Arthurian prose here)

That's nice prose, but hardly a plan. For all of the control and guidance women really seek (a nice way to say dominance) in a man, it really comes down to the direction of his vision. Is she confident in you? The biggest meta-shit test you will ever face as a Man is in replacing the plan of the Feminine Imperative with your own. How audacious! How cocky! How dare you?!

Begin with the ending in mind. As per the first *Iron Rule of Tomassi*, she enters your *Frame*, she enters your reality, she is the curious actor, she is the inquisitive one, she explores the world you create for her, it's your friends, family and cohorts she encounters. If you feel the reverse is true in your relationship, you've enter her reality, and the narrative, the question, of whose plan is in effect is answered for you.

AFTERWORD

As I mentioned in the introduction, my first impulse in deciding to publish a third book was prompted by a need to definitively outline just what the Red Pill is. I get asked quite often if I believe the Red Pill, as the Manosphere defines it, will ever go mainstream. In some respects it has, at least in a very bastardized sense. At the time of this writing there are several ideological factions that have appropriated The Red Pill as a moniker for their agendas.

The Red Pill as it refers to intersexual dynamics awareness does not preclude other men (and women) from attempting to profit by selling men a template upon which they believe others should follow. The term 'Red Pill' has evolved to the point where it's become a brand unto itself. This leaves its popularity up for exploitation and reinterpretation to suit the commercial interests of whomever has a personal agenda or ideology they wish to promote as 'Red Pill'. That term 'Red Pill' (not the intersexual praxeology) then becomes a convenient substitute for whatever subjective truth the one (or party) appropriating it would have others believe.

This bastardization of the Red Pill is something I've predicted for some time now. In November of 2011 I wrote an essay titled *Could a Man Have Written This?* My concern then was that women would eventually appropriate and redefine 'The Red Pill' to serve the Feminine Imperative by bastardizing it to mean whatever best fit women's purposes. The point in that essay was that, in our feminine-primary social order, it is only women who are allowed to speak with authority about intersexual dynamics and that any man attempting to apply a measure of critical thought to those dynamics will immediately be accused of male bias and misogyny. As such, only women would be allowed to decide what aspects of the Red Pill praxeology ought to be part of the Red Pill brand.

This is what we're beginning to see today. Just as in *Male Space* in this volume, the Manosphere is beginning to see this redefinition of what 'Red Pill' should mean according to the dictates of what best serves the Feminine Imperative. The Manosphere is predominantly a Male Space and as such we're beginning to see it being assimilated by female *overseers in the locker room*. Furthermore, we're also beginning to see vichy-male enablers ready to water down the most unflattering aspects of the 'true' Red Pill for women in order to advance their own commercial interests as "life coaches". In the 15 or so years that the Red Pill has risen to what it is today the Manosphere has become a popular niche market for men and women whose profit model centers on accepting only the parts of the Red Pill that might lead men to a self improvement that would make them more acceptable to the Feminine Imperative, yet entirely dismiss the aspects that would in any way make women accountable for the misgivings of their own natures and their own sexual strategies.

As such it becomes easy to bash Red Pill men as bitter or angry. 'Angry truth' is what I've heard it called, but it is truth regardless. We now have several other profiteers making similar claims about what the Red Pill really is and who ought to be able to redefine it to best serve their own motives. All of these factions have one common purpose; to reinterpret whatever bastardization of The Red Pill as a brand that will be a proxy for 'truth' whatever it is they are selling or what would affirm their ideology. Usually this is focused on unresolved Blue Pill ideals that are just to comforting to let go of.

We have a blatant attempts to reinterpret what the "red pill" is really all about by conflating the Red Pill brand with being the opposite side of a White Knight® coin. And again, it's packaged in TL;DR easily digestible feints at humor. Anyone versed in The Red Pill praxeology understands just how Blue Pill their assertions are, but this is the same *Purple Pill* sugar coating of Red Pill truths I've been warning against for years now. And it becomes potentially danger-ous to men because it encourages them to follow the *Children with Dynamite* path with regards to Game. Learning Game becomes a quest of acquiring only enough understanding of the nature of women and intersexual dynamics (the ones that are palatable to the profit model) to achieve a Blue Pill idealistic goal-state monogamy that brought these men to look for their own answers in the first place. They believe they are selling the key to a Blue Pill dream.

Ultimately, they're selling this same, comforting, Blue Pill idealism, and a means to achieving it packaged as Game, while personally defining the 'Red Pill' based on little or no understanding of the praxeology of it.

I should add here that a lot of ideological factions have appropriated The Red Pill in recent years as a proxy for validating their own social agendas. The Red Pill was always about intersexual dynamics from as far back as I've been familiar with it. I can remember using it as a term for awareness about men's feminine-centric conditioning from at least 2002 on the SoSuave forums. We didn't even refer to it as "Red Pill" as such so much as we'd call what we know as Blue Pill men (AFCs) as being trapped in the Matrix – unaware of their con-ditioning.

I'll still continue to use The Red Pill as a term for the praxeology we use to come into an awareness of true intersexual dynamics, but I realize it's becoming a bastardization. However, the point is that whatever The Red Pill is renamed as it will still be a branding effort on the part of those who see it as a niche market opportunity.

The Red Pill is the theory while Game is the practice and the fieldwork experimentation. Both inform the other, and one suffers without the other. This is what is at the heart of The Red Pill and it's what shocks men into a new awareness and a new experience in life. It is not founded in pessimism, cynicism or misogyny, but rather, honest, unvarnished assessments and correlated experiences of men. Those assessments are often disconcerting, but they are only upsetting to a mindset that holds Blue Pill conditioned ideals as a correct interpretation of them. That can lead to those outside a practiced knowledge of it to believe that the awareness the Red Pill brings is a net negative. What is undeniable is the appeal of the truth The Red Pill presents and that appeal is attractive to men who are still trapped in their Blue Pill idealism.

Their want is to find some way to achieve a Blue Pill idealistic goal with the very harsh reality a Red Pill awareness brings to them. They want to be reinserted back into the Matrix, but with just enough Red Pill awareness to make their Blue Pill hopes a reality. They don't believe The Lady in Red is real, but they do believe that she's attainable and can be made real because they have the Red Pill awareness to effect it. They want for a sort of lucid dreaming in a Blue Pill paradigm.

There really is no going back once you have a grasp of the praxeology of the Red Pill, but it's a comforting fiction for Blue Pill men (who've yet to kill their inner Betas) to believe they can achieve those Blue Pill goals with just enough Red Pill awareness (the pro-feminine parts they think women will approve of). This false hope, one that conveniently ignores the uncomfortable parts of Red Pill awareness, is what will be sold by profiteers no matter what title they apply to it.

I'm leaving you with this warning because I believe it's vitally important for men to realize that there may come a time when the mainstream recognizes the significance of what the Red Pill really is and what the Manosphere has become, and will develop into. As I've mentioned in this book, it's my belief that the Red Pill must remain fundamentally apolitical, non-racial and non-religious because the moment the Red Pill is associated with any social or religious movement, you co-brand it with an ideology, and the validity of it will be written off along with any preconceptions associated with that specific ideology. This association is exactly what we're seeing play out in the mainstream in 2017. Political and social elements like the Alt-Right and the mens (human) rights movement appropriate the brand identity of 'The Red Pill' and their personal ideology becomes an associated extension of what the Red Pill was never intended to be aligned with. The mainstream has accepted the "Red Pill", but the mainstream also needs an easy foil; a perfectly hateable enemy for their narrative, one their audience can feel justified in hating.

The mainstream wants crazy, but the Red Pill isn't crazy. It's rational, it's well-thought, it asks questions based on evidence that delivers uncomfortable, unflattering answers – particularly for women. The mainstream dismisses the real Red Pill as misogynists as it always does when men point out unflattering realities about women's nature – but more so because it's not interested in well-reasoned debate about them. It just wants crazy. So they conflate "Red Pill" with racism, sexism, conservatism, rape apologists, etc. They look for the outrage brokers who have little to lose and a lot to gain by selling themselves, the Manosphere and the true Red Pill out to the mainstream's need for a villain. They cash in on their association with 'The Red Pill', some more successfully than others, to make a new name for themselves in a hope to rebrand themselves and garner some celebrity they can get paid for in their 'Red Pill' association.

I wrote and compiled this book in an effort to give men some actionable ideas on how to better themselves with Red Pill awareness. I don't hope to tell men how to live better lives, I hope I give them the tools and information necessary for them to build better lives themselves. While I believe mindset is a necessary component to men making themselves better men, I also understand that even 'mindset development' is branching off as a market of its own within the Red Pill brand umbrella now. Practical, pragmatic Red Pill awareness becomes an aside to mindset motivators, again, cashing in on the identity of the Red Pill.

These are factions and elements I believe Red Pill aware men need to be aware of in the coming years we see the Manosphere and Red Pill (praxeology) awareness develop. I'm ending with this because I believe that men need to be wary of how the Red Pill can be distorted in the future. Red Pill awareness is a life-saving, life-changing set of information for men. While I don't aspire to give men a formula to change their lives I hope the information in this volume has given you some actionable suggestions as to how you might go about changing your mind and changing your self to better benefit from a new reality, now and to come.

– Rollo Tomassi

ACKNOWLEDGMENTS

The "Manosphere", is a very broad consortium of blogs, forums and men's issues sites dedicated to questioning and challenging the ideals of feminine social primacy while raising awareness of how the social changes initiated by those ideals adversely affect men. The Manosphere also encompasses Red Pill / Game and PUA theory and practice resources with the purpose of educating men about the social and psychological influences they find themselves subjected to in contemporary society.

There's a lot to sift through in the Manosphere, and the risk becomes one of men being bogged down in specific issues that agree with their own ego-investments or appear to salve a particular hurt they may have.

As is my habit in all of my books, I'm going to detail a few of the online resources I think best define a Red Pill perspective. I endorse these sites, but also bear in mind that everyone of them has their own niche, and their own pros and cons. Also, I am catering my acknowledgment selections here to be relevant to the content I've covered in this book. Thus, you'll see new entries that I believe speak best to the material covered.

The Rational Male
therationalmale.com/
I'll begin with my own blog. If you're reading this book you've probably got an idea of the content I publish. Many of the essays you've just read are (edited and abridged) versions of my blog posts. I like to stay as objective as possible, knowing that's not really possible, but (to my knowledge) I run the only truly unmoderated comment forum in the manosphere.

If I have a mission statement it's that the only way an idea's strengths and merit can be proven is in the crucible of an open discourse. This is what I make efforts to provide at The Rational Male.

The Family Alpha
thefamilyalpha.com
The Family Alpha is a great complement to the Red Pill Parenting section of this book. It is founded in Red Pill awareness but its niche is the married (or wants to be married) demographic of the Manosphere. While I'm on record for

not endorsing marriage in our current social environment, if this is your pre-disposition as a man I found that what The Family Alpha covers is a solid Red Pill (if a bit traditional) offering. Much of what he goes into is founded on men accepting their Burden of Performance and applying it in creating a Red Pill marriage and fatherhood.

Chateau Heartiste – Roissy
heartiste.wordpress.com
Roissy, the original proprietor of what is now Chateau Heartiste, is the inarguable godfather of the modern Manosphere. His revelations on Game and the psycho-social underpinnings of why Game works have formed the encyclopedic backbone of Red Pill awareness for over a decade.

At some point around 2009 Roissy passed the torch on to a collective of bloggers who now carry on for him. He and his collective of bloggers aren't the most accessible, and at times can be socially and politically sidetracked, but his early essays are the go-to reference points for every current Manosphere blogger.

The Red Pill – subreddit
reddit.com/r/TheRedPill/
At present the Red Pill subreddit (TRP) boasts over 215,000 subscribers and with good reason; it's easily the best warehouse of Red Pill discussion on the net. It's well moderated to stay focused on the Red Pill / Game topics as well as current affairs that affect and influence Red Pill awareness and application.

I can't praise this forum enough. In just a short time TRP has become a hub of Red Pill thought and it's not limited to PUA techniques, but covers a wide variety of Red Pill outreach and subdomains (married men Red Pill, etc.). In 2017 this Reddit sub made a shift to include more content on Positive Masculinity and self-improvement for men.

Dalrock
dalrock.wordpress.com/
Thoughts from a happily married father on a post feminist world.
I don't specifically focus on religious topics on The Rational Male unless some aspect of religion is directly related to Red Pill relevant intersexual relations. It's no secret that I've been a regular follower of Dalrock's blog for over five years now. Along with Dal I also consider *Donalgraeme's* blog and a few other bloggers in the 'Christo-Manosphere' Red Pill colleagues if not good friends. I've always held Dalrock as a sort of Red Pill brother since both our blogs came up around the same time. I've quoted and credited him in both my prior books and I'd be remiss if I didn't do the same in this volume.

If you have religious reservations about the 'morality' of the Red Pill Dalrock is the best at handling that awareness in a religious context. His blog is the best of what I call the Christo-Manosphere. He's also a consummate, well researched statistician with regard to modern marriage and divorce trends and their social implications. I highly recommend him to any Christian who discovers the Red Pill.

The Married Red Pill – subreddit
www.reddit.com/r/marriedredpill/
The married Red Pill subreddit is an offshoot forum from The Red Pill Reddit forum that's gained a lot of traction in the relatively few years it's been up. I'm acknowledging this forum in this book because a lot of the ideas debated there gave rise to many of the essays in both the parenting and positive masculinity sections in this book. The Married Red Pill (MRP) is a consortium of married (and some divorced) men that subscribe to The Red Pill (TRP) philosophy of sexual strategy, and in particular, applying it in marriage or in Long Term Relationships. This sub was created independently to address the needs of married men to discuss relationships issues. They focus primarily on how to become stronger men to lead in marriage and LTRs to happiness.

The SoSuave Discussion Forum
www.sosuave.net/forum/index.php
The SoSuave forum was the incubator of my earliest Red Pill ideas. I owe most of my own formal awareness to the years of discussion on the Mature Men's board. While I am n o longer a moderator on this board, I still participate in occasional threads and hash out ideas there. If you're interested in reading some of my earliest Red Pill ideas just do a basic member name search for "Rollo Tomassi" and you can see the archives of how it all began.

I would also like to extend my most heartfelt thanks to my fellow Red Pill bloggers and life-travelers:

Sam Botta – livefearless.com/
Christian McQueen – realchristianmcqueen.com
Golmund Unleashed – goldmundunleashed.com/
Tanner Guzy – masculine-style.com/
Ed Latimore – edlatimore.com
Anthony Johnson – www.the21convention.com
Nick Krauser – krauserpua.com
Anthony "Private Man" Hansen – theprivateman.wordpress.com

All of you and so many more have in some way influenced or promoted all of my literary work and I cannot thank you enough. When and if the Manosphere and Red Pill awareness reaches a positive societal acceptance it will be our names and the names of those I don't have space to recount who will look back and say we had a part in building it.

And to you, my readers, the men who bit by bit, part by part, contribute to the greater whole of the men's experience that constitutes the praxeology of understanding intersexual dynamics, take heart and know that you can indeed change your life for the better because of it. Thank you for continuing to contribute you to the greater whole of the Red Pill.

Made in the USA
Coppell, TX
26 September 2021